THE UNIVERSITY OF MICHIGAN

CENTER FOR SOUTH AND SOUTHEAST ASIAN STUDIES

MICHIGAN PAPERS ON SOUTH AND SOUTHEAST ASIA

Ann Arbor, Michigan
USA

KARAWITAN

SOURCE READINGS IN JAVANESE GAMELAN AND VOCAL MUSIC

Judith Becker
editor

Alan H. Feinstein
assistant editor

Hardjo Susilo
Sumarsam
A. L. Becker

consultants

Volume 1

MICHIGAN PAPERS ON SOUTH AND SOUTHEAST ASIA
Center for South and Southeast Asian Studies
The University of Michigan

Number 23, 1984

Library of Congress Catalog Card Number: 82-72445

ISBN 0-89148-027-7

Publication of this book was assisted in part by a grant from
the Publications Program of the National Endowment for the
Humanities. Additional funding was provided by the National
Endowment for the Humanities (Translations); the Southeast
Asia Regional Council, Association for Asian Studies; The
Rackham School of Graduate Studies, The University of Michigan;
and the School of Music, The University of Michigan.

Printed in the United States of America

CONTENTS

This work is complete in three volumes.

Volume 1

Articles and monographs by Martopangrawit, Sumarsam,
Sastrapustaka, Gitosaprodjo, Sindoesawarno,
Poerbapangrawit, and Probohardjono.

Volume 2

Articles and monographs by Warsodiningrat, Sumarsam,
Gitosaprodjo, Purbodiningrat, Poerbatjaraka,
Sindoesawarno, and Paku Buwana X.

Volume 3

Appendix 1: Glossary and index of technical terms
mentioned in the texts. Appendix 2: Javanese cipher
notation (*titilaras kepatihan*) of musical pieces
mentioned in the texts. Appendix 3: Bibliographies
of authors. Bibliography of sources mentioned by
authors, translators, editors, and consultants.

For information on obtaining the original versions
of these translated texts, write

Center for South and Southeast Asian Studies
Publications
130 Lane Hall
The University of Michigan
Ann Arbor, Michigan 48109
USA

PREFACE

Judith Becker

The last millenium of Javanese civilization was a period of prolific
literary activity. In his three-volume annotated catalogue of Javanese
literature from 900 to 1900 A.D., Pigeaud has included tens of thousands of
entries grouped under four general categories: Religion and Ethics; History
and Mythology; Belles Lettres; and the final potpourri category, Science,
Arts, Humanities, Law, Folklore, Customs, and Miscellanea. Many of these
texts were written in Javanese poetic meters and were intended to be
recited, chanted, or sung aloud, for oneself or for an audience. While
references to music, to gamelan, to dance, and to song are frequent, texts
dealing specifically with the history or craft of music are rare. The most
famous of the references to music, from the nineteenth-century manuscripts
Panji Semirang, *Sastra Miruda*, *Pustaka Raja*, and *Serat Centhini*, are
discussed in volumes 1 and 2 (Poerbatjaraka, Warsodiningrat,
Martopangrawit, Sindoesawarno). With the exception of the aforementioned,
if an old manuscript includes a section about music, it will most likely
give only the titles of *gendhing* appropriate to accompany particular scenes
in a *wayang* performance (Pigeaud 1967[2]:51, 80, 417, 690). Writing whole
treatises exclusively about gamelan, dance, or *tembang* is a twentieth-
century phenomenon which seems to have been stimulated by the interest of
Dutch scholars and more recently by the establishment of Western-style
conservatories of music. Books, articles, and manuscripts about *karawitan*
are now plentiful and have become a necessary adjunct study for the Western
student of the gamelan tradition. The texts included here were written
over a forty-five-year time span (ca. 1930-1975) and were selected by the
editor and translators from articles and manuscripts to which we had access
during the period 1969-1978.

The men who wrote these texts were well acquainted with the long
Javanese tradition of historical, literary, and didactic scholarship in
which certain kinds of questions are asked and certain other kinds of
questions are not asked. The particular assumptions of their literary
tradition mold the ways in which they think, talk, and write about music.

We, the translators, come from a different scholarly tradition with our own presuppositions and criteria of evaluation. The author's subjectivities are translated and filtered through our own subjectivities, resulting in a body of texts which cannot presume to be objective. We are presenting interpretive scholarship: our interpretations of the interpretations of our authors about gamelan music.

In preparing these manuscripts for an English-speaking, primarily Western, late-twentieth-century audience, we are removing them from their context, from the intentionality and language of their authors. In so doing, we have "broken their moorings from the psychology of their authors" (Ricoeur 1971:534). But these are old problems, well known to generations of literary critics and translators, which nonetheless continually reveal new facets and new solutions to those undeterred by the awesomeness of the undertaking.

In like manner, we have not hesitated to pursue this utopian task with high enthusiasm and strong confidence in the worthiness of our effort. We have severed the ties of these manuscripts to a particular time and place, enlarging their horizons to include an international scholarly community.

> The essential vocation of interpretive anthropology [musicology] is not to answer our deepest questions, but to make available to us answers that others . . . have given, and thus include them in the consultable record of what man has said. (Geertz 1973:30)

"The consultable record of what man has said" often needs to include more than simply the text in focus. A discussion of the manner of the saying, the intention of the author, and the tradition within which he wrote can help to bridge the ravine between distant texts and their readers (Becker, A. L. 1979:211-43). These authors did not all have the same audience in mind, nor did they write at the same time, but in one respect they are similar; they share a particular attitude toward the writing of a text, a presupposition about scholarship itself. The texts are not "original" in the sense that their authors are putting forth ideas and interpretations that are unique or lacking roots in traditional thought. Rather, it is accumulated wisdom that is presented here, the scholarly aspects of karawitan (the combined vocal and instrumental music of the gamelan), which have been preserved and transmitted primarily as oral tradition, but also through manuscripts. Java, until the twentieth century, belonged to a chirographic tradition, that is, a manuscript tradition with its own "noetics," or the system of shaping, storing, retrieving, and transmitting knowledge (Ong 1977:96). Many of the authors of these texts cite earlier manuscripts, many refer to the teachings and writings of other scholars, and nearly all, at one point or another, pay homage to the ancestors from whom they received the gamelan tradition. The author of a traditional Javanese text is often rewriting a previous text or texts. Sometimes an author will cite his sources (see Sulaiman Gitosaprodjo in this volume); more often they need not be mentioned. It is expected that readers will share the scholarly assumptions of the authors. A comparison of the texts, *Noot Gendhing lan Tembang*, attributed to Paku Buwana X, and *Wedha Pradangga*, by Warsodiningrat (see volume 2), underlines the continuity of a manuscript tradition as well as the uniqueness of each author's treatment of a prior manuscript. Both authors follow the coherence system of the chronograms called *candra sangkala* and both cite the prior text, *Sastra Miruda*. But, even within a scholarly tradition in which originality and individuality are not highly valued, and in which practice must find precedence in the past, the particular mind and personality of the author still inevitably surfaces. The contrasting interpretations and styles of three successive teacher-student generations, Warsodiningrat-Martopangrawit-Sumarsam (see volumes 1 and 2), point again to the facet of individuality within the continuation of a tradition.

The literary background of all these manuscripts, the tradition from which they derive and to which all show clear ancestry, is the Javanese-Balinese chirographic tradition, the *lontar* tradition. "Lontars" are traditional palm-leaf manuscripts produced in Java until the nineteenth century and still produced in Bali. Texts dating back a thousand years have been preserved by repeated "copying," which also includes editing, borrowing, adding, and rearranging. In contrasting the noetics of "fixed form" printed books with the chirographic noetics of Bali, Zurbuchen has this to say:

> . . . each new copy of a lontar is rather like a new "edition"
> from the point of view of the copyist, who may make alterations,
> substitutions, and deletions as his own knowledge and experience
> dictate. Balinese scholars will sometimes look over a number of
> manuscripts of a work and engage in "horizontal borrowing" in the
> creation of a new copy . . . this borrowing, sometimes called
> "contamination" by critical editors . . . can effect all levels
> of the text from spelling and word-grouping to large sections of
> content. In typographic tradition, books are standardized
> containers of knowledge; the verbal entities within them must be
> identical between copies, indexable, citable, and referenced when

quoted. In the case of Balinese lontars, elements can more or
less freely be reshaped, excerpted, expanded, condensed, and
otherwise altered. (Zurbuchen 1981:127)

Even though the manuscripts presented here appear with the format of a
typographic tradition, the authors are more strongly influenced by their
own literary heritage (the lontar tradition), with its copyist perspective,
than by Western traditions of scholarship. In *Serat Sulukan Sléndro*, by
Probohardjono, the combination of technical information, religious lore and
ritual, linguistics, and history is in no way meant to be original and is,
as the author says, "Selections from oral and written knowledge for the
student dhalang." Its sources are multiple, its author a teacher who has
compiled his information to facilitate transmission. He is not the
"author" of the information.

An organizational device which appears often enough in these texts to
suggest a culturally conventional way of writing about karawitan is the use
of numbered categories, each followed by a discussion. The categories
themselves are fairly consistent, usually including the following:

1. instruments/gamelan
2. laras
3. pathet
4. irama
5. gendhing

The order and contents of these categories are freely "reshaped,
excerpted, expanded, condensed and otherwise altered" (Zurbuchen 1981:127).
Some authors add other categories such as *ethos* and *notation*
(Gitosaprodjo), *developments* (Purbodiningrat), *cèngkok* and *style*
(Sindoesawarno 1955; see volume 2), *instruments* and *garap* (Sindoesawarno
1955) or *lagu* (Martopangrawit).

Another trait shared by some of these texts, and also shared with the
Javanese-Balinese lontar tradition, is organization around various areas of
expertise of the author rather than an abstracted, unifying topic.

In many cases, a lontar seems less a replica of one work in its
entirety and more a personal collection or compendium of one
person's knowledge and interests. (Zurbuchen 1981:127)

This method of cohesion is particularly striking in the manuscript of
Martopangrawit which presents a theory of *pathet* and *laras* from the

perspective of a *gender* player rather than the more usual theoretical
abstractions of both Javanese and Western theory.

In addition to the stylistic and organizational conventions which
these texts often share with the lontar tradition, they sometimes include
the same formulaic devices. The formal apology and self-deprecation of the
author, called *pangaksama* (from Sanskrit *ksam* 'to forgive, be patient')
link these texts to the literary conventions of Old Javanese poetry and
present-day rhetorical style as well. In the *kakawin* tradition, the
pangaksama is one of several boundary markers and may occur at either the
opening or the closing of the text. Compared to this instance of a
fifteenth-century kakawin pangaksama,

> But I myself am far from being endowed with the talent of
> composing sweet-sounding words in verse,
> For how could I achieve all that a poet longs for,
> exceedingly dull as I am?
> Thus indeed I cannot but incur the utmost derision of others;
> My one hope, however, is that this may succeed in being an
> aid in my search for the Absolute.
> (Teeuw et al. 1969:69, translation of canto 1, v. 3)

the apology of Sindoesawarno is closer to the expectations of twentieth-
century scholars,

> Informed readers will freely add and subtract, alter and contest,
> or completely throw out these theories and replace them with new
> ones. (*Ilmu Karawitan*; see volume 2)

But, the spirit of personal modesty and humility is consistent in both.

Within recent history (ca.1750-1875 A.D.), Surakarta was the scene of
a literary renaissance under the rulers Paku Buwana III-VII and Mangku
Negara IV-V (Drewes 1973-1974:199-215). Descendants of the great literary
figures of the nineteenth century still reside in that city. Given the
circumstance that the Akademi Seni Karawitan Indonesia (ASKI) is situated
in Surakarta, it is perhaps not surprising that the preponderance of
contemporary musical texts were written there. Two of these texts, *Noot
Gendhing lan Tembang* and *Wedha Pradangga* (a history of gamelan traditions
and compositions from the perspective of the Surakarta court), reiterate
the chronological framework found in the nineteenth-century text *Pustaka
Raja*, by the poet R. Ng. Ranggawarsita, in which he "fills in" the history
of Java from the end of the *Mahābhārata* (whose heroes are considered
ancestors of Javanese kings) to the time of the rise of the East Javanese

kingdoms in the twelfth century A.D. Each date given, in the form of a
candra sangkala, provided a story with key words and numbers which
themselves could be used as objects of contemplation and from which
insights into hidden realities might be extracted (Becker, J. 1980:231). By
the use of candra sangkala, these authors evoked a period of Javanese
history when sacred knowledge, literature, and history were transmitted
through private study and the oral recitation of lontars.

Another manuscript whose antecedents are deeply rooted in pre-Islamic
Java is the *Wědha Pradangga Kawedhar* by Sastrapustaka. The association of
the names of the first three keys of the gamelan instruments with parts of
the body suggests the Tantric doctrine of the subtle body and its important
cakra points located in the head, the neck, and the chest. Assigning names
associated with the five sense faculties and six perceptions (*rasa*) to the
remaining two keys also relates to earlier Buddhist traditions in Java
(Campbell 1974:330-31; Zoetmulder 1974:180-81).

Most of the manuscripts were written for the purpose of communicating
to students. Those of Gitosaprodjo were written for his students in
Malang, East Java, during the 1960's and early 1970's (before the advent of
cassette recordings and television and far from the centers of Central
Javanese traditions), and for students (like many Western students of
gamelan) with no direct access to the performance and scholarly traditions
of Surakarta and Yogyakarta. Others, such as the texts by Warsodiningrat
and Martopangrawit, were written for students at KOKAR (Konservatori
Karawitan Indonesia, now Sekolah Menengah Karawitan Indonesia--SMKI) and
ASKI, the secondary- and college-level institutes for the study of Central
Javanese music, whose students are often very knowledgeable as well as
proficient musicians. Gitosaprodjo conveys basic information (derived from
his teachers at KOKAR), while Martopangrawit sometimes explores the limits
of the knowable in karawitan. The manuscript closest in style of
presentation to the expectations of a late-twentieth-century audience is
Inner Melody in Javanese Gamelan, by Sumarsam, originally written in
English. A comparison of the style of this manuscript with the one
attributed to Paku Buwana X illuminates the different assumptions that
inform scholarship from different traditions.

Two basic transformations have been performed on these texts by the
consultants, translators, and editors: the process of translating itself
(see "Preface," by A. L. Becker, volume 2); and the process of changing the
format of the texts from a chirographic tradition to a printed-book
tradition. As editor, I have imposed standardization of spelling and word

division, and a system of capitalization not present in the originals.
Though providing clarity and conforming to one of the most rigid
constraints of printed-book technology, this standardization also
eliminates certain features that associate the texts with a particular time
and give them a tone of elegance or old-fashioned quaintness. Javanese
script, derived from the *Pallava* script that spread from South India
throughout Southeast Asia, has no word division. When Javanese script is
transcribed into Romanized script, word divisions are added. While all the
texts here were originally written in either Romanized Javanese or
Indonesian, the names of places, mythological or historical people, and
names of gendhing and *sekar* do not have an official Romanized form.
Different authors will choose different alternatives. For example, the
name of the gendhing *Gambir Sawit* in Javanese script looks like this:

Modern writers using Romanized script may choose any of the following
alternatives: Gambirsawit, Gambir-sawit, Gambir-Sawit, or Gambir Sawit. No
one form is more "correct" than another, but they do differ in
"archaicness," that is, closeness to Javanese script.

In our translations, word boundaries are marked with a space even if
they were not marked in the original or were marked with a hyphen. The
reason for this choice is to help those with only a little knowledge of
Sanskrit, Old Javanese, or modern Javanese to decipher the component parts
of names of gendhing, names of gamelan, and technical terms. However,
compound words joined by *sandhi* (letter fusion) are not separated, e.g., a
lokananta (from *loka* plus *ananta*, or *loka* plus *nata*); nor are compound
words joined by an epinthetic nasal, e.g., *asmarandana* (from *asmara* plus
dana). Hyphens are retained only for reduplicated words, e.g., *abon-abon*,
and for complementary pairs such as *padhang-ulihan*.

Transliteration from Javanese script also involves the choice of a
spelling. The open-sided, square, pillared, audience hall of traditional
Javanese nobility may be spelled *pendapa*, *penḍapa*, *pendhapa*, *pendopo*,
penḍopo, or *pendhopo*, depending upon whether the palatalized *d* is marked by
dh, by *ḍ*, or not marked at all, and whether the sound ɔ (aw) is spelled
with o or a. Another kind of variation can occur in the use of a Javanese
or Indonesian spelling of a word, such as *panerus* rather than *penerus*,
suggesting a reverence toward the subject, or a preference for Javanese
spellings--often a clue to the age of the author or the time the text was
written. For example, those writers who consistently use *badhaya*, rather

than *bedhaya*, convey a quaint antiquity. (The variants *bedaya*, *bedaya*,
bedhoyo, *bedoyo*, and *bedoyo* have been eliminated from these texts.)

A few variants have been retained, in some cases because both are
common and in others because the variations in spelling may partially
determine their meaning. For the vast majority of untranslated technical
terms, and for spellings of names and places, we have eliminated all
variations but one. The spelling conventions followed here conform to the
decisions of the Indonesian government spelling reform of 1972 and the
unofficial Javanese spelling standardization used in Javanese-language
newspapers. The sound formerly written *d* is now *dh*, (palatalized *d*); *t* is
now *th* (palatalized *t*); *oe* is now *u*; *dj* is now *j* (as in *j*udge); *tj* is now *c*
(as in *c*hurch); and the sound [ˈɔ], formerly written *o*, *å*, or *a*, is now
written *a*. Exceptions to this policy are the names of living authors who
have not modernized the spelling of their names, e.g., "Gitosaprodjo"
rather than "Gitasapraja"; or deceased authors whose names appear in
library catalogues under an older spelling, e.g., "Poerbatjaraka" rather
than "Purbacaraka." In Romanized Javanese the letter *e* represents two
phonemes. Unmarked *e* is pronounced [ə]. Marked *e* represents two
allophones: *é* is [e] and *è* is [ɛ]. Our guide for the use of diacritics
is the Javanese-Dutch dictionary by Pigeaud (1938).

The policy concerning capitalization is to try to indicate to the
reader for whom all these terms are new the degree of their specificity or
generality. For example, when a category of gamelan is referred to, lower-
case letters are used, e.g., "gamelan kodhok ngorèk." When a particular
set of instruments is meant, capitalized words and italics are used, e.g.,
"Gamelan *Guntur Sari*." Sometimes a string of generalized category-terms
precede a specific name, in which case only the specific name is
capitalized, e.g., "sekar" (song), "macapat" (metric-melodic category),
"dhandhang gula" (more specific meter-melody), and "*Lik Suling*" (name of
song). A special problem presents itself with the terms *ayak-ayakan*,
srepegan, and *sampak*, which are used as terms for generalized categories
and also as specific pieces. Usually it is clear from the context which is
meant and we have indicated our judgement by lower- or upper-case letters,
e.g., "the gendhing ayak-ayakan, srepegan, and sampak are used for the
accompaniment of wayang. . . ," or "*Srepegan*, sléndro pathet nem is used in
the first part of a wayang performance." One could argue that even
"*Srepegan*, sléndro pathet nem" represents a category rather than a specific
piece, but that is true only from an abstracted overview, looking at all
the variants of "Srepegan, sléndro pathet nem." Each author generally has

a specific srepegan in mind when he speaks of "*Srepegan*, sléndro pathet nem."

Many terms in Indonesian and Javanese may be unmarked for singular or plural. Rather than add the English plural marker *s*, we have decided to retain the original form of the word as both the singular and the plural form, for example, "the many gamelan found in the kraton. . . ." as well as "a gamelan may consist of as many as thirty instruments."

Any term, phrase, or sentence enclosed within brackets has been added for clarification by the translator and is not part of the original manuscript. Any term, phrase, or sentence enclosed within parentheses is part of the original manuscript. If the word in parentheses is English, the author enclosed the equivalent passage or word within parentheses. If the word in parentheses is Indonesian or Javanese, the translator has added the original passage immediately following the English translation; when a passage is ambiguous or a word has multiple meanings, the original has been added for the benefit of those who can read it.

For the convenience of the reader, Javanese cipher notation appearing within the texts has been standardized. Unless otherwise indicated, G = gong and kenong struck simultaneously, N = kenong, and t = kethuk. Cyclic units are enclosed within brackets.

The translation and preparation of these materials for publication has been a cooperative effort in which several individuals were involved with every text--the translator, the editors, at least two consultants, and sometimes the author as well. Often, one or several of these persons made significant interpretive comments in the form of footnotes. Thus, we may have four or more sources for footnotes in a single manuscript.

The important role played by our assistant editor, Alan Feinstein, and our consultants, A. L. Becker, Sumarsam, and Hardja Susilo, is not discernible from a scrutiny of the table of contents. Either Sumarsam or Hardja Susilo examined each translation, line by line, checking it against the original. Alan Feinstein painstakingly rechecked the original against each translation. As a result, passages in every manuscript were rewritten. A. L. Becker provided decisions, counsel, suggestions, warnings, and encouragement at every stage in the preparation of these texts. Without the efforts and patience of these fine scholars we would have far less confidence in the work we have produced.

By applying her considerable editorial talents to these manuscripts, Janet Opdyke, publications editor at the Center for South and Southeast

Asian Studies, transformed the ragged efforts of scholars into professionally formatted volumes. R. Anderson Sutton and Susan Pratt Walton contributed unstintingly of their expertise in the final editing of several sections of these volumes. Appreciation is due to René Lysloff, Carole Moody, and Dwight Thomas for typing and laying out the final version of the manuscripts. We are also grateful to Martha King for preparing drawings and diagrams that called for her considerable artistic skills.

We have received funding from various sources during ten years of work on these translations. The National Endowment for the Humanities has been the major source of support, awarding a Research Materials, Translations grant to the project (1979) and a publications subvention to the Center for South and Southeast Asian Studies (1982-1985). Contributions also were received from the Southeast Asia Regional Council of the Association for Asian Studies (1976) and the Rackham School of Graduate Studies at the University of Michigan (1974, 1975, 1983-1984). Finally, the School of Music, University of Michigan, has been generous in providing additional support.

CATATAN-CATATAN PENGETAHUAN KARAWITAN

[Notes on Knowledge of Gamelan Music]

Volume I

Radèn Lurah Martopangrawit

Translated from Indonesian by Martin F. Hatch

Surakarta: Akademi Seni Karawitan Indonesia
and Pusat Kesenian Jawa Tengah, 1972

[Second edition, 1975]

INTRODUCTION
[from 1972 Edition]

At this time, the Student Council of the Akademi Seni Karawitan
Indonesia [A.S.K.I., 'Academy of Indonesian Performing Arts'] has succeeded
in publishing this manuscript on *karawitan*. The Student Council feels very
fortunate that it is able to publish this manuscript by R[adèn] L[urah]
Martopangrawit. The value of this book for students at A.S.K.I. is
inestimable. Furthermore, the Student Council hopes that since this book
will be reaching a wider circle of readers, it will also increase the
understanding of and interest in karawitan.

The Student Council expresses its deep appreciation to R. L.
Martopangrawit, one of our mentors, for his permission to publish this
book. Also, we thank Drs. S. D. Humardani, director of the Pusat Kesenian
Jawa Tengah ['Center for the Arts of Central Java'], in Surakarta, who
cooperated fully in bringing it into print.

Surakarta, January 1972
Student Council
Akademi Seni Karawitan Indonesia

A NOTE FROM THE TRANSLATOR
[of the Original Javanese][1]

   The compiler of this book [Martopangrawit], hoped that the information
set forth herein would reach a wide audience. His original manuscript, to
which he gave the title *Budel* ['legacy'], is in Javanese. In our opinion,
with this translation into Indonesian his goal will be better achieved.
This translation was done freely, but without changing either the intent or
content of the original. Only those few Javanese terms which have a close
connection with Javanese music--for example, "*garap*," "*kalajengaken*,"
"*minggah*," and others--are left untranslated, and some of these terms are
explained in footnotes.

AUTHOR'S FOREWORD
[from 1972 and 1975 Editions]

I have begun this work precisely on the day of my seventh *tumbuk* [which falls every eighth birthday], that is, my fifty-sixth birthday according to the Javanese calendar. According to records left me by my parents, I was born on Rabu Wagé, the third day of Mulud, in the year Jimawal (the Javanese year 1845), or, April 4, 1914 [A.D.]. It is customary for Javanese people, depending on their financial ability, to hold a *slametan* ['ritual celebration'] on tumbuk days by inviting close friends and relatives.

On this, my seventh tumbuk, I am not able to assemble any of the ritual requirements [for a slametan]: "ora ana sarat-saraté" ('I cannot afford it'). Even so, I still wish to make a sort of remembrance of this occasion in place of the celebration I was unable to hold. Hence, this book.

In Javanese music circles, I am a performer ('one-who-does', a musician). For this reason, my analysis reflects the views of a performer.

May this book be useful, especially to the younger generation of Javanese musicians.

Surakarta, 4 Mulud 1901
21 May 1969
Martopangrawit

The System of Gendhing

In my foreword, I mentioned that this book would be based on [musical] practice. Because of this, it will do no harm to acquaint the reader with some of the ins and outs of *garap* ['performance practice'], though only a few, in order that he may understand better the meaning of the book. The reader must first know the system of *gendhing*.

Karawitan

What is "karawitan"? Actually, the meaning of "karawitan" is very broad, but here we will use the specific meaning that relates to the system of gendhing. Karawitan is the art of producing sound using the *sléndro* and *pélog* tuning systems. Any vocal or instrumental (i.e., gamelan) music that uses sléndro or pélog can be called "karawitan." However, as our discussion now concerns the system of gendhing, our use of the term shall be restricted to the music of the gamelan, i.e., gendhing.

The Contents of Karawitan

There are two basic ingredients in karawitan: *irama* and *lagu*.

1. Irama

As with the word "karawitan," "irama" has a broad meaning. In connection with gendhing, however, we can narrow the definition. "Irama" is the relative width of *gatra*. To clarify this, we have supplied the diagram below; there it can be seen just what is meant by "irama" in the special sense relative to gendhing. Irama can also be understood as the levels of filling in the gatra--beginning with each gatra containing four dots, each dot signifying one pulse [*slag*, from Dutch; 'beat', 'pulsation'] of the *balungan*, increasing by multiples until one balungan pulse can be filled in with sixteen dots. This, then, is the meaning of "irama" in gendhing.

Figure 1.   A Diagram of Irama

    a.   6532

    b.   .6.5.3.2

    c.   ...6...5...3...2

    d.   ....6.......5.......3.......2

    e.   ....6...............5...............3...............2

    d.   ....6.......5.......3.......2

    c.   ...6...5...3...2

    b.   .6.5.3.2

    a.   6532

It is clear from the figure of irama above that the relative distance between balungan pulses in one arrangement of the balungan depends on the number of dots that fill in the space. Who has the responsibilty of occupying the spaces between the balungan pulses? These spaces will be filled in by the playing of the melodic instruments--i.e., by the cèngkok of the gendèr, gambang, bonang, and others. Among all the players of cèngkok, the instrument whose notes fall on each individual dot is the *saron panerus*. For this reason, we can utilize the saron panerus as the indicator of differences in irama.

We must now touch upon the tempo of the *saron panerus*. This tempo cannot be scientifically measured, because, in karawitan, tempo depends on the player who sets the irama (*pamurba irama*) ['supervisor of irama'], i.e., the *kendhang* player. Since each player has his own individual sense of tempo, and since the function for which the gendhing is used may be different (e.g., for accompanying *wayang kulit*, in which the tempi are generally faster than in concert music [*klenèngan*]), tempo in karawitan is variable.

Although this is the case, one can still distinguish three basic tempi in karawitan:

    1. *tamban* ['slow']

    2. *sedheng* ['medium']

    3. *seseg* ['fast']

Tempo in karawitan is called "*laya*," not "irama."

Returning to the matter of the tempo of the saron panerus, each pulse
lasts approximately half a second.

We have already touched on the terms "laya" and "irama." But, in
everyday speech, the term "laya" is never heard; "irama" is invariably
used. Even so, all master musicians automatically know what the term
"irama" means [in different usages]. For example, the sentence, "Iramané
ketambanen" ['The irama is too slow'], clearly refers to laya, not irama.
But, in the sentence, "Mengko iramané lancar waé" ['We'll use irama lancar
later on'], irama in its true sense is referred to, not laya.

There are five types of irama, each with a separate name. Line (a) in
figure 1 is called "*irama lancar*." At this level, the saron panerus cannot
fill in with variations between balungan pulses, but plays the same number
of pulses as the balungan melody [carried by the other saron instruments].
In this case, I use the sign "1/1" to mean one balungan [pulse] to one
saron panerus [stroke]. Line (b) is called "*irama tanggung*," with the sign
"1/2" [i.e., one balungan pulse to two saron panerus strokes]. Line (c) is
called "*irama dados*," with the sign "1/4." Line (d) is called "*irama
wilet*," with the sign "1/8." Line (e) is called "*irama rangkep*," with the
sign "1/16." There is also another level of irama--faster than irama
lancar--usually called "*irama gropak*," with the sign "2/1."

2. Lagu

With regard to lagu, we will likewise limit ourselves to its
relationship to gendhing. The meaning of "lagu" is 'an ordered arrangement
of tones that sound pleasant when played'. The arrangement of tones, then,
must take a certain form. Many different forms have arisen and these are
called "*gendhing*." So, for example, the title "Gendhing *Gambir Sawit*"
refers to melodic elements [*lagu-lagu*] arranged into a form, in this case
the form *mérong kethuk kalih* ['2'] *kerep;*[*] this is called a gendhing, and
the gendhing is entitled *Gambir Sawit*.

---

[*]This will be explained further in the section "Gendhing," number 8a.

The Names and Functions of
Instruments in Karawitan

A. Instruments that
   relate to irama

   1. kendhang
      a. kendhang gedhé
      b. kendhang kalih
      c. ketipung
      d. ciblon
   2. kethuk
   3. kempyang
   4. kenong
   5. kempul
   6. gong
   7. kecèr (for wayangan)

Instruments that
relate to lagu

   1. rebab
   2. gendèr gedhé
   3. gendèr panerus
   4. gambang
   5. bonang gedhé
   6. bonang panerus
   7. slenthem
   8. demung
   9. saron barung
   10. saron panerus
   11. celempung
   12. suling

B. The respective function of irama-related instruments

   1. kendhang (serves as supervisor of irama [*pamurba irama*]):

      a. determines the form of the gendhing

      b. sets the irama and the course of the tempo (*laya*)

      c. determines the *mandheg*[*] and the ending

   2. kethuk (serves as an upholder of lagu [*pamangku irama*]):

      a. reinforces the kendhang in determining the form of the
         piece

      b. indicates the level of irama

   3. kenong (serves as an upholder of irama):

      a. determines the limits of the gatra, according to the form
         of the gendhing

   4. kempul (same as number 3 above)

---

[*]"Mandheg" [or "*andhegan*"] is a technique in which all the
instruments stop playing (though the piece is not yet over), and the piece
begins again with a vocal introduction.

5. gong (serves as an upholder of irama):

   a. reinforces the kendhang in determining the form of the gendhing

   b. serves as the *pada* [punctuation mark denoting the end of a stanza] and demarcates the final tone (*finalis*)

C. The respective functions of lagu-related instruments

   1. rebab (serves as the supervisor of lagu [*pamurba lagu*]):

      a. determines the lagu

      b. plays the *buka* for *gendhing rebab*

   2. gendèr gedhé (serves as an upholder of lagu [*pamangku lagu*]):

      a. beautifies the lagu with all its *cèngkok*

      b. plays the buka for *gendhing gendèr*

      c. plays the buka for *gendhing lancaran* when the *bonang gedhé* cannot do so

   3. bonang gedhé (serves as an upholder of lagu):

      a. beautifies the lagu with all its *cèngkok*

      b. plays the buka for *gendhing bonang*

      c. plays the buka for gendhing lancaran

   4. gambang (serves as an upholder of lagu):

      a. beautifies the lagu with all its *cèngkok*

      b. plays the buka for *gendhing gambang*

   5. celempung, gendèr panerus, bonang panerus (all serve as upholders of lagu)

      a. adorn the lagu

   6. slenthem, demung, saron barung (all serve as upholders of lagu):

      a. play the scheme of the lagu, termed "balungan"

   7. saron panerus (serves as an upholder of lagu):

      a. provides a pulse which may be used as a guide to the various levels of irama

Explanation. We will pause in our discussion to come back to the new terms we have used in this section.

a. Cèngkok. In gendhing, the word "cèngkok" has two completely different meanings: (1) 'playing style' or 'treatment' (*garap*); or (2) the number of *gongan* in one gendhing. Cèngkok, in the sense of a playing style, is a permanent, unchanging melody, either vocal or instrumental. For example, cèngkok "*ayu kuning*" ['pretty yellow maiden'] always has the following melody:

$$6 \quad \overset{.}{1} \quad \overset{.}{3} \quad \overset{.}{2} \quad 6 \quad 3 \quad 3 \quad 2 \quad 2 \quad 1$$

a - yu ku-ning bén-trok ma-ya ma-ya

Examples of variations are:

a. .6.1233.52.3653.32.31

b. . 6 . 1 23 3 .5 2 .3 65 3 .3 2 .3 1

A - yu   ku - ning   béntrok ma-ya ma-ya

c. 62 1 6 12 3 61 2 35 3 16 3 .6 21 62 1

A - yu   ku-ning   béntrok ma-ya ma- ya

It is clear that the above examples have the same motif, which is called "ayu kuning." But, the method of filling in the motif is different. These differences in, and types of, filling in are called "*wiletan*." So, the melodies above are the same in cèngkok, but different in wiletan.

The term "cèngkok" can also refer to the total number of gongan in a gendhing. Usually this usage is applied only to gendhing lancaran and above.[*] *Ayak-ayakan*, *srepegan*, *sampak*, and the like are thus not included.[**] Also, the word "cèngkok" is used in this sense only to refer

---

[*] I.e., in compositions whose gong structures are as long as, or longer than, lancaran. See the section "Gendhing," number 5 and following.

[**] See the section "The Names of Gendhing Forms," numbers 1-3.

to one section of a gendhing (to differentiate between the *mérong* and *inggah* sections). When a gendhing has both a one-gongan mérong and a one-gongan inggah section, one would not say that it has two cèngkok, but that the mérong section has one cèngkok and the inggah section has one cèngkok. So much for the term "cèngkok."

Now we shall consider another issue. After discussing the function of the instruments--both melodic and rhythmic--there may be some questions concerning the terms "supervisor" (*pamurba*) and "upholder" (*pamangku*).

b. Pamurba. It is easy enough to comprehend the term "supervisor," but what is its connection with karawitan? A supervisor is one who has the right to make decisions; he may also be called the leader. Thus, the supervisor of irama (*pamurba irama*) is the player with the authority to set the irama. Such is the case with the supervisor of lagu, also. The rebab--i.e., the rebab player--has the authority to make decisions, and can also be called the leader. The rebab player determines the course of the melody.

All decisions relating to irama, such as speeding up, slowing down, and changing from one irama to another, are under the absolute leadership of the kendhang player. As to choosing the gendhing, choosing whether to play in the sléndro or pélog tunings, or deciding whether or not to move to the higher register (*ngelik*),[*] the rebab player is in charge.

c. Pamangku. The upholding instruments are those that carry out a task to enable the supervisor's ideas to reach fruition. For example, the supervisor of irama may wish to change from one level of irama to another, and the instruments that uphold the irama--like soldiers--must not deviate. They should not set their own tempi, for not only will their efforts be in vain, but they will disrupt the flow of the gendhing. The case is similar with the supporters of lagu, also. If the supervisor of lagu determines the gendhing in the *buka*[**] of, say, Ladrang *Moncèr*, but after the gong the gendèr player proceeds to play Ladrang *Wilujeng*--thus, disobeying the supervisor of lagu--the result will be a breakdown of the gendhing. It is necessary to note here also that if there is no rebab, the bonang gedhé or the gendèr barung replaces the rebab as supervisor of lagu.

---

[*]See the section "Structures Found in Gendhing," number 3, below.

[**]See the section "Structures Found in Gendhing," number 1, below.

The Influence of Irama
on Lagu and Cèngkok

It is now best for us to return to the system of gendhing. Here we
shall talk about the influence of irama on lagu and cèngkok, for irama can
sometimes force lagu itself to change and cèngkok to be limited. This
occurs when the level of irama is accelerated--for examplè, in transition
from one irama level to another. A change in irama can effect a change in
lagu in many--though not all--gendhing. For example, in the gendhing
Ladrang *Pangkur*:

```
                                                    N
        a:    3   2   3   7      3   2   7   6

        b:  . 3 . 2 . 3 . 7    . 3 . 2 . 7 . 6

                                                    N
        a:    7   6   3   2      5   3   2   7

        b:  7 7 . . 6 6 7 2    3 2 5 3 . 2 . 7

                                                    N
        a:    3   5   3   2      6   5   3   2

        b:  . . . 3 6 5 3 2    3 2 5 3 6 5 3 2

                                                    G
        a:    5   3   2   7      3   2   7   6

        b:  6 7 3 2 6 3 2 7    . 3 . 2 . 7 . 6
```

Note: a = irama 1/1, 1/2, 1/4; b = irama 1/8, 1/16.

Here it can be seen clearly that a change in irama can affect both lagu and
cèngkok.

The Influence of Lagu on Irama

Although the influence of irama on lagu is very strong, there are also
lagu that are inflexible and cannot be presented in just any irama. They
have special irama associated with them, and are never presented in other
irama--for. example, the inggah[*] section of *Gambir Sawit Pacar Cina*, *Ela-
ela Kali Beber*, and others. These gendhing are associated with a
particular irama [or sequence of irama], and it is not possible to play

---

[*]See the section "Structures Found in Gendhing," number 7.

them in another irama.   There are also lagu that can be played only in
several specific irama.   Lagu of this type are called "*lagu mati*" ['fixed
lagu'] in karawitan.

Gendhing

We mentioned above that when lagu is organized into a form, that form
is called "gendhing." But in the field of karawitan the term "gendhing" is
only used to signify compositions that have a form consisting of *kethuk
kalih* and longer. Shorter forms [i.e., from *sampak* through *ladrang*] are
indicated with specific names.

The Names of Gendhing Forms

1. Sampak

```
      P   P   P   P   P   P   P   P
    N N N N N N N N N N N N N N N N
    3 2 3 2 3 2 5 3 5 3 5 3 2 1 2 1 2 1
```

The irama of sampak is always irama 1/1. Of the several rhythmic
instruments, only *kempyang* is not used in sampak. The *gong* used is the
gong suwukan.[*] The number of balungan or kenong strokes in each gongan is
not fixed.

2. Srepegan

```
        P       P       P       P       P
    t N t N t N t N t N t N t N t N t N t N t G
    . 3 . 2 . 3 . 2 . 5 . 3 . 5 . 3 . 2 . 1 . 2 . 1
```

The explanation of the structure of this form is much the same as that for
sampak, above.

3. Ayak-ayakan

```
      t   N   t   G   t   N   t   G   t   N   t   G   t   N   t   G
    . . . 3 . . . 2 . . . 3 . . . 2 . . . 5 . . . 3 . . . 2 . . . 1

      t   t N t   t G t   t N t   t G t   t N t   t G
    . 2 . 3 . 2 . 1 . 2 . 3 . 2 . 1 . 3 . 5 . 3 . 2
```

---

[*]The gong suwukan is smaller than the the the *gong ageng*, but larger
than the *kempul*. It is usually tuned to pitch *gulu* [2].

The initial irama of *Ayak-ayakan* [after the buka] is *irama gropak* [i.e., 2/1], followed by irama 1/1, and finally, irama 1/2. One irama-indicating instrument that is not used is the kempyang. Ayak-ayakan has many peculiarities, including the following:

a. It does not use the gong gedhé except for the final gong.

b. In ayak-ayakan [sléndro] pathet nem and sanga, all nonfinal gong are replaced by the kempul.

c. The irama undergoes three changes--first to irama gropak (2/1), then to irama lancar (1/1), then to irama tanggung (1/2).

d. In irama gropak and lancar, the kethuk plays once per kenong, but in irama tanggung, twice per kenong.

e. Irama tanggung is the basic irama for ayak-ayakan; however, the irama can also change to irama dados. For accompanying certain wayang scenes--notably *babak unjal* [the arrival of visitors in the first audience scene] in pathet nem and *alas-alasan* [scene of the hero in the forest] in pathet sanga--irama lancar is used throughout.

4. Kemuda

```
           P       P       P        P
   t tNt tNt tNt tNt tNt tNt tNt tNt tNt tG
   .2.6.2.6.2.6.2.6.3.3.2.3.2.1.2.1.6.5.4.5
```

This form is the same as sampak [insofar as there are two kenong beats per kempul beat]; the only difference is that it can be easily presented in irama lancar or irama tanggung. In wayang gedhog, kemuda in irama lancar serves as a replacement for srepegan, and in irama tanggung it is used to replace *Ayak-ayakan*, pélog pathet nem.

5. Lancaran

```
a.  [balungan nibani]:  t   t N t P t N t P t N t P t G
                        . 6 . 5 . 3 . 2 . 3 . 2 . 6 . 5

b.  [balungan mlaku]:   t   t N t P t N t P t N t P t G
                        6 3 6 5 6 3 6 5 6 3 6 3 6 1 3 2
```

Of the irama-indicating instruments, only the kempyang is not used for lancaran. Gong gedhé is used. Each gongan has a fixed number of balungan

pulses and kenongan. In examples (a) and (b) above each has its own
kendhang part.

6. Ketawang

The term "ketawang" actually refers to all forms in which each gongan
consists of two kenongan (thus, the second kenong occurring simultaneously
with the gong). In karawitan, the term "ketawang" is used in two ways:
(a) gendhing kethuk kalih [2] and longer, in which there are two kenongan
per gongan, are known as "ketawang gendhing"; and (b) ketawang in which the
kempul is used are known simply as "ketawang." For example: (a) Ketawang
Gendhing *Karawitan*, kethuk 4 kerep, laras sléndro pathet nem; (b) Ketawang
Puspa Warna, laras sléndro pathet manyura.

7. Ladrang

```
 p t p        p t p N      p t p P      p t p N
 5 3 1 6      5 3 1 6      3 3 2 3      6 5 3 2

 p t p P      p t p N      p t p P      p t p G
 3 2 3 5      6 5 3 2      1 6 5 3      5 6 1 6
```

All of the irama-indicating instruments are used. Each gongan has a fixed
number of kenongan [i.e., four].

8. Mérong

a. mérong kethuk 2 [i.e., kalih/loro] kerep

```
       t                   t           N
. 6 5 .    5 6 1 2    . 3 2 1    6 5 3 5


       t                   t           N
. 6 5 .    5 6 1 2    . 3 2 1    6 5 3 5


       t                   t           N
2 3 5 6    3 5 3 2    5 3 2 5    2 3 5 6


       t                   t           G
1 1 . .    3 2 1 6    3 3 5 6    3 5 3 2
```

Neither kempyang nor kempul is used in this form. The term "kethuk kalih
[2] kerep" here indicates that each kenongan consists of two kethuk
strokes. "Kerep" ['frequent'] means that the first kethuk stroke and the

second are close together (8 intervening balungan pulses), as distinguished from "kethuk arang" ['infrequent'] in which there are 16 balungan pulses between kethuk strokes (see examples below).

b. mérong kethuk 4 [i.e., sekawan/papat] kerep

```
      t                 t
 . . 6 5   3 3 5 6   2 3 2 1   6 5 3 2 ⎫
                                       ⎬ x 4 = one gongan
      t             t           N      ⎭
 . . 2 3   6 5 3 2   5 3 2 3   5 6 1 6 ⎭
```

See the explanation for (a) above.

c. mérong kethuk 8 [i.e., wolu] kerep

```
  t                   t
 . . . .   5 3 5 6   . 5 . 3   . 5 3 3 ⎫
      t                 t              ⎪
 5 5 . .   5 3 5 6   . 5 . 3   . 5 2 3 ⎪
                                       ⎬ x 4 = one gongan
      t                 t              ⎪
 5 5 . .   5 3 5 6   . 5 . 3   . 5 2 3 ⎪
      t                 t       N      ⎭
 6 6 . .   6 6 7 6   5 3 2 .   1 2 3 2 ⎭
```

See the explanation for (a), above; note that there is no such form as "kethuk 8 arang."

d. mérong kethuk 2 [i.e., kalih/loro] arang

```
          t
 . . 2 3   1 2 3 2   . . 2 3   5 6 5 6 ⎫
                                       ⎬ x 4 = one gongan
          t                 N          ⎭
 . . . .   2 1 6 5   3 3 6 5   2 3 5 3 ⎭
```

e. mérong kethuk 4 [i.e., sekawan/papat] arang

```
          t
 . 1 . 1   . 1 . 1   . 6 1 2   . 1 6 5 ⎫
          t                            ⎪
 . . 5 2   3 5 6 5   1 1 . .   1 2 1 6 ⎪
                                       ⎬ x 4 = one gongan
          t                            ⎪
 . . 6 1   6 5 3 5   1 1 . .   1 2 1 6 ⎪
          t                 N          ⎭
 . . . .   1 6 5 3   2 3 5 3   2 1 2 1 ⎭
```

9. Inggah

a. inggah kethuk 2 [i.e., kalih/loro]

This form is the same as the ladrang form. Thus, there are ladrang that may serve as inggah, although many can also stand alone. Ladrang that function as inggah--for example, Ladrang *Tlutur*, sléndro pathet sanga, Ladrang *Bang-bang Wétan*, [sléndro pathet manyura,] Ladrang *Kawit*, [sléndro pathet manyura,] and others--are ladrang that cannot be presented without a preceding mérong. Further, though there are ladrang that can be played independently, if they are presented after a mérong, they are considered as inggah.

b. inggah kethuk 4 [i.e., sekawan/papat]

```
p t p     p t p     p t p     p t p N
7 6 7 5   7 6 7 2   3 5 3 2   7 6 7 5     x 4 = one gongan
```

c. inggah kethuk 8 [i.e., wolu]

```
p t p     p t p     p t p     p t p
3 6 3 5   3 6 3 5   3 6 3 5   2 2 3 2 ⎫
                                      ⎬ x 4 = one gongan
p t p     p t p     p t p     p t p N
3 2 1 6   5 3 5 2   5 3 2 3   5 6 5 3 ⎭
```

d. inggah 16 [i.e., nem welas]

```
p t p     p t p     p t p     p t p
. 6 3 5   6 7 5 6   . 5 3 2   . 5 . 3 ⎫
                                      ⎪
p t p     p t p     p t p     p t p   ⎪
. 6 3 5   6 7 5 6   . 5 3 2   . 5 . 3 ⎬ x 4 = one gongan
                                      ⎪
p t p     p t p     p t p     p t p   ⎪
. 6 3 5   6 7 5 6   . 5 3 2   . 5 . 3 ⎪
                                      ⎪
p t p     p t p     p t p     p t p   ⎭
. 4 . 2   . 4 . 1   . . 1 2   . 4 . 5
```

Explanation. In the performance of the inggah form, all the instruments of the irama-indicating group are played; in inggah kethuk 4, 8, and 16, however, the kempul is not played.

10. Exceptional Forms

It is natural to expect that, where there are rules (*pathokan*), there are bound to be exceptions to those rules (i.e., irregularities). This is also true of Javanese gendhing. For example, in the mérong form there should be four kenong to one gongan, but there are cases where there are five kenong to one gongan. Similarly, in one kenongan there may be three kethuk strokes [instead of the usual two or four]. These exceptions are referred to as *pamijèn* ['irregular'].

Structures (*Komposisi*) Found in Gendhing[*]

1. buka
2. mérong
3. ngelik
4. umpak
5. umpak inggah
6. umpak-umpakan
7. inggah
8. sesegan

9. suwukan[**]
10. dados[***]
11. dhawah
12. kalajengaken
13. kaseling

1. Buka

Buka [literally, 'to open'] is a melody that is used as an introduction, or as an "opening" for a gendhing. The buka is performed by only one instrument. There are buka that can be performed by a vocalist; these are called *buka celuk*.

Examples of buka:

a. buka bonang

$$\text{2} \quad \text{2 1 6 5} \quad \text{. 6 5 .} \quad \text{5 6 1 2} \quad \text{1 3 1 2} \quad \text{2 1 6 \overset{G}{5}}$$

b. buka rebab [Ketawang *Taru Pala*, sléndro pathet manyura]

$$\text{6} \quad \text{6 1 6 5 3 6 5 6 2 1 3 2 3 1 . 2 } \overset{G}{6}$$

---

[*]I have been criticized for my use of the word "komposisi" ['composition'] as a generic term for numbers one to thirteen, above. A reader has suggested the term "struktur" ['structures'] instead. I concur.

[**]By this we do not mean gong suwukan.

[***]By this we do not mean irama dados.

c. buka gendèr [Ladrang *Moncèr*, sléndro pathet manyura]

$$. \quad . \quad \underline{3 \quad 5} \quad \underline{6 \quad .\overset{\cdot}{2} \; \overset{\cdot}{1} \quad 6} \quad \underline{\overset{\cdot}{1} \quad 6 \quad 5 \quad 3} \quad \underline{5 \quad 65 \quad .5 \quad \overset{-\;-}{6}} \quad G$$
$$. \quad 2 \quad . \quad . \quad \underline{. \quad 5 \quad 3 \quad 2} \quad \underline{\overset{\cdot}{1} \quad 6 \quad \overset{\cdot}{5} \quad 3} \quad \underline{5 \quad 6 \quad 21 \quad \overset{\cdot}{6}}$$

d. buka gambang [Ketawang *Undur-undur Kajongan*, sléndro pathet

   manyura]

$$\qquad\qquad\qquad\qquad\qquad\qquad\qquad\qquad\qquad\qquad\qquad G$$
$$\underline{. \; . \; . \; 2} \; . \; \underline{2} \; . \; \underline{3} \quad \underline{. \; 5} \; . \; \underline{3} \; \underline{5 \; 3} \; . \; 2 \quad \underline{. \; 5} \; . \; \underline{2} \; . \; \underline{3} \; \underline{5 \; 6} \quad \underline{. \; . \; 5 \; 6} \; . \; \underline{5} \; . \; \overset{\cdot}{3}$$
$$\underline{. \; . \; . \; 2} \; . \; \underline{2} \; . \; \underline{3} \quad \underline{. \; 5} \; . \; \underline{3} \; \underline{5 \; 3} \; 2 \; . \quad 5 \; . \; 2 \; . \; 3 \; . \; \underline{5 \; 6} \quad . \; . \; 5 \; 6 \; . \; 5 \; . \; 3$$

e. buka kendhang [Gendhing carabalèn *Pisan Bali*]

$$\overline{t \quad p} \quad \overline{p \quad p} \quad \overline{p} \quad . \quad \overline{b \quad p} \quad \overset{G}{b}$$

   [Note: t = "tak"; p = "dhung"; b = "dhah"]

f. buka celuk [Ketawang *Langen Gita Sri Naréndra*, pélog pathet

   barang]

$$6 \quad 7 \quad \overset{\cdot}{3} \; \overset{\cdot}{4} \quad \overset{\cdot}{2} \; \overset{\cdot}{3} \quad 6 \quad \underline{7 \quad 6} \quad 5 \quad . \quad 3 \quad . \quad \underline{7 \quad 2} \quad 3 \quad \underline{2 \quad 2} \quad \underline{7 \quad \overset{\cdot}{6}}$$

Si-nga   tir - ta   ka- wi   dha - yoh   wi -   nang   gi - ta

Explanation. Besides serving as the introduction to a gendhing, the
buka also helps to determine the category of the piece. For example, a
gendhing that uses a buka bonang usually falls in the category of gendhing
bonang (with the exception of lancaran). Gendhing that begin with a buka
gendèr are usually classed as gendhing gendèr, etc.

Commentary. In my opinion, categorizing gendhing on this basis is
unsatisfactory for the following reason. After the gong at the end of the
buka, the musical style of the rest of the gendhing is not distinguishable
[according to the instrument which plays the buka]. For example, the style
of a gendhing gendèr (with the buka played by the gendèr) would be the same
if the piece were introduced by the rebab.

2. Mérong

Mérong is one of the sections of a gendhing that provides an opportunity for a refined and calm playing style. In the mérong section the players must aim to create an effect [of refinement and peacefulness]. In addition, the mérong cannot stand alone; it must be followed by another piece or section. The continuation of a mérong is called "inggah"* and thus every mérong always has its corresponding inggah.

3. Ngelik

Ngelik is a section [of a gendhing] which is not essential, but which one has an obligation to play. By "obligation" we mean that it is not compulsory; if necessary, for lack of time or some other reason, one may omit the ngelik section. This should not present a problem in the performance of a gendhing. For example, a performance of Gendhing *Gambir Sawit* in which, for some reason, the ngelik is not played, would not be problematic and would still rightfully be called *Gambir Sawit*. Any piece in the gendhing form can have a ngelik section, but not every gendhing does.

It should be added here that many of the compositions of Mangku Negara IV violate the above rule [concerning the expendability of the ngelik] and the ngelik has become an inseparable part of the basic lagu of those compositions. In fact, the characteristic feature of a gendhing by Mangku Negara IV is that before the ngelik is played the gendhing is not yet distinguishable--one cannot guess its identity. For example, [in laras pélog,]

```
                              N
     .   2   .   3   .   2   .   1

             P               G
     .   3   .   2   .   1   .   6
                             .
```

This is possibly either [Ketawang] *Wala Gita*, or [Ketawang] *Ganda Mastuti*. We can identify it only after the gendhing has moved to the ngelik section. [Or, in another example,]

```
                              N
     6   6   .   .   2   3   2   1
     .   .
             P               G
     3   2   1   6   2   1   6   5
                 .           .   .
```

---

*See number 7, "Inggah," in this section, below.

Is this [Ketawang] *Raja Swala* or [Ketawang] *Sinom Parijatha?* No one can say for sure before hearing the ngelik that follows this melody. Many of the gendhing composed by Mangku Negara IV have this characteristic. Thus, a confusion in terminology has unwittingly arisen in karawitan. With the existence of the aforementioned kinds of gendhing, the term "umpak" arose, signifying the section of a gendhing which precedes the ngelik. Unfortunately, before the term came to be understood in this sense it already had another connotation, which we shall explain below.

4. Umpak

Umpak is the section of a composition that is used as a bridge from the mérong to the inggah section. So, if a mérong is to "minggah," that is, 'to move to the inggah', it cannot do so without going by way of the umpak. The player who signals the umpak is the supervisor of lagu (*pamurba lagu*). It should be noted that not all gendhing have umpak sections.

5. Umpak Inggah

This structure has a similar explanation to number 4, above. The main difference is that *umpak inggah* is signalled by the supervisor of irama (*pamurba irama*), whereas it is the supervisor of lagu (*pamurba lagu*) who signals the transition to umpak. Both umpak and umpak inggah have the [gong structure] characteristic of mérong. Not all gendhing have an umpak inggah section. In order to clarify these points, examples will be presented below.

6. Umpak-umpakan

Umpak-umpakan [is a kind of umpak that] does not have the form [i.e., gong structure] of mérong, but of inggah, and is used as a transitional passage to the main portion of the inggah.

7. Inggah

Inggah is a section of [a gendhing] that is used as a place for elaboration, ornamentation, and variation. Thus, inggah usually has a lively character. Inggah (or "minggah" [the verb form of the root "inggah"]) is a continuation of the mérong, although certain inggah can be played independently, that is, they need not follow a mérong section.

There are two types of minggah: (a) *minggah kendhang*, and (b) *minggah gendhing*.

In minggah kendhang, the kendhang alone plays a part specific to minggah, whereas the melody played is still the kernel lagu of the previous mérong section. The only difference is that, whereas the mérong is in the *balungan mlaku* style, the minggah is in the *balungan nibani* style.[*] Whereas the mérong uses simple and calm cèngkok, the minggah uses varied or lively cèngkok. Because of these differences in the character of mérong and inggah, we sometimes fail to recognize that the motif of the lagu is the same, especially if there has been a change in irama. [The melody of] minggah kendhang usually derives completely from the melody of the mérong. But, there are also instances where the minggah kendhang melody derives its motifs gatra by gatra, or, alternatively, derives them from larger melodic phrases (*kalimat lagu*).

In minggah gendhing the melody is not derived from the lagu of the preceding mérong, and may be in the balungan mlaku or balungan nibani styles. Gendhing with minggah ladrangan [i.e., in the ladrang form] may use either minggah kendhang or minggah gendhing.

Examples. The examples below are intended to clarify the explanations above; also, for those who have an interest in composing gendhing these examples will provide a basis for comparison.

  a. Gendhing *Gliyung*, kethuk 2 kerep, laras sléndro pathet manyura. The inggah to this gendhing is 100 percent minggah kendhang. The derivation of the lagu of the inggah is from each gatra of the mérong.

	I	II	III	IV
mérong (a)	. . 1 2	1 6 5 3	6 5 3 2	. 3 5 6 (N)
	5 5 . .	5 5 6 5	1 6 5 3	5 3 2 3 (N)
	6 5 3 5	3 2 1 2	6 6 . .	3 3 5 6 (N)
	3 5 6 1	6 5 3 2	. 1 6 5	1 2 3 2 (G)

---

[*]See example (a), below.

```
                                                    N
inggah (b)   . 3 . 2   . 5 . 3   . 5 . 2   . 5 . 6
             ‾‾‾‾‾‾‾‾   ‾‾‾‾‾‾‾‾   ‾‾‾‾‾‾‾‾   ‾‾‾‾‾‾‾‾

                                      .             N
             . 3 . 5   . 6 . 5   . 1 . 6   . 5 . 3
             ‾‾‾‾‾‾‾‾   ‾‾‾‾‾‾‾‾   ‾‾‾‾‾‾‾‾   ‾‾‾‾‾‾‾‾

                                                    N
             . 6 . 5   . 3 . 2   . 5 . 6   . 5 . 6
             ‾‾‾‾‾‾‾‾   ‾‾‾‾‾‾‾‾   ‾‾‾‾‾‾‾‾   ‾‾‾‾‾‾‾‾

                                                    G
             . 2 . 1   . 3 . 2   . 6 . 5   . 1 . 6
             ‾‾‾‾‾‾‾‾   ‾‾‾‾‾‾‾‾   ‾‾‾‾‾‾‾‾   ‾‾‾‾‾‾‾‾
```

b. Ketawang Gendhing *Kawit*, kethuk 2 kerep, minggah ladrang, laras
    sléndro pathet nem. The inggah to this gendhing is also 100
    percent minggah kendhang. The derivation of the lagu of the
    inggah from the lagu of the mérong is based on melodic phrases
    [i.e., not gatra per gatra].

```
                  I          II         III        IV
                                                            N
mérong (a)    . . . 3    . 1 2 3    . 1 2 3    . 1 2 3
              ‾‾‾‾‾‾‾    ‾‾‾‾‾‾‾    ‾‾‾‾‾‾‾    ‾‾‾‾‾‾‾

                                                            G
       (b)    2 2 . .    2 2 3 2    3 5 6 5    3 2 1 2
              ‾‾‾‾‾‾‾    ‾‾‾‾‾‾‾    ‾‾‾‾‾‾‾    ‾‾‾‾‾‾‾

                                                            N
       (c)    . . . .    2 2 3 2    3 5 6 5    3 2 1 2
              ‾‾‾‾‾‾‾    ‾‾‾‾‾‾‾    ‾‾‾‾‾‾‾    ‾‾‾‾‾‾‾

                                                            G
       (d)    3 3 . .    3 3 5 3    . 6 . 1    2 3 5 3
              ‾‾‾‾‾‾‾    ‾‾‾‾‾‾‾    ‾‾.‾‾‾‾    ‾‾‾‾‾‾‾

                             .           N                  .           N
inggah (a')   5 3 5 6    1 6 5 3    5 3 5 6    1 6 5 3
              ‾‾‾‾‾‾‾    ‾‾‾‾‾‾‾    ‾‾‾‾‾‾‾    ‾‾‾‾‾‾‾

                                         N                              G
       (b')   2 2 . .    2 2 3 2    3 5 6 5    3 2 1 2
              ‾‾‾‾‾‾‾    ‾‾‾‾‾‾‾    ‾‾‾‾‾‾‾    ‾‾‾‾‾‾‾

                                         N                              N
       (c')   3 2 3 5    6 5 3 2    3 2 3 5    6 5 3 2
              ‾‾‾‾‾‾‾    ‾‾‾‾‾‾‾    ‾‾‾‾‾‾‾    ‾‾‾‾‾‾‾

                                         N          .                   G
       (d')   3 3 . .    3 3 5 3    5 6 1 6    5 3 2 3
              ‾‾‾‾‾‾‾    ‾‾‾‾‾‾‾    ‾‾‾‾‾‾‾    ‾‾‾‾‾‾‾
```

It is unnecessary to give an example of minggah gendhing here, since there is no similarity between the lagu of the mérong and the lagu of the inggah in this form.

Below is an example of an inggah of mixed composition--part minggah kendhang, based on the melodic phrases, and part minggah gendhing. The example is Gendhing *Onang-onang*, kethuk 2 kerep, laras sléndro pathet sanga:

	I	II	III	IV
mérong (a)	. . 5 3	6 5 3 2	. . 2 3	5 6 3 5 (N)
(b)	1 1 . .	1 1 2 1	3 2 1 2	. 1 6 5 (N)
(c)	. . . .	5 5 3 5	6 6 . 5	3 3 5 6 (N)
(d)	3 5 6 1	6 5 3 5	2 3 5 6	3 5 3 2 (G)
(e)	6 6 . .	6 5 3 5	2 3 5 6	3 5 3 2 (N)
(f)	5 5 . .	5 5 2 3	5 6 5 3	2 1 2 1 (N)
(g)	3 2 1 2	. 1 6 5	2 2 . 3	1 2 3 2 (N)
(h)	. . 2 3	5 3 2 1	3 5 3 2	. 1 6 5 (G)
inggah (a')	. 6 . 5	. 3 . 2	. 3 . 2	. 6 . 5 (N)
(b')	. 2 . 1	. 2 . 1	. 3 . 2	. 6 . 5 (N)
(c')	. 6 . 5	. 1 . 6	. 5 . 3	. 5 . 6 (N)
(d')	. 5 . 6	. 3 . 5	. 6 . 5	. 3 . 2 (G)

```
                                            N
(e')  . 3 . 2   . 6 . 5   . 6 . 5   . 3 . 2
      _____

                                            N
(f')  . 3 . 2   . 6 . 5   . 6 . 5   . 2 . 1
                                    _____

                                            N
(g')  . 2 . 1   . 6 . 5   . 6 . 5   . 3 . 2
      _____

                                            G
(h')  . 3 . 5   . 2 . 1   . 2 . 1   . 6 . 5
      _____                         .   .
```

The greater part of the inggah is minggah kendhang and derives from the lagu of the mérong, based on melodic phrases [i.e., not gatra]. But, let us observe more closely that:

1. Line (a') is based on each melodic phrase.

2. Line (b') is based on each gatra.

3. Line (c') is based on two melodic phrases.

4. Line (f') is minggah gendhing, except for the last gatra. Thus, according to the above explanation, the common perception that the meaning of minggah kendhang is an inggah section that does not use the kendhang ciblon, is incorrect.

There are other matters concerning inggah that should be noted:

1. There are mérong that do not have inggah and thus must borrow their inggah sections from other gendhing.

2. There are mérong that have more than one [alternative] inggah section.

3. There are also inggah that have more than one [alternative] mérong associated with them.

Explanation. A mérong that utilizes a borrowed inggah actually has its own inggah--either minggah kendhang or minggah gendhing. But that inggah is not used, for one reason or another. We will use Gendhing *Laler Mengeng*, kethuk 2 arang (fourth kenong, kethuk 2 kerep), laras sléndro pathet sanga, as an example. This gendhing actually has its own inggah kendhang, but that inggah is never used. Rather, performers prefer to borrow the inggah of Gendhing *Tlutur*, which has an inggah ladrangan, called Ladrang *Tlutur*. The reason is that to use the inggah kendhang to *Laler*

Mengeng would mean breaking a rule concerning the sequence of inggah that can follow mérong sections.   This rule is summarized in the table below.

mérong	inggah
kethuk 2 kerep/arang	ladrang/kethuk 4
kethuk 4 kerep/arang*	ladrang/kethuk 4/kethuk 8
kethuk 8 kerep/arang**	kethuk 16

So, why does *Laler Mengeng* never use its own inggah?   Because of the above rules.[2]

There is another gendhing--Ketawang Gendhing *Randhat*, kethuk 4 kerep, laras sléndro pathet manyura--which always borrows its inggah from a different gendhing, but not because of the rules outlined above.   Gendhing *Randhat* actually does have its own inggah, Ladrang *Randhat*. But this ladrang is never used in performance as the inggah; rather, Ladrang *Kandha Manyura* is substituted.   This is true to this day.   In fact, the "ulterior motive" for using *Kandha Manyura* is merely to have an inggah in which there is a gérong part.   The lagu of *Kandha Manyura* and *Randhat* are nearly identical.   If the two ladrang are played instrumentally with *sindhèn* [but without gérong], the similarity of the two is evident--provided the musicians are sufficiently skillful.   But, it would be a shame if Ladrang *Randhat* were never performed.   (It cannot be presented separately since, coming as it does from a mérong, it does not have its own buka.)   This is the reason that at some subsequent time it came to be used as the inggah to Ketawang Gendhing *Merak Kasimpir*, kethuk 2 kerep, laras sléndro pathet manyura.   This has now become common practice.   Let this suffice as our explanation of borrowed inggah.

It is not necessary for us to go into great detail about mérong that have more than one inggah.   We shall only give the names of several examples: Gendhing *Gambir Sawit*, which, in laras pélog pathet nem can use as its inggah either *Pacar Cina*, *Jangga Lana*, or its own inggah.   In laras sléndro, *Gambir Sawit* can either use its own inggah [kethuk 4] or use *Sembung Gilang* (i.e., not the lancaran of that name).***

---

*However, kethuk 4 arang cannot be followed by an inggah kethuk 4.

**Gendhing in laras sléndro do not have mérong kethuk 8 kerep.

***The mérong of Gendhing *Gambir Sawit*, with its various inggah, has a very beautiful transition between umpak inggah and inggah.   The supervisor of lagu [pamurba lagu, i.e., the rebab player] need not inform the other musicians ahead of time as to which inggah he will choose, for it will be

As to inggah that have more than one merong, it shall suffice to give some examples--for instance, the inggah *Randha Maya* or *Èsèk-èsèk*. *Randha Maya* serves as the inggah to either Gendhing *Lungkèh* or Gendhing *Mongkok Dhelik*, both in laras sléndro pathet nem and both kethuk 4 arang. *Èsèk-èsèk* can be used as the inggah for several gendhing such as Gendhing *Rembun*, Gendhing *Banthèng Warèng*, or Gendhing *Pucung*, all in laras sléndro [pathet manyura]. It can also be performed in laras pélog pathet nem as the inggah to Gendhing *Méga Mendhung* or Gendhing *Kinanthi*.

There are also inggah that can stand alone--for example, *Kinanthi*, laras sléndro pathet manyura, kethuk 4, which is introduced by the buka celuk "Padhang bulan. . . ." Also, the inggah to Gendhing *Sinom* can stand alone, introduced by the bawa sekar ageng *Kusumastuti*.

8. Sesegan

The term "sesegan" should be distinguished from the term "seseg." Seseg has to do with laya [tempo], while sesegan can be categorized as a structural element in a gendhing. That part of a composition is used especially in accelerated tempi. In the general sense of sesegan as 'accelerated tempo', all gendhing can be considered to have sesegan. Gendhing that have sesegan [in the specific sense of a separate melody used only when the tempo speeds up] include: [Gendhing] *Bremara*, [Gendhing] *Jalaga*, [Gendhing] *Gobed*, Ladrang *Playon* [all in laras pélog pathet lima], and various gendhing bonang in laras sléndro.

9. Suwukan

"Suwukan" should be distinguished from "suwuk." "Suwuk" refers to the conclusion of a gendhing, whereas "suwukan" is one of the structural elements of gendhing, that is, the part of a gendhing that is used only when the gendhing is about to conclude. Not all gendhing have suwukan; some that do are [Gendhing] *Bremara*, [Gendhing] *Jalaga*, [Gendhing] *Babar Layar*, all in laras pélog pathet lima, [Ladrang] *Semang*, Ladrang *Bedhat*, etc.

---

clear from the umpak inggah. This is different from other similar gendhing, such as *Ganda Kusuma* (which can have either Ladrang *Ganda Suli* or Ladrang *Clunthang* as its inggah) or Gendhing *Sumedhang* (which can have either Ladrang *Clunthang* or Ladrang *Kapi Dhondhong* as its inggah). In the cases of *Ganda Kusuma* and *Sumedhang*, the supervisor of lagu must confer beforehand with the other musicians şince there is no distinguishing signal [in the transitional sections from merong to inggah].

10. Dados

"Dados" refers to the transition from one gendhing to another with the same gong structure--for example, "Ladrang *Sembawa* dados Ladrang *Playon*."

11. Dhawah

"Dhawah" refers to the transition from a vocal introduction, or bawa, to a gendhing--for example, "bawa sekar ageng *Manggala Gita* dhawah Gendhing *Onang-onang*."

12. Kalajengaken

"Kalajengaken" refers to the transition from one gendhing to another (other than from merong to inggah), the second of which does not have the same gong structure as the first--for example, "Ladrang *Pangkur* kalajengaken Ketawang *Sinom Parijatha*."

13. Kaseling

"Kaseling" refers to the interruption of one gendhing by another gendhing, which then returns to the first gendhing--for example, "Ladrang *Sembawa* kaseling Ladrang *Dhandhang Gula Mas Kentar*" [which indicates a transition from *Sembawa* to *Dhandhang Gula* and then a return to *Sembawa*].

Examples of Types of Structures

1. Gendhing *Jalaga*, kethuk 8 kerep, minggah kethuk 16, ketawang gendhing, laras pelog pathet lima (gendhing bonang). Types of structures found in Gendhing *Jalaga* are: buka, merong, umpak, inggah, umpak-umpakan, sesegan, and suwukan.

buka: adangiyah[*] . 3 . 3 . 3 2 1 . 3 1 2 3 5 6 $\overset{G}{5}$

mérong

```
[  .... 5356 .5.3 .523 55.. 5356 .5.3 .523
                                          N
   55.. 5356 .5.3 .532 66.. 5676 532. 1232


   .... 2235 6532 1232 .... 2235 6765 4.24
                                          G
   .521 ..24 .521 3212 ..23 5676 .53. 2353


   ...3 6521 66.. 2165 ..53 6532 .126 2165
                                          N
   ..53 6532 .126 5612 35.2 6532 .216 5456


   456. 3.32 .216 5456 456. 3.32 .444 2165
                                          G
   .... 5561 2165 7767 .... 7765 35.2 3565


   .... 5567 .653 .523 55.. 5567 .653 .523
                                          N
   55.. 5567 .653 6532 66.. 5676 532. 1232


   .... 2235 6532 1232 .... 2235 6765 4.24
                                          G
   .521 ..24 .521 3212 ..23 5676 .53. 2353


   ...3 6521 66.. 2165 ..53 6532 .216 2165
                                          N
   ..53 6532 .126 5612 35.3 6532 .216 5456


   456. 3.32 .216 5456 456. 3.32 .444 2165
                                          G
   .... 5561 2165 3323 .... 3321 .312 3565 ]
```

---

[*]A portion of the buka; not every buka will have an *adangiyah*. [The
adangiyah in pelog lima is: ...3 .... 2165 ...3 .... 2165 .]

umpak

```
                                                        N
    [ ..53 6532 .216 5612 35.3 6532 .216 5456
            ·    ··                        ····

      456. 3.32 .216 5456 456. 3.32 .444 2165
      ···       ·    ···· ···            ··
                                          G
      33.. 6532 66.. 66.1 22.. 2321 .653 2365

      ..53 6532 ..26 5365 ..53 6532 ..26 5365
      ··   ··   ··   ····  ··   ··   ··   ····
                                          N
      ..53 6532 ..26 5365 2356 532. 6656 2356
      ··   ··   ··   ····       ···  ···· ····

      .124 .126 .124 .126 .124 2123 .333 2165
           ·         ·                      ··
                                          G
      .55. 5532 .55. 5523 55.. 5356 5563 6535 ]
      ··   ···· ··   ···· ··   ···· ···· ····
```

inggah

```
    [ .22. 2356 5563 6535 .22. 2356 5563 6535
      ··   ···· ···· ····  ··   ···· ···· ····
                                          N
      .22. 2356 5563 6535 2356 532. 6656 2356
      ··   ···· ···· ····       ···  ···· ····

      .124 .126 .124 .126 .124 .123 .333 2165
           ·         ·                      ··
                                          G
      .55. 5532 .55. 5523 55.. 5356 1216 5322
      ··   ···· ··   ···· ··   ···· ···· ····

      .35. 2356 1216 5322 .35. 2356 1216 5322
      ··   ···· ·    ···· ··   ···· ·    ····
                                          N
      .35. 2356 1216 5322 .356 532. 6656 2356→
      ··   ···· ·    ····      ···  ···· ····

      .124 .126 .124 .126 .124 .123 .333 2165
           ·         ·                      ··
                                          G
      .55. 5532 .55. 5523 .55. 5356 5563 6535 ]
      ··   ···· ··   ···· ··   ···· ···· ····
```

umpak-umpakan

```
    →.124 1126 .124 .126 .124 2123 5653 2165
          ·         ·                      ··
                                          G
     3635 3632 3635 3632 3635 3632 3132 3635
     ···· ···· ···· ···· ···· ···· ···· ····
```

sesegan

```
[ 3635 3632 3635 3632 3635 3632 3132 3635
  ••••  ••••  ••••  ••••  ••••  ••••  ••••  ••••
                                              N
  3635 3632 3132 3635 2356 532. 6656 2356
  ••••  ••••  ••••  ••••  ••••  ••    ••••  ••••

  .124 .126 .124 .126 .124 2123 5653 2165 →
      •        •         •                ••
                                              G
  3635 3632 3635 3632 3635 3632 3132 3635 ]
  ••••  ••••  ••••  ••••  ••••  ••••  ••••  ••••
```

suwukan

```
                                      G
  → .... 5532 ..23 5535 ..23 55.3 6532 .3.5
         ••••      ••••      ••  ••  ••••  • •
```

2. Gendhing *Gobed*, kethuk 4 kerep, minggah 8, laras pélog pathet nem
(gendhing rebab). Types of structures found in Gendhing *Gobed* are: buka,
mérong, umpak inggah, inggah, and umpak-umpakan.

buka: adangiyah

```
                                                              •        G
[ 1̄2 3 . 2̄3 1 6 . 6 1̄2 3 . 3̄2 1 6 ] 2 1 6 1  2 3 5 3  1 6 . 5  3 2 1 2
       •          •                •
```

mérong

```
                                              N
  [ ..23 1232 ..24 .521 ..12 3216 ..61 2353
                             •             •
                                              N
    ..35 .653 6542 4521 ..12 3216 ..61 2353
                             •             •
                                              N
    ..35 .653 6542 4521 ..12 3216 ..65 6356
                             •             •
                                              G
    .... 66.. 6676 5421 612. 2212 33.. 1232
                        •         •
                                              N
    ..23 1232 ..23 5653 .523 5654 2.44 2165
                                              ••
                                              N
    .... 5535 66.. 1653 22.1 3216 ..63 2132 →
         ••••  ••   •••       •        •
                                              N
    .444 2126 .444 2123 .... 33.. 33.2 3521
         •                        •
                                              G
    .6.3 2132 3123 2123 .... 3353 6535 3212 ]
     •
```

umpak inggah

```
                                              N
  → .444 2126 .444 2165 .5.5 .2.6 ..76 5421
         •
                                              G
    .111 2321 .111 6124 .44. 4456 5424 2165
                        •                 ••
```

inggah

```
                                                        N
     [ ..6. 5.63 ..35 6532 3235 6535 4216 5612
                                                        N
       3216 5323 ..35 6532 3235 6535 4216 5612
                                                        N
       3216 5323 ..35 2.26 2.26 2.26 2123 2165
                                                        G
       .55. 5532 .55. 5532 .62. 62.3 5654 2165

                                                        N
       ..6. 5.63 66.. 6532 3235 6535 4216 5612
                                                        N
       3216 5323 ..35 6532 3235 6535 4216 5612
                                                        N
       3216 5323 ..35 2.26 2.26 2.26 2123 2165 →
                                                        G
       .55. 5532 .55. 5532 6323 5253 5154 2165 ]
```

umpak-umpakan

```
                                                        N
   → 3635 3635 3635 2232 3216 5352 5323 5653
                                                        N
     6563 6563 6563 2232 3216 5352 5352 5653
                                                        N
     6563 6563 6563 2.26 2.26 2.26 2123 2165
                                                        G
     3635 3632 3635 3632 3635 3632 3532 3635
```

3. Gendhing *Asri Katon*, kethuk 2 kerep, minggah kethuk 4, laras pélog pathet barang. Types of structures found in Gendhing *Asri Katon* are: buka, basic mérong, mérong ngelik, umpak inggah, and inggah.

```
                      G
buka:  .667 6523 ..35 6532 7732 .756
```

basic mérong

```
                              N
        [ ..67 5676 ..67 2327
                              N
          ..32 .767 2343 2767
                              N
          .3.2 .756 3567 6523
                              G
          ..35 6532 7732 .756 ]
```

mérong ngelik

```
                            N
            77.. 7765 .676 5323
                            N
            77.. 7765 .676 5323
                            N
            55.. 55.. 55.. 6356 →
                            G
            ..35 6732 7732 .756
                  ..     ...
```

umpak inggah

```
                            G
            → .5.6 .3.2 .3.2 .7.6
                              . .
```

inggah

```
                            N
            [ .7.6 .2.3 .5.3 .2.7
                .                .
                            N
            .2.7 .2.3 .5.3 .2.7
                .                .
                     .      N
            .3.2 .7.6 .2.7 .5.3
                            G
            .5.6 .3.2 .3.2 .7.6 ]
                              . .
```

4. Gendhing *Méga Mendhung*, kethuk 2 arang, minggah *Èsèk-èsèk*, kethuk 4, laras pélog pathet nem. Structures found in this gendhing are: buka, mérong, and inggah.

```
                          G
buka: .223 1232 .23. 3235 .632 1232
```

mérong

```
                              ..      N
      [ ..23 1232 ..23 5656 .... 2165 3365 2353
                              ..      N
        2132 ..12 3312 .126 .... 2165 3365 2353
                                  ..    N
        2132 ..12 3312 .126 .... 6656 1126 5323
                                      G
        .23. 323. 323. 1232 323. 3235 .632 1232 ]
```

inggah

```
                        N
[ .3.2 .3.1 .2.6 .3.2
                        N
  .3.2 .3.1 .2.6 .3.2
      .   .   .   . N
  .5.3 .2.1 .2.1 .2.6
    .       .     G
  .2.6 .3.5 .1.6 .3.2 ]
```

5. Ladrang *Wilujeng* kalajengaken Ketawang *Puspa Warna*, laras sléndro pathet manyura. [Both the ladrang and the ketawang comprise a basic melody (*lagu pokok*) and ngelik melody (*lagu ngelik*).]

Ladrang *Wilujeng*

```
                     G
buka: .132 6123 1132 .126
                        .
```

basic lagu

```
                N         N
[ 2123 2126 33.. 6532
        .
                N         G
  5653 2126 2123 2126 ]
                     .
```

lagu ngelik

```
        . .N     .    N
  .666 1516 3561 6532
        . .N          G
  .66. 1516 1132 .126
                     .
```

Ketawang *Puspa Warna*

basic lagu

```
          N         G
[ .2.3 .2.1 .3.2 .1.6 ]
                     .
```

lagu ngelik

```
              N
           ....      .  G
  .... 2321 3265 1653
          N         G
  ..32 5321 .3.2 .1.6
                     .
          N         G
  .2.3 .2.1 .3.2 .1.6
                     .
```

6. Ladrang *Sembawa* (gérong bedhayan) dados Ladrang *Playon*, laras
pélog pathet lima.

```
                          G
buka: .323 5653 5323 1212
                             N        N
                     [ .111 2321 .111 2353
                             N        G
                       .356 7653 5323 2121 ] →
```

lagu ngelik

```
                        ..  . N ...    N
                       ..32 .165 1216 5356
                          N        G
                       .653 6535 6621 2353

                          N        N
                       .323 2121 .111 2353
                          N        G
                       .356 7653 5323 2121 ]
```

Ladrang *Playon*

```
                          N        N
                   → .542 1245 .542 1245

                          N        G
                     .542 1245 66.7 5676
```

ngelik

```
                          N        N
                     .654 2212 ..24 5.65
                          N        G
                     6542 1645 .612 1645
                       •••   •   •••
```

basic lagu

```
                          N        N
                     .612 1645 3365 3216
                       •    •••        •
                          N        G
                     5612 3212 1654 2465
                       ••    ••• ••••
```

The foregoing are several examples of structures found in gendhing.
Lagu kaseling is well known enough that I need not provide an example. I
think that this is enough discussion concerning the system of gendhing to
equip us and to facilitate probing more deeply into the study of karawitan.

The Sléndro and Pélog Tuning Systems

I already mentioned that karawitan is a music which uses the sléndro
and pélog tuning systems. In the sléndro tuning system, there are five
tones in one *gembyangan** with [relatively] equal intervals between tones.
Pélog has seven tones in one gembyangan, with unequal intervals. In order
to clarify this, we have produced a table, kept in the Research Department
of the Conservatory (figure 2). This table shows the difference in
measurement of intervals between the pélog and sléndro tuning systems and
the diatonic scale. The intervals shown in the table are only approximate;
if we study the intervals on an actual gamelan, we may find many
differences in interval size. In karawitan, the variability of interval
size is called "*embat*."

Figure 2. [Comparison of Interval Size in the Sléndro and Pélog Tuning
            Systems and the Diatonic Scale]

laras pélog:

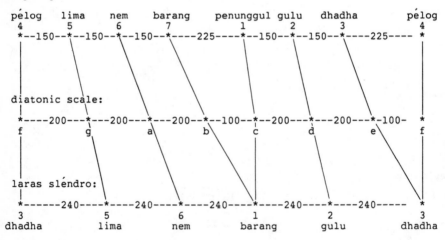

[Note: The above figures are approximate and indicate measurements in
cents.]

---

  *"Gembyangan" can be conceived as identical to "octave," but,
because "octave" means the eighth level, while "gembyang" does not
necessarily imply an eighth level, it is necessary to differentiate between
the terms.

In my opinion, there are two kinds of embat found in karawitan--
natural embat (*embat alam*) and fabricated, or artificial, embat (*embat
buatan*). Natural embat is the shift each tone undergoes after a change in
mode,* so that after a change in mode there must be one or more tones that
shift. It is exceedingly difficult to construct a gamelan based on natural
embat, because each time the mode changes, the pitches have to be changed.
As a result, the policy in gamelan tuning is to take the embat that pleases
the gamelan maker. This is what I call "fabricated embat." The fabricated
embat have had a great influence on the [perceived] characteristics of each
set of gamelan instruments; some gamelan are felt to be majestic, others
lively, others melancholy, and so on. It is not surprising that, if a
person owns more than one gamelan, the gamelan will probably have different
embat and will differ in absolute pitch.

There are those who claim that there are two kinds of embat--"embat
nglarasati" and "embat nyenggani"**--and that the intervals between tones
in the former are large, while intervals between tones in the latter are
small. In my opinion, this statement is confusing, for how could this be
so? Since the basic intervals in a gembyangan are always the same, if all
the tones had large intervals between them, what would happen to the
interval of one gembyangan? It would be stretched, and even more so in
succeeding gembyangan. So, the intervals in a gembyangan cannot possibly
be all large or all small. In figures 3 and 4, I have presented tables
that illustrate this point. These tables give some idea of the varieties
of embat realized in [actual] gamelan sets. It turns out that, among all
these gamelan, no two are alike. For, only the principle of tuning is the
same; gamelan sléndro has fairly even intervals, while gamelan pélog has
five small and two large intervals. This can be seen in figures 3 and 4.

---

*In this instance "mode" may be defined as an order of intervals
(*rèntètan jarak nada*) that is established or fixed. For example, the order
456 - 12 - 4 has the same interval structure as the order 123 - 56 - 1,
that is, narrow-narrow-wide-narrow-wide. Since the sequence of intervals
in the two series of tones is the same, they can be said to have the same
mode. This is distinguished from a series of tones such as 2 - 456 - 12
which has the sequence of intervals wide-narrow-narrow-wide-narrow [and
thus represents a different mode].

**"Nglarasati" refers to the personality of the wayang character
[Dèwi] Larasạti; "nyenggani" refers to the personality of the wayang
character [Dèwi] Senggani.

Figure 3. Embat in Gamelan Sléndro, Interval Measurements [in Cents]

	1	2	3	5	6	i
1. Kyai Manis Rengga Kraton Surakarta	219	226	266	232	257	
2. Kyai Kanyut Mèsem Istana Mangku Negaran	263	223	253	236	225	
3. Dalem Kusumayudan Surakarta	231	218	275	230	246	
4. [Gamelan donated by] Paku Buwana X Pura Paku Alaman, Yogyakarta	229	226	252	231	262	
5. Kyai Harja Mulya Kraton Yogyakarta	215	249	215	261	260	
6. Kyai Madu Kèntar Pura Paku Alaman	220	268	240	242	230	
7. Kyai Pangawé Sari Pura Paku Alaman	249	251	233	254	245	
8. Dalem Joyodipuran Yogyakarta	238	239	231	234	245	
9. Kabupatèn [Mojokerto] Mojokerto	250	244	228	240	238	
10. Gamelan Pusaka Majapahit Mojokerto	257	250	228	221	254	
11. Gamelan Konservatori Karawitan Indonesia [acquired] 1952	236	236	246	236	246	

Figure 4. Embat in Gamelan Pélog, Interval Measurements [in Cents]

	1	2	3	4	5	6	7
1. [Kyai] Kaduk Manis [Kraton] Surakarta	114	137.5	272.5	113.5	137	192.5	233
2. [Kyai] Kanyut Mèsem Mangku Negaran	125	146.5	251.5	165.5	99.5	166.5	245.5
3. [Dalem] Kusumayudan Surakarta	135	157.5	296	110	91	176	235
4. [Gamelan donated by] Paku Buwana X Pura Paku Alaman	140	144.5	274	114.5	114.5	72.5	240
5. [Kyai] Harja Mulya [Kraton] Yogyakarta	103.5	133.5	284.5	134.5	123	158.5	265.5
6. [Kyai] Sirat Madu [Kraton] Yogyakarta	103.5	149.5	278.5	131	139.5	149	249
7. [Kyai] Telaga Muncar Pura Paku Alaman	98	124.5	283	144	91.5	155	304
8. [Dalem] Joyodipuran Yogyakarta	94	204	249.5	106	127	181.5	238
9. Kabupatèn [Mojokerto] Mojokerto	145	113	262	132	128	145	275
10. Kabupatèn [Pasuruhan] Pasuruhan	132	150	338	98	105	142	234
11. [Gamelan] Konservatori [Karawitan Indonesia] [Acquired] 1952	120	140	270	140	120	140	270

Now we must know what is meant by natural embat. To explain natural embat, we must distinguish between laras sléndro and laras pélog, because the two laras are idiosyncratic.

Laras Sléndro

In one gembyangan of laras sléndro there are five tones, which can be considered to have equal intervals between them. When these tones take the form of keys, they are arranged in the following order.

Figure 5. [The Tones in Laras Sléndro]

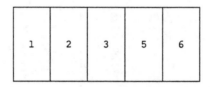

If we read (sing) the sléndro tones in order, from low to high, or vice versa, and listen to them carefully, we will find both large and small intervals between them. The small interval is situated in between the larger ones. This would appear in diagram form as follows:

Figure 6. [Sequence of Sléndro Intervals]

This is what we mean by "natural embat" (*embat alam*), or, more emphatically, "*embat kodrat*" ['embat based on universal laws, laws of nature']. This embat was the progenitor of embat used in gamelan, although we do not know for sure who first formulated embat alam in gamelan instruments. In fact, we no longer know who first created the arrangement of gamelan instruments found today. For, not only the arrangement of instruments, but also the style of playing the gamelan is based solely on tradition, which must be perpetuated.

In the past, there have been several innovations; these have not represented essential differences, but only added improvements. For

example, an additional key, pitch 6, was added to the thirteen-keyed
gendèr. Two kempul were added to make a total of five. But, principal
elements such as those we pointed out above have not changed. For example,
the sléndro rebab must always be tuned to 6 and 2, and the sléndro kethuk
must always be tuned to pitch 2 (gulu). So too, when we introduce embat
alam into the sléndro gamelan, we must be able to choose between [three
pre-existing possibilities]:

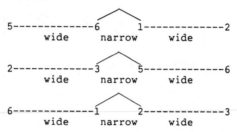

We are free to choose one or another embàt alam for application to the
gamelan. But "free to choose" does not mean the choice is easy; to
understand this we must first discuss pathet. When we apply one of the
embat above to a particular pathet, another pathet played in relation to
that same embat relationship may not produce pleasing results.

Usually we have a particular pathet in mind before we choose an embat.
Then we can consider the effect of the embat we chose on other pathet. If
it turns out that our choice is not appropriate to another pathet, then the
[embat of the] first pathet must be adjusted--the influence of the embat
must be diminished so that another pathet will [sound acceptable]. This
process is extremely difficult and requires the services of an expert. Let
us consider figure 7 and note how gamelan makers of old realized embat alam
in gamelan instruments.

Pathet

What is pathet? This question is always on my mind. I think no
definition has yet been satisfactory, due to the fact that the word
"pathet" has so many different uses, and each use fulfills a particular
need. So if one is to offer an explanation of pathet, the explanation must
be relevant to the particular need at hand. For example, I once asked an
ironsmith, "What is a knife?" He answered, "A knife is a kind of machete,
but smaller." It is understandable that his definition had to do with the

Figure 7.   [A Comparison of the Embat of Ten Sléndro Gamelan, with Indication of
Interval Size, in Cents (numbers refer to figure 3)]

No.	Gamelan							
1.	[Kyai] Manis Rengga	3	266	5	232	6	257	1̇
2.	[Kyai] Kanyut Mèsem	1	263	2	223	3	253	5
4.	[Gamelan donated by] Paku Buwana X / Paku Alaman	5	236	6	225	1	263	2
5.	[Kyai] Harja Mulya	3	252	5	231	6	262	1̇
6.	[Kyai] Madu Kèntar	6	260	1	215	2	249	3
7.	[Kyai] Pangawé Sari	6	230	1	220	2	268	3
8.	[Dalem] Joyodipuran	2	251	3	233	5	254	6
9.	[Mojokerto] Kabupatèn Mojokerto	2	239	3	231	5	234	6
10.	[Gamelan] Pusaka Majapahit	5	240	6	238	1	250	2

shape of the object, since as a toolmaker and vendor, he assumed that the questioner was a prospective customer and would want to calculate the cost of the object. However, when I asked a noodle vendor the same question, I got a very different answer. He said that a knife is an instrument used to cut onions, cabbage, and the like, while a machete is an instrument used to split wood. He wanted to impress upon the customer that he was a man who kept things clean and would not mix dirty and clean implements.

So it is with pathet. If we ask a dhalang what "pathet" means, he might answer that pathet refers to a "period of time." For, in wayang performances, gendhing of a particular pathet are associated with a particular time period [i.e., division of the play] which is referred to as "pathet." In fact, the pathet of a gendhing may be determined by the "pathet"--division of the play--in which it is used. For example, a gendhing that is actually in pathet manyura but is played during "pathet nem" [i.e., the section of the play when gendhing in pathet nem are usually played], will be considered as pathet nem as well.

If we ask a man who likes to perform songs what "pathet" is, we will probably get a different answer. He will say that pathet is "key," in the sense in which it is used in Western music. Thus, when he wants to perform a song, he need only find the key [i.e., pathet] that accommodates the range of his voice.

If we ask this same question of a practicing gamelan musician, such as myself, we will get the following explanation. Pathet is performance practice or treatment (*garap*), and to change pathet means to change treatment. Let me clarify this.

The Tones in Laras Sléndro

Laras sléndro has five tones, each with its own traditional name.

1. panunggul (pn)

2. gulu (gl)

3. dhadha (dh)

4. lima (lm)

5. nem (nm)

Some interpret these as follows:

1. panunggul = 'head'

2. gulu = 'neck'

3. dhadha = 'chest'

4. lima = 'hand', 'fingers'

5. nem = (meaning unclear)

If we understand the names of the tones, we know the sequence of the keys
and how to arrange the keys and gongs of each gamelan instrument. So, when
the gamelan is played--each instrument played according to the technique
appropriate to it--we do not need to be told what tones we are hearing.
(This is particularly true for someone who fully understands the playing
techniques of all the instruments.) For this reason, the term "pathet"
came into use to refer to the different treatments associated with pieces
in different pathet. For instance, if we take Ladrang *Pangkur* in sléndro
pathet manyura and in sléndro pathet sanga, the vocal melody [in both
pathet] may be the same, but the instrumental parts will certainly be
different. This point can be proven by studying the bonang part for
Ladrang *Pangkur*; the pathet manyura part will be inappropriate for pathet
sanga. Not only will the pitch level be shifted upward or downward (what
is known as "transposition" in Western music), but in some sections the
part will be significantly different. Thus, each instrument--with its
characteristic treatment and playing techniques--can delineate differences
in pathet. The instrument that can demonstrate these differences most
clearly is the *gendèr gedhé* (referred to in Yogyakarta as *"gendèr barung"*).
Let us proceed to examine the matter of the relationship of gendèr gedhé to
pathet.

Gendèr Gedhé [and Its Relationship to Pathet]

I shall not bother to provide a complete description of the shapes and
names of the various parts of the gendèr gedhé, for the instrument should
be well known to most readers.

The Number of Keys on the Gendèr Gedhé

By "keys" (*wilahan*) here, I mean the part of the instrument that is
struck [with a mallet]. Archaic gendèr gedhé had only ten keys. The
sequence of the pitches, from left to right, is illustrated in figure 8.

Figure 8.   [The Keys of the Gendèr Gedhé]

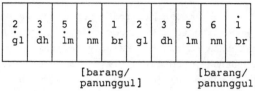

2 gl	3 dh	5 lm	6 nm	1 br	2 gl	3 dh	5 lm	6 nm	i br

[barang/   [barang/
 panunggul]   panunggul]

    I have yet to see a gendèr like the one outlined above. The gendèr
with which I am familiar have twelve, thirteen, and sometimes fourteen
keys, as shown in figure 9. For most musicians skilled in playing the
gendèr, a gendèr with thirteen keys is sufficient for executing all the
most beautiful cèngkok. So even if someone shows the initiative to add
another key, it will be of little use for the professional; in fact, one
could say that such a key is almost never used. The intention of the
innovator is probably to merely beautify the appearance of the gendèr, or
to make it symmetrical (i.e., so that each set of support pins will flank
two keys).

Figure 9.

    Gendèr with twelve keys

1 br	2 gl	3 dh	5 lm	6 nm	1 br	2 gl	3 dh	5 lm	6 nm	i br	2 gl

    Gendèr with thirteen keys

1 br	2 gl	3 dh	5 lm	6 nm	1 br	2 gl	3 dh	5 lm	6 nm	1 br	2 gl	3 dh

    Gendèr with fourteen keys

6 nm	1 br	2 gl	3 dh	5 lm	6 nm	1 br	2 gl	3 dh	5 lm	6 nm	1 br	2 gl	3 dh

Cèngkok as It Relates to Performance Practice

When we hear a full gamelan playing a gendhing, we hear each
instrument played according to its characteristic performance technique.
Among all the instruments no two use exactly the same technique. Although
the slenthem, saron barung, and demung essentially play the same part,
sometimes the technique used differs (for example, when playing *pinjalan*).
If we differentiate between the types of performance practice, or treatment
(*garap*), for all the instruments, there are three basic types.

1. *gumathok* ['fixed', 'set']: a playing technique that is not melodic
    and not tied to the melodic movement of the balungan, but to the
    form [gong structure] of the piece. The instruments that utilize
    this technique serve to indicate irama.

2. *sekaran* [from *sekar* 'flower']: a type of playing that involves
    inserting other melodies (*lagu*) into the basic melody (*lagu
    pokok*). This technique is characteristic of the kendhang ciblon
    as well as the bonang barung and bonang panerus when the latter
    two utilize the technique known as "*imbal*."

3. *cèngkok*: a playing technique that is guided by the pattern of the
    balungan and dependent upon the course of the balungan melody.
    All of the melodic (lagu) instruments utilize this playing style.

Gembyang and Kempyung in Gendèr Gedhé

If we listen to the gendèr playing of master musicians of Central
Java--particularly in Surakarta and Yogyakarta--and if we pay close
attention to the movements of their right and left hands, which seem to be
moving almost independently, we find that almost invariably at the end of a
cèngkok [i.e., at the sèlèh, or cadence] the hands will strike the interval
of a *gembyang* or *kempyung*. What is a gembyang? It is the interval
produced by striking two keys that flank four other keys [as illustrated
below]:

gembyang

A kempyung is the interval produced by striking two keys which flank two other keys. [Thus:]

```
        o o o o
        *     *
        ───────────
        kempyung
```

The Range of Sèlèh

We said above that a gendèr with thirteen keys is sufficient to play all kinds of cèngkok. And these cèngkok must, by definition, have a final tone (*sèlèh*). The sèlèh are restricted to a specified range on the gendèr, that is, a cèngkok, upon reaching the sèlèh, must fall within the prescribed range. This range is pictured in figure 10.

Figure 10. [Range of Sèlèh in] Gendèr with Thirteen Keys

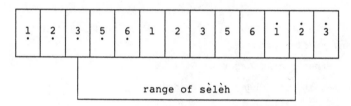

Let us examine what we find in the range of sèlèh pictured in this figure.

a. There are eight tones in the range of sèlèh.

b. The tones are 2, 3, 5, 6, 1, 2, 3, 5.

c. There are two 2's (gulu), two 3's (dhadha), and two 5's (lima); there is only one 1 (panunggul) and one 6 (nem).

Of the two gendèr mallets held in the right and left hands, the one held in the left hand indicates the sèlèh. The right hand has the task of striking either the kempyung or the gembyang above the key struck by the left hand. So there is only one sèlèh tone for each cèngkok.

According to tradition, there are only three pathet in laras sléndro-- sanga, nem, and manyura. How is one to divide the cadential tones (sèlèh) among these three pathet?

Pathet and the Range of Sèlèh on the Gendèr

It is probably clear by now that a pathet has a basic tone, or *tonika*
[from the Dutch "*tonica*"]. In the slèndro tuning system, there are five
tones with approximately equal intervals between them. So, it would seem
that all five tones could function as a tonika, or *dhong*, and could be
linked theoretically in a circle such as that pictured in figure 11.

Figure 11. [Circle of Dhong Tones]

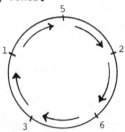

Figure 11 clearly shows that the slèndro tuning system can, in fact,
have as many as five pathet:

a.   a pathet with dhong tone 5 (lima)

b.   a pathet with dhong tone 2 (gulu)

c.   a pathet with dhong tone 6 (nem)

d.   a pathet with dhong tone 3 (dhadha)

e.   a pathet with dhong tone 1 (barang/panunggul)

Based on these dhong tones we can arrange the tones according to their
functions.

Figure 12.

	lower kempyung	dhong	upper kempyung	pelengkap	dhing
I.	1	5	2	6	3
II.	5	2	6	3	1
III.	2	6	3	1	5
IV.	6	3	1	5	2
V.	3	1	5	2	6

Three of the pathet in figure 12 [numbers I, II, and III] have been given names by our ancestors: the pathet with dhong 5 [number I] is called "pathet sanga"; the pathet with dhong 2 [number II] is called "pathet nem"; and the pathet with dhong 6 [number III] is called "pathet manyura." The pathet with dhong 3 [number IV] and dhong 1 [number V] were not used by our ancestors and thus were not given names. For our own purposes, we will call these pathet "X" and "Y," respectively.

This gives rise to the question, "Why do dhong tones 3 and 1 not merit their own pathet?" To answer this question we must continue the explanation begun above. Let us rearrange the tones in figure 12 (see figure 13).

Figure 13.

	lower kempyung	upper kempyung	dhing	dhong	pelengkap
pathet sanga	1	2	3	5	6
pathet nem	5	6	1	2	3
pathet manyura	2	3	5	6	1

Figures 12 and 13 clearly show that the interval between one pathet and another is one kempyung. When we apply the interval of a kempyung to the keys of a gendèr, the picture shown in figure 14 will emerge.

Figure 14.

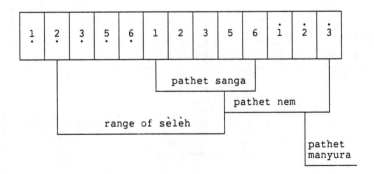

Considering the situation represented in figure 14, we should not try to make five pathet, for even pathet sanga presents some difficulty in that one of its tones, pitch 6, lies outside the range of sèlèh.

Let us first look at pathet manyura, for it lies farthest from the range of sèlèh. Let us try to move this pathet so that it falls within the range of sèlèh. We can lower pathet manyura one gembyangan, as in figure 15.

Figure 15.

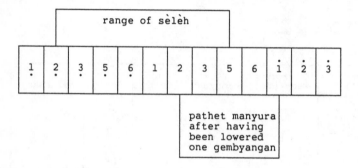

This results in a situation in which two tones remain outside the range of sèlèh (see figure 15). We should move on to a second step in our efforts (see figure 16).

Figure 16.

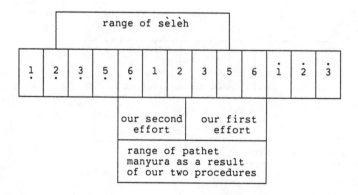

In our second step, we lowered tones 6 and 1̇ one gembyangan. Having accomplished these two steps, all the tones of pathet manyura lie within the range of sèlèh. The order of tones is now as in figure 17.

Figure 17.

dhong	pelengkap	lower kempyung	upper kempyung	dhing
6̣	1	2	3	5

We have succeeded in moving pathet manyura into the range of sèlèh. We should now deal with pathet nem, but, because so many of the tones of pathet sanga already fall within the range of sèlèh, and if we were to move pathet nem before pathet sanga, we would have to shift the tones of pathet sanga that already lie in the range of sèlèh. For this reason, we will work with pathet sanga first.

We will lower the two top tones of pathet sanga one gembyangan (see figure 18). Why? If only pitch 6 of the pathet lies outside the range of sèlèh, why should we move pitch 5 as well? We will do so because, if we moved only pitch 6, there would be no difference between pathet sanga and pathet manyura.

Figure 18.

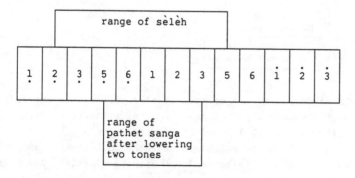

If we arrange the tones of pathet sanga according to modal practice, figure 19 results.

Figure 19.

dhong	pelengkap	lower kempyung	upper kempyung	dhing
5̣	6̣	1	2	3

Now pathet sanga is in the range of sèlèh and its area is clear. Let us compare the diagrams of pathet manyura and sanga in their original positions (see figure 14). The two pathet were previously two kempyung apart, but now are only one tone apart (see figure 20).

Figure 20.

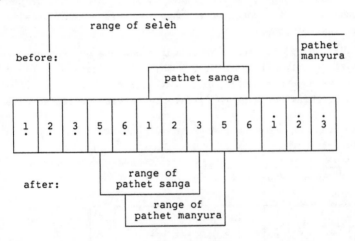

We must now arrange pathet nem so that it will fall within the range of sèlèh. Most of the tones of pathet nem are outside the range (e.g., pitches 6, 1̇, 2̇, 3̇). Only pitch 5 is within the range of sèlèh. If we look at the tones in the range of sèlèh not taken by pathet sanga and pathet manyura, we see that only pitches 2 and 3 are available. For this reason it is necessary to lower only pitches 2 and 3 of pathet nem into the range of sèlèh. It is not necessary to move pitches 6 and 1. In addition to the fact that these tones are already the property of pathet sanga and pathet manyura, even if they were moved they would not be

consecutive with the other moved tones (2, 3, 6, and 1). Figure 21 shows
the three pathet in the range of sèlèh.

Figure 21.

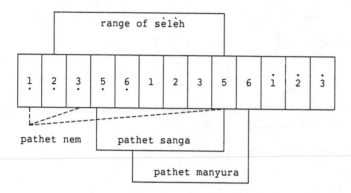

This is the position of pathet nem in the range of sèlèh. How is it
played? I will discuss this later. Now I shall explain gembyang and
kempyung on the gendèr gedhé.

The Range of Gembyang and Kempyung on the Gendèr

    In gendèr playing the cèngkok must have sèlèh ['cadences'], and these
sèlèh must fall in the range of sèlèh. There are only two possibilities
for sèlèh--sèlèh gembyang and sèlèh kempyung. Gembyang and kempyung also
have a specific range of occurrence on the gendèr. Let us look at this
range of sèlèh gembyang and sèlèh kempyung in figure 22.

Figure 22.

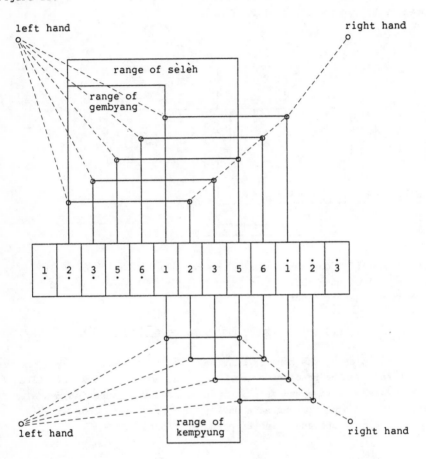

We note in figure 22 that:

a. Pitch 1 can be used as either sèlèh gembyang or sèlèh kempyung.
    (In pathet manyura, pitch 1 is used as sèlèh gembyang and in
    pathet sanga as sèlèh kempyung.)

b. Pathet nem has two gembyang and one kempyung [in its range], while
    the other two pathet have two gembyang [i.e., manyura: 6 and 1;
    sanga: 5 and 6] and two kempyung [manyura: 2 and 3; sanga: 1 and
    2]. This is a [relative] weakness of pathet nem.

For this reason, people whose appreciation of Javanese music is limited
will often have trouble differentiating between pathet nem on the one hand,
and pathet manyura or sanga on the other.

Moreover, there are people who are so bold as to claim that pathet nem
is a mixture of pathet manyura and pathet sanga. As far as I am concerned,
this opinion is incorrect. It is true that a mixture of pathet (*modulasi*
[from Dutch]) is common in Javanese gendhing--especially in Surakarta; in
fact, it can be said that there are almost no gendhing that do not include
a mixture of pathet. But, even so, the principal pathet will be clearly
felt. There are also a few gendhing whose pathet is ambiguous or seems
forced, for example, those for which the pathet should be manyura, but is
labelled "nem."

In figure 22 the [traditionally] established sèlèh gembyang and sèlèh
kempyung are clearly illustrated and these cannot be added to, nor can
their ranges be expanded. To add more keys [to the gendèr] would be a
simple matter, but the difficulty lies in creating new cèngkok. At most,
only new wiletan can be created. And, in fact, even this possibility has
not proved to be true; rather, the number of wiletan would seem to have
decreased over time. For, the number of wiletan created by our forebears
has actually dwindled and we have already lost many of the musical ideas
previously bequeathed to us. For instance, a set of bonang has been added
to the gamelan ensemble that accompanies the wayang kulit (*gamelan
wayangan*), and this is called "progress" (*perkembangan*). But, when seen
from the point of view of gendèr playing, this innovation could be
considered regressive. For, with the addition of the bonang, the gendèr
cèngkok played for sampak, srepegan, and lancaran[*] have become extinct.
(Very few individuals remain who know how to play those cèngkok.)

The question has occasionally been raised as to whether new cèngkok
could be created by merely transposing (*transposisi*) already existing
cèngkok up or down one pitch level. My answer to this is that it is just
too difficult. Cèngkok in manyura, for instance, can be easily transposed
to pathet sanga [and cèngkok in sanga to manyura] by merely lowering [or
raising] the melodies by one pitch level, though occasionally there are
cèngkok that can only be forcibly transposed [in that manner]. If we try
to transpose to pathet nem, however, the awkwardness is quite apparent.
Listeners experienced in Javanese gendhing would only laugh to hear the

---

[*]The meaning of "gendèr cèngkok for lancaran" here refers to
gendèran in irama lancar (1/1).

following attempt to transpose the cèngkok "*puthut gelut*" [from sanga/ manyura to pathet nem].

```
                         ·     · ·
pathet sanga:            1  6  1 2
                         ‾‾‾‾‾‾‾‾‾‾
                         1  6  5 2
                            · ·


                         ·  · · ·
pathet manyura:          2  1 2 3
                         ‾‾‾‾‾‾‾‾‾
                         2  1 6 3
                              ·


pathet nem:              5  3 5 6        (hypothetical)
                         ‾‾‾‾‾‾‾‾‾
                         5  3 2 6
                         ·  · · ·
```

The Strength of a Tone Based on Its Position

Before we discuss the strength of a tone based on position, let us look at figures 23 and 24.

Figure 23.

			I	II	III	IV	V	
pathet sanga			5.	6.	1	2	3	
	I	II						III
pathet nem	2.	3.						5
			I	II	III	IV	V	
pathet manyura			6.	1	2	3	5	

Figure 24.

	dhong	pelengkap	lower kempyung	upper kempyung	dhing
	I	II	III	IV	V
pathet sanga	5̣	6̣	1	2	3
pathet nem	2̣	3̣	5̣		
pathet manyura	6̣	1	2	3	5

Explanation

I. <u>Dhong</u>. This tone is also called the "*nada dasar*" ('basic tone'), which means that it serves as the basic tone in a pathet. Both vocalists and instrumentalists orient themselves to only one tone, the dhong tone. It serves as a guide to the pathet. When the dhong tone is used as a sèlèh, it will feel more resolute than the other tones. For this reason, this tone is the strongest of all the tones. If the dhong is the sèlèh in a cèngkok, the gendèr player will play gembyang.

II. <u>Pelengkap</u>. When this tone is used as sèlèh, it will seem weak or irresolute. It will seem unpleasant if used as a sèlèh tone. Nevertheless, its use does still clearly delineate the pathet, since it has special cèngkok associated with it in each pathet. The pelengkap also serves to reinforce the strong position of the dhong tone. If this tone falls as the sèlèh, the gendèr player will play gembyang.

III. <u>Lower Kempyung</u>. If this tone falls as the sèlèh, the feeling is resolute, but not as strong as the dhong tone. Because of this the lower kempyung also serves to strengthen the position of the dhong tone. That is, without the lower kempyung, the strength of the dhong tone would seem less pronounced. Let us take an example from pathet nem: the lower kempyung is 5̣, but because it does not follow consecutively with the other sèlèh tones in nem (see figure 23), the cèngkok used will be taken from pathet sanga (where 5̣ is the dhong tone) or manyura (where 5̣ is the dhing tone). For this reason, the dhong of pathet nem (2) is not as strong in that position as is tone 5̣ for pathet sanga or tone 6 for pathet manyura.

•

As a result of the weakness of the dhong tone in pathet nem, the difference
in relative strength of the sèlèh tones in pathet nem is less noticeable.

IV. Upper Kempyung. This tone is much weaker in pathet sanga than in
pathet manyura because the upper kempyung in sanga (pitch 2) requires the
same cèngkok as for pitch 2 in manyura (where it serves as the lower
kempyung). That is, the gendèr cèngkok required for pitch 2 will always
end on the interval of a kempyung. If occasionally one hears gendèr
players using a different cèngkok (leading to pitch 2), it is merely their
attempt to provide variation; in fact, there is no need to provide such
variation beyond attempting to differentiate sèlèh 2 in pathet sanga and
pathet manyura.

The case is different for pathet manyura, however, where the upper
kempyung is strong within the pathet, though weaker than the lower
kempyung. Why? Because there is no pathet whose pitch level lies higher
than manyura and thus the upper kempyung tone in manyura [3] will require
cèngkok that are exclusive to manyura.

The upper kempyung tone in pathet sanga [2] can also be strong, if it
is preceded or followed by a cadence (*kaden*)[*] typical of pathet sanga:

$$1 \quad 3 \quad 1 \quad \overset{\downarrow}{2} \qquad 1 \quad \underset{•}{6} \quad 1 \quad \underset{•}{5} \quad \text{(with sanga cadence following)}$$

$$1 \quad \underset{•}{6} \quad 1 \quad \underset{•}{5} \qquad 1 \quad \underset{•}{6} \quad 1 \quad \overset{\downarrow}{2} \quad \text{(with sanga cadence preceding)}$$

[Note: Arrows indicate sèlèh on upper kempyung, pitch 2.]

When such an arrangement of tones occurs, pitch 2 (the upper kempyung of
pathet sanga) is strong.

Pathet nem does not have an upper kempyung (see figure 20) because
pitch 6 is a part of pathet manyura and pathet sanga. So, when in pathet
nem compositions the sèlèh is pitch 6, usually either a manyura or a sanga
cèngkok is borrowed, depending on the preceding and/or following phrase.
In pathet nem, a sèlèh on pitch 6 usually requires a borrowed cèngkok.
Nevertheless, it is possible to increase the feeling of pathet nem (in
cèngkok to pitch 6) by having strong pathet nem tones, such as 2 and 3,
accompany pitch 6; for example, 2 3 5 6 or 5 3 5 6 . I will explain
more about this in the section on melodic direction (*arah nada*) below.

---

[*]"Kaden" (*cadens* [from Dutch]) refers to a particular sequence of
tones in a melodic phrase (*kalimat lagu*).

V. <u>Dhing</u>. Dhing is the weakest tone; it usually becomes the forbidden
tone in the pathet. Whenever dhing is used as a sèlèh tone in a pathet--
even if it is used only as the ending tone of a melodic phrase (not to
mention as a final sèlèh)--it will result in a feeling of awkwardness. In
fact, it can transform the atmosphere of the pathet.[*]

Pathet nem does not have a dhing tone and thus does not have a
prohibited tone. Although pathet nem has only a few tones, each of them is
strong. According to the theory of pathet, pathet nem has a dhong tone 2;
thus, its dhing theoretically must be pitch 1. However, sèlèh on pitch 1
(dhing) found in pathet nem gendhing are not felt to be awkward at all,
because cèngkok can be borrowed from pathet sanga or pathet manyura. The
dhing tone in a particular pathet does not have cèngkok associated with it
to serve as cèngkok for sèlèh. When [the dhing tone falls as a sèlèh],
cèngkok from another pathet must be used.

Mixing Pathet

The meaning of "mixing pathet" is about the same as the meaning of the
term "modulation" (*modulasi* [from Dutch]) in Western music. I touched on
the issue of mixing pathet above where I explained that of all Central
Javanese gendhing, especially in Surakarta, very few do not mix pathet.
However, the basic pathet remains clearly apparent. If we examine figure
25 (the circle of kempyung), we will see that the manner of mixing has
specific limits--pathet may not be mixed arbitrarily or without
limitations. Only adjacent pathet can be mixed, as illustrated in
figure 25.

---

[*]See, for example, Gendhing *Lonthang Kasmaran*, laras sléndro pathet
sanga.

Figure 25. [The Circle of Kempyung]

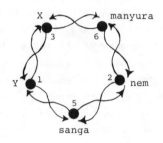

In this figure, we see that pathet can only mix with (modulate to) the
adjacent pathet. Because there are only three traditional pathet in our
music, only the pathet with dhong tone 2 (pathet nem) can mix in both
directions. For this reason, when pathet nem has manyura cadences, it
often uses cèngkok from pathet manyura, and when pathet nem has sanga
cadences, it often uses cèngkok from pathet sanga. Thus, only pathet nem
has the flexibility to use cèngkok from two other pathet.

Pathet manyura is able to mix only with the pathet to its left [i.e.,
facing the inside of the circle] because the pathet to its right is not
found. Pathet sanga is able to mix only with the pathet to its right
because the pathet to its left is not found. Thus, these two pathet (sanga
and manyura) are able to modulate to pathet nem only. A forced marriage
between pathet sanga and manyura would produce very awkward-sounding
results. Examples of this sort are Gendhing *Kuwung-kuwung*, laras sléndro
pathet manyura, and Gendhing *Lonthang Kasmaran*, laras sléndro pathet sanga.
We cannot speak for the individual listener's response to the feeling of
these gendhing in their arrangement of strong and weak tones.

In response to the question, "What about gendhing that have pitches 1
and 3 as dhong [cadence] tones," my response is that neither of these two
dhong tones can [be the basis for separate] pathet, because there is no
room for such a pathet in the range of sèlèh. Besides, there is a more
important reason: our ancestors have left us cèngkok in only three pathet
(sanga, nem, and manyura) and to this day we are not capable (or not yet
capable) of adding to these. Thus, when confronting gendhing that have
dhong [cadence] tones 1 or 3, like it or not, we must use the cèngkok of
the three given pathet. For example, if there is a gendhing that has the

dhong [cadence] tone 3, we may draw from manyura or nem cèngkok for pitch
3, but we may not draw from cèngkok in sanga, since pitch 3 is the
forbidden tone (dhing tone) in pathet sanga. If there is a gendhing with
the dhong [cadence] tone 1, we may draw from sanga or manyura cèngkok for
the pitch 1, but not from cèngkok in nem, since pitch 1 is not present in
the hierarchy of tones in pathet nem. Even were it present, it would be
the dhing tone. Cèngkok-borrowing among the three main pathet is shown in
figure 26.

Figure 26.

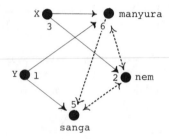

Explanation

A. Pathet manyura can borrow from pathet Y (i.e., for playing dhong
    tone 1), or from pathet X (i.e., for playing dhong tone 3).

B. Pathet nem can borrow from pathet X only.

C. Pathet sanga can borrow from pathet Y only.

From figure 26 we can see that pathet manyura is the strongest of the
pathet because it can borrow from two other pathet, while the other main
pathet can borrow from only one other pathet. For this reason, when a
composer notates a melody whose pathet is as yet indeterminate, or which
has yet to be accompanied by the gamelan, the composer will usually notate
the melody in pathet manyura.

Issues Related to Pathet

Padhang-ulihan

   Padhang-ulihan is found in many disciplines--dance, carving,
discourse, behavior, etc. In short, everything has padhang-ulihan.
"Padhang" ['bright', 'light', 'clear'] is something that is clear, but
whose ultimate purpose is still unknown. That which clarifies the final
purpose is "ulihan" ['return', 'coming home']. For an example, let us
imagine that we see a man walking to the bath, and we are unaware of his
intentions. Will he take a bath, or wash his face, or merely inspect the
condition of the bathwater? In other words, we know the padhang, but not
the ulihan.

   It is clear that each padhang may have 1,001 different ulihan. But it
is necessary that there be a harmonious match between padhang and ulihan.
If we saw a man enter the bath and straightaway lie down to take a nap, we
would certainly laugh, since his intentions are not in agreement with the
original appearance of his actions.

   It is necessary to keep in mind that there are different levels of
padhang-ulihan. For example, if a man goes to the bath with the intention
of washing his face, this set of padhang-ulihan [i.e., action, final
intention] can itself become a padhang [which will then be balanced by a
larger ulihan]. For example, the scheme of *dhandhang gula*, [laras]
sléndro:

3	6	1̇	1̇		1̇	2̇	3̇	3̇	3̇	3̇	
Wer-	di	ning-	kang		war-	si -	ta	ji-	nar-	wi	
	padhang					*ulihan*					⎫
3̇	3̇	3̇	2̇		2̇	2̇	1̇	1̇	1̇	1̇	⎬ *padhang*
Wruh	ing	ku -	kum		i -	ku	wa -	teg -	i -	ra	
	padhang					*ulihan*					⎭
1̇	1̇	1̇	1̇		1̇	1̇	6	6			⎫
A	- doh	ma -	rang		ka -	nis -	tha-	né			⎬ *ulihan*
	padhang					*ulihan*					⎭

This example should suffice [to show something about the levels of padhang-ulihan in Javanese vocal music]. As for instrumental music, there are two types of padhang-ulihan: as a part of cèngkok, and as a part of gendhing.

Padhang-ulihan as a Part of Cèngkok

The first of two cèngkok will serve as the padhang, while the second will serve as the ulihan. Each cèngkok has a fixed length. The gendèr part most clearly shows the limits of padhang and ulihan. Figure 27 shows the limits of gendèr cèngkok arranged by gatra as they are related to each level of irama.

Figure 27.

gatra I				gatra II				
padhang				ulihan				
3	2	3	1	3	2	1	6	irama lancar
3	2	3	1	3	2	1	6	irama tanggung
3	2	3	1	3	2	1	6	irama dados
. 3 . 2		. 3 . 1		. 3 . 2		. 1 . 6		irama wilet
. 3 . 2		. 3 . 1		. 3 . 2		. 1 . 6		irama rangkep
padhang		ulihan		padhang		ulihan		

In reference to figure 27, I must insert an explanation concerning the connection between irama and padhang-ulihan in cèngkok. In the world of karawitan, the term "rangkep" ['doubled'] has two usages: rangkep for cèngkok (i.e., cèngkok rangkep), and rangkep for irama (i.e., irama rangkep). For example, in the case of the gendhing, Ladrang *Mugi Rahayu*, and the inggah to Gendhing *Mudhatama*, in which the irama [usually used] is irama dados with kendhangan ciblon, if the irama is doubled (*dirangkepkan*) the gendhing would still be irama wilet (and not yet irama rangkep). However, the cèngkok of the gendèr and kendhang, for instance, would be cèngkok rangkep. The padhang and ulihan also would be the same as in irama dados, although according to figure 27 the padhang-ulihan in irama wilet are usually half as long as in irama dados.

In my personal opinion, if the levels of irama and their relationship to the divisions of padhang-ulihan (as illustrated in figure 27) were not a

tradition inherited from our ancestors, I would take issue with them, for
they tend to arouse confusion. Still, were we to change them we would
encounter great difficulties, for these rules have become habitual for us.
If I were to suggest a change in these rules, I would divide irama into two
parts: the smooth (*luwes*) irama would be called "*sabetan*," while I would
substitute "rangkep technique" (*tehnik rangkep*) or "rangkep treatment"
(*garap rangkep*) for what is [now] called "irama rangkep."

Padhang-ulihan as a Part of Gendhing

Here I mean the padhang-ulihan ordered into melodic phrases for
gendhing. Thus, the meaning of "padhang" is an unresolved melody, and
"ulihan" is a resolved melody (*lagu sumèlèh*). This is the same in vocal
pieces except that in gendhing [instrumental pieces] the length of padhang
and ulihan depends on the form of the gendhing. In other words, each
gendhing has its own rules. These will be easier to understand if I
explain them one at a time.

Padhang-ulihan melodic phrases in the sampak form:

Explanation. The sampak form is composed of several melodic phrases.
In each phrase a stress is felt; that stress is then bounded by an ulihan
that carries a sense of resolution (*rasa sèlèh*). However, this sèlèh is
less resolute than the ulihan that ends with a gong [stroke], in which case
the previous ulihan will appear lighter, and this ulihan will in turn serve

as padhang [to the stronger ulihan that coincides with the gong stroke].
Analogously, the gong tones that previously felt resolute will still be
less resolute than the final gong. This is what we mean by "levels" [in
the relationship of padhang-ulihan]. Gendhing forms with the same padhang-
ulihan as sampak are srepegan, ayak-ayakan, and kemuda.

Padhang-ulihan melodic phrases in the lancaran form:

Example (a) [Lancaran *Ricik-ricik*, laras sléndro pathet manyura]:

```
                                                    G
buka:    . . . 6    . 3 5 6    . 5 3 2    . 3 5 6
            p          u          p          u

         N          N          N          .   G
    [ . 3 . 5    . 6 . 5    . 6 . 5    . 1 . 6
         p          u          p          u

       N          N          N          .   G
     . 3 . 2    . 3 . 2    . 3 . 2    . 1 . 6 ]
         p          u          p          u
```

Example (b):

```
                  .          .                G
buka:          . 1 . 6    . 1 . 6    5 3 2 3
                  p          p          u

         N          N          N          G
    [ . 5 6 3    . 5 6 3    . 5 6 3    5 2 3 5
         p          p          p          u

       N          N          N          G
     . 3 6 5    . 3 6 5    . 3 6 5    3 2 1 2
         p          p          p          u

       N          N          N          G
     . 1 3 2    . 1 3 2    . 1 3 2    5 6 5 3 ]
         p          p          p          u
```

Explanation. In this illustration, (a) represents a lancaran form
with *balungan ndhawahi* and (b) represents a lancaran form with *balungan
mlampah*. Each kenong[an] represents a melodic phrase. Each gong[an]
comprises four kenongan (i.e., four melodic phrases). The first three
kenong[an] have the feeling of padhang, while the last kenong[an] (i.e.,
ending with a gong), has the feeling of ulihan.

The order described above represents [historically] the first scheme
of padhang-ulihan devised for lancaran. Eventually, composers felt that
this form was too narrowly conceived and placed extreme limitations on

gendhing lancaran, since it was very difficult to compose such melodic phrases. Then came a new idea concerning the form of melodic phrases in lancaran. In lancaran with more than two gong[an], the final gong could be composed of only two melodic phrases (rather than four as in the older style), in order to provide a smooth return to the opening phrase. For example:

Example (c) [Lancaran *Béndrong*, sléndro pathet manyura]:

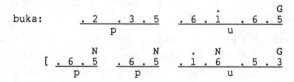

In this lancaran, the last gong[an] has only two melodic phrases [i.e., "padhang" and "ulihan"].

There is another form of lancaran in addition to the two forms described above. In this form each gong[an] is composed of three melodic phrases--the first two gatra make up two melodic phrases and the last two gatra make up one melodic phrase. For example, with balungan ndhawahi [nibani]:

Example (d):

```
          N              N              N              G
  . 5 . 3      . 5 . 3      . 5 . 2      . 3 . 5
      p              p              u

          N              N              N              G
  . 6 . 5      . 6 . 5      . 3 . 2      . 1 . 2
      p              p              u

          N              N              N              G
  . 3 . 2      . 3 . 2      . 6 . 1      . 6 . 5 ]
      p              p              u
```

And, an example with balungan mlaku [/mlampah]:

```
              N              N              N            G
buka:    . 3 5 .      2 3 5 6      2 3 2 1    6 5 3 5
              p            p            u

            N              N              N            G
[ 6 3 6 5      2 3 5 6      2 3 2 1    6 5 3 2
      p            p            u

            N              N              N            G
  3 1 3 2      3 1 3 2      5 6 5 3    2 1 6 5 ]
      p            p            u
```

Around 1930, I first heard the *adegan jaranan* [the horse-riding scene]
in the *wayang gedhog* accompanied by the gendhing, Lancaran *Tropong Bang*,
laras pélog [pathet nem], with Ketawang *Langen Gita* inserted into it, but
played in a lancaran style. To this day, this practice is still prevalent
in the accompaniment of wayang purwa. It is not clear who originated it.
The practice of forcing the melodic phraseology of ketawang into the gong
structure of a lancaran probably led to the appearance of several other
lancaran composed without regard to the traditional melodic phraseology
found in older lancaran. The composers following this trend merely made
sure that the piece was melodic, and that the number of beats fit the
lancaran form. For example, here is a [lancaran in] balungan nibani, which
actually uses the phraseology of a ketawang:

Example (e): [Lancaran *Witing Klapa*, sléndro pathet manyura]:

```
                                                          G
buka:      . 6 1 2      . 6 . 3      . 6 . 5      . 3 . 2
                p            u            p            u
                     p                         u

              N              N              N              G
[ . 5 . 6      . 5 . 3      . 5 . 3      . 2 . 1
      p            u            p            u
            p                         u
```

```
           N              N              N        .   G
         . 2 . 1      . 2 . 3      . 5 . 6      . 1 . 6
           p            u            p            u
              p                         u

           N              N              N        .   G
         . 3 . 5      . 6 . .      . 2 . 3      . 2 . 1
           p            u            p            u
              p                         u

           N              N              N        .   G
         . 3 . 2      . 6 . 3      . 6 . 5      . 3 . 2 ]
           p            u            p            u
              p                         u
```

Another example, with balungan mlaku:

```
                                                        G
buka:      1 5 1 6    5 3 2 1    6 1 2 3    6 5 3 2
             p          u          p          u
                 p                     u

             N          N          N                    G
     [ 3 1 3 2    5 3 2 1    6 1 2 3    6 5 3 2
         p          u          p          u
             p                     u

             N          N          N                    G
       3 5 3 2    5 3 2 1    6 1 2 3    6 5 3 2
         p          u          p          u
             p                     u

           N      .   . N          N                    G
       6 6 . .    1 5 1 6    3 5 6 1    6 5 3 2
         p          u          p          u
             p                     u

       .   . N          N          N                    G
       1 5 1 6    5 3 2 1    6 1 2 3    6 5 3 2 ]
         p          u          p          u
```

Lancaran that use the melodic phrasing of ketawang have not provoked discussion, since most listeners' emotional appreciation [of the music] is unaffected. People are content just to enjoy these "ketawang-as-lancaran." But, in the formal study of the rules of karawitan, there must be a special understanding of the structuring of melodic phrases in the various gendhing forms.

There has arisen another kind of lancaran, which includes a vocal part, and whose melodic phrases are even more chaotic, because the vocal part has obviously been composed first and the balungan rather arbitrarily

tacked on afterward. The function of the balungan in these pieces is not
to serve as a point of reference, but merely to accompany the vocal part.
Such a compositional process is unfortunate since it gives no thought to
the form of melodic phrases which must be used in the composition of
gendhing. It also tends to violate traditional instrumental practice.
Here is an example of such a composition.

a.	.	.3	33	3	.5	6 12	6 .5	3	
		Na - li-ka	ni - ra		ing	da - lu			
b.	3	3	5	3 (N)	5	6	5	3 (N)	

a.	.	.3	3 .3	61 .	.1	2 .3	12 1	6	
		Wong	agung	mang-sah	se - me -	di			
b.	.	.	3	5 (N)	6	1	5	6 (G)	

a.	.2	1	.6	12 .	.6	1 .2	2 .3	3. 2	
	si - rep	kang	ba - la	wa - na - ra					
b.	2	1	6	2 (N)	6	1	2	3 (N)	

a.	.1	.3	3 35	2	. 12	3	12 1	6	
		sa - daya	wus	sa- mi	gu - ling				
b.	1	1	3	2 (N)	.	1	2	6 (G)	

a.	.5	3	2 2	2	.6	12	23	3	
	na - dyan	a - ri	su - dar - sa - na						
b.	5	3	2	. (N)	6	1	2	3 (N)	

```
        —       .      —              ——       ——
a.    .6     1     2 6   5     .  35  6     35 3  2
      wus    da  - ngu   den  -  i - ra     gu - ling

                              N                  G
b.     6     1     6     5     3     2     1     2
```

In the example, the vocal part (a) was composed first, and only then
was the balungan (b) affixed and made to agree with the vocal melody.
Then, the composer(s) added a buka and a so-called umpak to the beginning
of the piece, and named the vocal part "ngelik." The irama of the umpak
section is to be irama tanggung, and for the transition to the ngelik in
irama dados the drummer must give a peremptory signal on the drum--"*tung
bleb.*" The melodic phrasing [of the balungan] is as follows.

```
                                                           G
buka:        . 3 5 2    6 1 2 3    6 1 6 5    3 2 1 2
                p        ·  u          p          u
                    p                       u

[umpak:]
                        N           N       .  N        G
a.       [ 3 1 3 2     6 1 2 3     6 1 6 5    3 2 1 2
              p         ·  u          p          u
                   p                       u

[ngelik:]
                        N           N           N     .  G
b.         3 3 5 3     5 6 5 3     . . 3 5    6 1 5 6
              p            u          p          u
                   p                       u


                        N           N           N        G
c.         2 1 6 2     6 1 2 3     1 1 3 2     . 1 2 6
              p            u          p          u
                   p                       u


                        N           N       .  N        G
d.         5 3 2 .     6 1 2 3     6 1 6 5    3 2 1 2 ]
              p         ·  u          p          u
                   p                       u
```

I mentioned above that I considered this kind of composition
regrettable since it extensively violates proper instrumental practice.
Let us examine the matter more closely:

(1) The movement from the fourth gatra of line (a) to the first gatra
     of line (b) presents technical problems for the gendèr player,
     and the feeling is awkward.

(2) Line (c) presents technical problems for the bonang player.

(3) The melodic phrasing is that of a ketawang [and not of a
     lancaran] and the only elements characteristic of lancaran are
     the number of beats per gong[an] and the gong structure.

(4) The movement from the second to the third gatra of line (d)
     presents technical problems for the gendèr player, and the
     feeling is awkward.

<u>Padhang-ulihan Melodic Sentences in the</u>
<u>Ketawang and Ladrang Forms</u>

The principles of padhang-ulihan in ketawang and ladrang are
identical, but the final sèlèh [cadence] is different. For example,

ketawang: notation with N and G markers, padhang and ulihan phrasing

ladrang: notation with N markers

If we examine the melodic phrasing of ketawang and ladrang, we realize that
all the forms of gendhing have their own rules of melodic phrasing and of
padhang-ulihan. One should not compose merely by filling in the correct
number of beats. We have to consider existing standards [of taste] and
have to know, feel, and differentiate between light sèlèh (those in the
middle of a phrase), and heavy sèlèh (those at the end of a phrase).

I once tried to compose a ladrang without paying attention to proper
melodic phrasing, only observing the right number of beats [per line]. As
it turned out, the piece was rejected by those who heard it; many

considered it laughable, though some of those who laughed were the very ones who also compose gendhing without attending to the rules of proper melodic phrasing. As an example of a composition that ignores melodic phrase structures, please consider the gendhing notated below:

```
                       N                          .        N
(a)  [ 2  1  2  6  .  3  5  6    (b)  3  5  6  i  .  6  5  3

                       N                                   N
       3  5  3  2  .  1  2  6         2  1  2  6  3  3  .  .

                       N                                   N
     .  6  5  6  5  3  2  3         6  5  3  2  5  6  5  3

                       G                                   G
       2  1  2  6  3  3  .  6         2  1  2  6  .  1  2  3 ]
```

<u>Padhang-ulihan Melodic</u>
<u>Phrasing in the Mérong Form</u>

Mérong kethuk 2 kerep [Gendhing *Gambir Sawit*, sléndro pathet sanga]:

```
          t                    t              N
[  . . . 5   2 3 5 6    2 2 . .   2 3 2 1
   ─────────────────    ─────────────────
          p                    u

          t                    t              N
   . . 3 2   . 1 2 6    2 2 . .   2 3 2 1
   ─────────────────    ─────────────────
          p                    u

          t                    t      .       N
   . . 3 2   . 1 6 5    . . 5 6   1 6 5 3
   ─────────────────    ─────────────────
          p                    u

          t                    t              G
   2 2 . 3   5 3 2 1    3 5 3 2   . 1 6 5 ]
   ─────────────────    ─────────────────
          p                    u
```

Since gendhing unequivocally in the form mérong kethuk 2 arang are rare in sléndro (most are in mixed form, such as Gendhing *Laler Mengeng*), the example below is taken from a pélog gendhing.

Mérong kethuk 2 arang [Gendhing *Laranjala*, pélog pathet lima]:

```
              t                        t              N
  [ ..21    2165   ....   55.6   11..   11.2    3323   2121
           ••
    ─────────────     ────────────────────────────────
        p                            u

              t                        t              N
    ..21    2165   ....   55.6   11..   11.2    3323   2121
           ••
    ─────────────     ────────────────────────────────
        p                            u

              t                      ...    ...t       N
    .21.    2165   ....   55.6   11.2   3216    5424   5645
           ••
    ─────────────     ────────────────────────────────
        p                            u

              t                        t              G
    ....    55..   5456   5424   .24.   4565    21.5   6121 ]
                                                 •      •
    ────────────────────────     ────────────────────────
              p                            u
```

This example demonstrates that there is a certain latitude in the composition of kethuk arang melodies [i.e., the padhang and ulihan phrases are not necessarily of equal length]. The designation of the number of kethuk beats in a kenongan (i.e., "kethuk 2," etc.) serves also to indicate the number of melodic phrases in each kenongan. Thus, kethuk 2 kerep and kethuk 2 arang both have two phrases in one kenongan, the difference lying in the number of gatra [in a phrase] and the placement of the kethuk strokes.

Mérong kethuk 4 kerep [Gendhing *Damar Kèli*, sléndro pathet manyura]:

```
      t           t           t           t        N
  [ ..65    3356   2321   6532   ..23   6532   5323   5616
     ••    ••••           ••••    ••    ••••   ••••   •• •
    ──────────────    ──────────────    ─────────────────
         p                  u                 p          u

      t           t           t           t        N
    ..65    3356   2321   6532   ..23   6532   5323   5616
     ••    ••••           ••••    ••    ••••          •• •
    ──────────────    ──────────────    ─────────────────
         p                  u                 p          u

      t           t           t           t        N
    ..65    3356   2321   6532   ..23   6532   5323   5616
     ••    ••••           ••••    ••    ••••   ••••   •• •
    ──────────────    ──────────────    ─────────────────
         p                  u                 p          u

      t           t           t           t        G
    33..    33..   33.2   5321   ....   1123   6532   .126 ]
                                                       •
    ──────────────    ──────────────    ─────────────────
         p                  p                 u
```

I have chosen this gendhing since it shows an instance of *balungan gantungan* ['hanging balungan']: 3 3 . . 3 3 . . . . According to the conception of our ancestors, balungan gantungan is not considered a part of a melodic phrase until it is completed by a subsequent phrase.

Mérong kethuk 4 arang, laras sléndro, with mixed melodic phrases
[Gendhing *Mawur*, sléndro pathet sanga]:

```
                 t                              t
[ 22..    2321    .216    .2.1    65..    55.6    123.    1232
        p                               u


                 t       . .                    t              N
  .126    ....   1561    6535    1656    5321    3216    .2.1
                         p                       u


                 t                              t
  65..    2321    .216    .2.1    65..    55.6    123.    1232
        p                               u


                 t       . .                    t              N
  .126    ....   1561    6535    1656    5321    .216    .2.1
                         p                       u


                 t                              t
  65..    2321    .216    .2.1    65..    55.6    123.    1232
        p                               u


                 t       . .                    t              N
  .126    ....   1561    6535    1656    5321    3212    .165
                         p                       u


                         t                              t
  11..    3216    3565    2232    ..25    2356    3565    2232
        p               u               p               u


                 t       .                      t              G
  11..    11.2    3516    3532    161.    1312    .321    6535  ]
                 p                       p               u
```

Mérong kethuk 4 arang, laras sléndro, with eight melodic phrases per
kenongan [Gendhing *Rondhon*, sléndro pathet sanga]:

```
        t
   ..    ....      ....     .            t      ..   ...
[ 11..  1121    3212   .165    ..52  3565    11..  1216
      p            u            p            u

        t                                   t            N
 ..61  6535    11..  1216    ....  1653   2353  2121
      p            u            p            u

        t      .                           t            N
 55.2  6535   1656  5321    .111  2321   3212  .126
      p            u            p            u
                                                         .
        t      .                           t   .        N
 ....  1653   22.3  5635    ....  55.6   1656  5321
      p  ...      u  ...  ....     p            u

        t      .            .              t            
 .111  2321   5616  5321   5616  5321   3532  .126
      p            u            p            u
                                                         .
        t      .                           t   .        N
 ....  1653   22.3  5635    ....  55.6   1656  5321
      p  ...      u  ...  ....     p            u

        t      .                           t
 33..  6532   .321  6535   2356  3532   ..25  2356
      p  ....      u  ....  ....     p  ...     u  ....

        t      ....  .                     t   ....     . G
 11..  1121   3212   .165   35..  5561   3212   .165 ]
      p            u            p            u
```

Mérong kethuk 4 arang, laras pélog [Gendhing *Klentung*, pélog pathet lima]:

```
         t                          t
[ ..32  .161   245.   5421    ..32  .161   245.   5421
         •                          •
          p                          u

         t                          t                 N
  .23.  123.   123.   1216    ..1.  6.5.   4.24   5645
                                          •  ••   ••••
          p                          u

         t                          t
  .456  5452   ..24   .245    .456  5452   ..24   .245
  •••   ••••    ••    •••     •••   ••••    ••    •••
          p                          u

         t                          t                 N
  ..24  5.24   5.54   2121    77..   77..   7765   4565
   ••   •  ••  •  ••
          p                          u

         t                          t
  .456  5452   ..24   .245    .456  5452   ..24   .245
          p                          u

         t                          t                 N
  44..  44..   44..   2245    ..56  .2.1   6123   2121
                                          •
          p                          u

         t                          t
  ..32  .161   .245   5421    ..32  .161   245.   5421
         •                          •
          p                          u

         t                          t                 G
  44..  44..   44..   2245    ..56  .2.1   6123   2121 ]
                                          •
          p                          u
```

Mérong kethuk 8 kerep, laras pélog [Gendhing *Pangrawit*, pélog pathet lima]:

```
        t              t              t              t
[ ..31    .3.2    3.35    6532    .321    .3.2    3.35    6532
      p           u           p           u

    t              t              t              t         N
  .321    .3.2    3.35    6532    3.35    2321    ..12    3565
      p           u           p           u

    t              t              t              t
  ..57    .656    77653    6523    55.7    5676    77653    6523
      p           u           p           u

    t              t              t              t         N
  55.7    5676    77653    6532    52.3    6532    .4.2    4521
      p           u           p           u

    t              t              t              t
  ..13    .212    3.35    6532    .321    .3.2    3.35    6532
      p           u           p           u

    t              t              t              t         N
  .321    .3.2    3.35    6532    3.35    2321    66..    2321
      p           u           p           u

    t              t              t              t
  .216    .2.1    .216    .2.1    23..    6532    3216    2165
      p           u           p           u

    t              t              t              t         G
  15.6    2165    15.6    2165    66..    6676    .532    .5.3 ]
      p           u           p           u
```

Earlier I explained that there is no kethuk 8 kerep form in laras sléndro, but only in laras pélog. I cannot account for this fact. In fact, there are sléndro gendhing that have eight phrases per kenongan, but these gendhing are all in the kethuk 4 arang form. There are also mixed compositions; that is, each kenongan contains either four or eight melodic phrases. I have provided examples above of two kethuk 4 arang gendhing in laras sléndro, and one kethuk 4 arang and one kethuk 8 kerep gendhing in laras pélog, for comparative purposes.

After considering all of these examples, I would conclude that the ordering of melodic phrases in gendhing of the kethuk 4 arang form in laras sléndro is not fixed. In fact, one often finds melodic phrases characteristic of the ladrang form included in the longer form. It is

indeed difficult to arrange melodic phrases in the kethuk 4 arang form.
Moreover, a composer has to think of more than melodic phrasing when he
composes. He must also keep in mind the creation of a pleasing melody, the
performance practices characteristic of the various instruments, and so on.
I think this is one of the reasons composers are reluctant to work in this
lengthy form. The longest form of gendhing that modern composers attempt
is ladrang. Even there, composers generally compose the vocal melody
first; the balungan merely conforms, frequently causing difficulties and
awkwardness in performance. Contemporary composers have generally ignored
the gendhing kethuk 2 and longer forms; gendhing in these forms have been
inherited from our ancestors. In my opinion, even if there were composers
who worked in these forms, the new pieces would not be comparable, much
less superior, to the old ones.

This shall suffice as my explanation concerning padhang-ulihan and
melodic phrasing in gendhing. I have provided this explanation as a
prelude to a consideration of the direction of tones (*arah nada*), or
melodic direction in gendhing. Melodic direction is very important because
it can show how pathet is determined.

The Direction of Tones

We shall use the gendèr as our means of explaining the material in
this section. To order the tones of the gendèr from large [i.e., low] to
small [i.e., high], we proceed from left to right [that is, from the
larger, lower-pitched keys on the left to the smaller keys on the right];
and conversely, to order the tones from high to low, we proceed from right
to left. For instance, in the melody 2 3 5 6 , we have a motion from 2
to 6, by way of pitches 3 and 5, which serves to clarify the direction of
the melody from left to right. On the other hand, although the motion is
from 2 to 6 in the melody 2 1 2 6 , the direction of the melody is from
right to left.

Let me try to clarify this matter further. There is a gendèr
technique known as "*thinthingan*" that is very simple--almost anyone can
learn to play it--but which has great practical value. For, it makes clear
to the listener which pathet is about to be played. Thinthingan consists
of the four tones of the particular pathet, exclusive of the dhing tone,
played from right to left.

Figure 28.

	IV	III	II	I
thinthingan pathet sanga	5	6	i̇	2̇
thinthingan pathet nem	2	3	5	6
thinthingan pathet manyura	6	i̇	2̇	3̇

Thinthingan played on the gendèr also serves to indicate melodic direction.

Figure 29.

The direction of tones in pathet sanga

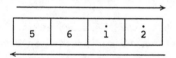

The direction of tones in pathet nem

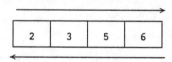

The direction of tones in pathet manyura

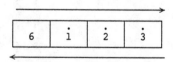

    Note that, since pathet nem has only two consecutive tones (2 - 3) [in the range of sèlèh], the melodic direction of pathet nem must always include these two tones, or at least one of them. For example, if there is a melody 6 . 6 5 (i.e., from pitch 6 to pitch 5, or, from right to left), the pathet is sanga, not nem. But if the rest [indicated with a dot] is filled in with pitch 3 (i.e., 6 3 6 5), thus adding a characteristic

pathet nem tone, the pathet will be nem. This can be further demonstrated
if we play these melodic phrases on the gendèr, since the gendèr [cèngkok]
required for the last-mentioned example will invariably be in the pathet
nem range. And, if, for example, there is a balungan phrase 3 . 3 2 ,
although pitches 3 and 2 are within the range of pathet nem, they are also
in the range of pathet manyura, especially since they are in middle
register. (Pitches 3 and 2 in the lower register [i.e., 3 and 2] are
unequivocally in the range of pathet nem.) So, if the phrase mentioned
above [3 . 3 2] is to become pathet nem, it must include either tone 6
or tone 5, or both. For instance, 3 6 3 2 and 3 5 3 2 , which
include one of these tones; or 3̅5̅ 6 3 2 and 3̅6̅ 5 3 2 , which include
both of them, are clearly identifiable as pathet nem. This is
reinforced by the pathet nem gendèr cèngkok that would be used in
playing these phrases.

Cèngkok Mati ['Fixed Cèngkok']

After our discussion of the structure of melodic phrases based on the
concept of melodic direction, we can proceed to a consideration of "*cèngkok
mati*." These are melodic phrases the pathet of which is predetermined and
not based on melodic direction. This is primarily a matter of intuition,
and is difficult to account for theoretically. The following are cèngkok
mati in three pathet of laras slèndro:

1. cèngkok mati, pathet sanga:

a.	3	5	3	2	. 1	2	6
b.	1̣	6	5	6	5 3	2	1
c.	5	6	1̇	6	5 3	2	1
d.	2	2	.	.	2 3	2	1
e.	1̣	6	5	6	5 3	1	2
f.	3	5	3	2	. 1	6̣	5̣
g.	5	6	5	3	2 1	2	1

2. cèngkok mati, pathet nem:

a.	5	6	5	3	2 1	6̣	5
b.	6	6	1̇	6	5 3	2	3
c.	.	1	6̣	5̣	1 2	1	6̣

3. cèngkok mati, pathet manyura:

$$
\begin{array}{llllllllll}
\text{a.} & 3 & 5 & 6 & \overset{\bullet}{1} & 6 & 5 & 3 & 2 \\
\text{b.} & 3 & 3 & . & . & 6 & 5 & 3 & 2 \\
\text{c.} & 3 & 5 & 6 & \overset{\bullet}{1} & 6 & 5 & 2 & 3 \\
\text{d.} & 5 & 6 & 5 & 3 & 2 & 1 & 2 & \underset{\bullet}{6} \\
\text{e.} & 5 & 6 & 5 & 3 & 2 & 1 & 2 & 1 \\
\end{array}
$$

Relative Strength in the Position of Tones

Each gatra is composed of four balungan beats, or *sabetan*. These four sabetan are named in accordance with the up-bow [*maju*] and down-bow [*mundur*] of the rebab. The names are as follows:

First sabetan = *sabetan maju* [i.e., 'forward']
Second sabetan = *sabetan mundur* [i.e., 'back']
Third sabetan = *sabetan maju*
Fourth sabetan = *sabetan sèlèh* [i.e., 'falling', or 'cadential']

Or, if these are written in graphic notation:

$$
\begin{array}{cccc}
1 & 2 & 3 & 4 \\
\bullet & \bullet & \bullet & \bullet \\
\text{maju} & \text{mundur} & \text{maju} & \text{sèlèh} \\
\end{array}
$$

The tones in an individual gatra are relatively strong or weak according to their position. For example, the arrangement of tones 6 5 2 1 is called "*nyiji*" ['one at a time'], meaning that no two tones repeat. The tones that fall on the maju beats [i.e., beats one and three] are relatively weak (light/thin/insubstantial). The tones that fall on the mundur beats [i.e., beats two and four] are relatively strong and emphatic. Since the tone that falls on the sèlèh beat is the strongest in emphasis, the cèngkok of the gendèr will be determined by those sèlèh tones. This can be demonstrated by noting the gendèr pattern used in playing the balungan mentioned above [6 5 2 1]; the cèngkok used aims toward the final sèlèh beat.

The balungan 6 3 6 5 , on the other hand, has a pattern called "*maju kembar*" ['repeated maju']. This kind of balungan tends to add emphasis to the tone on the mundur beat [i.e., beat two]. For this reason, the gendèr cèngkok will not only aim toward the sèlèh beat, but will utilize a "half-cèngkok" leading to the tone on the mundur beat. To

demonstrate this, let us consider the playing of the gendèr for balungan of
the maju kembar type:

$$
\begin{array}{ccccccc}
 & & & & & & & \text{N} \\
6 & 3 & 6 & 5 & 6 & 3 & 6 & 2
\end{array}
$$

$$
\begin{array}{ccccccc}
 & & & & & & & \text{G} \\
6 & 3 & 6 & 5 & 6 & 3 & 6 & 2
\end{array}
$$

If the repeated tone on the maju beat [beats one and three] is the dhing
tone, the result will be a change in pathet. The dhing tones are pitch 3
in pathet sanga, pitch 1 in pathet nem, and pitch 5 in pathet manyura. For
example, in the balungan melody . 6 . 5 in pathet sanga, if we fill in
the rests on the maju beats with pitch 3, the resultant melody, 3 6 3 2 ,
will be in pathet nem. Analogously, in the melody . 6 . 5 in pathet nem,
if we fill in the maju beats with pitch 1, the resultant melody, 1 6 1 5 ,
will become pathet sanga. To make this clearer, I have made a list of
balungan melodies into which the dhing tone can be inserted.

	Balungan				Pathet	Tone Added			Resultant Pathet
a.	.	3	.	2	manyura	+	5	→	nem
b.	.	3	.	2	nem	+	1	→	manyura
c.	.	2	.	1	sanga	+	3	→	manyura
d.	.	6	.	5	sanga	+	3	→	nem
e.	.	6	.	5	nem	+	1	→	sanga
f.	.	3	.	6	manyura	+	5	→	nem
g.	.	2	.	5	sanga	+	3	→	nem
h.	.	2	.	1	manyura	+	5	→	sanga

The tone that falls on the sèlèh beat is the strongest, but sometimes
its strength can be diminished, namely, when a tone one pitch degree higher
or lower than the sèlèh tone is repeated immediately after the sèlèh beat.
For instance, if the sèlèh tone 3 is followed by the repeated tone 2 or 5
(i.e., 1̇ 6 5 3   2 2 . . , or 1̇ 6 5 3   5 5 . .), then the strength of
the sèlèh tone will be sapped by the repeated tone which follows it. This
is evident in the third kenongan [of the mérong] of Gendhing *Gambir
Sawit*, sléndro pathet sanga:

$$
\begin{array}{cccccccccccccccc}
 & & & & & & & & & & & & & & \text{•} & \text{N} \\
. & . & 3 & 2 & . & 1 & 6 & 5 & . & . & 5 & 6 & 1̇ & 6 & 5 & 3
\end{array}
$$

$$
\begin{array}{ccccccccc}
2 & 2 & . & 3 & 5 & 3 & 2 & 1 & \text{etc.}
\end{array}
$$

Pitch 3 in the kenong position in pathet sanga is, in fact, quite awkward, but, because immediately following it there are the repeated tones, the feeling of pitch 3 is naturally sapped by the repeated pitch 2's. The composer of *Gambir Sawit* was truly masterful, not only in his use of the repeated 2's, but because the repeated tones lead naturally into a cèngkok mati for pathet sanga [thereby eliminating the ambiguity of pathet caused by pitch 3 in a cadential position].

Another example is the last gongan of the vocal gendhing, Ketawang *Sinom Parijatha*, laras slèndro pathet sanga, in which the final sèlèh tone is pitch 1. Because the beginning of the following gongan (the so-called umpak [see above in reference to the misuse of this term]) is a repeated pitch 6, the feeling of finality at the end of the gongan is diminished. So it is not surprising that some pesindhèn sing the melody as follows:

								N
balungan:	.	.	.	.	2	3	2	1
vocal melody:					. 2	2	13 2	1
					a – ma		ma – ngun	

								G
balungan:	5	2	1	6	2	3	2	1
vocal melody:	. 5	2	23 21	6	. 2	3 .5	23 21	1 61
	kar-ya	nak	cas		ing sa – sa – ma			

								N
balungan:	6	6	.	.	2	3	2	1

vocal melody: 6

The strength of the sèlèh tone can also be weakened if the tone that falls on the sèlèh beat in a padhang cèngkok for gendèr [i.e., the first of two cèngkok] also flanks the following tone. An example is 3 2 1 6 5 6 1 2 , in which pitch 6 serves not only as the sèlèh of the padhang cèngkok, but is also the same pitch as the second beat of the following gatra, thus flanking pitch 5 [i.e., the first beat of the gatra]. Or, in the balungan melody . 2 3 5 6 5 3 2 , the strength of pitch 5 on the

sèlèh beat of the first gatra is diminished by the flanked pitch 6 on the
first beat of the second gatra.

Analyzing a Gendhing

The above discussion of the ins and outs of karawitan, though
incomplete and with reference to laras slèndro only, should give some idea
of the complexity of our subject. We are, consequently, indebted to our
ancestors who have bequeathed to us the heritage of karawitan--gamelan,
gendhing, and so on. It is my considered opinion that unnecessary
innovation, adding or deleting something from the tradition, is improper.
Indeed, while we all wish to achieve progress, we would do well to remember
not to pursue progress for its own sake without considering the
consequences. For example, if we want to play a ketawang gendhing, we need
only look for [an existing] one that we like. We should not choose just
any gendhing kethuk 2 to be played as a ketawang gendhing, since the
melodic phrasing may not be appropriate. Or, if we insist on creating a
ketawang gendhing out of a gendhing kethuk 2, we should at least choose a
gendhing that tend toward the phrasing of a ketawang--for instance,
Ketawang Gendhing *Sumedhang*, which may be played as a ketawang with the
help of a vocal part. In contrast, Gendhing *Renyep* played as a ketawang
would sound awkward and forced.

There are other violations, such as a gendhing ladrang performed with
a gérongan vocal melody that has the melodic phrasing of a ketawang. This
is also very awkward, as, for example, in one kenongan of Ladrang
Clunthang, laras slèndro pathet sanga:

```
                                                              N
        .       1       .       6       .       3       .     5

____  ____  ____  ____  ____  ____  ____  ____  ____  ____
  . 6 2 1   6 2 1   . 2 5 2 5 1 6   2   . 2 3 2 1   . 5   2 2 2 6 5
```

If we pay very close attention to this example, its awkwardness will be
apparent. The melody of the gendhing has just reached the [second] kenong,
but the gérong melody already evokes the finality of the cadence leading to
the gong. Those who take pleasure in creating new gendhing or in
rearranging old ones should remember not to be careless. Vocal gendhing
such as *Mijil Lagu Dhempel*, *Mijil Ludira*, and Ketawang *Kesatriyan* should
never be altered. Though there is no sanction against such practices, they
are not really proper. In order to know better just what is correct or

incorrect in the arrangement of gendhing, let us proceed with the analysis
of a particular gendhing. As a first step, we shall study the types of
balungan.

The Types of Balungan

1. Balungan Mlaku ['Walking Balungan']

$$2 \quad 3 \quad 2 \quad 1 \quad . \quad 1 \quad 2 \quad \underset{.}{6}$$

Each beat (*sabetan*) is filled by either a balungan tone or a single
rest on the maju beat [i.e., beats one or three]. For the purposes of the
melodic instruments, the rest will be considered to be filled by the
preceding tone. That is, in the example above, pitch 1, [which ends the
first gatra, will be sustained through the following rest on the first beat
of the second gatra].

2. Balungan Nibani

Each of the maju beats [i.e., beats one and three] is filled by a rest
in balungan nibani. It is understood that, for the purposes of the melodic
instruments, this kind of balungan is directly derived from an [idealized]
balungan mlaku version of the same melody [i.e., from a filled-in version].
[Though this version is implied and not stated,] the players of the melodic
instruments will perform their parts according to the implied balungan
mlaku melody (see the section "Inggah," above).

3. Balungan Pin Mundur

$$2 \quad . \quad 1 \quad . \quad 2 \quad . \quad 2 \quad \underset{.}{6}$$

This kind of balungan [in which a rest occurs on a strong beat] is
particularly emphatic and requires that the melodic instruments follow
closely the tones of the balungan melody. (We should probably have dealt
with this matter above in the section "Strength in the Position of Tones,"
but since this sort of balungan melody is very rare, we chose to make note
of it here.)

4. Balungan Ngadhal

$$\overline{2\ 5}\ \overline{3\ 5}\ \overline{2\ 3}\ 1 \quad \overline{1\ 3}\ \overline{2\ 3}\ \overline{1\ 2}\ \underset{.}{6}$$

There are two or more tones per beat in this type of balungan. This can sometimes have the effect of changing the stress that particular tones receive.

5. Balungan Plèsèdan (/Mlèsèd) ['Sliding Balungan']

There are five varieties of balungan plèsèdan that apply to the solo female vocal part (*sindhènan*).

a. Plèsèdan Mbesut

$$
\begin{array}{ccccccc@{\qquad}c@{\qquad}cc@{\ }c@{\ }c}
 & & & & & & \text{N} & & & & & \\
2 & 3 & 2 & 1 & 3 & 2 & 1 & \underset{\cdot}{6} & 1 & 1 & . & .
\end{array}
$$

Following the sèlèh tone there is a repeated tone that is one step lower or higher than the sèlèh tone.

b. Plèsèdan Cèngkok

$$
\begin{array}{ccccccc@{\qquad}c@{\qquad}cc@{\ }c@{\ }c}
 & & & & & & \text{N} & & & & & \\
2 & 3 & 2 & 1 & 3 & 2 & 1 & \underset{\cdot}{6} & 3 & 3 & . & .
\end{array}
$$

Following the sèlèh tone there is a repeated tone that is more than one pitch degree higher or lower than the sèlèh tone.

c. Plèsèdan Tungkakan

$$
\begin{array}{cccccccccc}
 & & & & & & & \text{N} & & \\
3 & 5 & 6 & 5 & 2 & 2 & 3 & 2 & 6 & 6
\end{array}
$$

Preceding a repeated tone there is a tone that is not in the range of the sindhèn part.

d. Plèsèdan Jujugan

$$
\begin{array}{ccccccc@{\qquad}c@{\quad}c@{\ }c}
 & & & & & & & \text{N} & \cdot & \cdot \\
2 & 3 & 2 & 1 & 3 & 2 & 1 & \underset{\cdot}{6} & 1 & 1
\end{array}
$$

Following the sèlèh tone there is a repeated tone that is further than a gembyang away from the sèlèh tone.

e. Plèsèdan Wilet

$$
\begin{array}{ccccccc@{\qquad}ccc@{\ }c@{\ }c@{\ }c@{\ }c}
 & & & & & & & \text{N} & & & \cdot & & & & \\
2 & 3 & 2 & 1 & 3 & 2 & 1 & \underset{\cdot}{6} & 5 & 6 & 1 & . & . & . & .
\end{array}
$$

Following the sèlèh tone there is a melodic phrase that is the same length as the padhang and ulihan of a cèngkok (e.g., the padhang gatra has a rest on the [last] beat, and the following gatra consists of two or more rests). Another example would be the melody

```
                          N
2   3   2   1   3   2   1   6   3   5   .   .
```

in which, following the sèlèh tone, there is a padhang gatra that has balungan tones on only the first and second beats.

Now let us begin our analysis of a particular gendhing, using the terms we have outlined above (i.e., the types of balungan). For study purposes, let us take a well-known and easy gendhing, Ladrang *Pangkur*, laras sléndro [pathet manyura]:

```
                                    N
    (A)     3   2   3   1   3   2   1   6
                                        .
                                    N
    (B)     1   6   3   2   5   3   2   1
                .
                                    N
    (C)     3   5   3   2   6   5   3   2

                                    G
    (D)     5   3   2   1   3   2   1   6
                                        .
```

Melodic Phrases

If we analyze the melodic phrasing, we note that the phrases are appropriate to the ladrang form, and that there are no problematic spots. Everything is in its proper place, including padhang and ulihan.

Pathet

If we look at the notation of Ladrang *Pangkur*, above, we can immediately guess that the piece is in pathet manyura, for that is our instinctive reaction, and performers commonly use manyura treatment (*garap*) when confronted with this sort of notation. But why, and on what basis? The padhang and ulihan sèlèh could function in pathet sanga, since none of them fall on the dhing tone of pathet sanga [3]. Let us try to answer this question by performing an experiment. What would happen if we played the above-notated melody with cèngkok from pathet sanga? If in so doing we encountered sections that seem displeasing to the ear, perhaps we would find the answer to our question. [The notation which follows uses

the same balungan as noted above--that is, pathet manyura--with the gérong
notated as if the piece were in pathet sanga.]

```
                                                              N
(A)    3      2      3      1      3      2      1      6
                                                       .

      . 2  2  .   . 23 1      . 2  1  23 5   .2 16 .
                                                .
       Pa - rab -   é  sang     sma-ra       ba-ngun


                                                              N
(B)    1      6      3      2      5      3      2      1
              .

      . 1  6   1  .2 2     . 3  5   23 2  1
           .
       se - pat   dom - ba     ka - li   o  - ya


                                                              N
(C)    3      5      3      2      6      5      3      2

      . 3  5   5 3  2     . 3  5  61 5  .3 2
                                     .
       a - ja   do - lan     lan wong pri - ya


                                                              G
(D)    5      3      2      1      3      2      1      6
                                                              .

      . 56 3  .5 23 2  1     . 2  2  53 21 6
                                            .
       ge-rè - mèh  no -     ra pra - sa - ja
```

The section of the gérongan that sounds most unpleasant when played with
the above balungan is the first gatra of line (A). The reason for this
lies in what we said earlier about the strength of tones as related to
their position.

According to the position of the tones, the pathet of Ladrang *Pangkur*
notated above should indeed be manyura. It could be treated as pathet
sanga, but this would represent a violation, and, furthermore, would not
sound at all pleasing.

One may argue that the first gatra of line (A) alone prevents *Pangkur*
from becoming pathet sanga because there is the sanga dhing tone in both
maju beats. If this were indeed the reason, the issue could be resolved if
we replaced the gatra 3 2 3 1 with 2 3 2 1 . Thus,

```
                                                      N
(A)      2  3  2  1     3  2  1  6
                                   .
                                                      N
(B)      1  6  1  2     5  3  2  1
            .
                                                      N
(C)      3  5  3  2     6  5  3  2

                                                      G
(D)      5  3  2  1     3  2  1  6
                                   .
```

If we applied the pathet sanga gérongan to the above balungan, the effect
would be somewhat more pleasing. However, we would still have a problem in
the first gatra of line (C). We should realize that, although we have
changed the melody, we have not yet clearly established the pathet as
either pathet sanga or manyura. We cannot clarify this point further
through melodic changes. Master musicians and composers must now choose
for themselves and make their choice clear in the buka of the gendhing.
[Hypothetical] buka for the above-notated [hypothetical version] of Ladrang
Pangkur might sound as follows:

buka pathet sanga:
                                                         G
   2 2 2   1 1 2 1   5 6 1 2   3 2 1 6
                          . .   .
buka pathet nem:
                                                         G
      2   2 1 3 2   . 1 6 5   1 2 1 6
                             . .   .
buka pathet manyura:
                                                         G
      3   3 1 3 2   6 1 2 3   2 1 2 6
                       .   .

To make their choice more resolute, the performers would play pathetan in
the desired pathet before the buka.

The Direction of Tones and Performance Technique
[in Analyzing Ladrang *Pangkur*]

After examining the melodic phrases and the pathet of Ladrang *Pangkur*,
we turn to the matter of melodic direction of the tones in connection with
performance technique. Line (A) is [hypothetically] 2 3 2 1   3 2 1 6 ;
2 3 2 1 could be either pathet sanga or manyura. However, if we join this
gatra and the following, creating one phrase, the sèlèh tone of this line,
tone 6, will still be a very strong tone in pathet manyura. Thus, if
    .

we want to play this line as pathet sanga, we must precede and follow it
with melodies that are clearly and unambiguously in pathet sanga. For
example, either

        1 6 1 5   1 6 1 5   2 3 2 1   3 2 1 6

where the characteristic sanga melody [underlined in the example] precedes
the phrase (A); or,

        2 3 2 1   3 2 1 6   5 6 1 2   1 6 3 5

where the sanga melody [underlined] follows the phrase (A).

        Line (B) is written 1 6 1 2 5 3 2 1 ; the gatra 1 6 1 2 could be
pathet sanga or manyura. When this gatra is linked with the next gatra,
thus forming a single melodic phrase, the whole line becomes stronger in
pathet sanga because it ends on pitch 1, the lower kempyung in pathet
sanga. In pathet manyura, this tone is merely the pelengkap. (See the
section "The Strength of a Tone Based on Its Position.") So, conversely,
if we want to make this melodic phrase sound more like pathet manyura, we
must have melodies clearly in pathet manyura either before or after the
phrase; for example,

        3 3 5 6   3 1 3 2   1 6 1 2   5 3 2 1

where the characteristic manyura melody [underlined in the example]
precedes the phrase (B); or,

        1 6 1 2   5 3 2 1   6 1 2 3   2 1 2 6

where the manyura melody [underlined] follows the phrase (B).

        Line (C), which can be written 3 5 3 2 3 5 3 2 , is clearly in
pathet nem (see the sections "The Direction of Tones" and "The Strength of
a Tone Based on Its Position.") Line (C), as it is in the pathet manyura
version of Ladrang *Pangkur*-- 3 5 3 2 6 5 3 2 --is also pathet nem.
Although, according to the rules of performance practice, both pathet sanga
and pathet manyura make use of [phrases from] pathet nem, the composer's
wish is to keep the piece in pathet manyura. In line (B)
(1 6 3 2 5 3 2 1), if the gendèr player treated sèlèh 1 as a

gembyang (i.e., as pathet manyura) and then proceeded to treat the
following 6 5 3 2 as pathet nem, the result would be quite awkward. This
is because the mid-point of the gatra falls on pitch 5, which is the
avoided tone (dhing) for pathet manyura. If, however, the seleh 1 were
treated as a kempyung in the gender part (i.e., as pathet sanga), the
transition to the mid-point of the following gatra would be much smoother.
In all probability, the composer realized that once the gender player
reaches line (B)-- 3 5 3 2 6 5 3 2 --he is obliged to treat the line as
if it were . 3 . 2 . 3 . 2 , as in fact it is in irama wilet.

Ladrang *Pangkur* in irama dados and irama wilet, line by line:

```
        irama dados:    3   2   3   1     3   2   1   6 ⎫
                                                      .  ⎬ line (A)
        irama wilet:  . 3 . 2 . 3 . 1   . 3 . 2 . 1 . 6 ⎭
                                                      .

        irama dados:    1   6   3   2     5   3   2   1 ⎫
                        .                               ⎬ line (B)
        irama wilet:  1 1 . . 6 6 1 2   3 2 6 3 . 2 . 1 ⎭
                      . .       . .     . .

        irama dados:      .   3   .   2     .   3   .   2 ⎫
                                                          ⎬ line (C)
        irama wilet:    . . . 3 . . . 2   . . . 3 . . . 2 ⎭

        irama dados:    5   3   2   1     3   2   1   6 ⎫
                                                      .  ⎬ line (D)
        irama wilet:  6 1 3 2 6 3 2 1   . 3 . 2 . 1 . 6 ⎭
                        . . .
```

If we consider the gender part of Ladrang *Pangkur*--in pathet sanga or
pathet manyura--we can see clearly that its pathet is unequivocal and its
composition skillful. So it is not surprising that this gendhing has
become a beloved favorite of the people. But everything must have its
flaws and Ladrang *Pangkur* is no exception. Consider the second gatra of
line (B) in irama wilet

```
        3 2 6 3   . 2 . 1
        . .
        ‾‾‾‾‾‾‾   ‾‾‾‾‾‾‾
        padhang   ulihan
```

noting that an ulihan in irama dados is equivalent to a padhang plus an
ulihan in irama wilet. For the balungan of this ulihan [thus, . 2 . 1   ]

the gendèr usually uses the cèngkok called "*dua lolo*." For instance, in
the first gatra of line (A) in irama wilet, that cèngkok is used to great
effect. But the cèngkok "dua lolo" can only be used from sèlèh 6 or sèlèh
2 [to sèlèh 1]. The second gatra of line (B) must proceed from a sèlèh on
pitch 3 and thus "dua lolo" cannot comfortably be used there. So, each
gendèr player when treating this section of the gendhing will find his/her
own way of getting from sèlèh 3 to "dua lolo" based on his/her own personal
ability. It is hoped that prospective young composers of gendhing will
take note of problems such as these in order to avoid possible difficulties
in performance practice.

Ladrang *Grompol* and Ladrang *Mugi Rahayu*, Laras Slèndro

Let us continue and deepen our analyses of particular gendhing,
bearing in mind the current trend among young musicians for rearranging
pre-existing materials, and in order to remind them that their
rearrangements should not diminish the quality of the original works.

Ladrang *Grompol*, laras slèndro pathet nem:

```
                     .   . . . .   . . .               G
buka:      2   2 3 2 1   3 2 1 6   2 3 6 5


                                               N
      (A)        6  2  3  .   6  2  3  5


                                               N
      (B)        6  2  3  .   6  2  3  5


                                               N
      (C)        6  6  .  .   2  3  2  1


                                               G
      (D)        3  2  1  6   2  3  6  5
```

Ladrang *Mugi Rahayu*, laras sléndro pathet manyura:

```
                                              G
buka:     6  6 1 6 5  1 6 5 3  6 1 3 2
                                .
                                              N
 (A)      3 6 1 .  3 6 1 2
            .        .
                                              N
 (B)      3 6 1 .  3 6 1 2
            .        .
                                              N
 (C)      3 5 2 3  6 1 6 5
                     .
                                              G
 (D)      1 6 5 3  6 1 3 2
                     .
```

Ladrang *Grompol* is an old gendhing of anonymous composition, while Ladrang *Mugi Rahayu* was composed by K. R. M. H. [Kangjeng Radèn Mas Harya] Wiryadiningrat at the time of the invasion of the Netherlands by Nazi Germany during the Second World War, around 1940. I do not know whether it was deliberate or not, but it turns out that Ladrang *Mugi Rahayu* is the same gendhing as Ladrang *Grompol* but transposed up one kempyung (thus, gong 5 becomes gong 2, etc.). In Western music this is called "transposition," while in karawitan it is called "changing pathet" (see the section "The Tones in Laras Sléndro"). [See also "The Strength of a Tone Based on Its Position."]

Analysis of the Pathet in the Above Gendhing

We have already discussed pathet at length, so if we say that Ladrang *Grompol* is in pathet nem, there is no longer any room for confusion. But it is strange that, although the piece is in pathet nem, during its heyday it was never performed during the time reserved for pathet nem, but was more commonly played during the pathet manyura time slot. This is because the piece is played in an animated style (*gobyog*) not considered appropriate to the mood of pathet nem. There are, indeed, several other gendhing in pathet nem that are similar in mood to Ladrang *Grompol* and receive the same performance treatment.

Ladrang *Mugi Rahayu* is just as clearly in pathet manyura. Noteworthy in this piece are the following features: (a) the mixing of one pathet with another without lessening the character of the main pathet; and (b) the use

of a non-tonic tone as the gong tone--for it is a mistake to expect that
the tonic tone will always serve as the gong tone.

Analysis of the Performance Technique in the Above Gendhing

There is a section of Ladrang *Grompol* that presents a minor difficulty
in technical execution for the rebab: in the first gatra of line (A) and in
the second gatra of line (D) (i.e., leading up to the gong).

In Ladrang *Mugi Rahayu*, the most difficult technical problem is in the
gendèr part, from the second gatra of line (B) to the first gatra of line
(C). At that point there is a plèsèdan ['slide'] movement to the repeated
tone 3 [actually 3 5 2 3 , but with the effect of repeated 3] from pitch
2, and then an ulihan gatra that cadences on pitch 5. This movement is
difficult to execute [on the gendèr], and, in fact, the best solution is to
slide (*mlèsèd*) to low pitch 3 instead of to middle pitch 3. The only tones
from which the gendèr can slide to low pitch 3 are 2, 5, and 6. From pitch
1 and middle-range pitch 2 the gendèr can only comfortably slide to middle
pitch 3, as noted in figure 30.

Figure 30.

sèlèh	mlèsèd 3 (dhadha ageng)		
2 5 6	3 3 6 5 3 3 5 6 3 3 . . 3 3 . .	6 1 6 5	 3 3 5 6

sèlèh	mlèsèd 3 dhadha tengahan		
6 1 2	3 3 . . 3 3 1 2 3 3 1 2 3 3 1 6	6 5 3 2*	

*This is a cèngkok mati in pathet manyura.

A Note About the Patterns
of Cengkok for Gender

There are many terms for the patterns of gender cengkok. Some examples are "*kembang tiba*" ['falling flowers'], "*ukel pancaran*" ['twisting and radiating'], "*rangkep*" ['doubled'], "*lamba*" ['single, unattached'], and "*laku 1/ 2/ 4/ 8/ 16.*"

The significance of all these terms is, in my opinion, obscure. Indeed, I wish I myself could understand [the distinction between these terms], but whenever anyone attempts to explain them, he usually ends up providing extremely complicated explanations and not illuminating the issues at all. Therefore, in order to avoid further confusion, I will not explain [gender] cengkok with reference to the above terms. Rather, I will attempt to explain them with reference to the concept of irama. I will limit my examples to irama tanggung, irama dados, and irama wilet. Irama lancar and irama rangkep will appear only in diagram form, since irama lancar does not have fixed cengkok (*cengkok gumathok*), that is, the cengkok are determined by the inventiveness of the player; and irama rangkep clearly only doubles the cengkok of irama wilet (though, unfortunately, the method of doubling is not set and each player has his own particular way of playing irama rangkep).

What is the form of cengkok? What is the length of one cengkok? To answer these questions most simply, we will first provide the form of the vocal melody and then adjust it to the length of the cengkok of the gender gedhe [in each irama].

Figure 31. A Schematic Representation of Cengkok

irama 1/2 (tanggung)   saron panerus: . . . .

balungan: 2 1 2 6̣

vocal melody: .231.236
                e̱la e̱lo

irama 1/4 (dados)   saron panerus: . . . .

                           balungan: 2   1   2   6̣

                           vocal melody: ...2.3.1...2.3.6̣
                                            e‑la   e‑lo

irama 1/8 (wilet)   saron panerus: . . . .

                           balungan: 2   1   2   6̣

                           vocal melody: ....2...3...1.......2...3...6̣
                                        e - la   e - lo

It can be seen from reading figure 31 and singing the melodies in each
irama that the vocal melody is unpleasant in irama wilet (1/8), and would
be quite impossible in irama rangkep (1/16). The melody is most pleasant
when sung in irama dados (1/4). In karawitan this is called a "fixed
melody" (*lagu mati*), as distinguished from a "fixed cèngkok" (*cèngkok mati*)
in irama dados. Although it is still possible to sing this melody in irama
wilet (1/8), the effect would be most awkward. The instruments that
elaborate in a densely filled‑in style, that is, those that utilize the
doubling technique (*garap rangkep*), will only sound appropriate [if the
irama is changed from dados to wilet]. For an analogous reason, those
gendhing that can be played in irama rangkep‑‑which indeed call for garap
rangkep in the instrumental technique‑‑are not usually provided with a
gérong melody, because the effect would be unpleasant.

    To clarify this, I have drawn a figure (figure 32) of a fixed melody
(*lagu mati*) in irama lancar which can only be moved into irama tanggung by
using a rangkep technique.

Figure 32.

irama 1/1 (lancar)

saron panerus: .   .   .   .

balungan: .   5   .   6   .   5   .   6   .   5   .   6   .   3   .   2

vocal melody: .   .   ͵5   6   5   3   ͡5   6   2   .   5   6   1̇   5   3   2
                        É-pring pa-dha e-pring mas   Ke-tan su-ri-ka-ya

irama 1/2 (tanggung)

saron panerus:

. . . .

balungan:

.   5   .   6   .   5   .   6   .   5   .   6   .   3   .   2

vocal melody:

. . . . .͵5 . 6   . 5 . 3 .͵5 . 6   . 2 . . . 5 . 6   .1̇. 5 . 3 . 2
          É-pring   pa - dha e-pring   mas   Ke - tan su - ri- ka-ya

Figure 32 is an example of a melody in irama lancar (1/1) that can
only be played in one other irama--irama tanggung (1/2). There are also
melodies--"éla-élo" is the name of one example--that can be sung in a
"lower" irama [i.e., with more saron panerus pulses per balungan beat] as
well as a "higher" irama [i.e., fewer saron panerus pulses per balungan
beat]. The vocal melody "éla-élo" is clearly meant to be sung in irama
dados (1/4), but could also be sung in either irama tanggung (1/2) or irama
wilet (1/8)--in the latter case by using rangkep techniques (*garap
rangkep*). This differs from the melody in figure 32, which can be played
in a lower irama but not in a higher one. The only higher irama would be
irama gropak (2/1) [i.e., two balungan beats to one saron panerus stroke].
Because irama gropak can never be used for vocal melodies, our ancestors
never accepted it as a separate irama--though actually it is. However, no
gendhing can be played in irama gropak from beginning to end.

Figure 33. A Schematic Representation of Irama

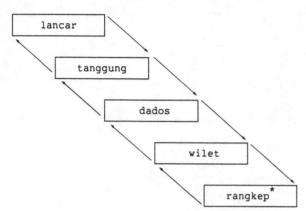

*It is highly probable that irama rangkep is a relative newcomer,
as proven by the fact that there are no fixed melodies in that irama.

After noting the use of fixed melodies in each irama, one might ask
about gendhing that have vocal parts in each irama. To answer this
question, we must relate the history [of such gendhing]. In Surakarta,
none of the elders [in former times] wanted [to use different vocal parts
in each irama]. If, for example, they played Ladrang *Pangkur*, they
proceeded straight from the buka to irama wilet, with only transitional
passages in irama tanggung and irama dados, since the fixed melody of
Ladrang *Pangkur* was considered to be in irama wilet. The reason these
elders did not wish to play the vocal melodies [for each irama in Ladrang
Pangkur] as they are generally played nowadays is that to them it seemed
like merely stringing together different melodies. In their view, there
ought to have been only one vocal melody. [This stringing together of
melodies is exemplified by the current practice of using, first,] the
"*rujak-rujakan*" melody in irama tanggung, then the "*parabé sang . . .*"
melody in irama dados, and, finally, the kinanthi melody in irama wilet.

It is true that the elders in former times, when playing gendhing in
which the fixed melody was conceived to lie only in irama wilet,
occasionally also played complete sections in irama tanggung and irama
dados. An example is the accompaniment to the Bondhan dance (Gendhing
[Ladrang] *Ginonjing*). But they only used gérong melodies in irama wilet;
the other irama were performed using only the instruments and sindhèn.

The custom of using a fixed melody in each irama, as in Ladrang *Asmarandana* and Ladrang *Pangkur*, began around 1933 as a result of influence from the accompaniment to the *Golèk Asmarandana* [a solo female dance] from Yogyakarta.

Since the cèngkok of vocal melodies can be accompanied on the gendèr, our predecessors chose melodies that were the same length as gendèr cèngkok. They chose fixed melodies in irama dados, since in this irama one gatra--either padhang or ulihan--is equal to one gendèr cèngkok. Gendèr cèngkok are sometimes two gatra long--both padhang and ulihan--and there are also half-gatra cèngkok for vocal melodies that are mixed. All of the gendèr cèngkok are distinguished according to the name of the particular vocal melody associated with them. The basic cèngkok patterns are given below. (Please note the ranges of gembyang and kempyung.)

1. Cèngkok "Éla-élo"

vocal melody: (2) . . . 5 . 6 . 3 . . . 5 . 6 . 2
                        $\overline{\text{e - la}}$ $\overline{\text{e - lo}}$

This cèngkok is used when the melodic motion is from one tone to a sèlèh tone of the same pitch, for example, from sèlèh 2 to sèlèh 2:

(2)   3   5   3   2

This cèngkok can be transposed up from 2 [to 3, and then to 5, etc.], up to pitch 1. The sèlèh tone is always treated as a gembyang.

saron panerus: . . .   .

vocal melody: (2)   . . . 5   . 6 . 3   . . . 5   . 6 . 2
                           e - la   e - lo

balungan: (2)   5   3   5   2

gendèr: [2]   3 5 3 .   3 5 3 1   3 5 3 .   3 5 3 2
        [2]   . . 1 2   3 3 3 3   . 1 . 3   . 1 . 2

Cèngkok "éla-élo" can also be used for melodic motion from a sèlèh kempyung to another sèlèh kempyung of the same pitch [e.g., from sèlèh 1 kempyung to sèlèh 1 kempyung]. This cèngkok can be transposed up to pitch 2 kempyung or pitch 3 kempyung by simply raising the melody one or two pitch degrees, respectively. For example:

```
    saron panerus:          . . .    . . .    . . .    . . .

    vocal melody: (1)    . . . 3  . 5 . 2   . . . 3  . 5 . 1
                               ‾‾‾‾‾‾‾‾           ‾‾‾‾‾‾‾‾
                                e - la             e - lo

       balungan: (1)        2          3          2          1

        gendèr: [5]     6 1 6 .    6 1 6 2    6 1 6 .    6 1 6 5
                [1]     . . 6 1    2 2 2 2    . 6 . 2    . 6 . 1
```

2. Cèngkok "Dua Lolo"

```
    vocal melody: (2)    . . 5 5    . . 6 6    . . 6 5    . . 6 3
                             du-a       lo-lo      lo-lo     lo-hing
```

This gendèr cèngkok is used for a melodic motion upward one pitch
degree. For example, from sèlèh pitch 2 to sèlèh pitch 3:

```
         (2)    5  6  5  3
```

This can be transposed up, with the following possibilities: from 2 to 3;
from 3 to 5; from 5 to 6; from 6 to 1. The final interval is always
gembyang.

```
    saron panerus:          . . .    . . .    . . .    . . .

    vocal melody: (2)    . . 5 5    . . 6 6    . . 6 5    . . 6 3
                             du-a       lo-lo      lo-lo     lo-hing
       balungan:
    (irama dados) (2)       5          6          5          3
    (irama wilet) (2)       .          5          .          3

        gendèr: [2]     5 3 5 2    5 6 5 3    2 1 2 5    . 3 5 3
                [2]     5 . 5 .    5 1 5 6    5 3 5 .    6 5 3 .
```

2a. Cèngkok "Jarit [Kawung]"

```
    vocal melody:           . . . .    . 6 1 5    . . . .    . 6 1 1 .
                                       ‾‾‾‾‾‾                ‾‾‾‾‾‾‾
                                       ja-rit                ka-wung
```

This cèngkok is used for the melodic motion from sèlèh 6 gembyang to
sèlèh 1 kempyung [sanga], or by transposition, from sèlèh 1 gembyang to
sèlèh 2 kempyung [manyura].

```
saron panerus:        . . .   . . .   . . .   . . .

vocal melody: (6)     . . . .   . 6 1̇ 5   . . . .   . 6 1 1
              .
   balungan:
(irama dados) (6)        1         5        2        1
                        .
(irama wilet) (6)        .         2        .        1

    gendèr: [6]    5 . 5 6    3 5 6 5    6 1 6̇ 2̇    6 1̇ 6 5
            [6]    . 1 5 2    6 . 1 5    . 6 5 6    1 2 3 1
            .        .          .         . .        .
```

3. Cèngkok "Gendhuk Kuning [or, "Kuthuk Kuning"] Adang Katul"

```
vocal melody: (2)     . . . .   6 6 6 6   . 3 . 2   . 3 . 5
              .
                      gen-dhuk ku-ning a - dang  ka-tul
```

This cèngkok is used for the melodic motion upward of two pitch
degrees. For example, from sèlèh 2 to sèlèh 5:

```
        (2)    3   6   3   5
         .     .   .   .   .
```

This can be transposed up successive pitch degrees, with the following
possibilities: 2 to 5; 3 to 6; 5 to 1. The final interval is gembyang.

```
saron panerus:        . . .   . . .   . . .   . . .

vocal melody: (2)     . . . .   6 6 6 6   . 3 . 2   . 3 . 5
              .
                      gen-dhuk ku-ning a - dang  ka-tul

   balungan:
(irama dados) (2)         6         3         6         5
                         .
(irama wilet) (2)         .         6         .         5
                                   .                   .
    gendèr: [2]    3 5 3 .    3 5 3 6    3 5 3 6    3 5 6 5
            [2]    . . 3 5    6 6 6 6    . 3 . 2    . 3 . 5
            .        .         . . .      . . .      . . .
```

This cèngkok can also be used for melodic motion upward two pitch degrees, ending with a kempyung interval. There are two possibilities: 5 to 1 [sanga] and 6 to 2 [manyura]. In this case, the gendèr cèngkok will be:

```
saron panerus:        . . .    . . .    . . .   . . .

vocal melody: (5)    . . . .   2 2 2 2   . 6 . 5   . 6 . 1
        .                      gen-dhuk ku-ning a - dang  ka-tul

   balungan:
(irama dados) (5)         2          3         2          1
              .
(irama wilet) (5)         .          2         .          1
              .

   gendèr: [5]    6 1 6 .    6 1 6 2    6 1 6 2    6 1 6 5
           [5]    . . 6 1    2 2 2 2    . 6 . 5    . 6 . 1
           .
```

4. Cèngkok "Ayo Yok-oyokan"

```
vocal melody: (2)    . . 2 3   5 . 5 6   2 . 2 3   5 6 1 6
        .                a-yo      a-yo     a-yo   yok-oyok-an
```

This cèngkok is used for melodic motion of a skip of three tones upward. For example, 2 to 6:

```
                  (2)   5   3   5   6
                   .    .   .   .   .
```

This cèngkok can be transposed up one pitch degree--thus, from sèlèh 3 to sèlèh 1 [gembyang].

```
saron panerus:        . . .    . . .    . . .   . . .

vocal melody: (2)    . . 2 3   5 . 5 6   2 . 2 3   5 1 5 6
        .                a-yo      a-yo     a-yo   yok-oyok-an

   balungan:
(irama dados) (2)         5          3         5          6
                                     .                    .
(irama wilet) (2)         .          5         .          6
                                     .                    .

   gendèr: [2]    5 6 5 .    5 6 5 2    5 3 . .    5 . 5 6
           [2]    . . 2 3    5 6 1 .    . . 2 1    6 1 5 6
           .
```

This cèngkok can also be used for a melodic skip of three tones that ends
on the interval of a kempyung. Thus, from 5̣ to 2 [kempyung]:

```
    saron panerus:        . . .    . . .    . . .   . . . .

    vocal melody: (5)    . . 5 6   1 . 1 2   5 . 5 6   1 3 1 2
           ̣                   a-yo      a-yo    a-yo yok-oyok-an
```

```
        balungan:
    (irama dados)  (5)        1        6        1        2
    (irama wilet)  (5̣)        .        3̣       .        2
```

```
        gendèr:     1 2 1 .   1 2 1 5   1 6 . .   1 2 1 6
                    . . 5 6   1 2 3 .   . . 5 3   2 3 1 2
```

This last cèngkok can be transposed up one pitch degree—thus, from sèlèh 6̣
to sèlèh 3 kempyung.

5. Cèngkok "Tumuruna"

```
    vocal melody: (3)    . . . .    6 6 6 5   . 3 5 3   2 5 3 2
                                    tumuruna  ngger se-dhé-la ba-é
```

This cèngkok is used for the downward motion of one step. For example,
from sèlèh 3 kempyung to sèlèh 2 kempyung:

```
        balungan:
    (irama dados)  (3)        6        5        3        2
    (irama wilet)  (3)        .        1        .        2
```

```
        gendèr:   [1]   5 6 5 1   5 6 1 6   1 2 1 .   1 2 1 6
                  [3]   . 1 . 3   . 1 2 6   . 1 6 1   2 3 1 2
```

This cèngkok can be transposed down one step; thus, from sèlèh 2
kempyung to sèlèh 1 kempyung. If the motion is from sèlèh gembyang to a
sèlèh gembyang one step lower (e.g., from sèlèh 1 gembyang to sèlèh 6
gembyang), the cèngkok is as follows:

```
        balungan:
      (irama dados)  (1)        3        2        1        6
                                                           .
      (irama wilet)  (1)        .        2        .        6
                                                           .
         .      .        .                           .
      gendèr: [1]    6 . 6 1   . 6 1 6   5 3 5 1   . 6 1 6
              [1]    . 2 3 .   2 3 5 2   1 6 1 .   2 1 6 .
                                                    .
```

This last example can be transposed down successive steps, with the
following possibilities: 1 to 6; 6 to 5; 5 to 3; 3 to 2.

6. Cèngkok "?"

This cèngkok is as yet unnamed, since there is no vocal melody
associated with it. The motion is from one sèlèh to a sèlèh two pitch
degrees below it. For example, from sèlèh 3 to sèlèh 1, sèlèh 2 to sèlèh
6, and so on. Perhaps one of the several reasons that this cèngkok is
nameless is that people tend to give it cipher names. For example, sèlèh 3
["*telu*"] to sèlèh 1 ["*siji*"] is called "*lu-ji*," sèlèh 6 ["*nem*"] to sèlèh 2
["*loro*"] is called "*nem-ro*," and so on.

From sèlèh 3 kempyung to sèlèh 1 gembyang is as follows:

```
         balungan:
      (irama dados)  (3)        2        6        2        1
      (irama wilet)  (3)        .        2        .        1
                .      .        .                           .
      gendèr (A): [1]    6 5 6 2   6 1 6 3   6 5 . .   6 5 6 1
                  [3]    2 1 2 .   6 1 2 .   . . 3 2   1 2 6 1
                                    .                   .
```

From sèlèh 3 kempyung to sèlèh 1 kempyung is as follows:

```
         balungan:
      (irama dados)  (3)        2        6        2        1
      (irama wilet)  (3)        .        2        .        2
                .      .        .      .      .      .     .
      gendèr (B): [1]    6 5 6 2   6 1 6 5   6 1 6 2   6 1 6 5
                  [3]    2 1 2 .   6 . 6 5   . 6 5 6   1 2 3 1
                                    .          . .     .  .
```

From sèlèh 2 kempyung to sèlèh 6 (pathet sanga), one uses cèngkok (A)
[i.e., to 1 gembyang] transposed down one pitch degree. From sèlèh 2
kempyung to sèlèh 6 (pathet manyura), the gendèr cèngkok is as follows:

balungan:

(irama dados)	(2)	.	1	2	6
(irama wilet)	(2)	.	1	.	6

gendèr (C): [6]   5 3 5 1   5 6 5 1   5 6 5 1   5 6 1 6
             [2]   1 6 1 .   . 5 6 3   . 5 3 5   6 1 2 6

From sèlèh 1 kempyung to sèlèh 5 (pathet sanga), one uses cèngkok (C) transposed down one pitch degree.

From sèlèh 1 gembyang to sèlèh 5 (pathet manyura), the following cèngkok is used:

balungan:

(irama dados)	(1)	6	5	3	5
(irama wilet)	(1)	.	6	.	5

gendèr (D): [1]   6 5 3 6   3 5 3 6   3 5 3 6   3 5 6 5
             [1]   6 5 6 .   . 5 3 2   . 3 2 3   5 6 1 5

From sèlèh 6 to sèlèh 3 [gembyang], and sèlèh 5 to sèlèh 2 [gembyang], one uses cèngkok (D) lowered one or two pitch degrees, respectively. From sèlèh 5 kempyung to sèlèh 2 kempyung, for gendèr that have a 3 key (*dhadha alit*), cèngkok (B) can be used by raising the melody one pitch degree. However, for a gendèr that has high 2 (*gulu alit*), the highest key, the cèngkok is as follows:

balungan:

(irama dados)	(5)	6	5	3	2
(irama wilet)	(5)	.	3	.	2

gendèr: [2]   1 6 1 5   1 2 1 6   1 2 1 .   1 2 1 6
         [5]   3 2 3 .   1 . 2 6   . 1 6 1   2 3 5 2

7. Cèngkok "Kemul Adem"

vocal melody: (3)   . . . .   . . 2 3   . . 2 3   . 1 . 6
                                ke-mul   ke-mul   a - dem

This cèngkok is used for the melodic motion of a downward skip of two tones, for example, from sèlèh 3 kempyung to sèlèh 6.

```
       balungan:
    (irama dados)  (3)        2        1        2        6
                                                         ·
    (irama wilet)  (3)        ·        1        ·        6
                                                         ·
```

```
                 ·                ·          ·  ·         ·  ·
    gendèr: [1]   5 6 5 1     . 6 1 6    5 3 5 1     . 6 1 6
            [3]   . 1 . 3     2 3 5 2    1 6 1 .     2 1 6 .
                                                       ·
```

This cèngkok can be transposed down successive pitch degrees: 2 kempyung to
5; 1 kempyung to 3 [gembyang]; 6 to 2 [gembyang]. In the case of sèlèh 6 to
sèlèh 2 [gembyang], the cèngkok is as follows:

```
       balungan:
    (irama dados)  (6)        3        5        3        2
                    ·         ·                 ·        ·
    (irama wilet)  (6)        ·        3        ·        2
                    ·                  ·                 ·
```

```
                 ·  ·  ·  ·      ·  ·  ·    ·  ·  ·       ·  ·  ·
    gendèr: [6]   3 5 3 6     . 5 3 2    1 6 1 3     . 2 3 2
            [6]   . 3 . 6     5 6 1 5    3 2 3 .     5 3 2 .
             ·       ·  ·      ·  ·        ·  ·  ·      ·  ·  ·
```

8. Cèngkok "Plèsèdan"

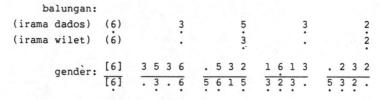

```
        sèlèh:          (2)
                         ·
    mlèsèd ['slide']:    1   2   3   5   6   1   3
                         ·   ·   ·   ·   ·
```

[This cèngkok has no particular vocal melody associated with it. It
is used for a melodic motion in which there is a sudden move from a sèlèh
tone to a new pitch level. For example, in the above illustration, the
sèlèh 2 can move suddenly, or "slide" (*mlèsèd*), to pitches 3, 5, 6, or 1.]
                                                         · · ·
The gendèr cèngkok is as follows:

```
    balungan: (2)    . . . 3    . . . 3
```

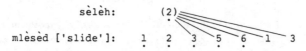

```
                 ·          ·         ·   ·  ·
    gendèr: [2]   3 . 5 3    5 . 5 3
            [2]   . 3 . .    . 6 5 3
             ·       ·         ·  ·  ·
```

For a plèsèdan to 5 gembyang and 1 gembyang, the above cèngkok can be
transposed up one, two, or three pitch levels, respectively.

For a plèsèdan from 2 gembyang to 1 kempyung, the gendèr cèngkok is as
                          ·
follows:

```
balungan: (2)    . . . 1    . . . 1

  gender: [2]    . 1 5 .    3 2 3 5
          [2]    . . . 5    . 6 . 1
```

The first example above is for plèsèdan to sèlèh gembyang; the second
example is for plèsèdan to sèlèh kempyung. (One should always keep in mind
the range of gembyang and kempyung.) But not every sèlèh tone can slide to
any other sèlèh tone; there is a limit of plèsèdan tones for each sèlèh
tone.

a. sèlèh 2 can slide to pitches 3, 5, 6, 1, and 3. A slide
    to 5 and 6 would require the same gendèr cèngkok as a slide
    to pitches 5 and 6.
b. sèlèh 3 can slide to pitches 2, 5, 6, 1, and 2.
c. sèlèh 5 can slide to pitches 2, 3, 6, 1, and 2.
d. sèlèh 6 can slide to pitches 3, 5, 1, and 2.
e. sèlèh 1 can slide to pitches 5, 6, 2, and 3.
f. sèlèh 2 can slide to pitches 6, 1, 3, and 5.
g. sèlèh 3 can slide to pitches 1 and 2.
h. sèlèh 5 can slide to pitches 2 and 3.

An exception is the slide from 1 [gembyang or kempyung] to 5, in which case
the gendèr cèngkok is:

```
[1]    . 5 6 5    6 . 6 5
[1]    5 . . .    . 1 6 5
```

This last example can be transposed up for slides from 2 [kempyung] to 6,
or from 3 [kempyung] to 1 [gembyang], by raising the pitch level one or two
degrees, respectively.

9. Cèngkok "Gantungan" ['Hanging' Cèngkok]

This cèngkok is used for balungan gantungan ['hanging' balungan], that
is, a balungan in which, following the mundur beat [the second beat], there
is more than one rest. The pitch on which the cèngkok "hangs" can be any
tone from 2 to 1 gembyang, with the cèngkok being transposed up or down the
necessary number of pitch degrees.

```
balungan: (2)        .       .        .        .

  gender: [2]    . 6 1 .    1 . 1 2   1 6 1 3   . 2 3 2
          [2]    . . . 5    3 2 . .   1 2 3 .   5 3 2 .
```

The same principle holds true for cases in which the hanging cèngkok begins from a kempyung, i.e., from any sèlèh kempyung from 1 kempyung to 5 kempyung.

```
balungan:  (1)           .        .        .        .

gendèr:  [5]    . . 3 5    3 . 3 5    . . 3 5    3 . 3 5
         [1]    . . . 5    6 1 . .    6 1 . 5    6 1 . .
```

This cèngkok could be transposed up or down the necessary number of pitch degrees.

The scheme of gendèran gantungan can be divided into two for gatra in which there are two successive rests: (a) when the rests come after the sèlèh beat [beat four], in which case the above gendèr cèngkok is used for the first half of the gatra [e.g., (5) . . 5 6, etc.]; and (b) when the rests come after the mundur beat [beat two], in which case the above cèngkok is used for the second half of the gatra [beats three and four; e.g., (5) . 5 . . , etc.].

The above shall suffice as our explanation of the scheme of gendèr cèngkok that are the length of one padhang or one ulihan [i.e., one gatra long]. There are also cèngkok that are the length of a complete padhang-ulihan. These cèngkok can usually be transposed only one pitch degree up or down, and some of them cannot be transposed at all. Most of these cèngkok also take their names from the vocal melodies associated with them.

10. Cèngkok "Ayu Kuning"

```
vocal melody:   . . . 6    . . 2 1    . 2 3 3    . . 5 2    . . . 3    . 1 6 3    . . 3 2    . . 3 1
                 a   -       yu         ku         ning       -          ma - ya    ma         ya

balungan:  (2)   6          1          3          2          6          3          2          1

(irama dados)  (3)  .        1          3          2          6          3          2          1
               (6)  .

(irama wilet)    .  .        .          .          3          .          .          .          1
                 .  .        .          .          2          .          .          .          1

gendèr:   . . 6    . . . 1   6 . 6 1   . 6 1 6   . 2 3 .   . 2 3 2 1   6 5 6 2   . 1 2 1
          . . 2 6  . . 5 1   . 2 3 .   . 2 3 5 2 . . 6 1   2 5 2 3     2 1 2 .   3 2 1 .
```

This cèngkok can be adapted to pathet sanga by transposing it down one pitch degree. Moreover, the second half of this [two-gatra-long] cèngkok can be used as a cèngkok from sèlèh 2 [kempyung] to 1 [gembyang], in pathet manyura, or from sèlèh 1 [kempyung] to 6 in pathet sanga.

11. Cèngkok "Ya Suraka" ("Dudukan")

```
vocal melody:  · · · · · 6 · 1 · · · 2   · 6 5 3 · 5 · 6   · 2 · 1 · · · 6   · · · 1 5
                        ya su     ̄       ra - ka            su - rak  i  -  ya

balungan:
  from (5)      2         3         5     3         2         1         6     5
  or (6/2/3)    5         6         5     3         2         1         6     5

gendèr from [5]:  · 3 5 6   · 5 6   5 · 1   6 · 6 1   6 · 1 2   6 · 6 3   6 · 6 2   6 1 6
           [5]:   · · · ·   2 3 ·   · 3 1   · 2 · 3   · 2 3 5   · 2 · 6   · 3 ·     · 3 ·     5 ·

                                    or

vocal melody:  · · · · · 6 · 1 · · · 2   · 6 5 3 · 5 · 6   · 2 5 3   · · · 1   2 1 6 6
                        ya su     ̄       ra - ka            su               rak i  -  ya

balungan:
  from (5)      2         3         5     3         2         1         2     6
  or (6/2/3)    5         6         5     3         2         1         2     6

gendèr from [5]:  · 3 5 6   · 5 6   5 · 1   6 · 6 1   6 5 6   6 5 6 1   · 6 5 1   5 6 1 6
           [5]:   · · · ·   2 3 ·   · 3 1   · 2 · 3   · · 3 2   1 2 6 1   · 5 · 3   · 5 · 6 ·
```

or

```
vocal melody:   · · · · · 6 · 1̇ · · · · 2̇   · 6 5 3   · 6 5 3   5 · 6   · 2 5 3   · · ·   · 1̇   · 6̇ 1 1
                          ya su      -        ra - ka      ka        su    -    rak     i̇ ÷   ya

balungan:
  from (5)        2        3        5              3        3        2        1        2        1
  or (6/2/3)      5        6        5              3        3        2        1        2        1

to sèlèh 1 gembyang

gendèr from [5]:  ·3 5 6  ·5 6  5 ·1̇·1̇   6 ·6̇1   6 5 6 2   6 5 6·   6̇ 1̇ 6 3   6 5 6·   6̇ 5 6̇ 1̇
          [5]:    ·· ··   ·2 3·  ·3 ·1    ·2 ·3    2 1 2·    2 1 2·   6̇ 1 2·    ··3 2    1 2 6̇ 1̇

to sèlèh 1 kempyung

gendèr from [5]:  ·3 5 6  ·5 6  5 ·1̇·1̇   6 ·6̇1   6 5 6 2   6 1̇ 6 2   6̇ 1̇ 6 5   6 1̇ 6 2   6̇ 1̇ 6 5
          [5]:    ·· ··   ·2 3·  ·3 ·1    ·2 ·3    2 1 2·    ·6 5 6·   6·1 5·    ·6 5 6·   1 2 3 1
```

12. Cèngkok "Ora Butuh"

This cèngkok is only used in pathet manyura or pathet nem from one of the sèlèh tones 5, 6, or 2 [leading to sèlèh 3 gembyang]. From sèlèh 5 or 6 the melody is as follows:

```
vocal melody:  .    .    .    .    6  5  6  5   6  5  3  5   .    .    .    .   2  3  5  6    .  2  5   .   5  6  3
                                   O-ra bu-tuh ka-é ka-é              [bu-tuh-ku sing   nyam-but  ga – wé]

balungan:
(irama dados) (5/6)     3                   5                   3                   5                   3

(irama wilet) (5/6)     .                   5                   .                   .                   3

gendèr: 3
```

From sèlèh 2, the melody is as follows:

```
balungan:
(irama dados) (2)       5                   6                   5                   1                   3

(irama dados) (2)       .                   5                   .                   .                   3

gendèr:
```

In my opinion, the cèngkok "ora butuh" can be transposed down one pitch degree to become pathet sanga, but almost no gendèr players do this. When there is a balungan . 3 . 2 in irama wilet in pathet sanga, most players use a cèngkok for 2 (gulu) in the middle range (for example, in the inggah of *Bondhèt* or *Menyan Kobar*).

13. Cèngkok "Puthut Gelut"

The name for this cèngkok is not derived from a vocal melody. "Puthut gelut" can only be played in pathet sanga or manyura, and moreover is used only in gendèran laku 8 [i.e., in which there are eight articulated subdivisions per balungan beat]. In gendèran laku 4, various gendèr cèngkok can be used depending upon the melodic phrase. For this reason these cèngkok cannot rightfully be called "puthut gelut"; hence, we can conclude that in laku 4 there is no cèngkok "puthut gelut." In irama wilet, this cèngkok is used only after sèlèh on pitch 6 or pitch 1 in pathet manyura, or after sèlèh on pitch 5 or pitch 6 in pathet sanga. If the balungan is mlaku [i.e., filled in], puthut gelut can proceed from sèlèh on pitch 2 in pathet manyura, or pitch 1 [kempyung] in pathet sanga. Below are the gendèr patterns for "puthut gelut" in pathet manyura. This can also be used in pathet sanga by simply lowering the melody one pitch degree.

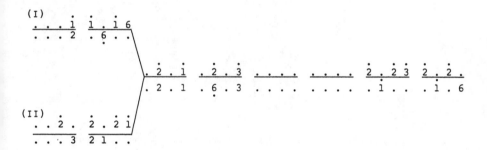

(The above notated pattern is only one-half of the entire pattern--the padhang. The ulihan follows below:)

```
 .  .   . .      . . .   . .  .   . .   . .    . .     . .    . . . .   . . . .
.1 . .  6 1 2 3  2 . 3 2  . 1 . .  1 6 1 .  . 1 . 6  1 6 . .  1 . 1 6
. . 3 5 . . . .  . 1 . .  6 . 6 3  . . . 3  5 . 5 .  . . 5 3  2 3 1 2
```

[Subphrase] (I) above follows sèlèh on pitch 6 and [subphrase] (II) follows sèlèh on pitch 1. If the balungan is not mlaku and the cèngkok follows a sèlèh on pitch 2 [kempyung], the cèngkok (I), above, can be used. The ulihan of "puthut gelut" can stand alone, in which case it is called "puthut semèdi" and is used to accompany phrases proceeding from sèlèh on pitch 6 to sèlèh on pitch 2 [kempyung] in pathet manyura.

Below are listed the types of balungan phrases which require the
cèngkok "puthut gelut."

```
(6)  ⎡3  3  .  .   6  5  3  2⎤
     ⎢                      ⎥
     ⎢3  3  .  .   3  5  3  2⎥        irama dados
     ⎢                      ⎥
     ⎢3  3  5  6   3  5  3  2⎥
(1)  ⎢3  3  2  3   6  5  3  2⎥                              pathet manyura
     ⎢                      ⎥
     ⎣   .     3      .     2⎦        irama wilet


(6)     3  5  6  i̇   6  5  3  2
                                     irama dados
(2)     6  5  6  i̇   6  5  3  2
```

```
(5)  ⎡2  2  .  .   2  3  2  1⎤
 ̇    ⎢                      ⎥
     ⎢2  2  .  3   5  3  2  1⎥        irama dados
     ⎢                      ⎥
(6)  ⎢2  2  .  .   5  3  2  1⎥
     ⎢                      ⎥                               pathet sanga
     ⎣   .     2      .     1⎦        irama wilet


(5)  ⎡i̇  6  5  6   5  3  2  1⎤
     ⎢                      ⎥
     ⎣i̇  2̇ i̇  6   5  3  2  1⎦        irama dados


(1)     5  6  i̇  6   5  3  2  1
```

14. Cèngkok "Deyang-debyung," or "Nya Tali Nya Emping"

The name of this cèngkok is derived from a vocal melody. "Debyang-debyung" is used only in pathet manyura and sanga and can only be used in laku 8. This cèngkok is used only from sèlèh on pitch 2 [kempyung] in pathet manyura or from sèlèh on pitch 1 [kempyung] in pathet sanga. For pathet sanga, the gendèr cèngkok notated above is lowered one pitch degree.

vocal melody: . 1 2 3 . 1 2 6 . 1 2 6 . 1 2 3 . 1 2 6 . 1 2 3 . 1 2 6 3 3 5 6 5 3 5 6 .

nya ta-li nya em-ping nya ta-li nya em-ping nya ta-li nya em-ping ja-luk ta-li jo-blang ja-bling

balungan: (a)	.	6	.	1	.	1	.	3
(pathet manyura, (b)	.	3	.	1	.	1	.	6
irama dados) (c)	.	2	.	3	.	6	.	3
(irama wilet) (d)	.	.	.	.	.	.	.	3

gendèr:
```
. . 1        . 1        . 5  . 5 6
. 1 2 3  . 1 2 .  . 1 2 3  . 1 2 .  . 1 2 3  . 1 2 .  . 3 5 6  6 3 5 6 .
```

The gendèr cèngkok notated above is only one-half of the entire pattern--the padhang. The ulihan is as follows:

balungan:(a)	.	6	.	1	.	1	.	2
(b)	.	3	.	1	.	1	.	2
(c)	.	6	.	3	.	3	.	2
(d)	.	.	.	.	.	.	.	2

gendèr:
```
. 1 . .  6 1 2 3  2 . 3 2  . 1 . .  1 6 1 .  . 1 . 6  1 6 . .  1 . 1 6
. . 3 5  . . . .  6 . 6 3  . 1 . .  6 . 6 3  . . . 3  5 . 5 .  . 5 3 2  2 3 1 2
```

The gendèr cèngkok for the ulihan is "puthut semèdi." The balungan for alternative (d) is irama wilet.

[The gendèr for the ulihan cèngkok (d) is irama wilet.]

The gendèr patterns enumerated above should suffice for now, since my
purpose here was only to give a view of the relationship of cèngkok to
irama. The gendèr cèngkok for irama dados and irama wilet are basically
identical; the application of these cèngkok to individual gatra differs.

Surakarta, November 17, 1969

Martopangrawit

NOTES

1. Volume 1 of *Catatan-Catatan Pengetahuan Karawitan* is a translation of a translation in Indonesian of the original Javanese manuscript. The translation into Indonesian was accomplished under the supervision of the author. No Javanese text was published. Volume 2 was published in Javanese. "A Note from the Translator [of the Original Javanese]" was written by the anonymous translator of the Javanese text.

2. It should be noted that the source of the irregularity is the original inggah to *Laler Mengeng*, which was kethuk 8 (see "Gendhing Appendix," volume 3). Since merong of kethuk arang or kerep cannot be followed by inggah longer than kethuk 4, this inggah can be considered to violate the above rule, and hence, according to the author, was replaced in common practice with another inggah.

3. The gendèr notation that appears here in brackets was left blank in the original text, with only indications by name of the required gendèr part: e.g., "cèngkok mlèsèd 3 separoh," or "cèngkok pipa landa." The notation supplied here is taken from Martopangrawit's gendèr handbook (Martopangrawit 1973:8, 59-60).

CATATAN-CATATAN

PENGETAHUAN KARAWITAN

[Notes on Knowledge about Gamelan Music]

Volume 2

by

Raden Lurah Martopangrawit

Translated from Javanese by

Martin F. Hatch

Surakarta: Pusat Kesenian Jawa Tengah and Dewan

Mahasiswa, Akademi Seni Karawitan Indonesia

1972

FOREWORD

These notes constitute the second part of the writings of our
colleague, Martopangrawit, compiled as a guide for his students at ASKI in
Surakarta. To save time, the original plan to translate this into
Indonesian in order to reach a wider audience had to be abandoned; so this
section is here reproduced in the original language [Javanese].

It is difficult to separate Martopangrawit's life from karawitan. For
that reason, it is easy to understand his great desire to preserve and to
conserve karawitan, among other ways, by revealing some of his
authoritative knowledge and passing it on to his students, as an important
inheritance of our cultural treasury. A desire and devotion of this type
have great meaning.

So it is appropriate here to offer our many thanks to our colleague
Martopangrawit for his intentions and tireless efforts.

Surakarta, February 1972
Central Java Art Center
Development Project
S. D. Humardani, Director

The Pélog Tuning System

Now I want to talk about the pélog tuning system. I have already explained the general meaning of laras pélog above, and so it is not necessary to discuss this further.

Which is Older, Laras Pélog or Laras Sléndro?

Because there are two tuning systems in karawitan, the question will certainly be asked, "Which of the two is older?" In my opinion, the intent of this question is unclear. Does it refer to the tuning system--the tones--or does it refer to the gamelan--the instruments?

Around 1935, the late revered old gentleman [Nga]bèi Mlayadimeja (the author of *Serat Titi Asri*), told me:

> Gamelan sléndro was made by Bathara Indra [Éndra] of Saléndra Bawana and was presenṭed to the King of Puṛwa Carita. "Slendro" took its namẹ from "Salendra Bawana." The pelog tuning system waṣ made by Radèn Panji Inu Kartapati of Jenggala Manik, so laras slendro is older.

This explanation clearly concerns the relative age of the instruments of the gamelan. He then told me, "The human voice, beginning from an infant's cry at birth, is in laras sléndro, so sléndro is the older tuning system." This statement clearly refers to the relative age of the tuning system-- the tones.

There are many other theories--both written and oral--concerning the age of the two laras. I presume that many of these theories are familiar to most readers, so I need not repeat them here. I do not want to dwell on these matters, realizing that I am not knowledgeable enough. I only want to pass on information concerning the performance practice (*garap*) found in the music of Central Java, specifically in Surakarta, information that deals with the question of which is older, performance practice in laras sléndro or in laras pélog?

Performance Practice (Garap) and Cèngkok on the Gendèr Gedhé

Cèngkok for the gendèr in the sléndro tuning system can be considered
already perfect [as they stand]; the melodic ranges are already defined in
terms of the range of gembyang and kempyung. Cèngkok that fall in the
gembyang range should [end on the interval of a] gembyang, and cèngkok that
fall in the kempyung range should [end on the interval of a] kempyung.
These cèngkok can be transferred to pélog without any changes; that is, the
sléndro cèngkok are used in the pélog tuning system. [The problem is that]
when some sléndro kempyung cèngkok are played in pélog, they do not yield a
kempyung interval.

Below is a portion of the gendèr part for Ladrang *Wilujeng*, laras
sléndro [pathet manyura], that can also be used in the gendèr part for
Ladrang *Sri Kuncara* in pélog [pathet nem].

```
             G                                       N
balungan:    6     2    1    2    3    2    1    2    6
             .                                       .

             G         .         .         .
gendèr:      6   5.56  .561  6.61  6561
             6   .12.  1231  .212  3.33
             .
```

This gendèr cèngkok can also be used in the gendèr part for Ladrang *Sri
Kuncara*, laras pélog [pathet nem], which has the [same] balungan, 2 1 2 3
2 1 2 6 . When played in laras sléndro, the gendèr part for the balungan
2 1 2 3 ends on kempyung and this results in the interval of a true
kempyung [i.e., a perfect fifth]:

                                 .
                                 1

                                 3

When this cèngkok is duplicated in pélog, the position is transferred as
is, but pitch 1 in pélog is not really a kempyung above pitch 3 [i.e., it
is not a perfect fifth higher, but closer to a minor sixth]. So, it is
clear that this cèngkok was conceived first in sléndro and that the sléndro
cèngkok is the older of the two.

An even clearer case of a pélog cèngkok merely copying a sléndro
cèngkok occurs if the cèngkok falls on pitch 6. In both laras sléndro and
laras pélog this sèlèh 6 must be treated as gembyang. Yet, if we compare
this with the sèlèh 3 example, which is treated as a kempyung but is, in
fact, not a kempyung [that is, a perfect fifth] in pélog, one could ask why
sèlèh 6 cannot be treated as kempyung. For, in laras pélog, pitch 6 does

indeed have pitch 3 as an interval exactly one kempyung higher [i.e., 3 is a perfect fifth higher than 6].

The derivation of cèngkok in laras pélog from laras sléndro is not only evident from gendèr cèngkok, but can be seen in rebab cèngkok as well. There are also cases of forced, or awkward, transpositions in rebab cèngkok from sléndro to pélog. These will be seen in the section on rebab fingering, below.

Gendèr Pélog Nem and Gendèr Pélog Barang

Legend has it that Radèn Panji Inu Kartapati created a pélog tuning system which used pitch panunggul [1], but not pitches pélog [4] or barang [7]. This tuning is known as pélog [pathet] nem.[*] Then, Dèwi Ragil Kuning created a pélog tuning which used pitch barang [7]. Therefore, according to legend pélog nem is older [than pélog pathet barang].

Whether or not the above story is true, I cannot say. I can only leave it to those of my children and grandchildren who are experts in history to decide. However, it seems possible that pélog nem is older than pélog barang. This will be clarified below.

Karawitan is called "*panca nada*" ['pentatonic']. Thus, although laras pélog has seven tones, the sequence of tones utilized clearly consists of five tones. Laras pélog, as a sequence of tones, consists of a group of three tones plus a group of two tones, as illustrated in figure 1.

Figure 1.

[Note: " ‿ " = narrow interval; " —— " = wide interval]

This grouping of tones, if portrayed in a line from left to right, or vice versa, will appear as in figure 2.

Figure 2.

---

[*]In Yogya, this is known as "pélog bem."

Knowing only the groups lined up as in figure 2, we cannot yet determine
the placement of particular tones, because these slots can be filled in any
one of the following ways.

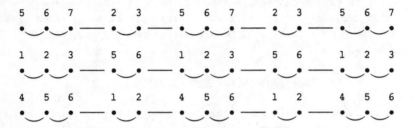

Let us vocalize one of these, then try to determine which pélog it is.

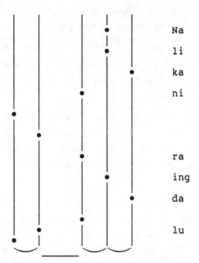

I am certain no one can guess what I am singing in the above example until
cèngkok are applied.

Above I showed, with examples, how cèngkok in laras pélog are borrowed
from cèngkok in laras sléndro. Here I will provide a further explanation.
The application of cèngkok in laras sléndro to laras pélog is accomplished
according to tonal considerations (*toonaliteit*). The distribution of the
ranges of gembyang and kempyung in laras pélog is the same as in laras
sléndro. This is illustrated in figure 3.

Figure 3.

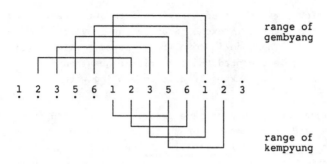

range of
gembyang

range of
kempyung

Once the division of ranges of gembyang and kempyung in sléndro is applied
to pélog, we can begin to figure out the pitches that are required in
figure 2.

But if we examine diagram 3 closely, we will notice that within the
range of kempyung there is an interval that is not really a kempyung [i.e.,
a perfect fifth], namely,

$$\dot{1}$$
$$3$$

Though the interval is not a kempyung [fifth], it is treated as if it were
a kempyung, as in sléndro [where $\frac{\dot{1}}{3}$ is a perfect fifth]. Thus, sléndro
manyura treatment as applied to pelog manyura is occasionally forced. In
order to [properly] apply sléndro manyura treatment to pélog, the grouping
of intervals should be changed, but without changing the tonality
[*toonaliteit*]. Thus, pitch panunggul (1) is replaced by pitch barang (7),
as in figure 4.

Figure 4.

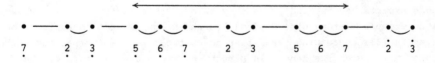

This arrangement of pitches allows for the same performance treatment in
pélog as in sléndro manyura. Based on this observation, I have concluded
that pélog nem (bem) is older than pélog barang.

Pathet in Laras Pélog

As I have said before, we inherited karawitan from our ancestors as a
finished product. This statement is exemplified in the proverbs, "The mat
is already spread out," or "The food is completely cooked." Like it or
not, the fact is that we have accepted the tradition bequeathed to us.
Accordingly, when I deal here with karawitan, I am dealing with something
that already exists.

The gamelan in laras pélog that we have inherited is divided into two
parts—pélog nem (bem) and pélog barang. Both are laras pélog. The use of
pélog barang is clear. It is used for gendhing in pathet barang,
regardless of what performance technique is chosen, and no matter what the
gong tone may be. It is only necessary that the sequence of tones (*modalé*
['store', 'capital']) contains the tone barang (7) for the pathet to be
recognized as barang. Pathet nem (bem), however, is traditionally used by
two pathet—pathet lima and pathet nem. Many people have tried to
understand the distinction between pathet lima and pathet nem, and many
theories have arisen. I will briefly recount the theories with which I am
familiar.

1. When I consider the names of the gendhing bequeathed us by our
ancestors, I am sometimes astounded. Beautiful or pleasing gendhing seem
to have been named quite arbitrarily with titles such as *Budheng-budheng*
['dull-sounding', 'dull witted'], *Okrak-okrak* [?], *Gobet* [?], *Lompong Kèli*
['leaf stem carried by a current'], *Cucur Bawuk* ['female genitalia during
menstruation or after birth'], and others. While these names do not have
bad connotations, they strike one as obscure. However, when I recall my
meetings with past masters of karawitan, I remember that most of them were
not expert in literature or language, and, in fact, many of them were
illiterate. This fact was also evident in their discussions or
explanations of karawitan—their style of speech was at the same time
simple and hard to grasp. So, a listener had to be able to guess what
these experts had in mind [when they held forth on matters of karawitan].
As an example, let me cite R[adèn] L[urah] Darmapradangga's explanation
given in 1933 concerning the difference between kethuk 4 kerep and kethuk 2
arang. "If; when the kenong is struck in a kethuk 4 kerep form, the
feeling is unpleasant, then the form must be kethuk 2 arang." For months I
searched unsuccessfully for the meaning of these words. I was able to
understand them only after hearing and appreciating many gamelan
performances. It is apparent that the meaning of the speaker related to

different *kalimat lagu* [melodic phrases] in the kethuk 4 kerep or kethuk 2 arang forms.

That is, a stroke of the kenong sounds awkward at the point in the balungan where it would fall if the piece were in kethuk 4 kerep form [and not kethuk 2 arang], because the melodic phrasing of the balungan is inappropriate [to the emphasis a kenong stroke provides].

A similar situation arose during a discussion I overheard between elder masters of karawitan at the home of R[adèn] Ng[abèhi] Mlayawiguna in Kemlayan.* Many aspects of karawitan were discussed. Among them was the subject of pathet and the ways to differentiate between pieces in pélog pathet lima and pélog pathet nem.** Their conclusion was, "If a piece has phrases that fall on pitch 1, the pathet is lima." Although the masters seemed to nod their heads in agreement, in my opinion the conclusion reached is still unclear. The thing I remember most vividly is the statement, "[pathet lima] falls on pitch 1."

I then studied the notation written in a book left to me by my parents, but my efforts were not rewarded; there were just as many phrases ending on pitch 1 in gendhing in pathet nem as in pathet lima. So I decided to search for proof in performance practice (*garap*) and to that end I applied myself diligently to learn to play. My research based on performance practice resulted only in findings pertaining to the sléndro pathet, as can be seen in volume 1 of this work. Alas, my effort was interrupted by the outbreak of the Second World War, and my research continued to be thwarted up through the "second military action."[1]

After the "second military action," I still did not resume my search for what was meant by those elders, because many of them (including R. Ng. Mlayawiguna) were victims of the Dutch occupation during this period.

2. One day I was shown a theory of pathet by some of my friends who were students at the Konservatori [Karawitan Indonesia]; the theory had come out of their studies at the Konservatori, and was worked out clearly in a scientific manner.*** I was delighted with what they told me. In fact, their view of laras sléndro was more or less identical to mine; the

---

*This was also in the year 1933, but I do not recall the business at hand.

**I merely listened silently.

***I need not unfold this theory here, since it is already well known, and there are many diagrams explicating the theory stored at the Konservatori.

only difference was in their mode of expression. As for pélog, their
conclusions were the same as for sléndro. I need not go into detail here,
but will show the gist of it only, in figure 5.

Figure 5.

	dhing	lower kempyung	dhong	upper kempyung	pelengkap
pathet lima	4	1	5	2	6
pathet nem	1	5	2	6	3
pathet barang	5	2	6	3	7

If the tones of each of the pathet in the diagram are arranged in order
from large to small (i.e., modally) they appear as in figure 6.

Figure 6.

	lower kempyung	upper kempyung	dhing	dhong	pelengkap
pathet lima	1	2	4	5	6
pathet nem	5	6	1	2	3
pathet barang	2	3	5	6	7

After we understand which are the tones in each pathet, we can
crystallize matters further: the difference between pathet lima and pathet
nem, besides the dhong tone, is that in lima there is no pitch 3 and in nem
there is no pitch 4.

The theory/exposition outlined in these diagrams is clear and
understandable; one pathet can be differentiated from another, and the
theory is scientific as well. However, I am still puzzled when I remember
the utterance of the masters of old, that "[pélog lima] falls on pitch 1."
This reawakened my search for pathet in laras pélog, because even this
scientifically explained theory had to be tested to determine the truth.

3. Did the statement of the old masters, that "[pélog lima] falls on
pitch 1," mean that the dhong or tonic (*toonica*) is panunggul (1)? To test
this possibility, I sought pieces whose gong tone was pitch 1, and found

two, one in which pitch 4 is used and one in which pitch 3 is used. Both
gendhing are considered to be in pathet lima.

a. The *unggah* of [Gendhing Bonang] *Dhenggung Laras*

```
                                            N
3 2 3 1   3 2 3 5   6 3 6 5   3 2 3 1
. 2 . 3   . 5 . 3   . 6 . 5   . 2 . 1
. 2 . 3   . 5 . 3   . 6 . 5   . 2 . 1
3 2 3 1   3 2 3 5   6 3 6 5   3 2 3 1G
```

b. The *unggah* of [Gendhing Rebab] *Laranjala*

```
                                            N
4 2 4 1   4 2 4 5   4 6 4 5   4 2 4 1
4 2 4 1   4 2 4 5   4 6 4 5   4 2 4 1
2 2 . .   2 2 . 4   5 6 7 6   5 4 2 1
6 6 . .   6 4 6 5   4 2 4 5   4 2 4 1G
```

The composers of both these gendhing are unknown. Such gendhing are
usually just called "old gendhing." Both are considered to be in pathet
lima by our elders and both have panunggul (1) as a sèlèh tone. One uses
pitch 3 and the other uses pitch 4. So, according to the above, pathet
lima does not depend on the presence or absence of pitch 3 or pitch 4.

If one judges the feeling of pathet in these pieces by intuition, it
seems clear that the feeling of pathet lima derives from the pieces having
pitch 1 as the sèlèh tone or dhong tone. As further proof of the elders'
belief that pathet lima has pitch 1 as the dhong tone, there are examples
in pathet nem in which the gong of the buka falls on pitch 1, or in which
there is a dhong tone on 1 in the buka--that is, in the *adangiyah* (opening
phrase of the buka). The adangiyah are identical in pathet nem and pathet
lima, except for the parts played on open strings (which in pathet nem are
tuned to pitches 6 and 2 [and to pitches 5 and 1, in pathet lima]).

If this is the case, the results are in agreement with another
opinion, that is, that the names of these pathet were originally based on
counting. That is the explanation, among others, for what is called
"pathet 8 [wolu]" in East Java (or "pathet 9 [sanga]" in Central Java),

based on counting from left to right the keys of the ten-keyed gendèr, as
illustrated in figure 7.[*]

Figure 7. A Ten-Keyed Sléndro Gendèr and a Ten-Keyed Pélog Gendèr

Sléndro

2	3	5	6	1	2	3	5	6	i

gulu dhadha lima   nem panunggul gulu dhadha lima   nem panunggul
                           (or barang)   (or barang)

Pélog

2	3	5	6	1	2	3	5	6	i

gulu dhadha lima   nem panunggul gulu dhadha lima   nem panunggul

<u>Garap</u>
<u>[Performance Practice, or Treatment]</u>

From the point of view of performance practice (*garap*)--especially
performance practice on the gendèr--the above-mentioned theory of my
colleagues from the Konservatori, taken in its entirety, more clearly
delineates the different treatment required in each pathet.

1. Pathet lima should be treated in the same way as pathet sanga in
    laras sléndro.

2. Pathet nem in laras pélog should be treated in the same way as
    pathet manyura in laras sléndro, although pitches 3 and 1 do not
    form the interval of an [acoustic] kempyung.

---

[*]This line of argument, which bases pathet on the counting of keys,
runs into a dead end, however, when confronted with the names for slendro
pathet manyura or pelog pathet barang.

3. Pathet barang should be treated in the same way as pathet manyura in laras sléndro, and pitches 3 and 7 do form the interval of an [acoustic] kempyung.

But note that in the gendhing left us by our ancestors, the actual performance practice is as follows.

1. Pathet lima requires mixed treatment. The final tone (*vinal*) [pitch 1] is not found in pathet manyura, and a sèlèh on pitch 1 (panunggul tengah) requires treatment as a kempyung on the gendèr. For example, the following excerpt from the umpak of Gendhing *Jalaga*, a gendhing rebab, represents a mixture of pathet sanga and pathet nem treatment.

G
33..   6532   55..   5535   ..56   7654   216.   5616
<u> nem </u>   <u> sanga </u>   <u> nem </u>

Another example, from the final gongan of Gendhing *Pasang*, represents a mixture of pathet nem and manyura treatment.

G
33..   6532   3216   5616
<u> manyura </u>   <u> nem </u>

The following example represents a mixture of pathet manyura and pathet sanga treatment.

N   G
....   2212   33..   1232   11..   5612   1312   .165
<u> manyura </u>   <u> sanga </u>

2. Pélog pathet nem can be treated with a mixture of pathet, or completely in pathet sanga or pathet manyura. Sèlèh on pitch 1 can be treated either as kempyung or gembyang. An example of mixed treatment is Ladrang *Kapi Dhondhong*; of pathet sanga treatment, Ladrang *Sri Kretarta*; and of wholly pathet manyura treatment, Gendhing *Randhu Kèntir* (the mérong of Ladrang *Ayun-ayun*).

3. The treatment of pathet barang is also mixed, but a sèlèh on pitch 7 must be treated as gembyang. In the example below, from the mérong of Gendhing *Bandhil Ori*, the gatra enclosed in brackets represents a pathet sanga cèngkok that requires treatment as gembyang.

```
                                  N
        .352   .352   5653   2767
                                  ....
               manyura

                                  N
        .3.2   .765   ..56   7232
               ...    ..     .
               sanga

                                  N
        35..   55..   5565   [3567]
               sanga

          . .                     G
        .3.2   .765   .7.6   .532
          sanga       manyura
```

An example of pathet barang that mixes pathet manyura cèngkok with
cèngkok in pathet nem is taken from the mérong of Gendhing *Bèlèk*
and is provided below. Note that the gatra enclosed in brackets
in the example represents mode number IV in pathet barang. (See
"Mode [Modus] in the Pélog Tuning System," below.)

```
    ..56  .356  .356  .532   5653  2756  33..  6532
                                    ...
              nem                   manyura

                                                  N
    5653  2756  33..  6532   5653  2767  .3.2  .756
                                    ...               ...
                    barang

    3567  6563  77..  3276   3567  6563  ..36  3567
    ....  ....  ..    ..     ....        ....
                    nem

                                                  N
    22..  22..  22.3  2767   .3.2  .767  [2343  2756]
                                    ...               ...
              manyura               manyura
```

Another example of pathet barang in which the cèngkok are all in
pathet manyura and the gong tone is 6 (nem) is taken from Ladrang
Wilujeng.

```
                N                       N
    2 7 2 3   2 7 5 6     3 3 . .   6 5 3 2
        .     . . .

                N                       G
    5 6 5 3   2 7 5 6     2 7 2 3   2 7 5 6
              . . .           .     . . .
```

A pélog barang example in which the cèngkok are wholly in pathet manyura with a gong tone on 2 (gulu) is taken from Ladrang *Sasangka*.

$$\begin{array}{ccccccc} & & & \overset{N}{} & & & & & \overset{N}{} \\ 3 & 2 & 7 & 6 & 3 & 5 & 3 & 2 & \quad & 3 & 2 & 7 & 6 & 3 & 5 & 3 & 2 \\ & & \cdot & \cdot & & & & & & & & \cdot & \cdot \end{array}$$

After studying these examples, we can conclude that the most unequivocal pathet is pathet barang, since, as we have mentioned before, the only prerequisite of pathet barang is that the range of tones include pitch 7 (barang) without any restriction on the treatment [as gembyang or kempyung on the gendèr, for example] of that pitch. However, in the case of pélog bem [encompassing both pathet nem and pathet lima], it is more difficult to determine what defines pathet lima or pathet nem.

Although it might seem that the modal system (*modus-modus*) in laras pélog is clear in number and form and the modes not hard to differentiate, in fact when these modes are arranged into gendhing (and we are speaking here only of the gendhing of Central Java), it becomes much more difficult to determine the pathet of a given gendhing. Most interpretations of pathet are merely based on the traditional association of a particular gendhing with a particular pathet.

Mode (Modus) in the Pélog Tuning System

The term "mode" in karawitan is borrowed from Western music terminology. "Mode," in karawitan, is a sequence of tones (*arah nada*) that may be read as well as sounded. This is not the case with, for example, 6 7 1; this sequence can be read, but not sounded. There are seven tones in laras pélog, but only a sequence of five tones can be sounded, as follows.

Mode I	no. 1:	4	5	6		1	2
	no. 2:	1	2	3		5	6
	no. 3:	5	6	7		2	3
	no. 4:	2	3	4*		6	7

---

*Even though there is no gamelan key for the tone 4, I have included it here because it is frequently used in vocal music.

Mode II	no. 1:	1	2		4	5	6	
	no. 2:	5	6		1	2	3	
	no. 3:	2	3		5	6	7	
	no. 4:	6	7		2	3	4	

Mode III	no. 1:	5	6		1	2		4
	no. 2:	2	3		5	6		1
	no. 3:	6	7		2	3		5
	no. 4:	3	∉		6	7		2

Mode IV	no. 1:	2		4	5	6		1
	no. 2:	6		1	2	3		5
	no. 3:	3		5	6	7		2
	no. 4:	7		2	3	∉		6

Mode V	no. 1:	6		1	2		4	5
	no. 2:	3		5	6		1	2
	no. 3:	7		2	3		5	6
	no. 4:	∉		6	7		2	3

The modes below represent an improved written form of those above.

Mode I	no. 1:	4	5	6		1	2		4
	no. 2:	1	2	3		5	6		1
	no. 3:	5	6	7		2	3		5
	no. 4:	2	3	∉		6	7		2

Mode II	no. 1:	1	2		4	5	6		1
	no. 2:	5	6		1	2	3		5
	no. 3:	2	3		5	6	7		2
	no. 4:	6	7		2	3	∉		6

Mode III	no. 1:	5	6		1	2		4	5
	no. 2:	2	3		5	6		1	2
	no. 3:	6	7		2	3		5	6
	no. 4:	3	∉		6	7		2	3

Mode IV	no. 1:	2		4	5	6		1	2
	no. 2:	6		1	2	3		5	6
	no. 3:	3		5	6	7		2	3
	no. 4:	7		2	3	∉		6	7

```
Mode V   no. 1:     6      1  2      4  5  6
         no. 2:     3      5  6      1  2  3
         no. 3:     7      2  3      5  6  7
         no. 4:     ∉      6  7      2  3  ∉
```

Indeed, these modes are used by performers--practicing musicians--as
sources of knowledge in areas such as embat, cèngkok for the gendèr,
fingering on the rebab, pathet, etc.

Fingering

Needless to say, the tones on the rebab are created by stopping the
string with the fingers. Players of karawitan also know that the duties of
each finger are determined by the given mode and are not merely arbitrary.
The following should be kept in mind: (1) the changes in mode or hand
position should not be awkward or uncomfortable; (2) the actual stopping of
the string by the finger should be accomplished with ease, keeping in mind
the natural limitations of the spread of the [individual player's] hand;
and (3) we should be able to understand the modes as based on the finger
positions. The rebab player must have especially sharp hearing because his
playing must conform to the embat of the gamelan, while not disregarding
natural embat (*embat alam*).

Figure 8. Natural Embat (*Embat Alam*)

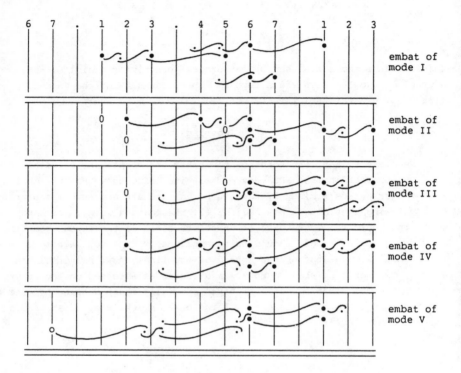

Figure 9.   Fingering (Stopping of the Strings) on the Rebab in Laras Pélog

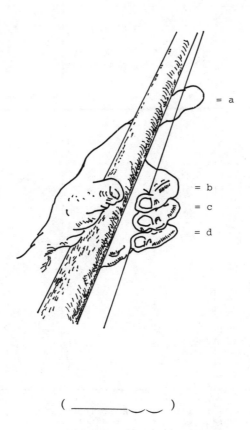

= a

= b

= c

= d

(_____ ‿‿)

The fingering illustrated in figure 9 will produce the following sequence
of tones in laras pélog.

Position	pélog barang	pélog bem
1	on the low string a = 3̣ b = 5̣ on the high string a = 7̣ b = 2 c = 3 d*	on the low string a = 3̣ b = 5̣ on the high string
2	a = 3 b = 5 c = 6 d = 7	a = 2 b = 4 c = 5 d = 6
3	a = 7 b = 2 c = 3 d = 4*	a = 6 b = 1̇ c = 2̇ d = 3̇

*In position 1, this finger has no function except to extend, or
beautify, other tones, but it does not have a clear tone of its own.
If the little finger (d) is pressed down, the tone 4̸ arises, but this
pitch is not present on our gamelan. Strangely enough, however, in
the third position, rebab players do use this fingering when there is
a pitch 4 in the balungan, as, for instance, in the ngelik section of
Ladrang *Pangkur* (4 3 2̇ 3).

Figure 10.

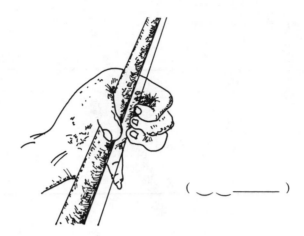

The fingering illustrated in figure 10 will produce the following sequence
of tones in laras pélog.

Position	pélog barang	pélog bem
1	on the low string	on the low string
	--- ---	--- ---
	--- ---	--- ---
	on the high string	on the high string
		a = 1
		b = 2
		c = 3
		d*
2	a = 5	a = 4
	b = 6	b = 5
	c = 7	c = 6
	d = 2	d = i̇

*Used only to extend, decorate, and beautify other tones.

Figure 11.

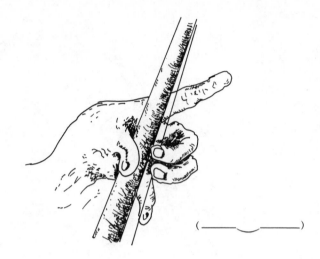

The fingering illustrated in figure 11 will produce the following sequence
of tones in laras pélog.

Position	pélog barang	pélog bem
1	on the low string	on the low string
	a = 3̣	a = 3̣
	b = 5̣	b = 5̣
	on the high string	on the high string
	a = 7̣	
	b = 2	
	c = 3	
	d = 4	
2	-- = --	a = 3
	-- = --	b = 5
	-- = --	c = 6
	-- = --	d = 1̇

The following figure represents these fingerings applied to the various
pélog modes.

Figure 12.

```
                    ┌ 4  5  6  .  .  1  2
                    │ 1  2  3        5  6
        Mode I      │ 5  6  7        2  3
                    └ 2  3  ∤        6  7
                      a  b  c        d
```

```
                    ┌ 1  2  .  .  4  5  6
                    │ 5  6        1  2  3
        Mode II     │ 2  3        5  6  7
                    └ 6  7        2  3  ∤
                      0  a        b  c  d
```

```
                    ┌ 5  6  .  .  1  2  .  .  4
                    │ 2  3        5  6        1
        Mode III    │ 6  7        2  3        5
                    └ 3  ∤        6  7        2
                      0  a        b  c        d
```

```
                    ┌ 2  .  .  4  5  6  .  .  1
                    │ 6        1  2  3        5
        Mode IV     │ 3        5  6  7        2
                    └ 7        2  3  ∤        6
                      a        b  c  d
```

```
                    ┌ 6  .  .  1  2  .  .  4  5
                    │ 3        5  6        1  2
        Mode V      │ 7        2  3        5  6
                    └ ∤        6  7        2  3
                      a        b  c        d
```

The sign "0" is used to designate a dhong tone that has no specified
fingering. These indefinite fingerings are clarified in the context of a
gendhing. When the above fingerings are applied to the strings of a rebab,
they will appear as in figure 13. In this figure I have diagrammed the
fingerings on a [hypothetical] single long string on the left side, while
on the right side I have indicated the fingerings on the [two strings of
the] rebab, so that the reader will understand the true modal schema as
well as the way they are realized on the rebab. For, the application of
these theoretical schema must be adjusted to the nature of the instrument.
Please note also the difference between these and the corresponding sléndro
fingerings and modal schema.

Figure 13. [Fingerings and Modes in Pélog]

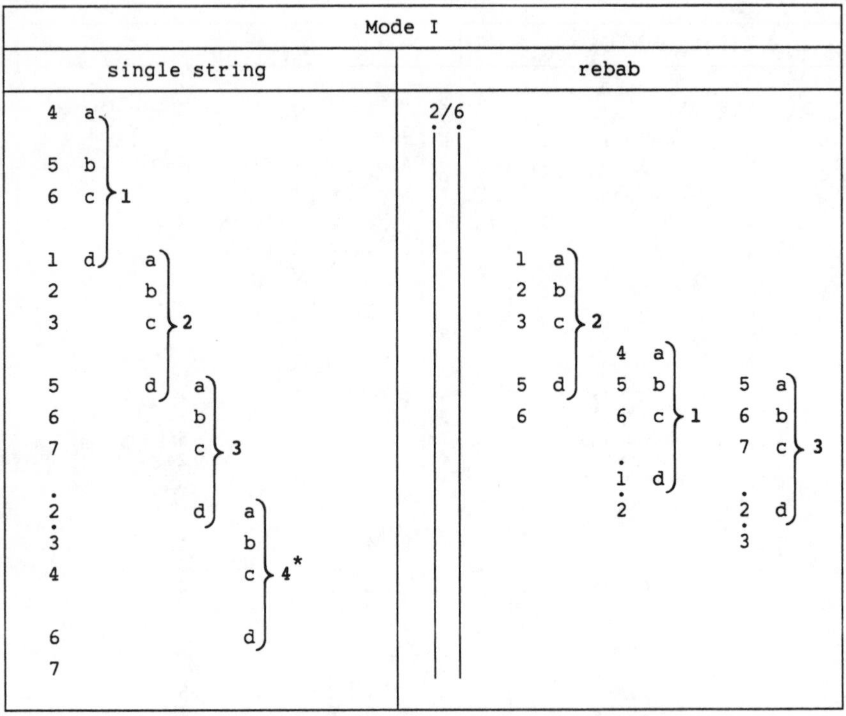

*I have not pictured this position on the rebab fingerings, because it is never used. I will not picture it in subsequent diagrams of the single string.

Mode II	
single string	rebab

```
single string                    rebab

1  0                      2/6
                          : :
2  a⎤
   ⎥                            1  0
4  b⎬1                          2  a⎤        2  0
5  c⎥   0                       ⎥
6  d⎦   a⎤                 4  b⎬1        3  a⎤
                          5  c⎥           ⎥
1       b⎬2              6  d⎦        5  b⎬3  5  0
2       c   0                       6  c       6  a⎤
3       d⎦  a⎤                      7  d⎦          ⎥
                                              ˙1  b⎬2
5          b⎬3                                ˙2  c
6          c                                  ˙3  d⎦
7          d⎦
```

Mode III	
single string	rebab

```
single string                          rebab

5  0                    2/6              6  0
                        :  :
6  a⎫                                    7  a⎫
   ⎬1                                    •  ⎬ ?*
1  b⎪                          2  0      2  b⎪
2  c⎪  2  0               3  a⎫          3  c⎭
      ⎧ 3  a⎫             5  b⎬2         5  0
4  d⎭ ⎪    ⎬              6  c⎫          6  a⎫     6  0
      ⎪ 5  b⎬2            •  ⎪          • ⎫      7  a⎫
      ⎨ 6  c⎫  6  0       1  d⎭          1  b⎬1   •  ⎬
        7  a⎫             2  c⎪        • ⎭      2  b⎬3
        •  ⎬3                            4  d⎭    3  c⎪
        2  b⎪                                    •  ⎪
        •  ⎪                                     5  d⎭
        3  c⎪
        •  ⎫
        5  d⎭
```

---

*When finger *d* is used here, pitch 4 (pélog) results, as an alternative
form of ⁴. Also, only [finger position] number 2 of this mode is used.
Number 1 is borrowed from mode II, number 2; number 3 is borrowed from
mode II, number 4.

Mode IV[*]	
single string	**rebab**

single string

```
2  a⎫
4  b⎬1
5  c⎪
6  d⎭ 6  a⎫
              1  b⎬2
.              2  c⎪
1              3  d⎭ 3  a⎫
                           5  b⎬3
        5       5       6  c⎪
                        7  d⎭

                           .
                           2
```

rebab

```
2/6
. .

2  a⎫
4  b⎬1            3  a⎫
5  c⎪             5  b⎬3
6  d⎭   5  b      6  c⎪      6  a⎫
        6  c      7  d⎭      1  b⎬2
.       7  d⎭              .  c⎪
1                  .       2  d⎭
                   2       .  
                           3

                           .
                           5
```

[*]The highest tone in this mode is never used.

Mode V*	
single string	rebab

```
 6  a⎤
    ⎟
 1  b⎬1
 2  c⎟
    ⎟   3  a⎤
 4  d⎦   ⎟
 5       5  b⎟
         6  c⎬2
             7  a⎤
         1  d⎟   ⎟
         2  ⎦   2  b⎟
                 3  c⎬3
                 5  d⎟
                 6  ⎦
```

```
 2/6
 :  :

              3  a⎤
              ⎟
              5  b⎟
              6  c⎬2   6  a⎤
              ⎟        ⎟       7  a⎤
              1  d⎟    1  b⎟   ⎟
              :  ⎦    :   ⎟   ⎟
              2       2  c⎬1   2  b⎟
                      :        3  c⎬3
                      4  d⎟   :   ⎟
                      :   ⎟   5  d⎟
                      5  ⎦   :   ⎦
                             6
```

---

*In this mode, only finger position number 2 is used. Also, the highest
tone is never used, but is merely touched upon [in passing] (*mbesut*), as in
mode I, numbers 1 and 3.

After you understand the application of the modes to the rebab (i.e.,
finger positions), you will see clearly that the numbers of the modes do
not necessarily correspond to the numbers of the fingering positions. For
example, mode I does not necessarily use, or occupy, position number 1. It
is especially difficult to establish the position of a mode when two modes
are fused through modulation. But, once you have a grasp of the fingering
positions and fully memorize them individually, you will determine easily
the mode and the number of the fingering position.

Let us now compare the fingerings and modes of the pélog tuning system
with those of the sléndro tuning system. I must explain first that these
matters are clearer in sléndro than they are in pélog. For that reason,
the modes and fingerings of sléndro can also indicate the pathet. However,
gendhing in pathet nem have a special range. This range on the rebab is on

the low string. However, the modes/fingerings lie on the high strings, as is illustrated in figure 14.

Figure 14. The Modes and Fingerings for Laras Sléndro

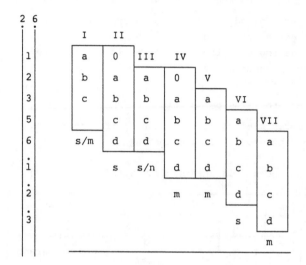

Key: "s" = sanga; "n" = nem; "m" = manyura.

I have diagrammed the modes and fingerings in consideration of the fact that many pieces in sléndro--such as *Gambir Sawit*, *Bondhèt*, *Pangkur*, and others--can also be played in pélog. For this reason we need to know whether the sléndro fingerings can be transferred to laras pélog--that is, whether the mode stays the same. This will become clearer when we examine the modes one at a time.

1. The fingering of laras sléndro mode I can be transferred directly to laras pélog bem or laras pélog barang, because the position of the fingers there is constant due to the nature of the instrument.

2. The fingering of laras sléndro mode II can be transferred to laras pélog bem with pélog tone 4 replacing sléndro tone 3. Finger *d* cannot slide to tone 1̇. This fingering cannot be transferred to laras pélog barang.

3. The fingering of laras sléndro mode III can be transferred to laras pélog bem with pélog tone 4 replacing sléndro tone 3.

Finger *d* cannot slide to tone i̇. This fingering cannot be
transferred to laras pélog barang.

4. The fingering of laras sléndro mode IV can be transferred to laras
    pélog bem or laras pélog barang, but finger *d* cannot slide.

5. The fingering of laras sléndro mode V can be transferred to laras
    pélog bem with finger *a* still sounding pitch 3, or occasionally
    pitch 4. This fingering can also be transferred to laras pélog
    barang, but finger *d* cannot slide.

6. The fingering of laras sléndro mode VI can be transferred to laras
    pélog barang but not to laras pélog bem.

7. The fingering of laras sléndro mode VII can be transferred to
    laras pélog bem but not to laras pélog barang.

Figure 15. [The Transfer of Modes (Fingerings) from Sléndro to Pélog]

Sléndro Modes (fingerings)	Pathet		Pélog Modes					Explanation
			I	II	III	IV	V	
I	s/m		?	?	?	?	?	bem or barang
II	s			1				bem
III	s/n					2		bem
IV	m	no.		3	2			barang or bem
V	m					3	2	barang or bem
VI	s		3					barang
VII	[m]					2		bem

When we examine the fingerings in laras sléndro and pélog, it becomes
clear that in gendhing in laras sléndro that are transposed to laras pélog
(e.g., *Gambir Sawit*) the finger positions are not simply transferred. This
is especially true of gendhing in laras sléndro pathet sanga that are
transposed to laras pélog bem, for there is no equivalent to mode VI in
pélog bem. Transposing a piece from sléndro sanga to pélog bem requires
changing to a mode in which the dhong is pitch 4--that is, mode I, number
1, in laras pélog, for which fingering V in laras sléndro can be used.

Mode and Gendèr Cèngkok

Now let us discuss these modes in laras pélog as applied to the gendèr. I will limit my explanation to the modes in laras pélog bem, because there is very little I need to explain about modes in laras pélog barang. This is because any mode with tone 7 can rightfully be called pathet barang.

I have already explained that some gendèr cèngkok in laras pélog are only imitations of laras sléndro cèngkok. For this reason, and to simplify matters, I will refer to them as the cèngkok of pathet sanga (s) and/or pathet manyura (m). I have not mentioned the cèngkok of [sléndro] pathet nem because [sléndro] pathet nem cèngkok in laras pélog are very thin (or weak and indistinct).

Figure 16 is a table of the modes, written from high to low tones-- thus, unlike the diagrams of the rebab.

Figure 16. [Pélog Modes with Respect to Gendèr]

Mode I		Mode II		Mode III		Mode IV		Mode V	
				4	1	1	5	5	2
								4	1
2	6	6	3						
1	5	5	2	2	6	6	3	2	6
		4	1	1	5	5	2	1	5
						4	1		
6	3								
5	2	2	6	6	3				
4	1	1	5	5	2	2	6	6	3
s/m	s/m	s	s	s	m	m	n	s/m	s/m

As is the case with modes in laras sléndro, in laras pélog there are modes that can be shared by two different pathet. The determination of the pathet of a phrase will depend upon the cadence (*kadens* [from the Dutch]) of the preceding or following phrases when they are arranged to form a

gendhing. In other words, the pathet [of a phrase] will depend on the
preceding or succeeding cadence (*kadens gandhèngané*).

If we examine treatment (*garap*) in each mode, we find that there are
two types in laras pélog bem: pathet sanga treatment and pathet manyura
treatment. Pathet sanga treatment is used for [pélog] pathet lima, while
pathet manyura treatment is used for [pélog] pathet nem. There is nothing
more to discuss on this matter, except perhaps the literature concerning
it.

However, although in gendhing--those left us by our ancestors--modes
in laras pélog are included in [pélog] pathet nem, many masters of
karawitan (*pangrawit*) considered pélog gendhing with entirely manyura
treatment to be "pathet manyura pélog" or "pathet nyamat." In other words,
such gendhing were not considered to be pélog pathet nem. Our willingness
to call these gendhing "pathet nem" comes only from the tradition that
laras pélog consists of three pathet--lima, nem, and barang. There are, in
fact, many gendhing that are played with completely manyura treatment.
After these gendhing are played, the pathetan melody (*lagu pathet*) played
will be taken from [sléndro] pathet manyura [transposed to pélog].
However, gendhing in laras pélog with sanga treatment will still be
considered [pélog] pathet nem. But, my children and grandchildren, let it
be known to you: the past masters did not refer to these gendhing as "pélog
pathet manyura" arbitrarily. Such a classification is based on the fact
that, in gendhing in pélog bem with manyura treatment, the treatment is
exactly the same as that of sléndro manyura, whether on the gendèr or on
the rebab. The only exception is that in laras sléndro the sèlèh on pitch
3 kempyung

$$\overset{\bullet}{1}$$
$$3$$

is a true kempyung [perfect fifth], whereas in laras pélog bem it is not.
For, the tone that lies a kempyung above pitch 3 (dhadha) in laras pélog is
pitch 7 (barang).

Thus, if we suppose that pélog pathet nem has a dhong--a basic tone
[tonic]--of pitch 2 (gulu), then it is [gendhing in] pélog bem played with
manyura treatment that must be called [pélog] pathet nem. To make this
clearer, please play the following [pélog] gendhing.

a. ladrangan with dhong 2 (gulu)

```
                                    G
 buka:  6   6 3 5 6    5 6 5 3    6 5 3 2

        t           t    N
        5 3 2 1    3 5 3 2

        5 3 2 1    3 5 3 2
                   . . . .              = manyura treatment
        6 6 . .    2 3 2 1
        . .
        3 2 6 3    6 5 3 2G
```

b. ladrangan with dhong 5 (lima)

```
                                    G
 buka:  2   2 3 2 1    3 2 1 6    2 1 6 5
                             .          .
        t           t    N
        1 2 1 6    2 1 6 5
            .          .
        1 2 1 6    2 1 6 5
            .          .          = sanga treatment
        2 2 . .    2 3 2 1

        3 2 1 6    2 1 6 5G
            .          .
```

c. ladrangan with dhong 2 (gulu)

```
                                    G
 buka:  6   6 5 4 2    5 4 5 6    5 4 1 2

         t          t    N
        . 4 5 6    5 4 5 2

        . 4 5 6    5 4 5 2          = manyura treatment

        6 6 . .    6 4 5 6

        5 6 5 4    6 4 1 2G
```

d. ladrangan with dhong 1 (panunggul)

```
                                    G
 buka:  5   5 6 1 2    2 1 6 5    1 1 . 5    6 1 2 1
        .   . .          . .                  . .
         t          t    N
        . 1 1 1    5 6 2 1
                   . .
        . 1 1 1    5 6 1 2
                   . .          = sanga treatment
        . . 2 3    5 5 6 5

        6 6 2 1    5 6 2 1G
                   . .
```

Explanation. Ladrangan (a) requires manyura treatment without pitch
4. Ladrangan (b) requires sanga treatment without pitch 4. Ladrangan (c)
requires manyura treatment without pitch 3. Ladrangan (d) requires sanga
treatment without pitch 4. Now that you have played these examples, decide
which of the four ladrangan are in [pélog] pathet nem--I leave it up to
you.

It has been previously stated that many of the modes in laras pélog
bem are included in [pélog] pathet nem. If that is the case, what is meant
by "pathet lima"? Many have tried to answer this question, but, in my
opinion, none satisfactorily. The reason derives from my analysis above.
Because I am not happy with the theories set forth thus far, I am
continuing my search for what, in fact, is pathet lima and what is pathet
nem. I have not yet determined the answers to these questions.

Here is one theory, the fruit of the research of some colleagues in
the field of karawitan--among others, Bapak Puspalalita and Bapak
Warsapangrawit. (Unfortunately, both passed away around 1949, during the
"second military action.") Originally, this analysis of gendhing (which I
subsequently have called the "theory of gendhing") revealed that the
following identifying characteristics were found in gendhing in pélog
pathet lima and not in gendhing in pélog pathet nem, and vice versa.

1. Characteristic of gendhing in pélog pathet lima, but not of
   gendhing in pélog pathet nem:

   a. pitch 1 (panunggul gedhé)

   b. pitch 4 (pélog gedhé)

   c. pitch 3 (dhadha tengahan) as a strong tone, frequently used
      as a seléh tone, but in varying positions

2. Characteristic of gendhing in pélog pathet nem, but not of
   gendhing in pélog pathet lima:

   a. pitch 1 (panunggul tengahan) treated as a gembyang (i.e.,
      treated as in a cengkok in manyura)

Later, the above-mentioned experts decided upon the following characteristic features of pélog pathet lima and pélog pathet nem.

1. Characteristic of gendhing in pathet lima:

    a. the lowest possible tone used is pitch 1 (panunggul gedhé)

    b. the use of pitch 4 (pélog gedhé)

    c. the prevalence of pitch 3 (dhadha tengahan)

    d. the treatment of seleh on pitch 1 (panunggul tengahan) as kempyung, i.e., treated as a cengkok in sanga

2. Characteristic of gendhing in pathet nem:

    a. the lowest possible tone used is pitch 2 (gulu gedhé)

    b. pitch 4 (pélog gedhé) is not used

    c. pitch 3 (dhadha tengah) is not a strongly emphasized seleh tone[*]

    d. seleh on pitch 1 (panunggul tengahan) are treated as either kempyung or gembyang

After examining the characteristics of pathet lima and pathet nem, the above-mentioned researchers considered my theory of pathet in laras slendro as seen on the gender (i.e., using the gender as the instrument for determining pathet). Their intention was to re-examine the previously discovered characteristics of the two pathet as seen on the gender, by "arranging the modes in pélog in sequence by kempyung, and lining these up with the [keys of the] gender," as seen in figure 17.

---

[*]In Gendhing *Miyanggong*, pitch 3 is found in various positions, but never as a seleh tone.

Figure 17. [Pélog Modes and the Keys of the Gendèr Barung Arranged in
            Sequence by Kempyung]

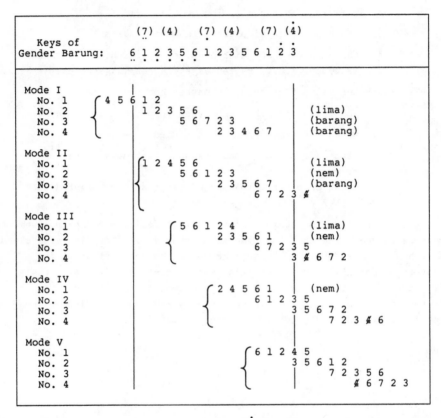

[Note: The vertical lines under "6" and "3" delimit the range of the
        gendèr barung.]

[The researchers] then selected only those pélog modes that were wholly
contained within the range of the keys of the gendèr barung (the area
delimited by vertical lines in figure 17). The results were:

Mode I: nos. 2, 3, and 4

Mode II: nos. 1, 2, and 3

Mode III: nos. 1 and 2

Mode IV: no. 1

Mode V: none

Then these modes were selected again according to the characteristics of pathet lima and nem, as described above. These are indicated [in parentheses] in figure 17. The results can be summarized as follows.

```
                        G
                        1 2 3 5 6            mode I, no. 2
                        . . . . .
                        G
pathet lima:            1 2 4 5 6            mode II, no. 1
                        . . . . .
                            G
                            5 6 1 2 4        mode III, no. 1
                            . .
```

```
                    G
                    5 6 1 2 3               mode II, no. 2
                    . .
                        G         .
pathet nem:             2 3 5 6 1           mode III, no. 2
                        G         .
                        2 4 5 6 1           mode IV, no. 1
```

```
                    G
                    5 6 7 2 3               mode I, no. 3
                    . .
                        G
pathet barang:          2 3 4 6 7           mode I, No. 4
                        G
                        2 3 5 6 7           mode II, no. 3
```

These groups can be further summarized as follows.

```
                        G     (4) G
        pathet lima:    1  2   3  5  6  1  2  4
                        .  .   .  .  .
```

```
                        G         G (4)           .
        pathet nem:     5  6  1   2  3  5  6  1
                        .  .
```

```
                        G         G     (4)
      pathet barang:    5  6  7   2  3   5  6  7
```

Pathet Lima in the Theory of Gendhing

According to the theory of gendhing, it is clear that pathet lima has
tones 1 and 5 for dhong tones (basic tones, tonics). This is indeed the
case in the gendhing left to us by our ancestors.

Dhong 1 and dhong 5 use cèngkok of pathet sanga; that is, any sèlèh on
pitch 1 (tengahan) must be treated as a kempyung.

Pitch 4 (pitch pélog in the low range) is only found in pathet lima
gendhing.*

The presence of pitch 4 (pitch pélog in the middle range) in pathet
lima gendhing is not obligatory (not necessarily present). Many gendhing
in pathet lima do not use middle tone 4--for example, Ladrang *Sembawa*.

Pélog Pathet Nem in the Theory of Gendhing

According to the theory of gendhing, pathet nem has pitches 5 and 2 as
dhong tones; dhong 5 is for sanga cèngkok and dhong 2 is for manyura
cèngkok. This also implies that sèlèh on 1 (panunggul tengahan) can be
treated either as kempyung [sanga] or gembyang [manyura], and this is, in
fact, one of the hallmarks of gendhing in pathet nem. (There are some
gendhing in pathet nem that use wholly sanga cèngkok or wholly manyura
cèngkok.)

There are no gendhing in pathet nem that use pitch 1 (panunggul gedhé)
or 4 (pélog gedhé). Pitch 3 (dhadha tengahan) is frequently used, but its
position is variable.

Pélog Pathet Barang in the Theory of Gendhing

According to the theory of gendhing, pathet barang has pitches 5 and 2
as dhong tones, and, indeed, this is borne out in the gendhing left us by
our ancestors. A survey of the approximately forty gendhing (excluding

---

*Ladrang *Tirta Kencana* uses low pitch 4. However, the man who
composed the piece (circa 1935-40), K[angjeng] R[adèn] M[as] T[umenggung]
Wiryadiningrat, classified it as pélog pathet nem. Many experts of the
time rejected the piece (though let's not worry about that), claiming that
it was awkward in its transition from the ngelik gongan back to the first
gongan. (The first gongan ends on low pitch 5 [allowing a natural return
to the beginning, which is low in register]; the ngelik gongan ends on
medium pitch 5, but straightaway returns to the low register of the first
gongan without any transition.)

ladrangan) in pathet barang bequeathed to us by our ancestors indicates
that only eight (or 20 percent) have pitch 6 as the gong tone.

Sèlèh on pitch 2 (gulu tengahan) and on pitch 3 (dhadha tengahan) must
be treated as kempyung in pathet barang. Sèlèh on pitch 7 (barang) must be
treated as gembyang, even in the context of a sanga cèngkok.

Note. The theory of gendhing is based on research on the gendhing
left by our ancestors. The conclusions about pathet nem and pathet barang
can be said to agree [with the material examined]. (I leave it up to the
reader whether or not he is satisfied [with those conclusions].) But with
regard to pathet lima, even those who derived the theory themselves are
uneasy with the results, because in the middle range only pitch 4 is found.
In fact, however, pitch 3 is not infrequently found in the middle range,
and it is clear that in those cases pitch 3 is not merely a borrowed tone,
but has a strong (or active [aktief]) position.

Thus, in the research referred to above, pathet lima remains obscure
(i.e., in the matter of agreement between theory and practice). The
practice-oriented musician at this time can only say that pathet lima is a
transposition from pathet barang. For example:

$$
\text{a.} \left\{
\begin{array}{lccccc}
\text{barang} & 2 & 3 & 4 & 6 & 7 \\
\text{bem} & 1 & 2 & 3 & 5 & 6
\end{array}
\right.
$$

$$
\text{b.} \left\{
\begin{array}{lccccc}
\text{barang} & 2 & 3 & 5 & 6 & 7 \\
\text{bem} & 1 & 2 & 4 & 5 & 6
\end{array}
\right.
$$

From the perspective of rebab performance practice, it is clear that the
position of the tones and fingerings in bem is no different from their
position in barang. If such is the case, why is it necessary to transpose?
The reasons are:

a. There is no pitch 4 in the pélog barang gamelan.

b. Any use of pitch 4 in pélog barang must involve borrowing that
    tone [and substituting it for pitch 5] -- (2 3 4 .   4 3 2 7) --
    causing a very different feeling to arise.

Furthermore, musicians consider pathet lima to be a transposition of pathet barang because of the following evidence.

a. In gendèr treatment (*garap*) in pathet lima, each sèlèh on pitch 1 (*panunggul tengahan*) must be treated as kempyung. This is in agreement with pélog barang treatment [transposed down one pitch degree], where each sèlèh on pitch 2 (*gulu tengahan*) must be treated as kempyung.

b. The lowest tone of pélog barang is pitch 2 (*gulu gedhé*). This agrees with the lowest tone of pathet lima, pitch 1 (*panunggul gedhé*) [transposed down one pitch degree].

Figure 18.

Tuning of Rebab Strings in Péloq Lima	Fingerings	Tuning of Rebab Strings in Péloq Baranq	Fingerings
1 5	5	2 6	6
	6		7
	1		2
	2		3
	3		4̸
	4		5
	5		6
	6		7
	1		2
	2		3
	3		4̸

[Note: Pitches 5 and 6 are open strings in pélog lima and pélog barang, respectively.]

Tuninq (Stem[m]inq)

Here I am using the term "stem[m]ing," ['tuning', from Dutch], which derives from Western music terminology, since there is no term in karawitan with the same meaning. I am using this term because I consider it close to the meaning intended: that is, "intervals (*sruti*) with a fixed embat that combine to form a pathet." The intervals that create a tuning are those in modes I, II, and IV, which have the following shape.

mode I   •⌣•⌣• — •⌣•   the tuning for [pathet] bem
                                 with sanga [treatment]

mode II   •⌣• — •⌣•⌣•   the tuning for [pathet]
                                 barang

mode IV   • — •⌣•⌣• — •   the tuning for [pathet] bem
                                 with manyura [treatment]

This can be clarified as follows. When mode I is sung, most assuredly
it becomes embat bem [with sanga treatment]. When mode II is sung, it must
become embat barang. When mode IV is sung, it must become embat bem with
manyura treatment.

Since each mode that gives rise to a tuning has its own embat (i.e.,
the intervals in the three groups are not the same), and, as we remember,
the tonality (*toonaliteit*) of the .treatment/cèngkok has already been
established, then the tones in each mode must also be fixed.

The tones for the bem/sanga tuning are:

$$1 \quad 2 \quad 3 \quad\quad 5 \quad 6$$
•⌣•⌣• — •⌣•

The tones for the barang tuning are:

$$2 \quad 3 \quad\quad 5 \quad 6 \quad 7$$
•⌣• — •⌣•⌣•

The tones for the bem/manyura tuning are:

$$6 \quad\quad 1 \quad 2 \quad 3 \quad\quad 5$$
• — •⌣•⌣• — •

If this is the case, is the phrase . 1 1 1   2 3 2 1   the same as
. 5 5 5   6 7 6 5 or . 4 4 4   5 6 5 4 ? The answer is, if this phrase is
hummed, without identifying the names of the tones, it will definitely
sound the same. But, if it is played on [gamelan] instruments, it will
clearly sound very different, because each cèngkok, or manner of treatment,
will have its own requirements. One difference is easy to detect: if we
play the phrase . 1 1 1   2 3 2 1   on the gendèr, the sèlèh on pitch 1 must
be treated as kempyung, but if we play . 5 5 5   6 7 6 5 on the gendèr,
the sèlèh on pitch 5 must be treated as gembyang, and so forth.

Analyzing Pathet in Laras Pélog Based on Tuning

If we consider pathet from the point of view of tuning, it is clear
that there are only three pathet. These are: (1) the tuning of mode I, (2)
the tuning of mode II, and (3) the tuning of mode IV. Because of the
position of the tones in the three modes as part of a series of tones,
intervals that are not [acoustically] kempyung [perfect fifths] are treated
as if the upper kempyung [*kempyung atas*] were the [acoustic] kempyung.
This is shown in figure 19.

Figure 19.

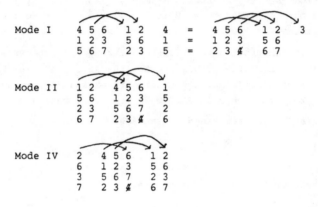

Mode I	4 5 6	1 2	4	=	4 5 6	1 2	3
	1 2 3	5 6	1	=	1 2 3	5 6	
	5 6 7	2 3	5	=	2 3 4̸	6 7	

Mode II	1 2	4 5 6	1
	5 6	1 2 3	5
	2 3	5 6 7	2
	6 7	2 3 4̸	6

Mode IV	2	4 5 6	1 2
	6	1 2 3	5 6
	3	5 6 7	2 3
	7	2 3 4̸	6 7

[Note: Arrows indicate tones one kempyung above (i.e., *kempyung atas*).]

Explanation [of Figure 19]

Mode I (bem tuning):

the upper kempyung of 4 is 1
the upper kempyung of 5 is 2
the upper kempyung of 6 is 3

When this tuning is ordered from left to right (from low to high), the
following intervals result: 4 5 6 1 2 3[*] or 1 2 3 5 6 7.

---

[*]Compare this with theory of gendhing, above.

Mode II (barang tuning):

> the upper kempyung of 2 is 6
> the upper kempyung of 2 is 6
> the upper kempyung of 4 is 1

When this tuning is ordered from left to right (from low to high), the following intervals result: 1 2 4 5 6 1 . Thus, each series can stand on its own. We therefore use 2 3 5 6 7 2 for pathet barang.

Modè IV (pélog manyura tuning):

> the upper kempyung of 2 is 6
> the upper kempyung of 4 is 1
> the upper kempyung of 5 is 2

When this tuning is ordered from left to right (from low to high), the following intervals result: 2 4 5 6 1 [2]. Here again, each series can stand on its own: the sequences 2 4 5 6 1 2 and 6 1 2 3 5 6 are used in pélog bem, because both use manyura treatment; the sequence 3 5 6 7 2 3 is included in pélog barang, because, as I said above, any order in which the tone 7 appears can be considered pathet barang. For this reason, in actual performance, treatment (*garap*) is a stronger determinant than tuning. For example, even if the tuning is barang, if the treatment is sanga, then the piece will be pathet sanga, and vice versa. If the tuning is manyura, and pitch barang [7] is found in the sequence of tones, then the pathet will be barang, and vice versa.

Since there is no pathet sanga or manyura in laras pélog, how can we refer to these entities and differentiate among them? I can only answer this question from the point of view of treatment, where the distinction is very clear. From the point of view of gendhing there is still confusion. In the end, I leave it up to the reader.

The Order of Tones in the Pélog Pathet According to Various Theories

1. pathet lima
$$\overset{G}{5}\ 6\quad 1\ 2\quad 4$$

   pathet nem
$$\overset{G}{2}\ 3\quad 5\ 6\quad 1$$

   pathet barang
$$\overset{G}{6}\ 7\quad 2\ 3\quad 5$$

The tones above do not derive from tuning, and use mode III. The treatment (*garap*) is as follows: for pathet lima, sanga treatment is transposed to pélog; for pathet nem, manyura treatment is transposed to pélog, with pitch 1 played as the kempyung above pitch 3, though the interval is not actually [i.e., acoustically] a kempyung; for pathet barang, manyura treatment is transposed to pélog.

2. pathet lima
$$\overset{G}{1}\ 2\quad 4\ 5\ 6$$

   pathet nem
$$\overset{G}{5}\ 6\quad 1\ 2\ 3$$

   pathet barang
$$\overset{G}{2}\ 3\quad 5\ 6\ 7$$

The order of tones above derives from the barang tuning, and uses mode II. The treatment is as follows: for pathet lima, sanga treatment is transposed to pélog; for pathet nem, sanga treatment is transposed to pélog; for pathet barang, manyura treatment is transposed to pélog.

3. pathet lima
$$\overset{G}{1}\ 2\ \overset{(4)}{3}\quad \overset{G}{5}\ 6$$

   pathet nem
$$\overset{G}{5}\ 6\ 1\quad \overset{G\,(3)}{2}\ 4$$

   pathet barang
$$\overset{G}{5}\ 6\ 7\quad \overset{G}{2}\ 3\ \overset{(\cancel{5})}{5}$$

According to the theory of gendhing, in the above sequence of tones pathet lima uses a mixture of sanga and manyura treatment, although a final cadence (*pada*) in archaic (*kuna*) gendhing will require sanga treatment, and a seléh on pitch 1 (panunggul) must be treated as kempyung. For pathet nem, the treatment will also be a mixture of sanga and manyura, except that the final cadence will sometimes require sanga and sometimes manyura

treatment. A sèlèh on pitch 1 (panunggul) will likewise sometimes be
treated as kempyung (as in pathet sanga), and sometimes as gembyang (as in
pathet manyura). For pathet barang the treatment will be mixed also, but a
sèlèh on pitch 7 (barang) will always be treated as gembyang.

Gendhing in Surakarta

According to the *Serat Centhini*,[2] there are only 157 pieces, including
ladrangan, used for *klenèngan*. In order to clarify this matter, I shall
quote excerpts from the *Serat Centhini* that were copied by Bapak Jayamlaya,
of the district Patangpuluhan in Sòlo. Unfortunately, he did not cite the
original pages or volumes from which these excerpts were taken. [Bapak
Jayamlaya's original notes] were written in Javanese characters; I have
transliterated them here into romanized characters.

Duk samana nèng pondokan lagi,	Then at their lodgings
Ki Amad lingnya lon,	Ki Amad spoke softly
Mangké ratri kakang dipun sarèh,	"Later this evening, older brother,
Pinarak mring wismané kiyai,	do not rush off,
Bawaraga miji,	We shall visit the home of Kyai
Pangrebab puniku.	Bawaraga, a specialist
	On the rebab.
Nyatahuni putunya pawèstri,	"He is performing a ritual upon the
Sru winantos-wantos,	first anniversary of his
Lalenggahan ing sakaparengé,	daughter's death.
Mirengaken kalenèngan tuwin,	We are urgently awaited,
Pangliking kang ringgit,	To sit and enjoy as we wish,
Binarung swara rum.	To listen to a klenèngan
	And the high, clear singing of a
	dancer
	Accompanied by gentle sounds."

Inggih adi saklangkung prayogi,

Bakda isya bodhol,

Ki Tengara kalawan tamuné,

Praptèng Bawaragan kyai panti,

Gupuh ngacarani,

Pinarnah nggènipun.

Sinambrama ing wicara manis,

Lumuntur kang sugoh,

Samya rahab sakèh tatamuné,

Miyarsakken gendhing Gambirsawit,

Jeng ngidung nyindhèni,

Wilet swara arum.

Mas Cebolang matur mring ki Panti,

Mboten-mboten ilok,

Lah, punapi punika gendhingé,

Teka nyenyos praptèng sanubari,

Wèh trenyuh kang myarsi,

Mrinding wulu puhun.

Bawaraga kathah amangsuli,

Babo mitraningong,

Gambirsawit puniku gendhingé,

Mas Cebolang matur mring ki Panti,

Paringa udani,

Gendhing manggènipun.

"Yes, younger brother, that is a
     fine idea."
They departed after evening prayer.
Ki Tengara and his guest
Arrived at the home of Kyai Bawaraga
Who greeted them eagerly,
Seating them,
With a felicitous welcome in
     flowing terms.
Copious food and drink were served,
Enjoyed by the many guests,
Who meanwhile listened to Gendhing
     Gambir Sawit.
A young girl sang the sindhèn
With pleasant-sounding wilet.
Mas Cebolang then said to the host,
"I have never heard this before.
Just what is the name of this
     gendhing?
It deeply touches my heart,
And stirs all who listen,
Raising the hairs on the back of
     the neck."
Bawaraga answered energetically,
"Well now, my friend,
The piece is Gambir Sawit."
Mas Cebolong asked his host
To tell him of
The nature of this piece.

Cagak lenggah tinimbang ngraosi,

Ing awoning uwong,

Bawaraga mèsem lon delingé,

Ènget kula manggèné kang
  gendhing,

Sendhon pathet nèki,

Samya ngenem likur.

Sesendhon nem* am Bondhan kinanthi,

Budheng-budheng Ménggok,**

Layu-layu Sabawa*** Pangawé,

Semang Rebeng Lonthang Sambul-
  gendhing,

Rangu Kaduk manis,

Mundhuk Mégamendhung.

Kapang-kapang ki Tamènggita ki,

Nèng Paséban Kabor,

Sarayuda Sambul talèdhèké,

Gonjanganom Ladrang Mangu tuwin,

Gandrungmangungkung gring,

Myanggong Gobet Rambu.

"It is useful for staying awake,

And better than gossiping about
  the faults of others."

Bawaraga smiled and spoke softly.

"As I remember it, the gendhing in

Each pathet number

Twenty-six altogether.

"In pathet nem* there are Bondhan
  Kinanthi,

Budheng-budheng, Ménggok,**

Layu-layu, Sabawa,*** Pangawé,

Semang, Rebeng, Lonthang, Sambul
  Gendhing,

Rangu, Kaduk Manis,

Mundhuk, Méga Mendhung,

"Kapang-kapang, Tamèng Gita,

Paséban, Kabor,

Sara Yuda, Sambul Talèdhèk,

Gonjang Anom, Ladrang Mangu, and

Gandrung Mangungkung Gring,

Miyanggong, Gobet, and Rambu.

---

*That is, pélog pathet nem.

**This could indicate the present-day "Mongkok."

***This could indicate the present-day "Sembawa."

Pathet sanga Lonthangkasmarané,	"In pathet sanga [the gendhing] are
Wangsaguna Rondhon,	Lonthang Kasmaran,
Danaraja Bontit Gègèrsoré,	Wangsa Guna, Rondhon,
Galagothang Ganggong Bawaragi,*	Dana Raja, Bontit, Gègèr Soré,
Mandhul a Malarsih,	Gala Gothang, Ganggong,
Bondhèt Surungdhuyung.	Bawa Raga,*
	Mandhul, Malarsih
	Bondhèt, Surung Dhayung,
Onang-onang Mawur Gambirsawit,	"Onang-onang, Mawur, Gambir Sawit
Candra Kencèngbarong,	Candra, Kencèng Barong,
Garompol myang Gendrèh kemasané,	Grompol, and Gendrèh Kemasan,
Ela-ela Gandakusuma di,	Ela-ela, Ganda Kusuma,
Gendhung** Sunggèng tuwin,	Gendhung,** Sunggèng,
Sumedhang Semèru.	Sumedhang, and Semèru.
Sendhon gangsal Muntab Candrasari,	"[The gendhing in] pélog pathet
Rarajala Gondrong,	lima are Muntap, Candra Sari,
Taliwangsa Jalaga rebabé,	Rara Jala, Gondrong,
Semanggita Gendrèh Larasati,	Tali Wangsa, Jalaga—the gendhing
Plajengan*** Pangrawit,	rebab,
Babarlayar Tlutur.	Semang Gita, Gendrèh, Laras Ati,
	Plajengan,*** Pangrawit,
	Babar Layar and Tlutur.

---

*That is, "Bawa Raga." [To follow the rules governing vowel quality at the end of a line, the *a* was changed to *i*.]

**This could indicate the present-day "Klenthung."

***This could indicate the present-day "Playon."

Singa-singa Goyang ing panggalih,

Jalaga bonang ndon,

Kembangmara Gulagul rebabé,

Kumbangmara Slébrak Duradasih,

Gendheng* Kendhung** Slasih ,

Bremara Majemuk.

Pathet nem*** Laranangis gendhing,

Bentaring kadhaton,†

Karawitan Babat Prihatiné,

Marasanja Kocak Kadukmanis,

Ramyang Galondhong-pring,

Tunjung-kroban Guntur.

Maskumambang Godheng†† Titipati,

Glendhèh Lelana njog,

Semukirang Lonthang Udansoré,

Peksibayan Talwi myang Pujanggi,

Menyanséta tuwin,

Jamba Semarmantu.

"Singa-singa, Goyanging Panggalih

Jalaga--the gendhing bonang,

Kembang Mara, Agul-agul--the
   gendhing rebab,

Kombang Mara, Slébrak, Dara Dasih,

Gendheng,* Kendhung,** Slasih,

Bremara and Majemuk.

"[The gendhing in] pathet nem***
   are Lara Nangis,

Kedhaton Bentar,†

Karawitan, Babat, Prihatin,

Mara Sanja, Kocak, Kaduk Manis,

Ramyang, Glondhong Pring,

Tunjung Karoban, and Guntur.

"Mas Kumambang, Godheng,††
   Titi Pati,

Glendhèh, Lana,

Semu Kirang, Lonthang, Udan Soré,

Peksi Bayan, Patalwé, Pujangga,

Menyan Séta,

Jamba, and Semar Mantu.

---

*This could indicate the present-day "Glendheng."

**This could indicate the present-day "Klenthung."

***That is, sléndro pathet nem.

†That is, "Kedhaton Bentar."

††This could have become the present-day "Godheg."

Sendhon barang Wedhikèngser Siring,
Ludira nDhol-endhol,
Cacatingrat Maraséba Bondhèt,
Semburadas Cangket Pramugari,
Jenthar ladrang Manis,
Bèlèk Kuwung-kuwung.

Sangupati Rimong Gandrungmanis,
Badhaya angGondrong,
Pan Ludira madura Gendrèhé,
Ejong mèru Babarlayar nèki,
Parigentang tuwin,
Tukung Lempunggunung.

Nahen pathet manyura amilir,
Sèdhet Pujangganom,
Talimurda Ramyang Kasmaranè,
Mènjep Gonjang Galéwang Semiring,
Randhat Damarkéli,
Lagu Cucurbawuk.

"[The gendhing in] pélog pathet
    barang are Wedhi Kèngser,
    Siring,
Ludira, Endhol-endhol,
Cacadingrat, Mara Séba, Bondhèt,
Sembur Adas, Cangket, Pramugari,
Jenthar, ladrang Manis,
Bèlèk, Kuwung-kuwung,
"Sangu Pati, Rimong, Gandrung
    Manis,
Bedhaya, Gondrong,
Ludira Madura, Gendrèh,
Jong Mèru, Babar Layar,
Pari Gentang,
Tukung, and Lempung Gunung.
"As for pathet manyura,
Sèdhet, Pujangga Anom,
Tali Murda, Ramyang, Kasmaran,
Mènjep, Gonjang, Gléwang,
    Semiring,
Randhat, Damar Kéli,
Lagu, and Cucur Bawuk.

Dhalangkarahinan Lambangsari,

Gandrungmangu Boyong,

Pujangganom madura Renyepé,

Jangga tawang Capang Mrakkasimpir,

Prénom* Gliyung Rindhik,

Lobong Pacarbanyu.

Ènget kula punika wus titi,

Cebolang nglingnya lon,

Satus sèket pipitu pétangé,

Awit pathet manyura myambaki,

Alangkung satunggil,

Dados pitu likur.

"Dhalang Karahinan, Lambang Sari,

Gandrung Mangu, Boyong,

Pujangga Anom Madura,Renyep,

Jangga Tawang, Capang, Merak

   Kasimpir,

Paré Anom*, Gliyung, Rindhik,

Lobong, and Pacar Banyu.

"As I remember it, those are all."

Mas Cebolang said softly,

"One hundred and fifty-seven in

   all,

Since pathet manyura is different,

Having one more than the others,

That is, twenty-seven."

Here I will end my quotation of the *Serat Centhini*, taken from the notes of Bapak Jayamlaya, for it shall suffice to give you an understanding of the total number of gendhing in use at the time of Paku Buwana IV.** In that work it is clearly explained that there were twenty-six gendhing in each pathet—with the exception of pathet manyura, which had twenty-seven. Thus, any gendhing not included in the *Serat Centhini* must be a gendhing composed after the time of Paku Buwana IV. However, please note that gendhing for the accompaniment of dance are not included in this work. This proves that in those times dance gendhing were not mixed with concert (*klenèngan*) gendhing. (In the *Serat Centhini*, gendhing for dance are treated in the section on dance.)

So the enumeration of gendhing will be clearer, I have written the names again, below, in a list according to pathet.

---

*That is, "Paré Anom."

**   *Serat Centhini* was composed by Paku Buwana V when he was still the Crown Prince (Pangéran Adipati Anom), thus, during the reign of Paku Buwana IV [reigned 1788-1820].[3]

No.	Gendhing in pélog pathet nem	Notes
1.	Bondhan Kinanthi	
2.	Budheng-budheng	
3.	Ménggok	This could be present-day "Mongkok."
4.	Layu-layu	
5.	Sabawa	"Sembawa" is now [classified as] pathet lima.
6.	Pangawé	
7.	Semang	
8.	Rebeng	
9.	Lonthang	
10.	Sambul Gendhing	
11.	Rangu	I have never come across this piece.
12.	Kaduk Manis	
13.	Mundhuk	
14.	Méga Mendhung	
15.	Kapang-kapang	The present-day piece with this title is a ladrangan.
16.	Tamèng Gita	
17.	Paséban	
18.	Kabor	
19.	Sara Yuda	
20.	Sambul Talèdhèk	
21.	Gonjang Anom	
22.	Ladrang Mangu	
23.	Gandrung Mangung Kung	
24.	Miyanggong	
25.	Gobet	
26.	Rambu	

No.	Gendhing in sléndro pathet sanga	Notes
1.	Lonthang Kasmaran	
2.	Wangsa Guna	
3.	Rondhon	
4.	Dana Raja	
5.	Bondhèt	
6.	Gègèr Soré	
7.	Gala Gothang	This could be present-day "Golo Gothang."
8.	Gangga	This could be the present-day "Ganggong."
9.	Bawa Raga	
10.	Mandhul	
11.	Amalarsih	Nowadays the gendhing called "Malarsih" is in sléndro pathet manyura.
12.	Bondhèt	
13.	Surung Dhayung	
14.	Onang-onang	
15.	Mawur	
16.	Gambir Sawit	
17.	Candra	
18.	Kencèng Barong	
19.	Grompol	Nowadays there are many gendhing called ""Grompol"; which is this?
20.	Gendrèh Kemasan	
21.	Ela-ela	Is this "[Ela-ela] Kali Beber" or "[Ela-ela] Pengantèn?"
22.	Ganda Kusuma	
23.	Gendhung	This could be present-day "Klenthung."
24.	Lungkèh[4]	The gendhing called "Lungkèh" is nowadays classified as pathet nem sléndro.
25.	Sumedhang	
26.	Semèru	

No.	Gendhing in pélog pathet lima	Notes
1.	Muntab	
2.	Candra Sari	
3.	Rara Jala	
4.	Gondrong	
5.	Tali Wangsa	
6.	Jalaga rebab	
7.	Semang Gita	
8.	Gendrèh	Nowadays there is no gendhing called "Gendreh" in pathet lima.
9.	Laras Ati	Nowadays the gendhing of this name is in slendro pathet nem.
10.	Plajengan	
11.	Pangrawit	
12.	Babar Layar	
13.	Tlutur	
14.	Singa-singa	This is a ladrangan.
15.	Goyang	
16.	Jalaga bonang	
17.	Kembang Mara	
18.	Gulagul	
19.	Kombang Mara	
20.	Slébrak	
21.	Dara Dasih	
22.	Gindheng	This could be present-day "Glendheng."
23.	Kendhung	This could be present-day "Klenthung."
24.	Slasih	I have never encountered this piece.
25.	Bremara	
26.	Majemuk	

No.	Gendhing in sléndro pathet nem	Notes
1.	Lara Nangis gendhing	
2.	Bentaring Kadhaton	This probably became present-day "Kedhaton Bentar."
3.	Karawitan	
4.	Babat	
5.	Prihatin	
6.	Mara Sanja	
7.	Kocak	
8.	Kaduk Manis	
9.	Ramyang	"Ramyang" is now classified as pathet manyura.
10.	Glondhong Pring	
11.	Tunjung Karoban	
12.	Guntur	
13.	Mas Kumambang	
14.	Godheng	This could be present-day "Godheg."
15.	Titi Pati	
16.	Glendhèh	I have never encountered this piece.
17.	Lelana	This could be present-day "Lana."
18.	Semu Kirang	
19.	Lonthang	
20.	Udan Soré	
21.	Peksi Bayan	
22.	Patalwé	I have never encountered this piece.
23.	Pujangga	
24.	Menyan Séta	
25.	Jamba	
26.	Semar Mantu	Nowadays "Semar Manṭu" is played in laras pelog.

No.	Gendhing in pélog pathet barang	Notes
1.	Wedhi Kèngser	
2.	Siring	
3.	Ludira	
4.	Èndhol-èndhol	
5.	Cacadingrat	
6.	Mara Séba	
7.	Bondhèt	
8.	Sembur Adas	
9.	Cangket	
10.	Pramugari	
11.	Jenthar	
12.	Ladrang Manis	
13.	Bèlèk	
14.	Kuwung-kuwung	
15.	Sangu Pati	
16.	Rimong	
17.	Gandrung Manis	
18.	Bedhaya	
19.	Gondrong	
20.	Ludira Madura	This could be present-day "Ludira Madu."
21.	Gendrèh	
22.	Jong Mèru	
23.	Babar Layar	
24.	Pari Gentang	
25.	Tukung	
26.	Lempung Gunung	

No.	Gendhing in sléndro pathet manyura	Notes
1.	Sèdhet	
2.	Pujangga Anom	
3.	Tali Murda	
4.	Ramyang	
5.	Kasmaran	I have never encountered this piece.
6.	Mènjep	I have never encountered this piece.
7.	Gonjang	This is a ladrangan.
8.	Gléwang	Nowadays there is a gendhing called "Glewang Gonjing."
9.	Sumirang[5]	Nowadays there is a gendhing called "Semiring" in sléndro pathet sanga.
10.	Randhat	
11.	Damar Kèli	
12.	Cucur Bawuk	
13.	Dhalang Karahinan	
14.	Lambang Sari	
15.	Gandrung Mangu	
16.	Boyong	Nowadays this is played in pelog barung.
17.	Pujangga Anom Madura	I have never encountered this piece.
18.	Renyep	Nowadays this is played in sléndro sanga.
19.	Jangga Tawang	This could be present-day "Pujangga Tawang."
20.	Capang	
21.	Merak Kasimpir	
22.	Paré Anom	
23.	Gléyong	There is nowadays a ladrang "Gleyong" in pelog pathet nem. This could be present-day "Gliyung."
24.	Rindhik	
25.	Lobong	
26.	Pacar Banyu	I have never encountered this piece.
27.	Lagu	

Note. The excerpts from *Serat Centhini* in Bapak Jayamlaya's notes
have the following comments written by him (in Javanese script) below the
text.

According to my notes, the gendhing bonang not included here are:
(1) *Sobanlah*; (2) *Kodhokan*; (3) *Kembang Gempol* minggah Ladrang *Bayem
Tur*; and (4) all gendhing bonang *Denggung*. Thus, these gendhing
bonang must have been composed after Sinuwun [Paku Buwana] V, since
the *Centhini* was written by him. Moreover, among other post-Paku
Buwana V gendhing not mentioned in the *Centhini* are those composed by
Radèn Demang Harjapradangga (Ridder). It is said that gendhing bonang
in laras slèndro were composed by Radèn Demang Gunasentika in the time
of Kangjeng Klèca [Patih Sasradiningrat IV].

In this list pathet nem is mentioned first. This certainly
suggests that pathet nem precedes pathet lima; then comes pathet sanga,
then pathet lima, and pathet nem slèndro.

Whether this last note has to do with the order of pathet in relation to
times of the day, or to the chronology of the composition of gendhing in
the various pathet, is unclear to me. If, however, the chronology of
composition is meant, then I am basically in agreement. For, in my
opinion, the creation of pathet lima must have come last, as I explained
above.

Slèndro Gendhing in Laras Pèlog

Gendhing are classified in the *Serat Centhini* according to pathet.
Those in slèndro are to be played only in laras slèndro and the same holds
for gendhing in laras pèlog. Thus, as far as laras is concerned, the *Serat
Centhini* can be used as an authority for determining whether gendhing were
originally pèlog or slèndro. As time passed, however, many gendhing
slèndro came to be played in pèlog. There are a variety of ways that the
laras of these gendhing can change. Some are transposed without additional
changes. The balungan of some are changed slightly to make them sound more
pleasant in laras pèlog. Some relate only slightly to their original form.
Some can be played alternately in the two laras. (This is not mentioned in
the *Serat Centhini*.) The following are examples of each type of gendhing.

1. Sléndro gendhing played in laras pélog without change:

   Ladrang *Ginonjing*, laras sléndro pathet manyura

   buka: 6̣ . 1 2 3 . 1 . 6̣ 3 3 5 6 3 5 3 ^G2

                                       N
          [5 6 5 3 5 6 5 2

                              .   N
           5 6 5 3 5 1 5 6

                     .   .   N
           5 2 5 1 5 3 5 6

                                       G
           5 3 5 6 5 3 5 2]

   Ladrang *Ginonjing*, laras pélog pathet nem

   buka: 6̣ . 1 2 3 . 1 . 6̣ 3 3 5 6 3 5 3 ^G2

                                       N
          [5 6 5 3 5 6 5 2

                              .   N
           5 6 5 3 5 1 5 6

                     .   .   N
           5 2 5 1 5 3 5 6

                                       G
           5 3 5 6 5 3 5 2]

   Ladrang *Ginonjing*, laras pélog pathet barang

   buka: 6̣ . 7̣ 2 3 . 7̣ . 6̣ 3 3 5 6 5 3 5 ^G2

                                       N
          [5 6 5 3 5 6 5 2

                                       N
           5 6 5 3 5 7 5 6

                                       N
           5 2 5 6 5 3 5 6

                                       G
           5 3 5 6 5 3 5 2]

2. Sléndro gendhing played in laras pélog with slight changes [with underlining indicating the altered sections]:

Gendhing *Bondhèt*, kethuk 2 kerep, laras sléndro pathet sanga

```
                                                        G
buka:  6 . 1 2 3  . 5 5 .  6 6 5 6  2 1 3 2  . 1 6 5
       .                                         .   .
                                                     N
          . . 5 3  6 5 3 5  2 2 . 3  5 6 3 5
              .    . . . .                     .
                                                     N
       [ . . 5 3  6 5 3 5  2 2 . 3  5 6 5 6
              .    . . . .                     .
                                                     N
         . . . .  6 6 5 6  3 5 6 1  6 5 2 3
                           _____
                                                     G
         . 3 3 3  5 6 5 3  2 3 5 3  2 1 6 5
                  _____  _____          .   .
                                                     N
         2 2 . .  2 2 . 3  5 6 5 3  2 1 6 5 ]
                           _____          .   .
```

Gendhing *Bondhèt*, kethuk 2 kerep, laras pélog pathet nem[*]

```
                                                        G
buka:  6 . 1 2 3  . 5 5 .  6 6 5 6  2 1 3 2  . 1 6 5
       .                                         .   .
                                                     N
          . . 5 3  6 5 3 5 ·2 2 . 3  5 6 3 5
              .    . . . .                     .
                                                     N
       [ . . 5 3  6 5 3 5  2 2 . 3  5 6 5 6
              .    . . . .                     .
                                              N
         . . . .  6 6 5 6  2 3 2 1  6 5 2 3
                           _____
                                                     G
         . 3 3 3  5 6 5 4  2 4 5 4  2 1 6 5
                  _____  _____          .   .
                                                     N
         2 2 . .  2 2 . 3  5 6 5 4  2 1 6 5 ]
                           _____          .   .
```

Gendhing *Bondhèt*, kethuk 2 kerep, laras pélog pathet barang

```
                                                        G
buka:  6 . 7 2 3  . 5 5 .  6 6 5 6  2 6 7 2  . 7 6 5
       .                                         .
                                                     N
          . . 5 3  6 5 3 5  2 2 . 3  5 6 3 5
              .    . . . .                     .
                                                     N
       [ . . 5 3  6 5 3 5  2 2 . 3  5 6 7 6
              .    . . . .                  _____
                                                     N
         . . . .  6 6 5 6  3 5 6 7  6 5 2 3
                                                     G
         . 3 3 3  5 6 5 3  2 3 5 3  2 7 6 5
                                            .   .
                                                     N
         2 2 . .  2 2 . 3  5 6 5 3  2 7 6 5 ]
                                            .   .
```

---

[*]The most frequent transposition is to pélog nem. Around 1959, I tried this gendhing in pelog barang for an RRI [Radio Republik Indonesia] broadcast by the karawitan instructors of the Konservatori Karawitan Indonesia (KOKAR).

3. Sléndro gendhing that can be played alternately in both laras in a
    single performance:*

    Kinanthi (the unggah of *Lobong*) irama 1/8, sléndro pathet manyura

<pre>
                                        N
    [. 1 . 6 . 1 . 6 . 2 . 1 . 3 . 2
                                        N
      . 3 . 1 . 2 . 6 . 2 . 1 . 3 . 2
                                        N
      . 3 . 1 . 2 . 6 . 3 . 2 . 3 . 1
                                        G
      . 2 . 1 . 2 . 1 . 3 . 2 . 1 . 6]
</pre>

    Kinanthi (the unggah of *Lobong*) irama 1/8, pélog pathet nem/bem

<pre>
                                        N
    [. 1 . 6 . 1 . 6 . 2 . 1 . 3 . 2
                                        N
      . 3 . 1 . 2 . 6 . 2 . 1 . 3 . 2
                                        N
      . 3 . 1 . 2 . 6 . 3 . 2 . 3 . 1
                                        G
      . 2 . 1 . 2 . 1 . 3 . 2 . 1 . 6]
</pre>

    Kinanthi (the unggah of *Lobong*) irama 1/8, pélog pathet barang

<pre>
                                        N
    [. 7 . 6 . 7 . 6 . 2 . 7 . 3 . 2
                                        N
      . 3 . 7 . 2 . 6 . 2 . 7 . 3 . 2
                                        N
      . 3 . 7 . 2 . 6 . 3 . 2 . 3 . 7
                                        G
      . 2 . 7 . 2 . 7 . 3 . 2 . 7 . 6]
</pre>

---

*If *Kinanthi* is played in irama 1/4, the laras does not shift. If
it is played in irama 1/8, with çiblon drumming, it can go back and forth
between laras pelog and laras slendro.

4. Pélog gendhing that have an indirect relation to the sléndro original:

Gendhing *Génjong*, kethuk 2 kerep, laras sléndro pathet sanga

```
                                                        G
buka:    5  . 6 1 2  . 2 . 2  1 1 2 1  3 2 1 2  . 5 6 1
                                                        N
         . . . .  1 1 2 1  3 2 1 2  . 1 6 5
                                                        N
      [ . 2 3 5  . . 5 6  1 2 1 6  5 3 1 2
                                                        N
        . 1 3 2  . 3 6 5  1 6 5 6  5 3 1 2
                                                        G
        1 1 . .  5 6 1 2  1 3 1 2  . 1 6 5
                                                        G
        . 6 2 1  . . . .  3 2 1 2  . 1 6 5 ]
```

Gendhing *Gonjit*, kethuk 2 kerep, laras pélog pathet lima
     (derived from *Génjong*)

```
                                                        G
buka:    5 5 6  . 5 3 2  1 1 . .  5 6 1 2  1 3 1 2  . 1 6 5
                                                        N
      [ . 6 2 1  . . . .  3 2 1 2  . 1 6 5
                                                        N
        2 2 . .  2 2 1 2  3 3 . .  1 2 3 2
                                                        N
        . . . .  2 2 1 2  3 3 . .  1 2 3 2
                                                        G
        1 1 . .  5 6 1 2  1 3 1 2  . 1 6 5
                                                        N
        1 1 . .  1 1 2 1  3 2 1 2  . 1 6 5
                                                        N
        . 6 2 1  . . . .  3 2 1 6  5 3 1 2
                                                        N
        . 3 6 5  . . . .  5 5 . 6  . 5 3 2
                                                        G
        1 1 . .  5 6 1 2  1 3 1 2  . 1 6 5 ]
```

Gendhing *Glondhong Pring*, kethuk 2 kerep, laras sléndro pathet nem

```
                                                    G
buka: . 2  . 2 . 1  . 3 . 2  . 2 . 3  . 6 . 5  . 3 . 5  . 3 . 2
                                          •    •      •      •    •
```

```
                                            N
   [ . . . .  2 2 . 3  5 6 1 6  5 3 2 3
              • •      • • • •  • • • •
                                            N
   6 5 3 5  . 3 2 3  5 6 1 6  5 3 2 3
   • • • •    • • •  • • • •  • • • •
                                            N
   6 5 3 5  2 2 3 2  . 3 2 1  6 1 3 2
   • • • •            •        •
                                            G
   5 6 5 3  2 1 6 5  3 3 6 5  2 2 3 2
            • • • •  • •      • • • •
                                            N
   . . . .  2 2 . 3  5 6 1 6  5 3 2 3
            • •      • • • •  • • • •
                                            N
   6 5 3 5  . 3 2 3  5 6 1 6  5 3 2 3
   • • • •    • • •  • • • •  • • • •
                                            N
   6 5 3 5  2 2 3 2  . 3 2 1  6 1 3 2
   • • • •            •
                                            G
   . . . .  3 3 5 3  6 5 3 5  3 2 1 2
                                            N
                                  •
   6 6 . .  6 6 5 6  3 5 6 1  6 5 2 3
                                            N
                                  •
   6 5 3 5  . 3 2 3  5 6 1 6  5 3 2 3
                                            N
   6 5 3 5  3 3 1 2  . 3 2 1  6 1 3 2
                                  •
                                            G
   5 6 5 3  2 1 6 5  3 3 6 5  2 2 3 2 ]
```

Gendhing *Pring Glendhengan*, kethuk 2 kerep, laras pélog pathet lima
   (derived from *Glondhong Pring*)

```
                                              G
buka: 5 5 6  5 4 2 4  . 5 5 6  5 4 2 1  5 6 1 2  . 1 6 5
                                         •         •  •
```

```
                                          N
   [ . . 5 6  2 1 6 5  . . 5 6  1 2 1 6
       • •            • •              •
                                          N
   . . 2 1  . 6 5 6  1 2 3 2  1 6 5 6
           • • •              • •
                                          N
   . . 2 1  . 1 6 5  2 4 5 6  5 4 2 4
                                          G
   5 5 . 6  5 4 2 1  5 6 1 2  . 1 6 5 ]
                     •  •         •  •
```

5. Gendhing played in either laras sléndro or pélog, the original laras
    of which is unknown:

Ladrang *Pangkur*, laras sléndro pathet sanga; irama 1/8

```
                                              G
   buka:   . 2 1 1   . 2 1 1   2 2 1 1   . 6 . 5
                                                  N
            [ 2    1    2    6     2    1    6    5  6

                                                  N
              6    . 5 5 6 1 2    1 5 2    1    6

                                                  N
              .    2    .    1     .    2 5 3 2 1  5

                                                  G
              6 2 1 5 2 1 6       2    1    6    5 ]
```

Ladrang *Pangkur*, laras sléndro pathet manyura

```
                                                  N
            [ 3    2    3    1     3    2    1    6  1

                                                  N
              1    . 6 6 1 2 3    2 6 3    2    1

                                                  N
              .    3    .    2     .    3 6 5 3 2  6

                                                  G
              1 3 2 6 3 2 1       3    2    1    6 ]
```

Ladrang *Pangkur*, laras pélog pathet bem (sanga treatment)

```
                                                  N
            [ 2    1    2    6     2    1    6    5  6

                                                  N
              6    . 5 5 6 1 2    1 5 2    1    6

                                                  N
              .    2    .    1     .    2 5 3 2 1  5

                                                  G
              6 2 1 5 2 1 6       2    1    6    5 ]
```

Ladrang *Pangkur*, laras pélog pathet bem (manyura treatment)

```
                                        N
    [ 3    2    3    1    3    2    1    6    1̇

      .    ‾‾   ‾‾   ‾‾   ‾‾               N
      1̣  . 6  6  1̇  2̇  3̇   2̇  6  3    2    1

                                        N
      .    3    .    2    .    3̄ 6̄ 5̄ 3̄  2̇ 6

      ‾‾   ‾‾   ‾‾                       G
      1̣ 3̣ 2̇ 6 3̣ 2 1    3    2    1    6̣ ]
```

Ladrang *Pangkur*, laras pélog pathet barang

```
                                        N
    [ 3    2    3    7    3    2    7    6̇ 7

      ‾‾   ‾‾   ‾‾   ‾‾                  N
      7  . 6  6  7  2̇  3̇   2̇  6  3    2    7̇

                                        N
      .    3    .    2    .    3̄ 6̄ 5̄ 3̄  2̇ 6

      ‾‾   ‾‾   ‾‾                       G
      7̇ 3̣ 2̇ 6 3̣ 2 7̇   3    2    7    6̣ ]
```

In addition to the examples given above, there is also the repertory of gendhing to accompany the *wayang madya*, all of which are gendhing in sléndro transposed to pélog.[*]

From the examples and explanations provided above, it is clear that only gendhing in sléndro can be transposed to pélog, and not vice versa. There are no gendhing in laras pélog that can be transposed to laras sléndro. It is said that the *wayang klithik* (in the palace [at Surakarta]) were previously--that is, before the reign of Paku Buwana X [1893-1939]-- accompanied by pélog gendhing transposed to sléndro. However, subsequently--that is, during the reign of Paku Buwana X--the accompaniment used was gendhing in laras sléndro. This is proof that the transposition [from pélog to sléndro] must have been unpleasant to the ear.

---

[*]According to Bapak R[adèn] Ng[abèhi] Atmacendana [later known as Nojowirongko], the *wayang madya* was created during the reign of K[angjeng] G[usti] P[angèran] A[rya] A[dipati] Mangku Negara IV [reigned 1853-1881]. The accompaniment was by the pélog gamelan, and many new gendhing were created for this purpose. But when Paku Buwana X [reigned 1893-1939] adapted the wayang madya form [at the Kraton Surakarta], the gendhing used were all sléndro gendhing transposed to pélog. The clowns, Capa and Capi, previously used, were [6] replaced by Semar, Garèng, and Petruk [as in the wayang purwa repertory].

I should add that when skilled players play sléndro gendhing on a
pélog gamelan, they are careful that:

   a. the theme (cèngkok), or basic material, of the gendhing is not
       lost;

   b. the sléndro gendhing should be transposed to a pélog pathet that
       is the counterpart of the sléndro pathet.

Sléndro pathet sanga can be transposed to pélog pathet nem; sléndro pathet
manyura can be transposed to pélog pathet manyura, pélog nyamat, or pélog
pathet barang. Sléndro pathet nem, however, cannot be transposed to pélog
pathet lima. If a gendhing in sléndro pathet nem is played on a pélog
gamelan, the pathet will remain sléndro pathet nem, made pélog.

Around 1938-39, Bapak R[adèn] T[umenggung] Warsadiningrat (then known
as Prajapangrawit) transposed a sléndro gendhing into pélog. The gendhing
was Ladrang *Éling-éling Kasmaran* and the piece was to accompany an episode
from the *wayang orang* lakon, "*Kéyong Mas*" in the *wayang gedhog* repertory,
for the scene of Radèn Panji Inu Kartapati and Sarag.* The gendhing was
transposed to pathet barang (not pathet nem), and this practice has been
perpetuated to the present time.

A few years ago, around 1967, Ladrang *Sri Karongron*, laras sléndro
pathet sanga, was transposed to pélog pathet barang. However, be aware
that, even though these two gendhing (Ladrang *Éling-éling Kasmaran* and
Ladrang *Sri Karongron*) were both originally pathet sanga and both
transposed to pélog pathet barang, the procedures for doing so were not
identical. In Ladrang *Éling-éling Kasmaran* the gong tone remained
unchanged (tone 2 [gulu]), while in Ladrang *Sri Karongron* it was raised one
key--from pitch 5 (lima) in sléndro to pitch 6 (nem) in pélog.

Ladrang *Éling-éling Kasmaran*, pélog barang, is frequently played now
and in fact a suitable mérong for it has been found. Usually Gendhing
Bandhil Ori is chosen as the mérong, and, indeed, this choice is very
agreeable to the ear. But the question arises, "When Ladrang *Éling-éling
Kasmaran* is played in sléndro sanga, its mérong must be *Renyep*, but when
the piece is transposed, why is *Renyep* not transposed as well?" This
question is normally answered, "It would be unpleasant." Just that is
said, without regard for the fact that both the mérong and the unggah
sections of the gendhing have gong tone 2 (gulu) [and thus should be
equally transposable]. Actually, there are reasons for this.

---

*The actor-dancers, of whom I was one, were all musicians.

First, we must examine the laras pélog gamelan. Our gamelan has seven
tones, ordered thus: 1 2 3 4 5 6 7 . These tones are divided into two, to
become pélog bem and pélog barang, of which pélog bem is divided in two, in
the following manner: part I is   1 2 3 5 6   and part II is   1 2 4 5 6 .
Each part has two kinds of treatment, that is, tone 1 as kempyung (sanga
treatment) and tone 1 as gembyang (manyura treatment). Thus, pélog bem is
quite broad in scope, accommodating sléndro pieces of any pathet. The case
of pélog barang (2 3 5 6 7) is different. It has only one part and the
treatment (*garap*) is also ·invariable, that is, tone 7 (barang) must be
treated as gembyang.

As a result, if we want to transpose a piece in laras sléndro to laras
pélog bem, we can do so almost without thinking. If pitch 1 in laras
sléndro is treated as kempyung, then in pélog bem we need only use sanga
treatment; if pitch 1 in laras sléndro is treated as gembyang, we need only
use manyura treatment. If the use of pitch 3 in pélog is not very
pleasant, we can substitute pitch 4 in its place, and vice versa. This is
not, however, the case in pélog barang. If we want to transpose a sléndro
gendhing to pélog barang, we must choose a gendhing that has gembyang on
pitch 1 (a pathet manyura gendhing) or we must choose a pathet sanga
gendhing without sèlèh on pitch 1 and transpose it up one pitch level (as
in the case of *Sri Karongron*, where pitch 5 is raised one pitch level to
become pitch 6).

Changes in the Balungan of Gendhing

By changes in the balungan of gendhing I do not mean those changes
that occur when transposing from one laras to another. For example, if the
balungan   3 5 6 1   in laras sléndro becomes   2 3 2 1   in laras pélog bem,
or   3 5 3 2   . 1 2 6   in laras sléndro becomes   3 5 3 2   . 7 5 6   in laras
pélog barang, there has been no real "change." In karawitan circles these
are not regarded as changes, because the motif (*motief*) of the balungan
remains the same. Here, I mean changes in the motif or in the sèlèh. I am
convinced that these changes from an earlier original version have
occurred, based on the following evidence.

   a. Many of our venerable musicians are in disagreement over sections
       of the balungan of particular gendhing.

b. There is an episode in the *Serat Centhini** that tells of the
    playing of Gendhing *Gambir Sawit* in a manner that differs from
    current practice.

sekar kinanthi [in the *kinanthi* meter]:

Nulya ki Jayèngragèku   [Then Ki Jayèngraga
Anyenggrèng rebabira ris,   softly touched the bow to the
Anganti sendhon pathetan,   rebab strings
Laju buka Gambir Sawit,   and played the pathetan,
Tibaning nem beming kendhang,   then the buka for *Gambir Sawit*,
Tibaning lima dèn-gongi.   the bem of the kendhang entered
                                     at pitch nem,
                                 and the gong fell on pitch lima.]

According to this excerpt from the *Serat Centhini*, in the buka for
Gendhing *Gambir Sawit* the kendhang stroke bem falls on pitch 6
(nem), whereas in present-day practice the kendhang bem coincides
with pitch 2 (gulu), as below.

$$
\overset{\text{G}}{
\underset{\bullet}{5} \quad . \; \underset{\bullet}{6} \, 1 \, 2 \quad . \; 2 \; . \; 2 \quad 1 \, 1 \, 2 \, 1 \quad 3 \, 2 \, 1 \, 2 \quad . \; 1 \; \underset{\bullet}{6} \; \underset{\bullet}{5}
}
$$
                                       b t t t
[Note: b = bem; t = tong]

In the days of the *Serat Centhini*, the buka could have been as
follows.

$$
\overset{\text{G}}{
\underset{\bullet}{5} \quad . \; \underset{\bullet}{6} \, 1 \, 2 \quad . \; 2 \; . \; 2 \quad 1 \, 1 \, 2 \, 1 \quad 3 \, 2 \, 1 \, \underset{\bullet}{6} \quad 2 \, 1 \, \underset{\bullet}{6} \; \underset{\bullet}{5}
}
$$
                                       b t t t

     With this in mind, let us consider Gendhing *Onang-onang*. According to
the words of the elders, this gendhing was originally in laras sléndro
pathet sanga. This is consistent with the information in the *Serat
Centhini*, where *Onang-onang* is classified as a gendhing in pathet sanga.
Today this gendhing is invariably played in laras pélog bem, because when
played in its original laras and pathet it sounds unpleasant (awkward),
which means that the gendhing does not want to return to its origins. Is

*The following excerpt is taken from a copy of the *Serat
Centhini* owned by Bapak Jayamlaya. The volume and page are not mentioned.[7]

this not caused by [historical] changes in the areas of laras and treatment (*garap*)? Such changes could cause the original to be misunderstood.

Gendhing *Onang-onang*, laras pélog pathet nem

<pre>
                                                               G
buka: 2 . 3 5 6 . 6 . 1 . 2 . 1 . 2 . 6 . 3 . 5
                                                               N
           [. . 5 3   6 5 3 2   . . 2 3   5 6 3 5
                                                               N
             1 1 . .   1 1 2 1   3 2 1 2   . 1 6 5
                                                               N
             . . . .   5 5 3 5   6 6 . 5   3 3 5 6
                                         ‾‾‾‾‾‾‾‾‾‾‾
                                              I
                                                               G
             2 3 2 1   6 5 3 5   2 3 5 6   3 5 3 2
                                 ‾‾‾‾‾‾‾‾‾‾‾‾‾‾‾‾‾‾‾
                                         II

                                                               N
             6 6 . .   6 5 3 5   2 3 5 6   3 5 3 2
                                 ‾‾‾‾‾‾‾‾‾‾‾‾‾‾‾‾‾‾‾
                                        III
                                                               N
             5 5 . .   5 5 2 3   5 6 5 4   2 1 2 1
                                                               N
             3 2 1 2   . 1 6 5   2 2 . 3   1 2 3 2
                                                               G
             . . 2 3   5 3 2 1   3 5 3 2   . 1 6 5]
</pre>

If this balungan, common today, were played in sléndro, it would sound unpleasant. Sanga treatment precedes the underlined section I, but then there is an immediate switch to manyura. Underlined sections II and III are clearly to be treated as manyura, but after section III there is a reversal to sanga treatment at the repeated tones 5 5 . . . If the piece used balungan [phrases] from sléndro sanga in the sléndro version, it certainly would be much more pleasant.

```
                                                    N
[ . . 5 3   6 5 3 2   . . 2 3   6 5 3 5
                                                    N
  1 1 . .   1 1 2 1   3 2 1 2   . 1 6 5

                                                    N
  . . . .   5 5 3 5   6 6 . 5   6 3 5 6
                              I
                                                    G
  2 3 2 1   6 5 3 5   1 6 5 6   3 5 3 2
                              II

                                                    N
  6 6 . .   2 1 6 5   1 6 5 6   3 5 3 2
                              III                   N
  5 5 . .   5 5 2 3   5 6 5 3   2 3 2 1

                                                    N
  3 2 1 2   . 1 6 5   2 2 . 3   1 2 3 2
                              minur
                                                    G
  . . 2 3   5 3 2 1   3 5 3 2   . 1 6 5 ]
```

Aside from the changes mentioned above, there are other changes in balungan that are caused by necessity. For example, when Ladrang *Kembang Pépé* is used to accompany the bedhaya dance, it must be altered to accommodate the vocal part, since the latter is so important in gendhing bedhayan. If no change were made, the vocal part would be uncomfortable to sing.

Ladrang *Kembang Pépé* (original [i.e., klenèngan] version):

```
                                      N
      [ .  1  .  6  .  5  .  3
                  •
                                      N
        .  5  .  2  .  5  .  3
                                      N
        .  5  .  2  .  5  .  3
                                      G
        .  1  .  2  .  1  .  6
                                      •
                                      N
ngelik: .  5  .  3  .  5  .  6
                                      N
        .  5  .  3  .  5  .  6
                                      N
        .  3  .  2  .  5  .  3
                                      G
        .  1  .  2  .  1  .  6 ]
                                      •
```

Ladrang *Kembang Pépé* (as used to accompany bedhaya):

```
                                      N
      [ .  3  .  2  .  5  .  3
                  •
                                      N
        .  5  .  2  .  5  .  3
                                      N
        .  5  .  2  .  5  .  3
                                      G
        .  1  .  2  .  1  .  6
                                      •
                                      N
ngelik: .  5  .  3  .  5  .  6
                                      N
        .  5  .  3  .  5  .  6
                                      N
        .  3  .  2  .  5  .  3
                                      G
        .  1  .  2  .  1  .  6 ]
                                      •
```

Because such changes usually make the piece more pleasant, the changed
version tends to be used even if circumstances do not call for it. Often,
changed versions are performed so frequently that the original becomes
unknown. Ladrang *Pangkur* is another example.

The old Ladrang *Pangkur*, played without the so-called lancaran section
is below.[*]

buka: . 3 . 2 . 3 . 2 3 7 3 2 . 7 5 6̤ (G)

[3   2   3   7   3   2   7   6̱ 7̄ (N)

  7   . 6̄ 6̄ 7̄ 2̇̄ 3̄   2̇̄ 6̄ 3   2   7 (N)

  .   3   .   2   .   3   .   2̱ 6̄ (N)

  7̇̄ 3̄ 2̇̄ 6̄ 3 2 7   3   2   7   6̣] (G)

This version of Ladrang *Pangkur* was traditionally played in the following
manner: after the buka, the piece is irama 1/2 to the first kenong; then it
becomes irama 1/4, slowing down to the gong, where it becomes irama 1/8
(usually with ciblon drumming); after becoming irama 1/8 it occasionally
becomes 1/16, ending eventually in irama 1/8. The balungan remains
unchanged throughout. Later, *Pangkur* with a gancaran section emerged—
possibly from Ngayogya [Yogyakarta]—having the following shape in irama
1/4 and 1/2.

[3   2   3   7̣   3   2   7̣   6̣ (N)

  7   6   3   2   5   3   2   7̣ (N)

  3   5   3   2   6   5   3   2 (N)

  5   3   2   7̣   3   2   7̣   6̣] (G)

_____

[*]Actually *gancaran*—lancaran is a form.

When this *Pangkur* gancaran is played with kendhangan ciblon in irama 1/2 or
irama 1/4, it is accompanied by a solo female vocal part called "*rujak-rujakan*."

```
                                                    N
  [ 3      2      3      7      3      2      7      6
                         .             .      .      .

                                                    N
    7      6      3      2      5      3      2      7
    .      .                                         .
               .   2  2  2   2  6   2  6  3  5  6  2  7  3
                  Ru-jak na- nas pan- tes den wa- dhahi ge-las, ya

                                                    N
    3      5      3      2      6      5      3      2
    7  3  7  2   2  2   2  2   7  7  6  3  6  7  2  6
    mas ya mas ti- was ti- was ngla- buh-i wong o- ra we-las, a-

                                                    G
    5      3      2      7      3      2      7      6  ]
    .                    .             .      .      .
    2  6  3  2   2  2   7  3   3  3  4  2  7     6
    la ba-pak balung pa-kel a- lok a- lok    ho-    se.
```

When *Pangkur* gancaran is played with kendhang kalih drumming in irama 1/4,
it has the following gérong part in the *salisir* meter.

As time passed, another *Pangkur* with gancaran appeared, this time in laras
sléndro pathet sanga, played in irama 1/4 with a *laras madya* melody in the
pangkur meter as the gérongan.*

							N
[2	1	2	6	2	1	6	5

. 2 2 2 1 .2   3 5 2 1 6   . 2 2 2 1   6 1 2 3 1 6 5 . 2
Sekar pangkur kang wi- nar- na,   lalabuhan kang kanggo wong urip, a-

							N
6	5	2	1	3	2	1	6

2 . 2 2 . 3 1 2 5 6 1   6 1   2 1 5   2 . 5 3 2 3 1 6
la lan be -cik pu- niku,   prayo- ga ka-wruha- na

							N
2	3	2	1	5	3	2	1

. 2 3 5 6 5 6 1 5 3 2 6 1
adat waton puniku dipun ka-dulu

							G
3	2	1	6	2	1	6	5]

. 5 1 5 2 . 2 3 2 1   6   . 2 2 2 1 5 . 2 3 1 6   5
wiwah ing-kang tata kra-ma   dèn ka-èsthi si-yang ra-tri

---

*This follows the views of both Bapak Jayamlaya and Bapak
Mlayasuteja.

Still another *Pangkur* gancaran evolved, to meet certain needs, that is, as
an accompaniment for a dance (what dance?). This *Pangkur* gancaran had a
balungan similar to the rujak-rujakan melody in irama 1/2.

```
                                    N
 [ 3    2    3    7      3    2    7   6
                                    .
                                    N
   7 6 . 6  6 7 2 3    2 6 3   5 6 7  2

                                    N
   7 2 7  ·6 7 2      . 6 7 6 5 3 2  .2

                                    G
  . 2 2 5 3 2 7      . 3 2 3 2 7 6 ]
                                    .
```

This *Pangkur* gancaran balungan is very much enjoyed by young people. It is
frequently used in klenèngan—and not just as dance accompaniment. Because
young people have greater mobility than their elders, this *Pangkur* balungan
spread quickly. For this reason, the general public has come to regard
this balungan as Ladrang *Pangkur*, while the original balungan has been
forgotten.

Pélog Pieces in Laras Sléndro

There have never been any Solonese gendhing originally in pélog that
were later transposed to sléndro. As I mentioned above, there are some
pieces that can be played alternately in pélog and sléndro, but the
original laras of these is unknown.

There are also sléndro gendhing from Yogya that are considered in Solo
to be originally pélog. For example, *Rujak Jeruk* (sléndro) from Yogya is
equivalent to *Rujak Senthul* (pélog) in Solo; Ladrang *Temantèn* (sléndro) in
Yogya is equivalent to Ladrang *Serang* (pélog) in Solo. However, Yogya and
Solo have different styles of rendering balungan; thus, even though the
basic motifs (*motiefe*) of these gendhing are the same, there are some
differences, as set out below.

```
                                          N
 Rujak Jeruk:  [ . . . 5  . . . 3  . . . 5  . . . 2

                                          N
 Rujak Sentul: [ . 5 2 .  2 5 2 3  6 5 3 5  3 2 1 2
```

```
                                              N
Rujak Jeruk:      . . . 5   . . . 3   . . . 5   . . . 2

                                              N
Rujak Sentul:     . 5 2 .   2 5 2 3   6 5 3 5   3 2 1 2

                           . .   . .   . . . .   N
Rujak Jeruk:      6 3 5 6   . 1 3 2   5 3 2 1   6 5 2 3

                                   . . . .       N
Rujak Sentul:     . 1 2 6   . . . .   2 3 2 1   6 5 2 3

                                   . .           G
Rujak Jeruk:      6 5 2 .   2 3 5 6   1 2 6 3   6 5 3 2 ]

                                              G
Rujak Sentul:     . 5 2 .   2 3 6 5   2 1 6 1   2 3 1 2 ]
                                        .


                              N                       N
Ladrang Temanten:[ 1 5 1 6   1 5 1 6   1 5 1 6   3 5 6 1
                     .   .   .   .     .   .   .   .
                              N                       N
   Ladrang Serang:[ 7 5 7 6   7 5 7 6   7 5 7 6   3 5 6 7
                   . . . .   . . . .   . . . .   .   .


                              N                       G
Ladrang Temanten:  2 3 2 1   6 5 6 3   6 5 3 5   6 1 5 6
                             .   .   .   . . . .     .
                              N                       G
   Ladrang Serang:  2 3 2 7   6 5 6 3   6 5 3 5   6 7 5 6
                     .       .   .   .   . . . .


                              N           .           N
Ladrang Temanten:  3 3 . 1   2 3 5 3     6 1 6 5   3 2 1 2

                              N                       N
   Ladrang Serang:  3 3 . .   3 3 5 3     6 7 6 5   3 2 7 2
                                                       .


                              N                       G
Ladrang Temanten:  3 2 1 6   5 3 5 2   5 3 2 3   5 6 5 3
                             .   .   .   . . . .   .   .
                              N                       G
   Ladrang Serang:  3 2 7 6   5 3 5 2   5 3 2 3   5 6 5 3
                     . .     .   .   .   . . . .   .   .


                              N                       N
Ladrang Temanten:  6 5 6 3   6 5 6 3   6 5 6 3   6 5 3 2
                   . . . .   . . . .   . . . .   . .   .
                              N                       N
   Ladrang Serang:  6 5 6 3   6 5 6 3   6 5 6 3   6 5 3 2
                   . . . .   . . . .   . . . .   . .   .


                              N                       G
Ladrang Temanten:  6 5 2 6   5 2 6 5   2 5 2 3   5 6 5 3
                   . . . .   . . . .   . . . .   . .   .
                              N                       G
   Ladrang Serang:  5 3 2 5   3 2 5 3   2 5 2 3   5 6 5 3
                   . . . .   . . . .   . . . .   . .   .
```

```
                                    N                           N
  Ladrang Temantèn:  6 5 6 3   6 5 6 3     6 5 6 3   6 5 6 1 ]
                     . . . .   . . . .     . . . .   . . . .
                                    N                           N
  Ladrang Serang:    6 5 6 3   6 5 6 3     6 5 6 3   6 5 6 7
                     . . . .   . . . .     . . . .   . . . .


                                    N                           G
  Ladrang Temantèn:  2 3 2 1   6 5 6 3     6 5 3 5   6 1 5 6 ]
                                 . . . .               . . . .
                                    N                           G
  Ladrang Serang:    2 3 2 7   6 5 6 3     6 5 6 3   6 7 5 6 ]
                       .         . . . .               . . . .
```

In 1961, I tried playing Ladrang *Tirta Kencana*, laras pélog pathet nem,* in sléndro sanga for the Ramayana ballet. I have notated the balungan of the two versions below.

Ladrang *Tirta Kencana*

```
                                  N                                 N
  pélog nem:    [ 2  1  2  6    2  1  6  5    2  1  2  6    2  1  6  5
                          .              .              .              .
                                  N                                 N
  sléndro sanga: [ 2  1  2  6    2  1  6  5    2  1  2  6    2  1  6  5
                          .              .              .              .


                                  N                                 G
  pélog nem:      1  5  6  1    3  2  1  6    5  4  2  4    5  6  4  5 ]
                     .  .              .        .     .        .     .
                                  N                                 G
  sléndro sanga:  1  5  6  1    3  2  1  6    5  3  2  3    5  6  3  5 ]
                     .  .              .        .     .        .     .
```

ngelik

```
                 __  __  __  __   __  __  __  N    __  __  __  __   __  __  __  N
  pélog nem:     56  12  56  12   56  12  16  5    56  12  56  12   56  12  16  5

                 __  __  __  __   __  __  __  N    __  __  __  __   __  __  __  N
  sléndro sanga: 56  12  56  12   56  12  16  5    56  12  56  12   56  12  16  5


                 .        .        .  .     N                           G
  pélog nem:     1  5  6  1     3  2  1  6    5  4  2  4    5  6  4  5 ]
                                             N                           G
  sléndro sanga: 1  5  6  1     3  2  1  6    5  3  2  3    5  6  3  5 ]
                    .  .              .        .     .        .     .
```

In 1967, I tried playing Gendhing *Bandhil Ori*, pélog barang, in sléndro, but I was unable to put it into the corresponding pathet (pathet manyura), and it turned out to be more pleasant in sléndro sanga.

---

*I consider it pélog pathet lima because it uses a low 4.

Gendhing *Bandhil Ori*

```
                                                                  G
  buka:  pélog barang:   .5  .5.5  3567  .7.7  .6.5  .7.6  .532
                                        .     . .                 G
         sléndro sanga:   .5  .5.5  3561  .1.2  .6.5  .1.6  .532

                                                                  N
  pélog barang:   [ .  3  5  2  .  3  5  2  5  6  5  3  2  7  6  7
                                                         .     .  N
  sléndro sanga:  [ .  3  5  2  .  3  5  2  5  6  5  3  2  1  2  1


                                                                  N
  pélog barang:    .  3  .  2  .  7  6  5  .  .  5  6  7  2  3  2
                               .  .        .  .  .                N
  sléndro sanga:   .  3  .  2  .  1  6  5  .  .  5  6  1  2  3  2
                               .  .        .  .  .


                                                                  N
  pélog barang:    3  5  .  .  5  5  .  .  5  5  6  5  3  5  6  7
                                                                  N
                                                                  .
  sléndro sanga:   5  5  .  .  5  5  .  .  5  5  6  5  3  5  6  1


                      .     .                                     G
  pélog barang:    .  3  .  2  .  7  6  5  .  7  .  6  .  5  3  2 ]
                      .     .        .              .             G
  sléndro sanga:   .  3  .  2  .  1  6  5  .  1  .  6  .  5  3  2 ]
```

When Gendhing *Bandhil Ori* is transposed to sléndro pathet sanga, the result
is very pleasant, whereas transposed to pathet manyura, it clearly is not.
The reasons are as follows.

1. *Bandhil Ori* has many sèlèh on pitch 5, which is the dhing
   (avoided) tone in pathet manyura; furthermore, there is a
   gantungan (repeated tone) on pitch 5. The dhing tone of a pathet
   may be found in the balungan of a piece, but it should be
   accompanied by tones that soften the effect of the dhing.

2. There should be a sèlèh tone immediately following (*ing saburiné*)
   the dhing tone that can counteract the effect of the dhing tone.

These two conditions are illustrated below.

1. Tones that soften the effect of the dhing tone are found in the
   following gendhing.

   a. Gendhing *Damar Kèli*, sléndro pathet manyura

   $$5653 \quad 2126 \quad 356\dot{1} \quad 6523 \quad ..35 \quad 6532 \quad .12\underset{.}{6} \quad 3532 \quad \text{N}$$

   $$5653 \quad 2165 \quad 33.6 \quad 3561 \quad .... \quad 1123 \quad 6532 \quad .126 \quad \text{G}$$

   b. Gendhing *Lobong*, sléndro pathet manyura

   $$22.. \quad 2321 \quad 3265 \quad 3356 \quad \text{G}$$

2. Sèlèh tones that counteract the effect of the dhing tone are found
   in the following gendhing.

   a. Gendhing *Genès*, sléndro pathet manyura

   $$\text{buka:} \quad 66\dot{1} \quad 6523 \quad .\dot{1}.\dot{1} \quad .\dot{2}.6 \quad .535 \quad 3212 \quad \text{G}$$

   $$55.. \quad 5523 \quad 5653 \quad 2126 \quad \text{N}$$

   _____/

   (Note: The bracket indicates a "cèngkok mati" in pathet
   manyura.)

Note. Actually, the themes (*motiefé*) in Gendhing *Bandhil Ori* are
rather unclear in sléndro sanga, because in pélog barang the sèlèh tone 7
is gembyang, while in sléndro sanga the sèlèh tone 1 becomes kempyung.
There is, of course, a great difference in feeling between kempyung and
gembyang. Gembyang has a soft and calm feeling while kempyung has an
energetic feeling. The difference influences the pathet as well. Thus,
changing laras sometimes can be based only on agreeableness, not on themes.

There are many cases where gendhing originally in laras pélog can be
transposed to sléndro--and not only necessarily to the corresponding
pathet--without merely raising or lowering the pitch levels. An example of
this is Gendhing *Sinom*, pélog pathet barang, which can be transposed to
sléndro pathet sanga.

Gendhing *Sinom*

```
                                                              G
buka:  pélog barang   . 3 . 3 . 2 . 7 . 2 . 6 . 3 . 2
                                          •       •         G
       sléndro sanga  . 2 . 2 . 3 . 1 . 2 . 6 . 1 . 2
                                                  •

                                                              N
barang:  [ ..27  .6.5  ..56  7567  ..73  .532  .327  .6.5
            •    •  •   •• •  •• ••             •  •  •  •
                                                              N
sanga:   [ ..21  6535  ..56  1121  ..13  1232  ..21  6535
            • •  •• ••  •• •                          •• ••
                                                     ••
                                                              N
barang:    ..56  .765  ..56  7567  ....  7767  22.7  .6.5
           ••    •• •   •• •  •• ••                   •  •
                                               ••••   •• •    N
sanga:     ..56  2165  ..56  1.21  ....  1121  22.1  6535
           ••    •• •   •• •                          •• ••

                                                              N
barang:    .2.7  .3.2  .327  .6.5  22..  2327  .2.3  .532
             •          •    •  •          •
                                                              N
sanga:     .2.1  .3.2  ..21  6535  22..  5321  22.3  1232
                            •• ••

                                                              G
barang:    .327  .6.5  .672  .765  22..  2327  .2.6  .3.2 ]
             •    •  •  •• •  •• •          •    •      •
                                                              G
sanga:     ..21  6535  .612  .165  22..  5321  .2.6  .3.2 ]
           • •   •• ••        •  •                •
```

To transpose a gendhing from pélog to sléndro one must be aware of the
following rules.

1. One must determine if the gendhing has dhing tones in the
    prospective pathet.

2. One must examine the sèlèh or balungan tones, weighing one against
    another to determine which become kempyung in a particular pathet,
    using the following formula.

```
a.   1   5   2   6                  ⎤
b.       5   2   6   3        .      ⎥   pélog bem
c.           2   6   3        1      ⎦


a.   7   5   2   6                  ⎤
b.       5   2   6   3              ⎥   pélog barang
c.           2   6   3   7          ⎦


a.   1   5   2   6                  ⎤
b.       5   2   6   3        .      ⎥   sléndro
c.           2   6   3        1      ⎦
```

Explanation. If the sèlèh tones of a pélog gendhing correspond to
those in the lines marked "a," above, then the gendhing will become pathet
sanga when transposed to laras sléndro. If the sèlèh tones correspond to
those in the lines marked "b," and if there are sèlèh on pitch 5, but not
on pitch 3, then the pathet will be sanga when the piece is transposed to
sléndro. If there are sèlèh on pitch 3, but not on pitch 5, then the
pathet will be manyura. Gendhing with sèlèh tones that correspond to those
in the lines marked "c" will be pathet manyura when transposed to sléndro.

Examples

A gendhing in pélog lima, like the following, with sèlèh on
pitches 1 and 3, will become pathet manyura when transposed to
sléndro.

```
                    N                    N
        1.   .111   2321    .111    2353

                    N                    G
             .356   7653    5323    2121
```

A gendhing in pélog lima, like the following, with sèlèh on
pitches 1 and 5, will become pathet sanga when transposed to
sléndro.

```
                    N                    N
        2.   .111   5621    .111    5612
                     ..                   ..
                    N                    G
             ..23   5.65    6654    2121
```

A gendhing in pélog nem, like the following, with sèlèh on
pitches 2 and 5, will become pathet sanga when transposed to
sléndro.

```
             N              N
   3.  ..56  1232   .216   5612
        ..           .     ..
                     N             G
        .235  .645   6621  3265
                            ..
```

Having sèlèh on pitches 2 and 6, and the repeated tone 3, this
gendhing in pélog nem will become pathet manyura when transposed
to sléndro.

```
             N              N
   4.  ..61  3216   3356   3532
         .      .
                     N             G
        5352  5352   5654  2126
                            .
```

A gendhing in pélog barang, like the following, with sèlèh on
pitches 7 and 5, will become pathet sanga when transposed to
sléndro.

```
             N               N
   5.  .555  3235    .555   3567
        ...   ....    ...    ....
                      N             G
        .723  4327    6765  3235
                .      ....  ....
```

A gendhing in pélog barang, like the following, with sèlèh on
pitches 7 and 3, will become pathet manyura when transposed to
sléndro.

```
             N               N
   6.  .767  2327    .767   2353
        ...   .       ...
                      N             G
        .356  7653    5323  2767
                             ...
```

APPENDIX I

This appendix concerns *bawa*, vocal [introductions to gendhing].
Although bawa can stand alone as vocal music, they are also closely
connected with instrumental music--gamelan. Thus, karawitan musicians
should understand them.

I once received a note from Bapak Jayamlaya with the following
message.*

<u>Advice from R[adèn] M[as] Sahirjan**</u>

1. The creator of *laras madya* was K[angjeng] P[angéran] Santakusuma, a
grandson of Paku Buwana V. He took the lyrics from the book [Serat]
Wulang Rèh.

2. The creator of bawa and gérong was K[angjeng] P[angéran]
Kusumabrata, and the first singer of bawa was R[adèn] M[as]
Hesmubrata, at the royal estate, Langen Harja. The bawa he sang was
[sekar ageng] *candra kusuma* as an introduction to the gendhing *Pangkur
Paripurna*, performed in honor of the visit of Kangjeng Gusti [Pangéran
Adipati Arya] Mangku Negara IV. The singer wore the *Langen Harjan*-
style costume.

3. The creator of *santi swaran* was Sumaningrat, who offered his
creation to [the *patih*, or prime minister] Kangjeng [Adipati]
Sasradinigrat ([Patih] Kléca). Melodies from gamelan gendhing were
later added.

According to this note from Bapak Jayamlaya, there were no bawa before
the time of Paku Buwana IX [reigned 1861-1893] and Mangku Negara IV
[reigned 1853-1881]. Since that time it has become common practice to
precede many gendhing with a bawa--whether *tembang gedhè*, *tembang macapat*,
or *tembang tengahan*.

In my opinion, before these tembang [poetic meters] were used as bawa,
only their laras was predetermined--their pathet was as yet undetermined.

---

*I still have the original, which is written in Javanese script.

**His home was in *kampung* Patang Puluhan.

Nowadays, the notation of tembang possessed by most vocalists will include
the specification of pathet, especially when the musical notation is
included. The pathet of a tembang used as a bawa to a particular gendhing
will agree with the pathet of the gendhing. On the other hand, tembang
that are not used as bawa are sometimes assigned a pitch level according to
what the writer of the notation arbitrarily considers to be the pathet.
This is shown by the following two versions of tembang *megatruh* in which
the melody is the same, but the pitch levels of the notation differ.

```
I.   7    5    6    7    . 7  6    7    5    3    5    6    7
     Si-  gra mi - lir   sang gè- thèk si - nang-ga ba- jul

     .    2    3    5    5    5    5    7 6  5
          ka- wan  da - sa   kang ja - gèn - i

     .    2    3    5    5    5    5    7    6
          ing ngar-sa mi- wah-ing pung-kur,

     .    2    2    2    2    2    3    2    7
          tan- a - pi  ing ka - nan ké- ring

     .    5    5    3    2    3    5    5 3  2
          Sang gè -thèk lam- pah- nya  a -  lon.


II.  3    1    2    3    . 3  2    3    1    6    1    2    3
     Si - gra mi - lir  sang    gè-thèk si - nang-ga ba - jul

     .    5    6    1    1    1    1    3 2  1
          ka- wan da - sa   kang ja - gèn - i

     .    5    6    1    1    1    1    3    2
          ing ngar-sa   mi - wah ing pung- kur

     .    5    5    5    5    5    6    5    3
          tan- a - pi  ing  ka - nan ké- ring

     1    1    6    5    6    1    1 6  5
     Sang gè-thèk lam- pah- nya  a -  lon.
```

Another example [this time of tembang gedhé], in which the same melody
is notated at different pitch levels, is [tembang gedhé] *bremara ngingsep
sari*, lampah 11, pedhotan 4-7 [eleven syllables per line, divided four-
seven], laras sléndro.

1. 0 5 5 6 . 5 5 6 . 6 ı̇ ı̇ 2̇ . 6 5 .3 2 .5 6 .5 3
    Ga-lak   u- lat   ka-di tha - thit am - ba-rung,

    3 .1 1 2̇3̇ 2̇ .6 1̇ 65 3 1 2 3 35 3 2 . 26 1̇ 65 3
    kang   pa - mu - lu   a-lus ma-nis ma - wèh   kung,

    6 53 5 6 . 2 1 6 . 6 6 ı̇ ı̇ 2̇ . 6 5 .3 2 .6 1̇ 65 3
    sem - ba - da kang de-deg man-da - ra   na -   kung,

    6 5̄3 5 6 . 2 1 6 . 1̄ 2 3 35̄ 2 5̄6 5   3
    a - go - rèh pan   da-dya pantes malat kung.

2. 0 3 3 5 . 3 3 5 . 5 6 6 ı̇ . 5 3 .2 1 .3 5 .3 2
    Ga-lak   u- lat   ka-di tha - thit am - ba-rung,

    2 .6 6 1̇2̇ 1̇ .5 6 53 2 6 1 2 23 2 1 . 15 6 53 2
    kang   pa - mu - lu   a-lus ma-nis ma - wèh   kung,

    5 32 3 5 . 1 6 5 . 5 5 6 6 ı̇ . 5 3 .2 1 .5 6 53 2
    sem - ba - da kang de-deg man-da - ra   na -   kung,

    5 3̄2 3 5 . 1 6 5 . 6̄ 1̇ 2 2̄3 1 3̄5 3   2
    a - go - rèh pan   da-dya pantes malat kung.

In tembang such as those above, the melody is clearly the most
significant part; pathet is of no consequence. But, when used as a bawa,
the pathet of the tembang must agree with that of the gendhing it
introduces. For example, when sekar ageng [tembang gedhé] *rara bèntrok* is
used as a bawa for Gendhing *Gambir Sawit*, sléndro pathet sanga, the tembang
rara bèntrok must be pathet sanga and use the proper pitch level for pathet
sanga.

```
0 5    5 6  1 2 . 6   6  61   6  5
  Kang ka-te-man  ra- ras ma - ra

. 5   5 .6  1 .5   6 53  2   . 2  22  35   5
  ra  -  ra  bén - trok    a-nglam-lam- i,

. 2   2   2   21 65  56 16   5 .2   5 32   1
  pa-ran tu-ma-mèng     ti - lam  rum

5   6 12   2 .3   1  2 15   2   2 .1   6
ba - ya  rum -  ing sa - ri- ran - ta

.   . 5  61  12   2 3  5 13   2 .1   6 16    5
     su- mar-ma  ma - du  me -  nuh - i

. 5   5  5  6 1  . 12   61  .5   6 53   2
 dhuh mas mi-rah   sang ku- su - ma

. 2   5  6  61  .5   2   23  2  1 6   61  12   2
 am-bu-ka gan- da-ning se-kar gam- bir sa-wit

6 1   1 .2  61 65   5
ma - ra - ta - ni.
```

The lyrics of this version of *rara bèntrok* clearly indicate that the tembang is to be used as a bawa for Gendhing *Gambir Sawit*. In fact, there is another *rara bèntrok* song, with a different set of words, which shows even more clearly that the tembang serves as a bawa for *Gambir Sawit*.

0 5   5 6 i 2 . 6   6 6i 6   5
Te-men-é   na   kang dèn an - ti

. 5   5 6i 2 2 2 23   2 16 5 .1 2 .1   6
Gam- bir   sa-wit du - rung   mu - ni,

2   i   2 .1 6 .3   3 35 3   2
tur i - ku no- ra mbo-sen - i

. 2 5 6 6 i 2   6 .2 i 65 2 .3 5 32 1
wit ku-na ngan -   ti   sa - i - ki,

. 5   5 6 i 53 2 3 5 .1   1 21 6   5
na - dyan sa - jam mu- ni ping tri

. 2 2 2   2 2   1 23 5 6 i .5 6 53   2
se-rengé durung ngen -   dhon - i

. 2 2 21 6 i 2   6 2 i 65 2 .3 5 32   1
pa-na-buh - é   ma - sih u - thi

6   6 i 1 2   2   6 1 1 .2 6i 65   5
tan-dha dhe - men trus- ing   a - ti

When we compare these two versions we can see that, although the melody and words differ, the notation for both is pathet sanga.

An interesting situation arises, however, when *Gambir Sawit* is played
in pélog pathet nem (bem). The gendhing is played as if there were no
change; that is, it is not raised or lowered as is, for example, Ladrang
Sri Karongron. But why are the tones of the bawa *rara béntrok* raised one
pitch level so that sèlèh on pitch 5 (lima) becomes sèlèh on pitch 6 (nem),
and so forth? Only later, in approaching gong, is the bawa melody rerouted
so that it has a sèlèh on pitch 5, since the gong tone of the gendhing is
fixed as pitch 5. The melody is as below.

```
0  6   6  i   2 3   . i   i   23  i  21   6
Te-men-é  na      kang dèn  an  -   ti

. 6   6 12   3  3  3    . 2   2 .i   6 .2   3 .2   i
Gam - bir  sa-wit   du - rung  mu  -   ni

3    2 32  i  65   6 i   . 6   54   .5   6 54   2
tur i  -  ku     no -  ra mbo-sen  -   i

2   4  5   6 12   i .6   5   16 53   2   1
wit ku-na  ngan -  ti  sa -  i  -   ki

. 3   5   16 53   2  3   . i   i   12 16   5
na-dyan sa - jam    mu-ni ping  tri,

. 1   2  2   2  .3   5   5 65   3   2
se-rengé  du-rung ngen-dhon  -  i

. 2   2 2   2   2   i   6 .i   2   5   i  6 53   2   1
pa-nabuh-é  ma  -   sih      u  -   thi,

. 3   5   56 53   2   61 23   1   12 16   5
tan-dha  dhe men trus - ing   a  -  ti
```

Tembang *rara béntrok*, above, has the same sèlèh tone at the words "-ra mboseni" as does the pathet sanga version. But, in fact, the version above uses the manyura/nyamat tuning for the tones 2 4 5 6 1̇ , as a transition to sanga treatment (*garap*).

Below I have provided another example to further prove that, when a pathet sanga melody is transposed to pélog, it is raised one pitch level to become nyamat. This is the tembang *sudira warna*, which is used as a bawa for Gendhing *Bondhèt*, laras sléndro pathet sanga.

5   6   1̇   2̇   6̇1̇ 6̇5   5
Lir sad pa - dèng - sun

5 5̄3̄ 2 3 5 .̄1̄ 1 2̄1̄   6   5
tu-mi- ling ma-ngu-lat - i

2   2   1 2̄3̄ 5 .̄2̄   5 .̄3̄   2 .̄1̄   6
puspi - ta   ing - kang

. 5   5   5 3̄2̄ 1 2̄3̄ 5   1 2̄3̄ 2 .̄1̄   6 5
   me-dem in-dah kang   war - ni

5   6   1̇   2̇   6̇1̇ 6̇5   5
mi-dar ing   ta - man

5 5̄3̄ 2 3 5 .̄1̄   1 2̄1̄   6 5
a-nom se - kar war-si - ki

2   2   1 2̄3̄ 5 .̄2̄   5 .̄3̄   2 .̄1̄   6
ku-me - nyut   ing   tyas

6   1̄2̄   1   6̄1̄   2̄1̄   6   5
ba- ya   ta ja - tu   kra-ma

Gendhing *Bondhèt*, sléndro sanga, like Gendhing *Gambir Sawit*, is sometimes
played in pélog. The contour of the melody does not change and when the
piece uses bawa it is introduced by the same bawa, tembang *sudira warna*.
In pélog, however, the title of the tembang is changed to tembang *sudira
wicitra*.

6 1 2 3 12 16 6
Lir sad - pa - dèng - sun

6   6 5   3 5   6 .2   2 23   1 21   6
tu- mi - ling   ma-ngu-lat - i

3 3   2 .3   5 65   4   6   5 .3   2 1
puspi - ta   ing - kang

. 6   6   6 65   3 .5   6   2 3   1 21   6
  mè-dem in-dah kang   war - ni

6 1 2 3 12 16 6
mi-der-ing   ta - man

6 65   3 5   6 .2   2   23   1 21   6
a-nom   se - kar war-si - ki

3 3   2 .3   5 65   4   6   5 .3   2 1
ku-me - nyut   ing - tyas

1   1 2   2   1 2   3 2   1 6   5
ba- ya   ta ja - tu kra- ma

All of tembang *sudira wicitra* has been raised one pitch level (in other
words, to nyamat or manyura), except at the place of the gong, where it
remains pitch 5 (lima) because the gong tone for Gendhing *Bondhèt* remains 5
when transposed from sléndro to pélog.

There are many more cases like these--far too many to be written down. However, I want to give another example, from a vocal gendhing, specifically from a santi swara gendhing. Melodies for santi swara are vocal melodies. This means that the melody is a vocal part, accompanied entirely by instruments from the irama group. Even so, in books of santi swara the pathet is specified--though only pathet nem and barang for pélog (there are none in lima) and pathet sanga and manyura for sléndro (there are none in pathet nem). I have selected the santi swara gendhing, Gendhing *Kudup Turi*, laras sléndro pathet sanga, for which the bawa is sekar ageng [tembang gedhé] *wegang sulanjari*,[*] lampah 20, pedhotan 8-12 [20 syllables per line, divided 8-12].

```
2 .3  1 .5  2 35  6 61  6 5  5 61  2   56 53  2 32  1
Tan- dya ba - la   Pan  -   dha  -   wa   mbyuk

. 1   1 .1  3 5   5 6  1 53  2 .3  1  35  3 2
  gu-mu-lung ma-ngung-sir   ing Sa-ta Ku-ra - wa

2 35  5 6  1 .5   3   2 .5  3 21  6 .5  6 1  2
kam - bah   kung-kih   sru  ka - ti- tih

. 5   5  . 6  1 .6  5 2  6 1  2  . 5   6  1  21 65   5
  mi-rut ké - rut   la - rut    ka-tut pa-ra Ra- tu

. 5   5  3  2 5  5 .6  1 .6  5 .3  2 .5  3 21  6 5  6 1 2
  tu-win sa -   gung           pra di - pa - ti

. 5   5  . 6  1 .6  5 2  6 1  2  . 5  6 1  2 .1  6 .5  5
  mi-rut ka - pa - la - yu   sigra prapta - ni - ra

. 5  5 3 25  5 .6  1 .6  5 .3  2  . 5  3 21  65  61  2
  A-swa-ta -  ma           ta - ta  nya-lah
```

---

[*]I know nothing of the name and I have chosen only the bawa version.

. 5̣ 5 . 6 1̄ .6̄ 5 2 6 1 2 6̄1̄ 6 5 . 3 3 .5̄ 2 3 2

pa-gé - né ta i - ki ywa pa- dha lu - ma - yu

This version of tembang *wegang sulanjari* is also used as a bawa for
Gendhing *Bango Maté* in santi swara. This gendhing has pitch 5 (lima) as a
gong tone. Even so, the bawa is clearly pélog manyura or nyamat, which
means it is raised one pitch level from *wegang sulanjari* in laras sléndro.

3 2̇ 6 3 5 6 1̇ 1̇ 2 1̇ 6 6 1 2 3 1̇ 2 1̇ 6 5 . 3 2

Sri Kresna ka - sreg - i ni - rup

. 2 2 .2 3 5 6 1̇ 2̇ .6 5 65 3 5 6 2 . 3 5 65 3

si-nèp li-ne-pas-an wa - ras - tra pi - na - reg,

3 .1̄ 1̄ 2̄3̄ 2̄ .1̄ 6 .5 3 1 23 3 6 5 6 2 3 1 .2 3

di - ra nga - deg ma - mu- ling - nga

. 6̇ 6 . 1̇ 2̇ 1̄6̄ 5 .3 1 2 3 . 6 1 2 3 .2 1 21 6

nga-we - ri la - rut- ing ba-la ra-ta re - bah,

. 6 6 5 3̄1̄ 1̇ 2̄3̄ 2̄ .1̄ 6 .5 3 . 6 5 6 2 3 1 .2 3

Bi-ma nge - bag le- pas - a muk -

. 6 6 . 1̇ 2̄6̄ 53 1 2 3 . 6̣ 1 2 3 2 1 21 6

ti-né ba-la re - bah ma-bag gajah ra - ta

. 6 6 5 3̄1̄ 1̇ 2̄3̄ 2̄ .1̄ 6 .5 3 . 6 5 6 2 3 1 2 3

bentar tre - nyuh si-nga na - rug

. 6̇ 6 . 1̇ 2̄6̄ 5 3 1 2 3 . 6 1 2 3 2 1 6̣ 5

ti-nem-bung- i - ra ring ga-da ka-su - la - yah

These vocal examples should be sufficient to demonstrate that the
counterpart of sléndro pathet sanga is pélog manyura or nyamat--that is,
raised one key [tone]. Raising one key [tone] is not ordinarily restricted
to pathet nyamat, but can also be pleasing in pélog barang. Thus, in
short, the basic principle is to raise the melody one pitch level. Below,
I have given the barang version [of tembang gedhé *wegang sulanjari*].

```
  3   2   6   3 56  7  72 76  6 72  3  72 76  5 .3  2
Sri Kresna ka -  sreg- i          ni - rup


 . 2   2 .2   3 5   6   7   2 .6   5 65  3  5 6   2  . 3   5 65 3
  si-nèp li-ne-pas-an    wa - ras - tra pi - na - reg,


 3 .7  7 23  2 .7  6 .5  3  7 23   3   6   5 6  2 3  7 .2 3
di - ra          nga - deg ma - mu- ling - nga


 . 6   6  . 7  2 76  5 .3  1 2  3  . 6  7  2  3 .2  7 27  6
 nga-we - ri la -  rut- ing    ba-la ra-ta   re - bah,


 . 6   6 5 37  7 23  2 .7  6 .5  3  . 6  5 6  2 3  7 .2  3
 Bi-ma nge - bag            le- pas - a   muk -


 . 6   6  . 7  26 53  7 2  3  . 6  7 2  3 2  7 27  6
 ti-né  ba-la re - bah    ma-pag gajah ra - ta


 . 6   6 5  37  7 23  2 .7  6 .5  3  . 6  5 6  2 3  7 2  3
 bentar tre - nyuh          si-nga na - rug


 . 6   6  . 7  2 6  5 3  7  23  . 6  7  2  3 2  7 6  5
 ti-nem-bung- i - ra   ring   ga-da ka-su - la - yah
```

Now that I have provided the transposition to barang, we must understand
that it is not usually necessary to raise a melody one tone as long as we
use the barang tuning (steming) 1 2 4 5 6 , which is the same as
2 3   5 6 7 . To make this clearer, I will notate the above melody in
such a form.

```
2 .4  1 .5  2 45  6  61 65  5 61  2  56 54  2 42  1
Tan- dya ba- la      Pan - dha  -  wa      mbyuk
```

```
. 1  1 .1   4   5   5 6  1 54  2 .4  1  45   4     2
 gu-mu-lung mang-ung-sir   ring Sa-ta Ku-ra - wa
```

```
2 45  5 6  1 .5  4  2  . 5  4 21  6 .5  6 1  2
kam - bah  kung-kih  sru ka - ti - tih,
```

```
. 5  5  . 6  1 .6  5 .2  6 1  2  . 5  6 1  21 65  5
 mi-rut  ké - rut  la - rut     ka-tut pa-ra Ra- tu
```

```
. 5  5 4 2 5  5 .6  1 .6  5 .4  2  . 5  4 21  6 5  6 1 2
tuwin sa -    gung              pra di - pa - ti,
```

```
. 5  5  . 6  1 .6  5 .2  6 1  2  . 5  6 1  2 .1  6 .5 5
 mi-rut  ka - pa - la- yu     si-gra prapta - ni - ra
```

```
. 5  5 4 2 5  5 .6  1 .6  5 .4  2 .5  4 21  6 5  6 1 2
A-swata -    ma               ta - ta - nya - lah
```

```
. 5  5  . 6  1 .6  5 2  6 1  2  61 6  5  . 4  4 .5  2 4 2
pa-gé - né  ta   i - ki   ywa  pa - dha lu - ma - yu
```

Although it is not necessary to raise the melody one tone to render it
into barang, vocalists and instrumentalists in the karawitan community are
unwilling to use such a version as the one given above because, when the
resultant melody is used as a bawa, the *thinthingan* played on the gendèr
does not agree with one tone of the vocal part, namely, pitch 4 [since

there is no pitch 4 on the gendèr]. Worse yet, this pitch is used more
than once or twice, so if played with the gendèr the feeling would be
unpleasant. If the vocal part is sung alone, however, the impression will
be of the embat of barang, or at least the barang tuning. Therefore, it is
preferable just to transpose it directly into barang, or, if it is in pélog
bem, to make it nyamat [i.e., manyura].

Once we have understood all this, a question may arise. If the
[original] melody is in sléndro manyura, should [the pélog barang version]
also be raised one tone? This answer is: if one is looking for
consistency, one must raise the melody one tone, tone 6 becoming tone 7,
etc., as in the example below.

[sléndro:] . 6   6 1   2   3   . 1   2   1 .6   6

            Kang kadi su -   da - ma gus - ti

[pélog:]   . 7   7 2   3   4̸   . 2   3   2 .7   7

            Kang kadi su -   da - ma gus - ti

But this sort of transposition has never been adopted in karawitan circles,
because pitch 4̸ is not used in vocal or instrumental performance practice.
Therefore, a means must be sought to avoid raising the melody one pitch
level, as with tembang *wegang sulanjari* above. But we must keep in mind
that each tuning (*stem[m]ing*) has its own particular characteristics.
Thus, for example, the nyamat tuning has a different character from the
barang tuning, even though the melodic motifs (*motiefé*) may be the same.

For example:

sléndro: . 6   6 1   2   3   . 1   2   1 .6   6

nyamat: . 6   6 1   2   3   . 1   2   1 .6   6

barang: . 6   7 2   . 2   2 .2   7 2   3   23 27   6

In fact, this condition can be considered predetermined by nature—it
is not planned, but built-in. The natural tendency of the fingers in the
playing of rebab also bears out this natural condition. There are only
three possible ways to spread the fingers, as shown in figure 23.

Figure 23.

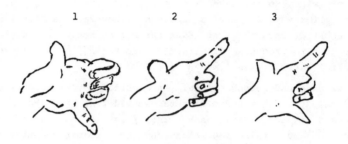

This way is impossible:

Both nyamat and barang utilize fingering (2) above; however, the stopping
of the string (*pathetane*) is different.

nyamat: . 6 6 1 2 3 . 1 2 1 .6 6
           a a b c d   b c b a a

barang: . 6 7 2 . 2 2 .2 7 2 3 23 27 6
           a a b   b b b a b c bc ba a

    My remarks above on vocal music merely relate what is already
evident--that is, they are not fabricated. Therefore, in accord with vocal
music, sléndro sanga has pélog nem with manyura treatment as its
counterpart. For, the dhong of sléndro sanga is pitch 5, while the dhong
of pélog nem (bem) is pitch 6--thus, it has been transposed up one pitch
level.

    As for sléndro pathet nem, the dhong of which is pitch 2, when
transposed to pélog the dhong tone must become pitch 1, thereby involving a
transposition *down* one pitch level. This would then be called "pathet

lima," and thus the counterpart of sléndro pathet nem is pélog pathet lima.
Is this not exceptional? The fact is that sléndro pathet nem is
exceptional in another respect--its range (*ambitus*). For, the range of
pathet sanga and pathet manyura (considered from low to high) is one
gembyang plus one kempyung, whereas that of pathet nem is one kempyung plus
one gembyang. This is illustrated in the diagram below.

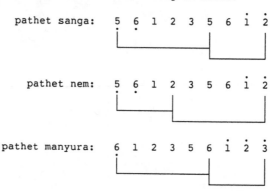

Note that the tones above and below the indicated ranges [thus, above
3 or below 5] are not included in vocal music, but are only utilized as
passing tones (*lintasan*). That is why our grandfathers, when confronted
with gendhing with seleh on pitches 2 or 3 (*gulu gedhé* and *dhadha gedhé*,
respectively), insisted that such seleh should not be treated vocally.
They reasoned that to sing those tones would be unpleasant because "such
[low] sounds are not natural [for the human voice]" (*wis dudu swarané
dhéwé*).

So, to be consistent, if pathet manyura were transposed to pélog, the
procedure should be the same as for pathet sanga--that the dhong tone 6 in
manyura be raised to pitch 7 in pélog. However, in view of the fact that a
dhong tone 7 requires a pitch ♯--which does not exist on gamelan or in
notation--dhong 6 in sléndro pathet manyura is merely transferred directly
as dhong 6 in pélog.

APPENDIX II

This appendix is in the form of notes concerning modulation between modes.

1. Mode I can only be transposed; it cannot modulate to another mode. If a gendhing in this mode modulates to another mode, the [melodic] patterns (*motiefé*) will be lost.

2. Modes II, III, and IV can be transposed or can modulate without obscuring the melodic patterns of the gendhing.

3. The same explanation as for mode I above holds for mode V.

CREATING OR COMPOSING GENDHING

If I were to count the Javanese gendhing I have composed, including those for which manuscripts are held in the Research Department of the Conservatory in Surakarta, those composed for the Ramayana Ballet at Rara Jonggrang [Candhi Prambanan] and for the Ramayana Festival, and those that are already widely known, the total probably would be no less than one hundred.

Here I would like to relate just what resources (*pawitan*) I drew upon to compose these gendhing, according to my own personal experience. I want to document this here so that succeeding generations (*anak putu*) can make use of this information if they wish to set about composing gendhing.

1. You must be familiar with the proper performance practice on all of the instruments [of the gamelan], so that the gendhing you compose will not have sections that are awkward to play.

2. If the gendhing you compose is to include a vocal part (*gérong*), both the instrumental and the vocal sections must be given equal consideration, so that neither one is overemphasized. In this way, both elements will go well together.

3. You must understand the direction of the melody (*arah nada*), for this is what determines pathet.

4. You must understand which tones can emphasize or de-emphasize the seléh tones, for if this is not understood, the pathet can be altered unwittingly.

5. You must understand the function (*fungsi*) of each of the tones in each pathet, for these are what serve to determine the pathet.

6. You must understand melodic phrasing (*kalimat lagu*), for this serves to determine the form of the gendhing.

7. You must understand the rules of sindhèn [solo singing], for these are closely related to melodic phrasing.

8. You must understand the structures of gendhing in order to avoid any discontinuity in the course of the gendhing.

9. You must understand the features of melody, since these will determine the character of the gendhing—whether dignified, pitiful, gay, excited, lively, etc.

10. You must understand the cèngkok mati [fixed cèngkok] so that in either pélog or sléndro you can avoid an awkward balungan.

11. You must understand lagu mati [fixed melodies] because they serve to determine the basic irama of the gendhing.

12. You must be able to change the density of the balungan (*lakuning balungan*)—for instance from balungan mlaku to balungan nibani, or to balungan ngadhal, and back again—so that the atmosphere of the gendhing can be manipulated.

13. You must understand the natural embat (*embat alam* [natural intervallic structure]) of each mode or tuning, so as not to cause the vocalists and the rebab player to play out of tune.

14. You must understand mode and tuning, for this will help the performers.

15. Finally, you must know how to transpose a gendhing in sléndro to pélog and vice versa. Below is a scheme for doing so.

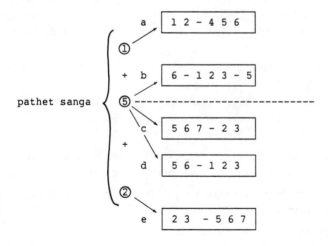

Explanation of the Above Scheme

Pathet sanga has its dhong tone on pitch 5. If a gendhing with sèlèh on pitches 5 and 1, and a dhong tone on pitch 1, is to be transposed to pélog, then the resultant mode will be 1 2 4 5 6 , or any pitches with the contour • • • • • . This is referred to as the barang tuning. The possibilities of the barang tuning are as follows.

       1 2   4 5 6
       2 3   5 6 7
       6 7   2 3 4
       5 6   1 2 3

If, however, a gendhing [with sèlèh on pitches 5 and 1, but] with a dhong tone on pitch 5, is to be transposed to pélog, the resultant mode will be 6   1 2 3   5 , or any pitches with the contour • • • •   • . This tuning is referred to as pélog nyamat. The possibilities of the nyamat tuning are as follows.

       6   1 2 3   5
       3   5 6 7   2
       2   4 5 6   1
       7   2 3 ǥ   6

If a gendhing in pathet sanga with sèlèh on pitches 5 and 2 [and a dhong tone on pitch 5] is transposed to pélog, the resultant mode will be 5 6 7   2 3 , or any pitches with the contour • • • • • . This tuning is referred to as pélog bem. The possibilities of the bem tuning are as follows.

       5 6 7   2 3
       2 3 ǥ   6 7
       4 5 6   1 2
       1 2 3   5 6

Pélog bem tuning can also be written as 5 6   1 2 3 , or any pitches with the contour • • • • • . The possibilities of this tuning are as follows.

       5 6   1 2 3
       2 3   5 6 7
       1 2   4 5 6
       6 7   2 3 ǥ

If, however, a gendhing [with sèlèh on pitches 5 and 2, but] with a
dhong tone on pitch 2, is transposed to pélog, then the resultant mode will
be 2 3   5 6 7 , or any pitches with the contour • •   • • • . This
tuning is referred to as pélog barang tuning (see the barang tuning,
above).

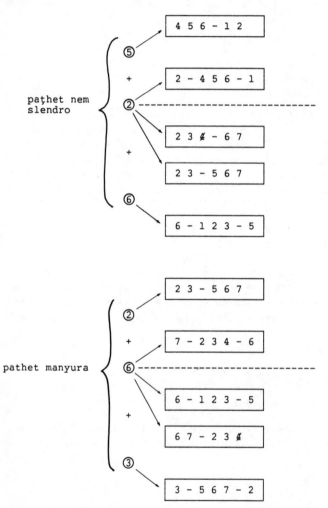

As for the two diagrams above [concerning transposition from sléndro
pathet nem and sléndro pathet manyura to pélog], it shall suffice to refer
[analogously] to the preceding diagram for pathet sanga.

APPENDIX IV

MINOR

The "minor" [from the Dutch, *minuur*] has been used in karawitan circles for some time, though it is difficult to know just for how long. The term clearly derives from the terminology of Western music. Javanese musicians do not understand its original meaning, but the term is used for, or taken to mean, a deviating (*miring*) tone or laras. Since laras sléndro is considered to have a "straight" (*jejeg*), or regular, sequence of intervals [i.e., more or less equal], sléndro is thus the only laras that can have miring tones.

There are three kinds of minor in sléndro.

	dhong	dhèng	dhung	dhang	dhing
regular sléndro:	●	●	●	●	●
minor no. 1:	●	●	●	●	●
	o	è	u	a	i

In minor number 1, the tones dhèng, dhang, and dhing are altered by deviating downward. But in this variety of minor, the dhong (tonic) tone itself changes. What was previously dhung now becomes dhong; if this contour is transposed to pélog, the result will be:

o è u a i o

A sequence of intervals (*sruti*) such as this is very close to what is called "*degung*" in Sunda [West Java].

	dhong	dhèng	dhung	dhang	dhing
regular sléndro:	●	●	●	●	●
minor no. 2:	●	●	●	●	●
	o	è	u	a	i

In minor number 2, the tones dhèng and dhang are altered by deviating downward, but the dhong (*toonica*) is not altered. If this contour is transposed to pélog, the result will be:

        o   è   u   a   i   o

A sequence of intervals such as this is approximately the same as what is called "*penangis*" in Sunda. (I am not positive about this matter; I have merely borrowed this term to differentiate the two types.)

	dhong	dhèng	dhung	dhang	dhing
regular sléndro:	•	•	╱•	•	╱•
minor no. 3:	•	•	•╱	•	•╱
	o	è	u	a	i

In minor number 3, the tones dhung and dhing are altered by deviating downward, while the dhong (tonic) does not change. However, a sequence of intervals such as this is not found in pélog, and therefore is untransposable to pélog. If a transposition to pélog is forced, the result will be [a kind of] degung that can only be realized on the rebab or in singing. In that case, the embat in laras pélog will be the same as that for 3 2 1 , but pitch 2 (gulu) will be the same pitch 2 used in 3 2 7 , that is, slightly higher than the pitch 2 that goes to pitch 1 in pélog. This sequence of intervals is approximately similar to the tuning known in Sunda as "*madenda*." In Central Java in general, and in Solo in particular, this form of minor (*madenda*) is never used in instrumental music. I am acquainted with its usage in the following vocal music.

1. It is used in the melody for the tembang macapat *asmarandana*.

2. It is used in the melody for a lullaby and for the children's song, *Brambang Bawang*.

These three melodies are provided below.

tembang *asmarandana* (dhong 6)

```
0  6   1  2   3  3   3  3   3
   ·
A- ja  tu- ru so- ré ka- ki,
```

```
.  3   6  1   2  1   6   3   3
   a - na Dé-wa nganglang Ja-gad,
```

```
.  2   1  2   3  2   1  6   1
   nyang-king bokor  kenca- na- né,
```

```
1   2  3   3  3   3  3   3
i - si-né  do-nga te-tu-lak
```

```
1  1   1  1   1  6   6
san-dhang ka-la- wan pa-ngan,
```

```
.  6   1  1   1  1   1  2   1
   ya  i- ku  ba-gé- yan-i- pun,
```

```
.  6   6  6   6  1   2  1   6
   wong me-lèk sa-bar na-ri- ma
```

The melody for the lullaby

```
0   0   6   1   1   2 3  2 1  2 1   1
    ·
    La - lé - la  lé - la  lé -  dhung,
```

```
.   .  3  3   3   2   1   6   2 1   6
    a- ngem- ban  a - nak- ku  kun -  cung,
```

```
.   .  3  6   1   1   2 3  2 1  2 1   1
    O- ra   tu - ru  nja - luk  a  -  pa,
```

```
.   .  3  3   3   2   1   6   2 1   6
    nja-luk  i - wak  ka - ro  se  -  ga
```

The melody for *Brambang Bawang*

```
0   0   6̄  1̄   1   2̄ ‾3   2̄ ‾1   2̄ ‾1   1
            •
        Kang ka-kang nggu -  yang    ja  - ran,

 .   3̄ ‾3   3̄  2̄ ‾2   1̄ ‾1   6̄ ‾6   2̄ ‾1   6
        ngri-ku wa- u  won-ten po- pok be- ruk kè- li,
                              •                 •

 .   .   6̄ ‾1   1   2̄ ‾2   6   2̄ ‾1   1
        po- pok- è  lu- rik  glondhong - an,
                   •        •

 .   .   3̄ ‾3   2   1   6   2̄ ‾1   6
        be- ruk-è  kir- u-  kir - an.
                •      •          •
```

[The translation of the lyrics to tembang *asmarandana* is as follows.]

    Don't sleep in the evening, son.

    There is a god wandering about the world

    carrying a golden bowl

    that contains prayers to prevent evil,

    food and clothing.

    Those are the gifts for

    those who stay awake, patient and receptive.

[The translation of the lyrics for the lullaby is as follows.]

    Laléla léla lédhung,

    Carrying my child with his shaven head,

    Who refuses to sleep but asks for something,

    He asks for meat with rice.

[The translation of the lyrics for *Brambang Bawang* is as follows.]

    Brother, older brother bathes the horse,

    Just now a long cloth and a coconut shell were washed away.

    The cloth was striped,

    The coconut shell carved.

I stated above that minor number 3 (madenda) is never used in Central
Javanese instrumental music, while both minor number 1 (degung) and minor
number 1 (penangis) are used. However, the latter are mixed together to
become one tuning. As an example of this, please note *Ada-ada hasta
kuswala*, sléndro pathet sanga, below.

```
5   5   5   5   5   5   5
Men-thang gen-dhé- wa  di-bya,

5   6̲1̲  i   i   i   i   2̲3̲  i
bin-ta - la  ri- nuk-mi  ga - dhing,

6̲   5   5   5   5   5   3̲5̲
ka- ya  ka- yu  ke- mu- ning,

3   3   3   3   3   3   3   3̲5̲ . 3̲2̲1̲
prap-tèng ja- ja  su- ra  ra - ra,
```

If this notation were written in pélog bem it would appear as below.

```
5   5   5   5   5   5   5
Men-thang gen-dhé- wa  di-bya,

5   6̲1̲  i   i   i   i   2̲3̲  i
bin-ta - la  ri- nuk-mi  ga - dhing,

6   5   5   5   5   5   4̲5̲
ka- ya  ka- yu  ke- mu- ning,

4   4   4   4   4   4   4   4̲5̲ . 3̲2̲1̲
prap-tèng ja- ja  su- ra  ra - ra,
```

If this notation is used, the pathet is clearly lima. The tones used are:

```
o   è   u       a   i
1   2   3       5   6
            4   5   6       1   2
            i   o   è       u   a
```

When unified, they become:

$$1 \quad 2 \quad 3 \quad\quad 4 \quad 5 \quad 6 \quad = \quad 4 \quad 5 \quad 6 \quad\quad 1 \quad 2 \quad 3^{*}$$

Thus, if a theory of pathet lima cannot be derived from a study of performance practice (*garap*), it may very well derive from a combination of the sléndro minor tunings, degung and penangis. If this is the case, then it is not surprising that differences of opinion would arise concerning the dhong (tonic) tone in pathet lima. There are those who hold that the dhong tone is 1 (panunggul), and others who maintain that it is 5 (lima).

In addition to the minor sequences of intervals mentioned above, there is yet another called *tlutur*. This is a form of the degung minor sequence but with continuous modulation. That is, the placement of the dhong tone (tonic) is variable; this also implies that the minor (miring) notes will differ according [to the placement of the dhong tone]. An example is Sendhon *Tlutur*, sléndro pathet sanga, below.

```
 .  1   1  1   1  1̄6̱   5   3————————5
    rah- nya ma - ra-ta -  ni- a /[umpak]
                    c
```

Explanation

a = •   / / •   •   /   =   dhong 1 (panunggul)
    •   • • •   •   •
    1   2 3   5   6

b = / / •   •   /   •   =   dhong 6 (nem)
   •   • •   •   •   •
    1 2   3   5   6

c = a

The umpak is sléndro pathet sanga [that is, with no miring tones].

APPENDIX V

BARANG MIRING

Sometimes minor is also called "laras *barang miring*" in Central Java. This name raises several questions.

1. What is "barang miring"?

2. Is it pitch barang [pitch 1 sléndro] that is considered "*miring*" [deviating]?

3. Is there an object (*barang*) that is *miring* [deviating]?

These questions have never received a firm and satisfying answer, but the designation of "barang miring" for "minor" is used continually.

Children, here is an explanation of why minor is called "barang miring." "Barang" means the barang tuning (or fingering) and "miring" means "not yet clear" (not yet fixed). The meaning of "miring" is demonstrated by the following.

Father: Son, I asked you to ask your uncle whether or not he is going. What did he say?

Son: He said, if he can borrow a vehicle, he will go--otherwise, he won't.

Father: Well, in that case it is still "miring" [unclear].

In the example above, it is clear that "miring" means "not yet clear/not yet definite." This is also the case with "barang miring," that is, "a *barang* that is not yet clear/a barang tuning system that is not yet definite."

Which barang tuning system is not yet clear? My explanation is as follows. Central Javanese minor must use the barang tuning, or fingering:

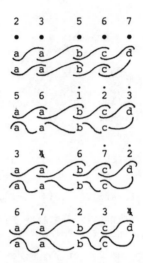

In the gamelan sekatèn repertory there is a gendhing Ladrang *Barang Miring*. This gendhing is always the first played in pathet barang. The notation for this gendhing is as follows.

```
                        N                    N
[ 6 7 6 5    7 6 5 3    6 5 3 5    6 5 3 2

                        N                    G
    5 3 2 3    5 3 5 6    3 5 6 5    3 5 6 7 ]

                                             G
                        [to] ngelik:   3 2 3 5


    ngelik
                        N                    N
[ 3 6 5 6    5 6 5 3    5 6 5 6    3 5 3 2

                        N                    G
    5 3 2 3    5 3 5 6    3 5 6 5    3 2 3 5 ]

                                             G
                                   3 5 6 7 ]
```

According to the notation, this gendhing is, in fact, wholly in laras/
pathet barang, and wholly in the barang tuning (*steming*) as well, since the
finger positions do not change.

```
2   3       5   6   7
a   a       b   c   d
```

However, you must understand that when the embat and the frequencies
of the pitches on the gamelan sekatèn are compared to those of other
gamelan, the intervals of the sekatèn gamelan fall somewhere in the
middle.[8]

```
            ┌─────────────────────────────────┐
            │      gamelan sekatèn tuning      │
            │   1   2   3   4   5   6   7      │
┌───────────────────────────────┼──────────────────────────────────┐
│ ordinary gamelan tuning [a]    │ ordinary gamelan tuning [b]      │
│  1   2   3   4   5   6   7      │ 1   2   3   4   5   6   7        │
└───────────────────────────────┼──────────────────────────────────┘
                              ┌──┴───────────────────────────────────┐
                              │ ordinary gamelan tuning [c]          │
                              │ 1   2   3   4   5   6   7            │
                              └──────────────────────────────────────┘
```

Thus, if Ladrang *Barang Miring* were transposed according to its embat [on
the sekatèn instruments] onto an ordinary pélog gamelan, the notation would
appear as follows.

```
                              N
2   3   2   1   3   2   1   6
                             .
                              N
2   1   6   1   2   1   6   5
        .           .      .
                              N
1   6   5   6   1   6   1   2
    .   .   .       .
                              G
6   1   2   1   6   1   2   3
.                   .
```

Even when notated this way, the tuning (*steming* [i.e., rebab fingering])
will still be the barang tuning; the result will be the barang tuning in a
bem embat. It is from this that barang miring got its name, for it refers
to a "barang (tuning) that is not yet clear."

THE END

Marsudiya kawruh jroning gendhing,
taberiya ngrasakké irama,
pangolahé lan garapé,
ngrasakna wosing lagu
witing pathet saka ing ngendi,
ing kono golèkana,
surasaning lagu
rarasen nganti kajiwa,
karya padhang narawang nora mblerengi,
tatas nembus Bawana.[9]

[Strive to understand the wisdom contained in gendhing,
be diligent in feeling its irama,
its development and treatment;
feel the essence of the lagu,
know where lies the origin of pathet,
seek there
the meaning of lagu,
feel it until your soul
is made clear, bright, and your view unclouded--
a clarity that penetrates the universe.]

Surakarta, 1 August 1970,
28 Jumadilawal 1902
Martopangrawit

1. The "second military action" (*clas II* 'second clash', in the
   author's Javanese, and often referred to in history books as the
   second "police action"), refers to the military attack launched on
   the new Republic of Indonesia by Dutch forces on December 18, 1948,
   in abrogation of the Renville truce of January of that year. (See
   Kahin 1952:332ff.; Dahm 1971:139ff.; Ricklefs 1981:213-14, 218-19.)

2. The *Serat Centhini* is described by Pigeaud (1967[1]:228) as a
   "wandering students' romance." He goes on to say:

   > A very elaborate text was composed in the first decades of the
   > nineteenth century in Surakarta by the court-scholars
   > Yasadipura II and Rangga Sutrasna, under the auspices of the
   > Crown Prince, later King Paku Buwana V. . . . Information of
   > all kinds on things Javanese, topography, art, music, magic,
   > divination, and erotics, but also religious speculation and
   > mysticism, was collected by order of the Royal patron to be
   > incorporated in the book. (Pigeaud 1967[1]:229)

   The complete *Centhini* consists of twelve manuscript volumes and
   contains 772 cantos (Soebardi 1971:331). The first four of these
   volumes are in fact a separate romance, the *Serat Cabolang*, that
   according to Pigeaud (1967[1]:228) became attached to the *Serat
   Centhini* some time in the nineteenth century.

   > Volumes V through IX [were] copied down in gold ink during the
   > reign of Paku Buwana VII (1830-1858) and provided with a new
   > introductory canto [dated] 1846. . . . [These five volumes]
   > were then divided into eight volumes . . . and presented as a
   > gift from the court of Surakarta to the Leiden University
   > Library. (Soebardi 1971:331n)

   This is the source of the published version in romanization,
   published in Batavia in 1912 (*Serat Tjentini* 1912).

   Based upon the detailed index and description of contents of
   several manuscript versions of the complete *Centhini* compiled by
   Pigeaud (1933), we can infer that the excerpts cited here by

Martopangrawit, from his brother Jayamlaya's notes, are taken from
volume 2 (hence, from the as yet unpublished *Serat Cabolang*), canto
112, in the *mijil* meter.

3. See note 2, above, as regards authorship and dating of *Serat
   Centhini*.

4. The list of gendhing in the quoted excerpt from the *Centhini* would
   seem to require Gendhing *Sunggèng* here, not Gendhing *Lungkèh*.

5. The list of gendhing in the *Centhini* excerpt includes Gendhing
   "*Semiring*," and not "*Sumirang*." The following comment in the
   "Notes" column, however, refers to gendhing "*Semiring*," so
   "*Sumirang*" is probably a typographical error.

6. On the genesis and development of wayang madya, see also Pigeaud
   1967[1]:247-50, and Drewes 1974:199-215.

7. This excerpt appears in *Serat Tjentini* (1912[8]:202), as canto 276,
   verse 25. The fifth line reads, "tibaning nem deming kendang," but
   Jayamlaya's reading, ". . . beming kendhang," would seem to make
   better musical sense.

8. In the drawing that appears in the original at this point, the
   individual tunings are not clearly marked, so the translator has
   taken the liberty of labeling each one. The translator understands
   the author's meaning to be that the tuning (or embat--since we are
   not speaking here of absolute pitch) of the gamelan sekatèn
   ensemble does not correspond to the embat of most ordinary gamelan
   (*gamelan umum*), but lies about a fifth higher in terms of embat.
   The absolute pitch of the four gamelan sekatèn in Yogya and Solo
   would seem to be somewhat lower than the pitch of the average
   gamelan (see Wasisto Suryodiningrat et al. 1969: table 6). Three
   possible "ordinary gamelan" tunings are provided in the diagram;
   the translator has marked these "a," "b," and "c." In the
   transposed notation of Ladrang *Barang Miring* below the diagram, the
   author refers to a transposition to tuning "b."

9. The first syllable of each line in this verse together make up an
   acrostic that reads "Martapang[ng]rawit ing Surakarta"
   ('Martopangrawit of Surakarta'). The practice of hiding the
   author's identity and other pertinent information about the writing
   of the text is very common in Javanese traditional literature; the
   practice is known as "*sandi asma*" ('concealed name'). For another
   translation of this verse, see Lindsay 1979:39-40.

INNER MELODY IN JAVANESE GAMELAN

Sumarsam

Middletown, Connecticut

Wesleyan University

1975

To

Maeny

in appreciation of our
married life together
and our collaboration
in the arts

and to

Tistha
and
Dwi

CONTENTS

CHAPTER I

SARON MELODY, BALUNGAN, AND NUCLEAR THEME

Theorists have long assumed that the melody in Javanese gamelan is contained in the *saron* melody.[1] This melody was first described by foreign analysts of gamelan as the nuclear theme or "cantus firmus" of the *gendhing*, or gamelan composition (Kunst 1973[1]:167, 247). Mantle Hood, in *The Nuclear Theme as a Determinant of Patet in Javanese Music*, accepted this idea. According to Hood, the nuclear theme, or principal melody, was the core of a gamelan composition. This core was used as a basis for elaboration by instruments such as rebab, gendèr, gambang, bonang, and celempung (Hood 1954:3). He noted, ". . . the nuclear theme and the instruments entrusted with this principal melody were the most important elements of the gamelan--elements which could provide a clue to the order and logic of Javanese musical expression" (1954:17). Hood and Susilo later used another term ("fixed melody") persistently, although it is similar in meaning to "nuclear theme." "The fixed melody, within the framework of musical form, mode, and tuning system, provides the melodic basis for orchestral improvisation" (Hood and Susilo 1964:15).

The terms "nuclear theme," "cantus firmus," "principal melody," and "fixed melody" represent Kunst's and Hood's interpretations of the Javanese terms "*balunganing gendhing*," or "*balungan*" (Kunst 1973[1]:167, 247; Hood 1954:9). But, in his recent work, Hood refers to balungan as an abstraction of the saron melody (fixed melody) which is played by bonang panembung or slenthem (1973:17).[2]

Similar concepts of melody in Javanese gamelan have also been proposed by Javanese theorists. Ki Sindoesawarno groups the gamelan instruments according to two functions: (1) the instruments that carry the melody; and

---

1. The saron melody is the melody played by the saron barung, demung, and slenthem.

2. This practice is commonly followed in Yogyanese gamelan style. Hood (1971:238) has questioned the validity of Kunst's term, "cantus firmus," as a description of saron melody.

(2) the instruments that carry the irama.[3] The first group is subdivided
into the instruments that carry the melody of the balungan and the
instruments that fill in the balungan with *kembangan* or ornamentation
(Sindoesawarno 1955:2). Although Sindoesawarno did not state clearly
whether balungan is equivalent to the saron melody, the concept of balungan
being ornamented by other instruments is similar to the concept of a
nuclear theme being elaborated by elaborating instruments. R. L. [Raden
Lurah] Martopangrawit has written that "saron barung, demung, and slenthem
perform the pattern of the melody called balungan" (1972[1a]:11). However,
in an interview during the summer of 1974, he told me that the members of
the saron group perform balungan within the melodic range of an individual
instrument. In other words, balungan is not equivalent to the saron
melody. We will return to this point in the next chapter.

   Actually, the concept of melody in Javanese gamelan encompasses the
relationships between the musicians' conception of the melodic motion of
the gendhing and the melodic patterns of each of the instruments. From
these two elements, we will find the melody as conceived by the musicians
themselves. This is indeed an involved problem, for we cannot easily
determine what musicians feel is the melody of a gendhing, since there are
different limitations in the melodic ranges of the gamelan instruments (see
figures 1 and 2). We must analyze the effect of these limitations, the
performance techniques of individual instruments, and the melodic ideas of
the musicians in order to understand more fully the role of melody in the
gamelan. The influence of these factors in the definition of gamelan
melody has not yet been studied in depth. It is precisely because of
theorists' failure to take into account the above factors that in
attempting to define *balungan* they have equated it with the saron melody.
In some cases, the melody of the saron moves in the opposite direction from
the melody of the other instruments, as in figure 3.

---

   3. Irama refers to the stretching or compressing of tempo and the
length of the melodic phrases. There are five irama: *lancar*, *tanggung*,
dadi, *wilet*, and *rangkep*.

Figure 1. Range and Pitch Level of Instruments and Vocalists in Sléndro
Tuning

	I		II					III					IV					V					VI					VII	
Octaves / Tones	5	6	1	2	3	5	6	1	2	3	5	6	1	2	3	5	6	1	2	3	5	6	1	2	3	5	6	1	2
Rebab								0	o	o	0	0	o	o	o	o	o	o	o	o	o								
Gendèr barung							●	o	o	o	o	o	o	o	o	o	o	o	o	o									
Gendèr panerus										●	o	o	o	o	o	o	o	o	o	o	o	o	o						
Gambang							●	o	o	o	o	o	o	o	o	o	o	o	o	o	o	o	o	o	o	o	●		
Celempung								o	o	o	o	o	o	o	o	o	o	o	o	o									
Bonang barung												●	o	o	o	o	o	o	o	o	o	o	●						
Bonang panerus																	●	o	o	o	o	o	o	o	o	o	o	●	
Suling													o	o	o	o	o	o	o	o	o	o	o	o	o	o			
Slenthem				●	o	o	o	o	o	o																			
Demung										●	o	o	o	o	o	o	o												
Saron barung												●	o	o	o	o	o	o	o										
Saron panerus																	●	o	o	o	o	o	o	o					
Kethuk kempyang										o						o													
Engkuk kemong																o	o												
Kenong										o	o	o	o	o															
Kempul			●	o	o	o	●																						
Gong suwukan			●	o																									
Gong ageng	o	o																											
Pesindhèn								o	o	o	o	o	o	o	o	o	o	o	o	o									
Penggérong				o	o	o	o	o	o	o	o	o	o	o	o														

Note: o = tones of the instruments and vocalists.
      0 = rebab tuning.
      ● = tones which might be absent from the instruments.

Figure 2. Range and Pitch Level of Instruments and Vocalists in Pélog
Tuning

Octaves	I	II	III	IV	V	VI
Tones	5 6 7	1 2 3 4 5 6 7	1 2 3 4 5 6 7	1 2 3 4 5 6 7	1 2 3 4 5 6 7	1 2 3 4 5 6 7
Rebab			0 0 0 0 0 0 0	0 0 0 0 0 0 0	0 0 0 0	
Gendèr barung bem		● o o o o o o	o o o o o	o o o o	o o	
Gendèr barung barang		● o o o o o o	o o o o o	o o o o o	o o	
Gendèr panerus bem			● o o o o o	o o o o o	o o o o	o o o
Gendèr panerus barang			● o o o o o o	o o o o o	o o o o o	o o
Gambang bem		● o o o o o	o o o o o	o o o o o	o o o o	o o o
Gambang barang		● o o o o o o	o o o o o	o o o o o	o o o o o	o o
Celempung bem		o o o o o	o o o o o	o o o o o	o o	
Celempung barang		o o o o o	o o o o o	o o o		
Bonang barung			o o o o o o o	o o o o o o o		
Bonang panerus				o o o o o o o	o o o o o o o	o o o o o o o
Suling			o o o o o o	o o o o o o	o o o o o o	o o o o
Slenthem		o o o o o o o				
Demung			o o o o o o o			
Saron barung				o o o o o o o		
Saron panerus					o o o o o o o	o o o o o o o
Kethuk kempyang			o		o	
Kenong				o o o o o o o		
Kempul		o o o o o o				
Gong suwukan	● ● o					
Gong ageng	o ●					
Pesindhèn			o o o o o o o	o o o o o o o	o o o o o	
Penggêrong		o o o o o o o	o o o o o o o	o o o o		

Note: o = tones of the instruments and vocalists.
0 = rebab tuning (pathet lima 1-5, pathet nem and barang 2-6).
● = tones which might be absent from the instruments.

Figure 3. Excerpt from Lancaran *Tropong Bang*, laras pélog nem

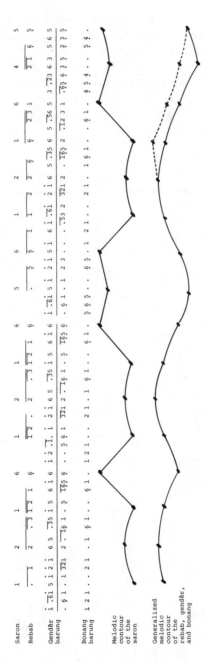

Saron

Rebab

Gendèr barung

Bonang barung

Melodic contour of the saron

Generalized melodic contour of the rebab, gendèr, and bonang

Note: In present-day Java, cipher notation is commonly used as a teaching device and for analyses. In sléndro the arrangement of tones is notated as follows: barang="1", gulu="2", dhadha="3", lima="5", nem="6". In pélog: penunggul="1", gulu="2", dhadha="3", pélog="4", lima="5", nem="6",barang="7". A dot in the place of a number indicates a rest. A dot above a number indicates the upper octave; below a number, the lower octave. A dash above a number, or numbers, indicates a fractional duration of the notes. In the gendèr notation, tones above the line indicate tones played by the right hand; tones below the line indicate tones played by the left hand.

[The following table (figure 4) is a comparative analysis of the saron part in the excerpt from Lancaran *Tropong Bang* (1216 1216 5612 1645 ; see figure 3) and the underlying idea of melodic motion in the rebab, gendèr, and bonang parts of the same piece (1216 1216 5612 1645 -- or, alternatively, for the last four notes, 3165 ; see broken line in figure 3). It is the author's contention that the melodic motion, 1216 1216 5612 1645 (or, 1216 1216 5612 3165), represents what Javanese musicians actually feel as the balungan.]

Figure 4.   Analysis of Saron, Rebab, Gender and Bonang Parts in an Excerpt
            from Lancaran *Tropong Bang* (see figure 3)

	Saron Part	Melodic Motion in the Rebab, Gender, and Bonang Parts

1-2 ascending conjunct motion   1-2 ascending conjunct motion

2-1 descending conjunct motion   2-1 descending conjunct motion

1-6 <u>ascending disjunct motion</u>   1-6 <u>descending conjunct motion</u>

6-1 <u>descending disjunct motion</u>   6-1 <u>ascending conjunct motion</u>

1-2 ascending conjunct motion   1-2 ascending conjunct motion

2-1 descending conjunct motion   2-1 descending conjunct motion

1-6 <u>ascending disjunct motion</u>   1-6 <u>descending conjunct motion</u>

6-5 descending conjunct motion   6-5 descending conjunct motion

5-6 ascending conjunct motion   5-6 ascending conjunct motion

6-1 <u>descending disjunct motion</u>   6-1 <u>ascending conjunct motion</u>

1-2 ascending conjunct motion   1-2 ascending conjunct motion

2-1 descending conjunct motion   2-1 descending conjunct motion

                                   (or 2-3 <u>ascending conjunct motion</u>)

1-6 <u>ascending disjunct motion</u>   1-6 <u>descending conjunct motion</u>

                                   (or 3-1 <u>descending conjunct motion</u>)

6-4 descending conjunct motion   6-4 descending conjunct motion

                                   (or 1-6 descending conjunct motion)

4-5 ascending conjunct motion   4-5 ascending conjunct motion

                                   6-5 <u>descending conjunct motion</u>

Note: The underlined portions indicate differences in the melodic motion.

Becker has pointed out that, when a melodic contour such as 1 2 1 6 is
played on the one-octave saron, the contour of the balungan is altered
(Becker, J., 1980:83). During the summer of 1974, the subject of melody in
Javanese gamelan arose in conversation with my colleagues and students at
the *Akademi Seni Karawitan Indonesia* (ASKI) in Surakarta, Java. We agreed
that balungan can be defined as the framework and melodic motion of a
gendhing that is felt by musicians but not necessarily played on the saron.
Because the saron is limited to only six or seven pitches, and because the
range of the melodic motion of the gendhing is often wider than this, the
saron cannot always follow the whole melodic contour of a gendhing. In a
previous article, written in collaboration with Vincent McDermott, I
speculated as to why saron with two or three more keys, to accommodate many
of the standard melodic patterns, have not been built.

> . . . we are not sure we have a thoroughly convincing answer but,
> though we have not polled them, it may be a general rule that
> Javanese musicians hear the downward pattern anyway, even in the
> saron, feeling it pass conjunctly from higher to lower saron, in
> other words that the line may be heard as passing stepwise from
> one instrument to another, ultimately to be swallowed by the gong
> ageng. It is true that sung melodies tend to start high and
> descend to a cadence and that the low sound of the gong is the
> protean element of central Javanese music, the beginning and end
> of pieces, the single most important sound out of which all other
> sounds are said to arise and to which they all descend in return.
> In any case, and without the metaphors, it seems that if a
> passage can be heard as conjunct it will be heard that way
> regardless of instrumental limitations and if it can be played
> conjunctly it will be done so. (McDermott and Sumarsam 1975:237)

We should keep in mind that we are not discounting or disallowing other
sorts of jumps or disjunctions in the melodic line. There are such jumps,
but they differ in character from the jumps executed by the saron melody.

It has been pointed out that balungan is not the same as the nuclear
theme of a gendhing or the saron melody. There are indications that
musicians have an intuitive understanding of the gendhing melody deeper
than balungan. We will discuss this deeper melody in the next chapter.

CHAPTER II

THE RANGE AND MOTION OF GAMELAN MELODY
AND HOW IT IS PLAYED ON THE INSTRUMENTS

It has been mentioned above that, based solely on what each individual instrument plays, it is difficult to determine what musicians feel is the melody of a gendhing. By examining how the musicians play the melody as they interact with each other, we will attempt to determine how it is conceived in their minds. The position taken here is that the musicians' conception of melody is the true and only essence of melody in Javanese gamelan music. Therefore, we have to analyze the playing of each instrument in the context of its melodic motion, melodic range, playing technique, and its position in the ensemble.

Rebab

Let us begin with the rebab, the instrument considered to be the leader of the ensemble. It is a two-stringed bowed lute which sounds bright, light, and clear. The melodic range of the rebab in sléndro tuning is two octaves and two tones, and in pélog tuning, two octaves and three tones. The range of the rebab constitutes the limits of melodic motion in a gendhing. Although all gendhing do not have the same melodic ranges, melodic movement in all gendhing is limited to the range of the rebab and gambang. These two instruments have the widest ranges in the gamelan.

Western musicologists have called the rebab the leader of the gamelan (Hood 1970:151; Kunst 1973[1]:223). Javanese musicians and theorists describe the function of the rebab as *pamurba lagu*, which means "that which has authority over melody" (Martopangrawit 1972[1a]:10). In performance the rebab plays *senggrèngan*, a short melody which indicates the tuning system (*laras*) and *pathet* of the following gendhing, and then an introduction (*buka*) that determines which gendhing the musicians are going to play.[4] However, I am not sure that the playing of senggrèngan and buka

---

4. Gendhing with a buka played by the rebab are sometimes called "*gendhing rebab*." However, not all gendhing are gendhing rebab. There are

by the rebab are the only reasons why the rebab is pamurba lagu.[5] A more substantial explanation for considering the rebab the melodic leader may be that throughout the gendhing the rebab gives direction to the melodic motion. Frequently, the rebab anticipates the notes that will appear in the following line (see figure 5).

But, not only the rebab's function of anticipating the melody suggests its role as melodic leader. The voicelike sound of the rebab, as opposed to the percussive sound of other instruments, makes it more suitable for guiding the melodic motion of the gendhing. It should be pointed out that "vocal characteristic" does not necessarily mean the kind of sound produced by a singer. Here we mean a continuous or smoothly flowing quality of sound such as the rebab melody, which underlies the feeling of the melodic motion of the gendhing.

Despite the importance of the rebab, how much does the rebab as pamurba lagu affect the other musicians? How much do other musicians listen to the rebab in the course of playing a gendhing? Sometimes the rebab cannot be heard clearly, as, for example, in gamelan accompaniment to dance. Usually this occurs because the sounds of soft instruments such as rebab, gendèr, gambang, and celempung are drowned out by the loud, exciting sounds of the dance drumming and interlocking bonang melodies.[6] In *bedhaya* or *serimpi* dance accompaniment, the rebab sound is sometimes covered by the sound of the large, mixed chorus. Furthermore, the rebab can be absent from the ensemble without making it difficult for other musicians to play their instruments. In *gendhing bonang* and *jineman* the rebab is never played. In some small ensembles, such as *cokèkan* and

---

also gendhing that have buka from the gendèr, bonang barung, kendhang, or gambang. When musicians use the terms "gendhing rebab," gendhing gendèr," or "gendhing bonang," they refer to gendhing forms longer than ketuk 2 kerep (a gendhing form determined by the length of the gongan phrases). Ladrang, ketawang, lancaran, ayak-ayakan, srepegan, and sampak are never classified as gendhing rebab, gendèr, or bonang.

  5. R. L. [Radèn Lurah] Martopangrawit adds one more elementary task to the rebab, that of giving the signal to others to move into the ngelik section (1972[1a]:13). Ngelik is the section of a gendhing that begins in the high register.

  6. Sometimes we get the impression from rebab, gendèr, or gambang players that, when accompanying dance, they do not pay too much attention to their playing, as if to say, "Nobody is going to listen anyway."

Figure 5.   Excerpt from Ladrang *Wilujeng*, laras sléndro pathet manyura

```
balungan:  2    1    2    3    2    1    2    6
                                            .

rebab:     ‾    ‾‾   ‾    ‾‾   ‾‾   ‾‾   ‾    ‾‾
           2 3  1 .2 2 3  3 12 1 2  1 .6 2 1  23.
                                        .
                  —> —>     ————————>        —>
                —————>     —>—> —  ————>
```

```
           3    3    .    .    6    5    3    2
           ‾    ‾‾         ‾    ‾    ‾‾   ‾‾   ‾
                          .                
           . 3  56.6 . 6  6 .1  . 3  1 .2 232  3 5
           —>     —>—>—>              —>—>—>
                                              ———>
```

```
           5    6    5    3    2    1    2    6
                                            .
           ‾‾   ‾‾        ‾    ‾‾   ‾‾   ‾‾   ‾‾
           3 56 6    165  5 6  6 2  1 .6 2 1  6
                                            .
           —> —>      —> —> —  ————>
           ———>                    ————————>
```

```
           2    1    2    3    2    1    2    6
           ‾    ‾‾   ‾    ‾‾   ‾‾        ‾‾
                ‾         ‾‾   ‾‾ ‾      ‾‾ ‾
           2 3  1 .2 2 3  5661 6 12 3    121  6
                —>
           ————————>     _____/
```

Note: Arrows indicate how the rebab directs the melodic motion of the gendhing by
        anticipating the tone or tones which will be approached. This rebab direction is
        the direction for the melody of the rebab and for the other instruments or vocalist
        as well. The bracketed portion where the rebab directs the other instruments and
        the pesindhèn (female soloist) to the high register. Arrows indicate the
        following:

                    —> = immediate anticipation
                 ————> = early anticipation
             —>——>——> = continuous anticipation

siteran, the rebab is not present. It is often absent from the village gamelan as well.[7]

All this leads to the conclusion that the rebab does not necessarily lead the melodic motion of the ensemble. Who, then, does direct the melodic motion of the gendhing? Why is the rebab called "pamurba lagu" if it can be absent or cannot at times be heard in the ensemble? In an attempt to answer the first question, let us briefly look at other instruments or vocal parts to see if in any way they might be responsible for guiding the melodic motion of gendhing.

A vocal part could assume leadership because of the similarity between vocal melody and that of the rebab. However, the *pesindhèn* (solo female singer) does not sing continuously. She usually sings towards the end of the melodic phrase (*sindhènan baku*), or sometimes near the beginning of the melodic phrase (*sindhènan isèn-isèn*), as exemplified in figure 6.[8]

Figure 6.

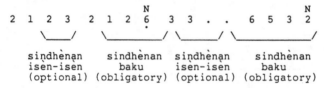

7. One might assume that village gamelan playing is a poor imitation of the palace gamelan style. However, no study has yet been devoted to the relationship between village and palace gamelan style. It might be that village gamelan style is an older form and that they both relate to each other closely.

8. A few compositions are based on the melody of the pesindhèn, for example, Jineman *Uler Kambang*, Jineman *Glathik Glindhing*, and srepegan *rambangan/uran-uran*.

The gérong (male chorus) sings almost continuously during a melodic phrase, but not every gendhing or section of gendhing has gérongan (see figure 7).[9]

Figure 7.

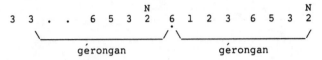

Perhaps the gendèr barung and the bonang barung could be considered melodic leaders. But, unlike the rebab, their sounds are not vocal in character. Their ranges are also not as wide as the rebab's; therefore, they cannot always follow the melodic motion of the gendhing.

Perhaps the gambang could be considered the leader. Its range is as wide as the rebab's. However, the highly percussive melodic line of the gambang makes it unsuitable for guiding the melodic direction of gendhing. Most of the time the gambang plays in fast speed (between MM.320 and MM.240) with *gembyangan* (octave-playing) technique. Embellishments are accomplished by doubling a stroke, changing the rhythm slightly, substituting a *kempyungan* (two notes separated by 2 keys) stroke, or playing two notes separated by six keys. Because of these embellishments, the melodic direction of the gambang is less clear than that of the rebab (see figure 8).

---

9. Sections of some gendhing, such as the ngelik section, may be inspired by the gerongan melody, for example, the ngelik of Ladrang *Wilujeng*, laras slendro pathet manyura, Ketawang *Laras Maya*, laras pelog pathet barang, Ketawang *Suba Kastawa*, laras slendro pathet sanga, and Ketawang *Ibu Pertiwi*, laras pelog pathet nem. R. L. Martopangrawit states that in many of Mangku Negara IV's compositions the ngelik section, which always has a gerongan part, is the basis for identifying the gendhing. This is true of Ketawang *Wala Gita*, laras pelog pathet nem, Ladrang *Ganda Mastuti*, laras pelog pathet nem, Ketawang *Raja Swala*, laras slendro pathet sanga, and Ketawang *Sinom Parijatha*, laras slendro pathet sanga (1972[1a]:24). Some gendhing are inspired by macapat songs, for example, Ketawang *Pucung*, laras slendro pathet manyura, Ketawang *Gambuh*, laras slendro pathet nem, and Ketawang *Mas Kumambang*, laras pelog pathet lima.

Figure 8. A Comparison of the Melodic Contour of the Rebab and the Gambang
gambang: • = MM.320-240

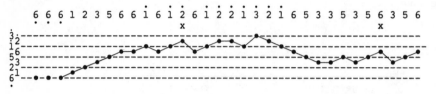

rebab:

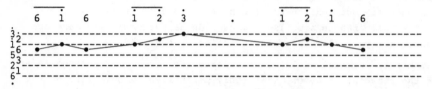

Note: Gambang plays gembyangan (octave-playing) technique. An "x"
        indicates that a right-hand note is doubled, with the following
        right-hand note a rest. Thus,

$$\overline{\overset{\cdot\cdot}{22.}}\ \overset{\cdot}{1}\ \overset{\cdot}{2}$$
$$\overset{\cdot}{2}\ 6\ \overset{\cdot}{1}\ \overset{\cdot}{2}$$

is written "2 6 1 2." Note that the rebab moves more clearly and
directly than the gambang.

It seems that no single instrument or vocal part in the ensemble is
solely responsible for guiding the melodic motion of a gendhing. I believe
the real "authority over melody" is a melodic idea sung in the minds of the
individual musicians. This directs the melodic motion. This melodic
conception could be called "inner melody." Inner melody is the melody that
is sung by musicians in their hearts. Inner melody is the essence of
melody in Javanese gamelan. My gamelan teacher often advised me "golèkana
lan rasakna wosing utawa surasaning lagu," that is, "search for and feel
the essence, or the soul, of a melody."

There is some evidence for the existence of an inner melody
unconsciously sung by musicians. Once, a group playing gamelan at ASKI
forgot a section of a gendhing that we had not played for a long time.
Even the teachers present had difficulty remembering the piece. My bonang
teacher rose and left the room. Sitting down in a corner of the building,
he tried to remember the piece by humming a melody. The melody he hummed

was not the bonang melody, nor was it the melody of any other part; rather, it flowed in the manner of all Javanese vocal music.[10] A friend of mine who is a famous drummer often hums melodies while drumming. And, according to one of my American students, when K. R. T. [Kangjeng Radèn Tumenggung] Wasitodipuro plays examples of gendhing on the gendèr, he frequently hums another melody at the same time.

If inner melody is the essence of gendhing, based on the inner feeling of the musicians, we may say that the range of the gendhing is actually comparable to the range of the musicians' voices. The range of the melodic motion of gendhing in sléndro covers two octaves and two tones.

$$2 \quad 3 \quad 5 \quad 6 \quad 1 \quad 2 \quad 3 \quad 5 \quad 6 \quad \dot{1} \quad \dot{2} \quad \dot{3} \quad \dot{5}$$

The range of the melodic motion of gendhing in pélog covers two octaves and four tones.

$$1 \quad 2 \quad 3 \quad 4 \quad 5 \quad 6 \quad 7 \quad 1 \quad 2 \quad 3 \quad 4 \quad 5 \quad 6 \quad 7 \quad \dot{1} \quad \dot{2} \quad \dot{3} \quad \dot{4} \quad \dot{5}$$

Only the lowest tone in sléndro (2) and the lowest tones in pélog (1 and 2) are below a musician's vocal range. In practice, however, gamelan teachers still express these lowest tones (albeit unclearly), or imitate the rebab part.[11] Use of the lowest tones beyond the vocal range is meant to create a *regu* ('venerable') or *wingit* ('revered') feeling.

---

10. I remember this event clearly since the rehearsal was in preparation for my lecture on Javanese gamelan to the younger generation in Jakarta on March 12, 1971, at Taman Ismail Marzuki. The gendhing was Ladrang *Semang*, laras pelog pathet nem.

11. The rebab in low register plays both strings simultaneously. Musicians will often use a sound such as *engrek*, *ngrek*, or *ngek*, to express the sound of the kempyung interval. In expressing 2, a gamelan teacher will sing 6, or in expressing 1, a gamelan teacher will sing 5. Here, the bowing technique of the rebab is called "*ngecrek*" or "*ngecek*" because the sound of the rebab is like the sound of a cricket. In the example below, the bracketed part is the ngecek bowing.

The range of the rebab is comparable to the range of the melodic
motion of gendhing, and the rebab can imitate the smooth texture of the
voice. Since it is the best-suited of all gamelan instruments to present a
vocal melody, the rebab has an important role in presenting the inner
melody. It provides the proper direction of melodic movement in gendhing
and is therefore regarded as the melodic leader, or pamurba lagu, of the
gamelan. Some gamelan teachers believe the rebab presents the "soul" of
the gendhing, and they call it the *pamurba yatmaka* ('that which has
authority in presenting the soul'). K. R. T. Wasitodipuro gives the
meaning of rebab as *karepé bab* ('the meaning of the contents').[12] It is
not important to debate this etymology since it is generally assumed that
the name "rebab" derives from *rabab*, a bowed lute from Western Asia which
is almost identical in form to the Javanese rebab. However, it is
important to take into account the way a venerable musician presents his
idea that the rebab has the melodically preeminent role in the ensemble.

We can safely say that the rebab melody is similar to the inner melody
of a gendhing, but traditional rebab playing frequently requires
elaboration. It is as if the bright sound of the rebab encourages
musicians to create more elaborate interpretations of the inner melody
(see figure 9).

---

12. Personal communication, October 1975.

Figure 9. A Comparison Between Various Vocal and Instrumental Melodies and the Author's Hypothetical Version of the Inner Melody

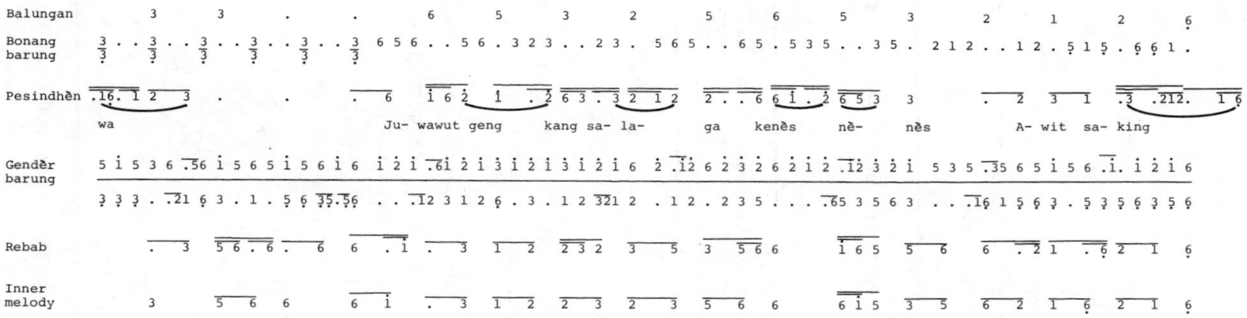

Possibly, in times past, the rebab melody was very close to the inner melody. Through evolution, the established standard patterns of rebab melody found today have emerged. Sometimes the standard patterns of the rebab are indicated by the names of the melodic patterns of other instrumental or vocal parts, for example, the *puthut gelut* pattern and the *ayu kuning* pattern. The puthut gelut pattern of the rebab derives from the name of the gendèr pattern. "Puthut" means 'disciple' and "gelut" means 'fight' or 'joking'. The joking disciple is indicated on the gendèr by the movement of the player's two hands with the *tabuh* (mallets) close to each other. The movement of the two tabuh is like two joking disciples running after one another (see figure 10).

Figure 10.   The Gendèr Pattern *Puthut Gelut* and the Associated Rebab Melody

```
balungan:          .        .        .        3        .        .        .        2

gender     .6.5.6.1.2.1.2.3⌈3.333.3321.1..61 2.232..2.1....61..1..1.6.3...356⌉
  barung:   .23.3.3.2.212163⌊..........6.35.. .1...61.6.6535.3.535635.2.612.2.⌋

rebab:       .    6    1   1̈ 2̈ 6    1    2   1̈ 2̈   2̈ 1̈ 6 3 2    1 6 1    2    2
```

Note: The circled part shows where the movement of the tabuh is like two
        joking disciples, puthut gelut.

The ayu kuning pattern played on the rebab derives from the melodic pattern of the same name sung by the gérong. A text that might be fitted to this gérongan part begins with the words "ayu kuning," and hence the name. "Ayu" means 'pretty', and "kuning" means 'yellow', 'light'. It refers to the image of a beautiful Javanese girl whose skin color is golden or light (see figure 11).[13]

---

13. Usually, the names of the patterns have interesting meanings that relate to the melodies.

Figure 11. The Vocal Pattern *Ayu Kuning* and the Associated Rebab Melody

balungan: 6   i̇   3̇   2̇   6   3   2   1

gérongan: . 6 i̇ 23 3 .5 2 12. 3 126 3   3 532 1
             A- yu   ku - ning   ben-trok   ma - ya

rebab: . 6 i̇ 12 6 i̇ 2 1 2 216563 2 1 1 2   6 1 .

Note: The circled part shows the section from which the name of the
       pattern is derived.

It should be mentioned that rebab patterns are not as standardized as
those of the gendèr. In the modern teaching of gamelan, the rebab teacher
must write out the entire rebab notation of a gendhing, but this is not
necessary for gendèr.

The bowing technique of the rebab has also been standardized. In a
melodic phrase the rebab should play with a particular kind of bowing.
There are ten kinds of bowing techniques (Djumadi 1972:57-63):

1. *mbalung* ('to act like *balungan*'), in which the speed of the bowing
    is the same as the pulses of the balungan;

2. *milah* ('to act like *wilahan*'), in which the rate of the bowing and
    its melody are the same as the pulses and the melody of the
    balungan;

3. *nduduk* ('in a hurry'), in which the rate of bowing is twice as
    fast as regular, or mbalung, bowing (see figure 11);

4. *kosok wangsul* (literally, 'to bow' and 'to return, come back';
    thus, 'bowing back and forth') which indicates back and forth
    bowing with a syncopated rhythm (see figure 12);

5. *sendhal pancing* ('jerk of a fishing pole, as when a fish is caught
    on the hook');

6. *nyela* ('to interrupt'), indicating bowing off the beat;

7. *ngecèk* or *ngecrèk* ('to make a cricketlike sound'), in which both
    strings of the rebab are bowed together (see footnote 11);

8. *ngikik* ('to convulse with laughter'), in which the bow seems to tremble on the strings;

9. *nungkak* ('to kick'), which indicates two extra bowings at the end of a pattern; and

10. *nggandhul* ('to hang'), in which there is a sense of delay or suspense to the bowing.

Figure 12. *Nduduk* Bowing

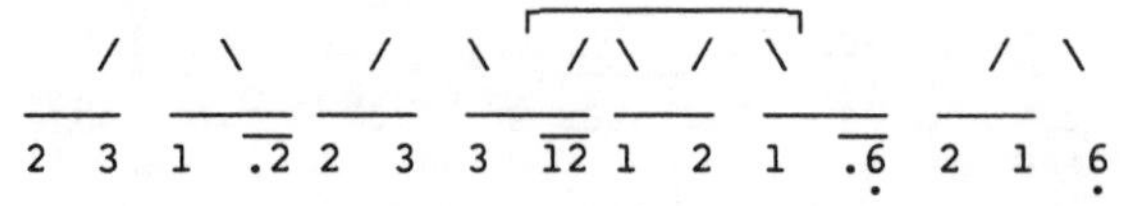

/ = forward bowing, i.e., moving the bow from right to left
\ = backward bowing, i.e., moving the bow from left to right

Figure 13. *Kosok Wangsul* Bowing

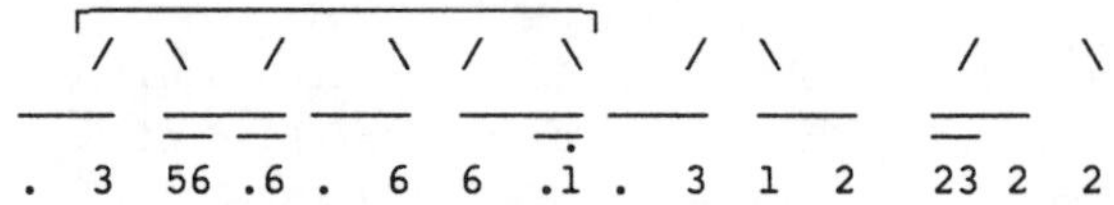

Gendèr Barung

The gendèr barung is a metallophone with bronze keys suspended by cords over tube resonators. It is played with both hands, and has a range of two octaves and two tones. However, because the instrument's range is divided between the player's two hands, melodies played on it only cover a maximum of one octave and three tones.

I believe gendèr playing has evolved over the ages. In my opinion, many different styles of gendèr playing used to exist. Perhaps a gendèr player creating a melody formerly might have followed the inner melody alone. Because the melodic range of the gendèr is only one octave and three tones, the player would coordinate his part with the flow of the inner melody. After years of evolution, gendèr playing style must have emerged with many of the standard patterns agreed upon by most present-day gendèr players.[14] The process of creating these standard patterns is very hard to reconstruct. They may have been created by a well-known gendèr player who passed them on to his students or other gendèr players. The establishment of gendèr patterns involves the determination of the use of gembyang and kempyung, since gembyang and kempyung are sounded at the ends of melodic phrases.

Most gendèr patterns have names. As I have previously stated in an article,

> . . . [the] names [are] based on melodic ideas from the vocal repertoire, gendèr melodic lines, or other technical gamelan terms. Some of these names are: *rujak-rujakan* ('a peppery fruit dish'), *aja ngono* ('don't be like that'), *gendhuk kuning* ('yellow maiden'), and *nduḍuk* ('hurrying'). Traditionally, in teaching gendèr a teacher calls out the céngkok by name to the student. The names have evocative meanings that relate to exciting melodies so they are easily remembered. (Sumarsam 1975:162)

The gendèr player often concentrates on creating a refined melodic flow. However, whenever there is a chance to express the motion of the inner melody, the gendèr player will do so (see figures 13 and 14).

---

14. I have previously discussed this in depth (Sumarsam 1975:161-71, and Sumarsam 1971). See also Martopangrawit 1973.

Figure 14. Excerpt from Gendhing *Damar Keli*, laras sléndro pathet manyura

```
balungan:        .      .      2      3      6      5      3      2
                                ·      ·      ·      ·      ·      ·

rebab:           6      6      6    3  6    6       . 6 6 6 6   6    6
                 ·      ·      ·       ·    ·         2 2 2 2   2    2
                 2      2      2       2    2         · · · ·   ·    ·
                 ·      ·      ·       ·    ·


gender:   1 . 1 ‾61 6 1 2 5 ‾35 2 5 6 5 3 2 ‾12 3 2 ‾23 2 1 ‾61 3 1 ‾23 2
barung:         ·  ·                                      ·
          . 6 ‾53 2 2 2 . . 3 5 . 2 ‾532 3 ‾56 6 . ‾56 1 5 ‾32 3 . ‾53 2 .
            ·  · · · · ·     · ·     ··· ·  ··        ··   ·  ··      ··  ·


balungan:        5      3      2      3      5      6      1      6
                 ·      ·      ·      ·      ·      ·      ·      ·

rebab:           5      3      6    3  ‾1 2 ‾1   2    1    . 6 2  1    6
                 ·      ·      ·       ·                     2         2
                 2                                          ·         ·
                 ·


gender:   5 .35 2 5 6 5 3 2 .12 5 2 .35 3 5 6 5 1 5 6 5 3 5 6 .‾1. 1 2 1 6
barung:   ‾53 5 . 5 ‾165 6 ‾53 5 . ‾65 3 . ‾16 1 ‾65 6 ‾653 . 5 3 5 6 6 6 .
          ·· ·   ·  ·· ·   ·· ·     ·· ·    ·· · ···      ·· · ··  · · · · ·
```

Note: Here the gender player can express both the flow of the inner melody and the refined melodic flow of his own part.

Figure 15. Excerpt from *Ayak-Ayakan*, laras sléndro pathet nem

balungan: 3   2   3   5   2   3   5   3

rebab: 6̄ 1̄ 2   2   2̄ 1̄ 6   2̄ 3̄ .   .   3   3̄ 3̄ 2   3̄ 5̄ 3   3̄ 5̄

gendèr barung: 3 2 3 .̄2̄3̄ 5 3 6 3 5 3 6 3 5 6 5 3 . 2 .̄1̄2 1 2 3 2 .̄3̄2 5 2 .̄3̄5 3
                . . .̄6̄5 6 3 5 2 . 3 2 3 5 5 5 . . 3 .̄6̄5 3 3 3 . .̄5̄3 5 . .̄6̄5 3 .

balungan: 5   2   3   5

rebab: .   3̄ 6̄   5̄ 6̄ 5̄   5

gendèr barung: 5 5 5 5 3 .̄2̄3̄ 6 3 5 3 6 3 .̄5̄6 5
                5 . . . .̄6̄5 6 . . 3 2 3 5 5 5 .

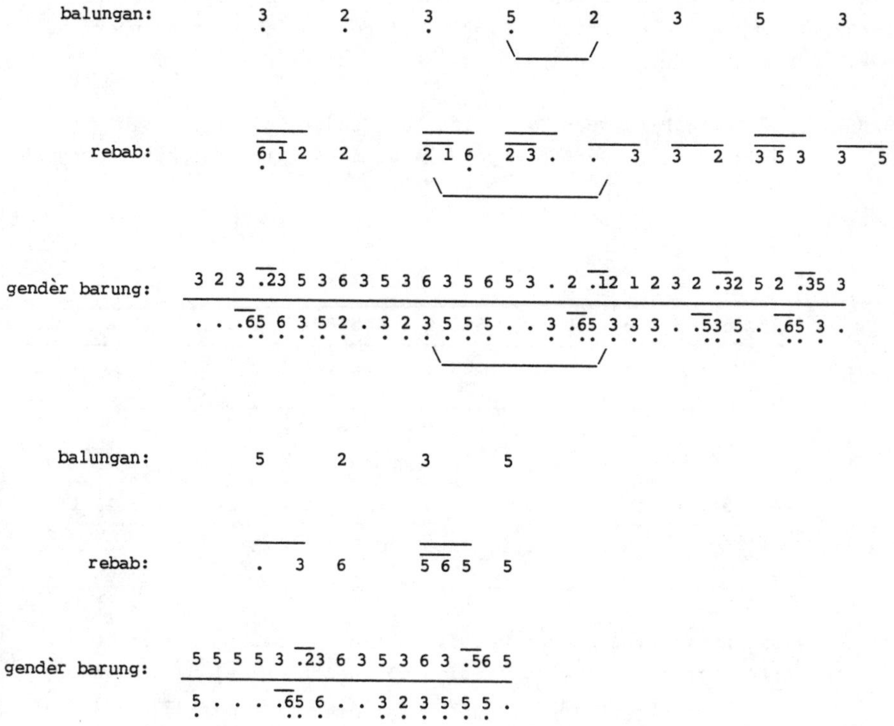

Note: The gendèr player concentrates on a refined melodic flow where he cannot follow
       the motion of the inner melody. The flow of the inner melody at the underlined
       part is ascending, but the gendèr plays conjunct downward motion, concentrating on
       linking melodic patterns.

Sometimes gendèr players may differ on the matter of choosing
realizations which either emphasize smooth connections between gendèr
patterns, or emphasize a strict following of the motion of the inner
melody. For a hypothetical comparison, see figure 16.

Figure 16.   Comparison Between Two Different Gènder Realizations of an
             Excerpt from Ladrang *Mugi Rahayu*, laras slèndro pathet manyura

balungan: 3   5   2   3   6   i   6   5

I.   5 . 6 i 6 .56 i . . 6 i 6 .56 i 6 5 6 2 6 i 6 5 3 .23 6 3 .56 5
gendèr
barung: . 3 . 1 .23 3 . . . . 1 .23 3 . . 2 . 6 1 2 3 1 6 5 6 . 5 6 1 5
            _____ A _____/ _____ B _____/

II.   5 . 6 i 6 .56 i . . 6 i 6 .56 i 6 . 6 . 6 . i 2 i . i 2 .6. i 2
gendèr
barung: . 3 . 1 .23 3 . . . . 1 .23 3 . . 5 . 5 . 5 3 2 . 3 2 3 5 5 3 5
            _____ A _____/ _____ B _____/

Note: In version (I), the gendèr melodic motion in phrase (B) is in the
        opposite direction from the motion of the inner melody. However,
        another gendèr player might play the (B) phrase flowing parallel to
        the motion of the inner melody (version II).

Saron and Balunqan

We shall include four types of instruments in our discussion of the
saron. The slenthem, providing the lowest octave of the saron group, has
bronze keys suspended by cords over tube resonators. The saron demung,
saron barung, and saron panerus (peking) have thick, heavy keys placed on
wooden frames that serve as trough resonators. The slèndro saron normally
consists of six keys, the pélog of seven keys. A saron is played with a
tabuh (mallet).

For the moment, our discussion of saron shall be limited to slenthem,
demung, and saron barung, which very often play the same melody. The saron
panerus will be discussed in the following section because of its idiosyncratic melody in relation to the other saron.

Balungan is an abstraction of the inner melody felt by musicians.   In
general, a saron plays balungan within the limitation of its range; thus,
no one saron plays the full balungan as it is felt or notated.   Musicians
take two factors into account when composing balungan: the direction of the
inner melody and the limitation of the saron range.   However, where these
two factors diverge, the inner melody often takes precedence.   As a result,
there may be places in the balungan where several interpretations are
possible.   The slenthem player may play a slightly different line from that
of the demung or the saron barung player.   However, with the passing of
time, standard balungan have evolved for almost every gendhing, especially,
of course, those for which balungan have been notated.   Musicians find
coordination of the inner melody with the saron range and uniformity in the
saron melody to be aesthetically pleasing.   There are even differences of
opinion among musicians as to what would be the standard balungan for some
sections of gendhing.   These differences arise because one musician may
stress following the range of the inner melody, while another stresses
refining the melody within the one-octave saron range.   Figure 17
illustrates such a case.

Figure 17. Excerpt from Gendhing *Kabor*, laras sléndro pathet nem

Note: In the underlined section, balungan (I) closely follows the motion of the inner
       melody (which is also close to the rebab part). Balungan (II) concentrates on a
       smooth line within the saron range.

We also find parts of gendhing in which the commonly accepted version of the balungan is organized with the aim of refining the melody within the one-octave saron range. In such cases, the balungan motion tends in an opposite direction from the motion of the inner melody. Only at the end of the melodic phrase will the balungan and the inner melody coincide on the same tone, although in different octaves (see figure 18).

Figure 18. Excerpt from Gendhing *Merak Kasimpir*, laras sléndro pathet manyura

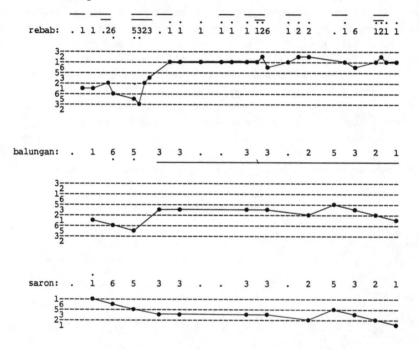

Note: The underlined section shows where the rebab and the balungan move in opposite directions, but at certain points coincide on the same tone.

In gamelan performance, the slenthem player is usually the strongest saron player, the player who knows the pieces best. The demung, and especially the saron barung, are often played by musicians who do not know the pieces very well. They often "hang on to" (*nggandhul*), or "float with" (*ngambang*), the slenthem or bonang barung. By "hanging on to the slenthem"

we mean that they try to follow by listening to the slenthem player or
seeing which key he is about to play. "Hanging" or "floating" also means
that a musician, unfamiliar with or forgetting some sections of a gendhing,
"hangs on to" or "floats with" the melody of other instuments while
figuring out his own part. Sometimes different interpretations of saron
parts among the saron players are resolved by one player adjusting to
another. Usually a younger player will respect seniority by adjusting his
interpretation to that of an older musician.

Basically, there are two kinds of balungan: *balungan mlaku* and
balungan nibani.[15] The latter is the more abstract. Most gendhing are
played in one of these balungan styles.

Figure 19. Balungan Mlaku (Ladrang *Mugi Rahayu*, laras sléndro pathet
manyura)

```
                   N                       N
      3 6 1 .   3 6 1 2   3 6 1 .   3 6 1 2
        .         .         .         .

                   .   N   .               G
      3 5 2 3   6 1 6 5   1 6 5 3   6 1 3 2
                                      .
```

Figure 20. Balungan Nibani (Ladrang *Gonjang Ganjing*, laras sléndro pathet
sanga, Excerpt)

```
                 N                       N
      . 2 . 1  . 6 . 5  . 2 . 5  . 2 . 1
                   .       .

                 N                       G
      . 2 . 1  . 2 . 1  . 2 . 1  . 6 . 5
                                   .   .
```

Another kind of balungan is *balungan rangkep* ('doubled'). The pulse
of balungan rangkep is double, or sometimes quadruple, that of balungan
mlaku and has a variety of rhythmic variations. Balungan rangkep is rarely
used throughout a gendhing, but only in certain sections. Sometimes
balungan rangkep can express the inner melody (see figure 21). There are
some gendhing that combine balungan mlaku and balungan nibani, or balungan

---

15. In balungan mlaku (*mlaku*) 'to walk'), the balungan melody
expresses the abstraction of the inner melody clearly. In balungan nibani
(*nibani* 'to fall upon'), the balungan notes are played only at certain
stressed points, and therefore represent a more abstract realization of the
inner melody.

nibani and balungan rangkep, or balungan mlaku and balungan rangkep, or
balungan mlaku, balungan nibani, and balungan rangkep. Examples are
Ketawang *Puspa Warna*, laras sléndro pathet manyura (combining balungan
nibani and balungan mlaku); Ladrang *Gonjang Sèrèt*, laras sléndro pathet
manyura (combining balungan nibani and balungan rangkep); and Gendhing *Ela-
ela Kali Beber* or Ladrang *Sri Karongron*, laras sléndro pathet sanga
(combining balungan nibani, balungan mlaku, and balungan rangkep; see
figure 22).

Figure 21. Balungan Rangkep (Ladrang *Pakumpulan*, laras sléndro pathet
            sanga, Excerpt)

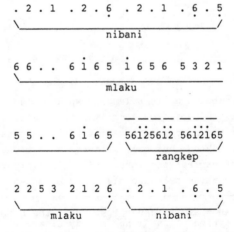

```
                        N                                 N
                       ___ __ ___                        ___
   .   2   .   1   .   5   .   6 2 126 .21265612   .   1   6   55.5

   ___ __ ___                 N                           G
   61.125.561312   .   1   6  5 6 6  . 6 5 3 2 3 5 6 5 2 1 6 5
```

Note: In this excerpt, the underlined part is a balungan rangkep that
       expresses the inner melody.

Figure 22. Excerpt from Ladrang *Sri Karongron*, laras sléndro pathet sanga

```
              . 2 . 1 . 2 . 6 . 2 . 1 . 6 . 5
              _____/
                            nibani

              6 6 . . 6 1 6 5 1 6 5 6 5 3 2 1
              _____
                            mlaku

              5 5 . . 6 1 6 5 56125612 5612165
              _____/ _____/
                                   rangkep

              2 2 5 3 2 1 2 6 . 2 . 1 . 6 . 5
              _____/ _____/
                    mlaku             nibani
```

     The melodic motion of srepegan and gendhing in the lancaran form
(gendhing lancaran) can be discussed in the context of our examination of

balungan. Although these pieces seem to be based on the saron range, their inner melodies are actually greater than the saron range. Especially in irama tanggung or dadi, the inner melody of gendhing lancaran is clearly suggested by other parts such as the rebab, vocal melody, and gambang. Even if a lancaran is played without rebab, vocalist, or gambang, the musicians have in mind the inner melody established earlier when these instruments were played. In any case, saron players are usually proficient performers on the other instruments.

Figure 23. Comparison Between Saron Melody and Balungan (Abstraction of Inner Melody) (Lancaran *Maésa Liwung*, laras sléndro pathet sanga, Excerpts)

```
                                               G
   saron:    . 6 . 5 . 2 . 1 . 2 . 1 . 6 . 5
                          .   .   .   .        G
   balungan:  . 6 . 5 . 2 . 1 . 2 . 1 . 6 . 5
                       ‾‾‾‾‾‾‾‾‾‾‾‾‾‾‾

                                               G
   saron:    . 6 . 5 . 2 . 1 . 2 . 1 . 6 . 5
                          .   .   .   .        G
   balungan:  . 6 . 5 . 2 . 1 . 2 . 1 . 6 . 5
                       ‾‾‾‾‾‾‾‾‾‾‾‾‾‾‾‾

              .                                G
   saron:    . 1 . 6 . 5 . 3 . 2 . 1 . 3 . 2
              .                                G
   balungan:  . 1 . 6 . 5 . 3 . 2 . 1 . 3 . 2

                                               G
   saron:    . 3 . 2 . 3 . 1 . 3 . 1 . 3 . 2
                                               G
   balungan:  . 3 . 2 . 3 . 1 . 3 . 1 . 3 . 2

                                               G
   saron:    . 3 . 2 . 3 . 1 . 3 . 1 . 3 . 2
                                               G
   balungan:  . 3 . 2 . 3 . 1 . 3 . 1 . 3 . 2

                                               G
   saron:    . 5 . 6 . 2 . 1 . 5 . 2 . 3 . 5
                          .   .                G
   balungan:  . 5 . 6 . 2 . 1 . 5 . 2 . 3 . 5
                       ‾‾‾‾‾‾‾‾
```

Note: The underlined portions indicate where the saron melody cannot follow the melodic direction of the balungan.

It is hard to determine whether or not gendhing lancaran are based on the vocal inspiration of inner melody. It is clear that, when lancaran gendhing are played in irama tanggung or dadi, the rebab is the melodic leader, while the gambang and vocalist follow the motion of inner melody. It is also certain that gendhing lancaran, such as *Maésa Liwung*, are composed in a wider range than that of the saron. There are only a few gendhing lancaran composed within the saron range. Examples of such gendhing lancaran are Lancaran *Manyar Sèwu* and Lancaran *Singa Nebah*, laras sléndro pathet manyura.

Usually srepegan is played in irama lancar without the rebab. Each pathet has its own srepegan. Like gendhing lancaran, srepegan is also composed in a greater melodic range than the saron range (see figure 24).

Figure 24. Comparison of the Balungan, Pesindhèn, and Gambang Melodies (*Srepegan*, laras sléndro pathet manyura, Excerpt)

balungan: 3 2 3 2

pesindhèn: . . $\overline{.\ 2}$ 3
Jar-wa

gambang: 2 1 2 3 2 $\underset{\cdot}{6}$ 1 2 2 1 2 3 2 $\underset{\cdot}{6}$ 1 2
x x

balungan: (5 6 $\dot{1}$ 6)

pesindhèn: $\overline{1\ \overline{.\ 3}}$ $\overline{.\ \overline{212}}$ $\overline{.\ 1}$ $\overline{\underset{\cdot}{6}\ \underset{\cdot}{6}}$
pur - wa

gambang: 2 1 3 2 1 $\underset{\cdot}{6}$ $\underset{\cdot}{5}$ $\underset{\cdot}{3}$ $\underset{\cdot}{3}$ $\underset{\cdot}{5}$ $\underset{\cdot}{3}$ $\underset{\cdot}{5}$ $\underset{\cdot}{6}$ $\underset{\cdot}{3}$ $\underset{\cdot}{5}$ $\underset{\cdot}{6}$
x

Note: The circled portion shows where the balungan--because of the limit of the saron range--moves in contrary motion to the inner melody suggested by the gambang and pesindhèn. The melodic movement of each reaches pitch $\underset{\cdot}{6}$, which is beyond the ambitus of the saron. The relatively recent development of saron sléndro with a $\underset{\cdot}{6}$ key does not change the saron melody of *Srepegan*, sléndro pathet manyura.

Looking at the melodies of srepegan and ayak-ayakan, we get the impression that they are related. It seems that srepegan is inspired by, or is an abstraction and modification of, the inner melody of ayak-ayakan.[16] If this is granted, it will explain why the motion of the inner melody of srepegan is greater than the saron range. Figure 25 shows how ayak-ayakan can be abstracted and modified to become srepegan.

Figure 25. *Ayak-ayakan* Compared with *Srepegan*, laras sléndro pathet manyura

```
                N   N     N   N     N   N                   N   G
Ayak-ayakan:  3 5 3 2   3 5 3 2   5 3 2 3 [. . . .  . . . .] 2 1 2 1

                N   N     N   N     N   N     N   N     N   N     N   G
  Srepegan:     3   2     3   2     5   3     5   3     2   3     2   1

                N   N     N   N     N   G     N   N     N   G
Ayak-ayakan:  2 3 2 1   2 3 2 1   3 5 3 2   3 5 3 2   5 3 5 6 [. . . .]

                N   N     N   N     N   N     N   N     N   N     N   G
                                                                  .
  Srepegan:     2   1     2   1     3   2     3   2     5   6     1   6

                N   N     N   N     N   N                   N   G
Ayak-ayakan:  5 3 5 6   5 3 5 6   5 3 2 3 [. . . .  . . . .] 6 5 3 2

                N   N     N   N     N   N     N   N     N   N     N   G
                .         .
  Srepegan:     1   6     1   6     5   3     5   3     6   5     3   2
```

Note: The circled portions indicate where modifications take place. Note also that there is a gong deleted in the second line of *Srepegan* where it would have been expected to occur based on the inner melody of *Ayak-ayakan*.

Saron Panerus (Saron Peking)

Saron panerus playing is based on the balungan. There are two main techniques of saron panerus: *nacah lamba* and *nacah rangkep*. In nacah lamba (literally, 'single chopping'), each tone of the balungan is played twice (see figure 26).

---

16. The only exception is *Ayak-ayakan* and *Srepegan*, laras sléndro pathet nem. More discussion of ayak-ayakan and srepegan may be found in chapter III, below.

Figure 26. Nacah Lamba

balungan: 2   1   2   3

saron panerus: 2 2 1 1 2 2 3 3

In nacah rangkep (literally, 'double chopping'), each section of nacah
lamba is played twice (see figure 27).

Figure 27. Nacah Rangkep

balungan: 2   1   2   3

saron panerus: 2 2 1 1 2 2 1 1 2 2 3 3 2 2 3 3

In balungan mlaku, as in figures 26 and 27, the saron panerus is
clearly guided by the balungan melody. But, in playing saron panerus for
balungan nibani, the player must mentally change balungan nibani into
balungan mlaku. He must fill in the gap between balungan nibani with
neighboring tones. After changing balungan nibani to balungan mlaku, he
plays nacah lamba or nacah rangkep, depending on the irama in which the
gendhing is played.

Figure 28. Excerpt from the *Inggah* of Gendhing *Paré Anom*,
            laras sléndro pathet manyura

balungan nibani: .   5   .   3   .   1   .   2

hypothetical
balungan mlaku: 6   5   2   3   2   1   3   2

saron panerus: 6655665522332233 2211221133223322

In some cases, awkward melodies may result if the saron panerus adheres
strictly to the above procedure. Therefore, the saron panerus player may
vary his part in order to refine the melody (see figure 29).

Another type of variation is based on the player's awareness of the
inner melody. This is not to say that musicians who play the parts in the
example in figure 29 are not aware of the inner melody. In the example,
the balungan, as the abstraction of the inner melody, gives clear direction
to the saron panerus player.

The player must be aware of the inner melody in playing *nggantung* or
gantungan ('hanging, sustaining') melodies. A gantungan melody is a

sustained melodic line which, in the balungan mlaku, is presented by
doubled tones (<u>2 2</u> 5 3), doubled tones and rest (<u>1 1</u> . .), or a rest
which sustains the preceding tone (2 3 2 <u>1</u> . . 3 2). Balungan nibani
cannot express gantungan melodies as the balungan mlaku do. A gantungan
melody must be felt or known by the saron panerus player as he listens to
other instruments such as rebab, gendèr, or bonang. If the saron panerus
player has internalized the inner melody of the gendhing, this gantungan
melody is a part of his inner melody. In other words, he does not
necessarily need to listen to the other instruments in order to determine
where the gantungan melodies are (see figure 30).

Figure 29. Excerpt from Ladrang *Gonjang Ganjing*, laras sléndro
pathet sanga

balungan nibani: .   2   .   1   .   6   .   5

two hypothetical
balungan mlaku: (3   2   2   1)   5   6   3   5

                    3   2   3   1   5   6   3   5

some hypothetical
saron panerus parts: 3322(33222211)2211 5566556633553355

                      33223322(33113311) 5566116633556655

                      3322332255332211 5566116633556655

                      3322112255332211 5566116633556655

Note: The circled parts identify places where the melody is awkward. The
awkwardness is caused by the presence of too many double tones or of
a disjunct melodic flow (when such disjunct motion could have been
avoided). Variations are created to prevent an awkward melody or to
create a more interesting melody. The underlined parts show places
where variations occur.

Sometimes the saron panerus player must be aware that the end tone of
a particular melodic phrase is stressed. This stressed tone is presented
clearly by other instruments. As in the gantungan melody, the saron

panerus player must replace the middle tone with the end tone of the melodic phrase. The underlined part in figure 31 illustrates such a case.

Figure 30. Excerpt from Ladrang *Gonjang Ganjing*, laras sléndro pathet sanga

balungan: . 1̇ . 6 (. 5̇ . 6

saron panerus: 221122115566556655665566116611̇66

balungan: . 5̇ . 6 . 3 . 5

saron panerus: 5566556611̇66116633553355665566556655

Note: The circled sections indicate where the saron panerus player must be aware of the inner melody (gantungan 6). The saron panerus must stress tone 6 (see oblique circle) even though in the middle of the phrase the balungan nibani is tone 5.

Figure 31. Excerpt from the Inggah of Gendhing *Gambir Sawit*, laras sléndro pathet sanga

rebab: . 2 2 .11 2 35565 612̇ 616̇ 5

balungan: . 2 . 1 . 6 . 5

saron panerus: 33223322553322113355335566556655

Note: The underlined part shows where the saron panerus must substitute tone 5 (instead of 6) in the middle of the melodic phrase.

Bonang Barung

The bonang consists of two rows of small horizontal gongs placed on cords strung through a wooden frame. The sléndro bonang normally covers a range of one octave and four tones. Sometimes two gongs are added, increasing the range to two octaves and one tone. The pélog bonang covers a range of one octave and six tones. The bonang is played with two tabuh, but, unlike the gendèr, its melodic motion covers its entire pitch range.

Basically, there are two bonang-playing techniques: *pipilan* (or *mipil*) and *imbal-imbalan*. "Pipilan" literally means 'to pick off one by one' or to 'play single notes one at a time'. "Imbal-imbalan" means 'interlocking'. In general, in pipilan technique the bonang functions as the melodic leader of the saron instruments. The bonang tells the saron player what tones will follow by anticipating a pair of balungan tones.

Figure 32. Pipilan Technique for Balungan Mlaku

balungan: 2 3 2 1

bonang barung: 2 3 2 . . 3 2 . 2 1 2 . . 1 2 .

Figure 33. Pipilan Technique for Balungan Nibani

balungan: . 5 . 3

bonang barung: . 5 . 2 2 5 . . 2 5 2 . 3 3 5 .

   As in the case of rebab, gendèr, and balungan, bonang techniques seem to have evolved also. Pipilan technique, which relates closely to the balungan, seems to have little to do with the flow of the inner melody. However, there may have been a time when bonang players, as they expressed the inner melody, played in many different styles and with more freedom than is possible in pipilan. R. L. Martopangrawit is of the opinion that pipilan is the newest development in bonang technique and points to the earlier bonang technique used in the *gamelan sekaten*.[17] In this archaic gamelan the bonang plays in a freer, more melodic style. Sometimes this is also found in Yogyanese-style bonangan. Pipilan may have been created to meet the need for a melodic leader to guide the saron. In this capacity the bonang could be a teacher of balungan. As I mentioned earlier, demung, saron barung, and saron panerus often "hang on to" or "float with" slenthem or bonang. Usually the bonang player is also a good slenthem player.

   In practice, the responsibility of the bonang player as melodic leader of the saron is limited. Within the pipilan technique, there are some practices that give clues to the motion of the inner melody. These techniques are *gembyangan* (octave playing) and *nduduk tunggal* (syncopated single tones). There are different kinds of gembyangan grouped according to their special uses in expressing the inner melody. To indicate the high register of the inner melody, unattainable on the bonang, various kinds of

17. Letter from R. L. Martopangrawit, dated October 17, 1975.

gembyangan are played. This also provides a smooth melodic connection for
the bonang itself (see figure 34).

Figure 34. Example of Gembyangan Used to Indicate the High Register of the
Inner Melody (Ketawang *Sukma Ilang*, laras slendro pathet
manyura, Excerpt)

```
balungan:     3    5    6    i̇    3̇    2̇    i̇    6


rebab:      . 6  i̇ 2  121  i̇ 12  6 12 3̇   121   6


bonang:  353. .53. 616. .i6. 2166 6.66 .66. 66.6
                                    6  6   6   6
                     _____/
                            gembyangan
```

Gembyangan technique is also used to indicate a gantungan melody in the
high or medium octave. In figure 35, *nduduk gembyang* (syncopated octaves)
is played.

Figure 35. Example of Nduduk Gembyang Technique Used to Indicate a
Gantungan Melody in the Middle or Upper Octave (Gendhing *Damar
Kèli*, laras sléndro pathet manyura, Excerpt)

```
balungan:     3    3    .    .    3    3    .    2


rebab:      . 3  3  .3.  3  3  .3.  3  2  161  2  2


bonang:  ..3..3..3..3..3..3..3..3.23.323.
            3  3  3  3  3  3  3  3
          _____/
                nduduk gembyang
```

Nduduk tunggal is played when expressing gantungan melody in the low
octave. In figure 36, the bonang plays single tones in the low octave.

Figure 36. Example of Nduduk Tunggal Technique Used to Indicate a
Gantungan Melody in the Low Octave (Gendhing *Cucur Bawuk*, laras
sléndro pathet manyura, Excerpt)

```
balungan:    6   5   2   3   .   .   3   6
             .   .   .   .           .   .

bonang:   656..56.232..32.3..3..3.363..63.
          ... .. ...  .. .  .  . ...  ..
                          _____/
                            nduduk
                           tunggal
```

In the other main bonang technique, imbal-imbalan, the bonang barung
and bonang panerus play interlocking patterns. Imbal-imbalan is played
during gendhing or sections of gendhing which have a lively or exciting
mood. In figure 37, the bonang does not lead the saron melodically or
express the motion of the inner melody. However, the inner melody has been
internalized by the bonang players. The imbal-imbalan is very much a
background function which creates, or adds to, the excitement of the piece.
In an important point of the melodic line, toward the end of the melodic
phrases, the bonang might play a "sekaran" (ornamentation) melody. A fancy
bonang player might even play sekaran in the middle of melodic phrases (see
figure 38).

The arrangement of the tones in interlocking patterns is based on the
ending tone of the melodic phrase and the pathet of the gendhing.

Figure 37. Interlocking Patterns in Bonang Imbal-imbalan Technique, Based
on Ending Tone and Pathet

Interlocking pattern		Ending tone	Pathet
. 1 . 3	bonang barung	3,2,1	manyura/nem
2 . 2 . 2 .. 2 .	bonang panerus		
. 6 . 2	bonang barung	5,6,1,2	sanga
1 . 1 .	bonang panerus		
. 3 . 6	bonang barung	5,6	sanga/nem/manyura
5 . 1 .	bonang panerus		

Figure 38. Sekaran in the Imbal-Imbalan Bonang Technique

        balungan: 3   6
                                     .   .

    bonang barung: . 1 . 3 . 1 . 3 . 1 . 3 . 1 . 3
                    _____/

    bonang panerus: $\frac{2}{2}$. $\frac{2}{2}$. $\frac{2}{2}$. $\frac{2}{2}$. $\frac{2}{2}$. $\frac{2}{2}$. $\frac{2}{2}$. $\frac{2}{2}$.
                    _____/
                              imbal-imbalan

        balungan: 1   2

    bonang barung: 2 1 6 3 . 6 . 1 . 2 . 6 3 6 1 $\frac{2}{2}$
                        .   .   .   .   .
                    _____/ .

    bonang panerus: 6 1 2 3 5 3 5 3 2 1 6 1 2 . 1 2
                    .   .
                    _____/
                              sekaran

    R. L. Martopangrawit suggests that imbal-imbalan bonang was created by
Paku Buwana V of Surakarta when he was still *pangéran adipati* (crown
prince) in the late eighteenth century.[18] However, interlocking technique
can be found in the gamelan carabalèn, which is believed to be ancient.
This interlocking technique is known as *klénangan*. Klénangan is also used
in the full modern gamelan for gendhing such as Ketawang *Suba Kastawa*,
laras sléndro pathet sanga, Lancaran *Liwung*, and Ketawang *Pisan Bali*, laras
pélog pathet barang.

---

18. Lecture notes, R. L. Martopangrawit, lecture at ASKI, 1967.

Figure 39. Imbal-imbalan Klénangan

```
        balungan:                    .              1
   bonang barung:  5 6 . . 5 6 . . 5 6 . . 5 6 . .
                     . .     . .     . .     . .
  bonang panerus:  . . 1 2 . . 1 2 . . 1 2 . . 1 2


        balungan:                    .              6
                                                   .
   bonang barung:  5 6 . . 5 6 . . 5 6 . . 5 6 . .
                     . .     . .     . .     . .
  bonang panerus:  . . 1 2 . . 1 2 . . 1 2 . . 1 2
```

Gendhing Bonang

Gendhing bonang can be distinguished from regular gendhing in that they are always played by gamelan bonangan. The gendèr, rebab, gambang, celempung, suling, and vocalists are absent from this ensemble. The *buka* (introduction) is played by the bonang barung. There is a point at which the inggah, or a section of the inggah (*sesegan*), must be played in irama tanggung.[19]

It may seem that gendhing bonang are purely instrumental pieces, lacking vocal ideas. However, gendhing bonang are also based on a songlike inner melody. It is possible that gendhing bonang were created in the following way. In a gamelan rehearsal or performance, some of the musicians occasionally may have arrived after the ensemble had begun to play, so that the ensemble had begun without a full complement of musicians. To compensate for this, the musicians may have played pieces from the repertoire for full ensemble (including vocalists), but in the reduced instrumentation of the gamelan bonangan.[20] Perhaps inspired by this experience of playing vocal gendhing in the bonangan style, musicians

---

19. In the larger gendhing forms, a gendhing consists of two sections. The first section is merong and the second section is inggah (see chapter III).

20. This happens even in present-day gamelan rehearsals or performances. In these cases, typical gendhing are Ladrang *Sywignya*, laras pelog pathet barang; Ladrang *Eling-eḷing Badranaya*, laras slendro pathet manyura; Ladrang *Singa-singa*, laras pelog pathet barang; Gendhing *Bolang-bolang*, minggah Ladrang *Agun-agun*, laras slendro pathet manyura; Gendhing *Okrak-okrak*, laras slendro pathet manyura; Ladrang *Semar Mantu*, laras pelog pathet nem; and Ladrang *Geger Sakutha*, laras slendro pathet sanga.

eventually composed gendhing bonang specifically for the reduced
instrumentation. Therefore, the process of composing gendhing bonang does
not exclude the concept of the inner melody as its basis.

The evidence for the above account of the origins of gendhing bonang
lies in the fact that all gendhing bonang are either in sléndro pathet nem,
pélog pathet barang, or pélog pathet lima. It is customary in daytime
gamelan performances for musicians to begin with pieces in sléndro pathet
manyura or pélog pathet barang. In evening gamelan performances, pieces in
sléndro pathet nem or pélog pathet lima normally are played at the
beginning. Therefore, it is likely that gendhing bonang were only composed
in the pathet used at the beginning of gamelan performances.[21]

Because the process of composing gendhing bonang is probably based on
the vocally inspired inner melody, a question arises as to whether rebab
can be played in the gendhing bonang. In answering this question,
R. L. Martopangrawit and other gamelan teachers at ASKI explained that it
is possible, though rather difficult.[22] This difficulty occurs because
some sections of gendhing bonang have arbitrary disjunct motion.

In figure 40, for example, the balungan melody from Gendhing *Tukung* is
not characterized by the smooth, conjunct motion of a proper inner melody.
It can be further seen how the bonang player approaches this problem of
arbitrary, disjunct motion.

The inner melody from section IA to section IB (circled in figure 40)
shows disjunct motion from 7 to 6. This leap from one register to another
could be conceived as smooth, if it were to receive a vocal treatment (for
example, 2 7 7 7 3 $\overline{56}$ 6 6), but this conception cannot be expressed by the
balungan. The balungan in this section confines itself to refinement of
the melody within the saron range, and the bonang resolves the disjunct
motion with the gembyangan technique.

In the circled sections marked IIA and IIB in figure 40 can be seen an
example of arbitrary, disjunct motion from 5 to 6 (i.e., from the end of
IIA to the beginning of IIB). However, the bonang playing disguises the
disjuncture by playing nduduk gembyang for the gantungan 5 melody; the
register of nduduk gembyang is inherently ambiguous and can suggest either
the low or the medium octave.

---

21. However, there are no gendhing bonang in sléndro pathet manyura.

22. I. M. Harjito, personal communication, 1975.

Figure 40. Example of Disjunct Motion in the Balungan Melody of Gendhing
Bonang (Gendhing Bonang *Tukung*, laras pélog pathet barang,
Excerpt)

```
        balungan:      .   6   5   3   2   3   5   3
        bonang barung: 6..6..6.535..35. 232..32.535..35.
                       6  6  6
```

```
        balungan:      6   7   6   5   3   2   7   2
        bonang barung: 676..76.656..56. 323..23.727..27.
```

```
        balungan:      .   .   7   .   5   6   7   2
        bonang barung: 2..2..2.7..7..7. 565..65.727..27.
                       2  2  2
```

```
                              IA                    IB
        balungan:      .   7   .   .    5   6   7   6
        bonang barung: 2..2..7..7..7..7 27666.66.66.66.6
                       2  2                 6 .6 .6 .6 .
```

```
        balungan:      5   4   .   2   4   5   4 2 1
        bonang barung: 545..45.424..24. 454..54.542.1..1
```

```
        balungan:      4   1   .   2   4   5   6   5
        bonang barung: 414..14.121..21. 454..54.65..5..5
                                                5  5  5
```

```
                                                IIA
        balungan:      .   .   .   .    5   5   .   .
        bonang barung: ..5..5..5..5..5. .5..5..5..5..5..
                         5  5  5  5  5   5  5  5  5  5
```

```
                      IIB
        balungan:      6   7   2   7    6   5   3   5
        bonang barung: 676..76.272..72. 656..56.353..53.
```

CHAPTER III

FORM AND MELODIC PHRASES IN GENDHING

Gamelan pieces are composed in equal metrical units. The playing of
hanging gongs (gong ageng, gong suwukan, and kempul) and horizontal pot
gongs (kenong and kethuk) marks the metrical units of the gendhing.
Gendhing forms fall into three categories, based on the length of the
gongan[23] and the position of gong, kenong, kempul, and kethuk in one
gongan.

I. In the gendhing forms in figure 41, each gongan consists of four
kenongan: lancaran, ladrang, mérong kethuk 2 kerep, mérong kethuk 4 kerep,
mérong kethuk 2 arang, mérong kethuk 8 kerep, and mérong kethuk 4
arang.[24]

II. In the gendhing forms in figure 42, each gongan consists of two
kenongan: ketawang; mérong kethuk 2 kerep, ketawang gendhing; mérong kethuk
4 kerep, ketawang gendhing; and mérong kethuk 8 kerep, ketawang gendhing.

III. In the gendhing forms in figure 43, each gongan is of
indeterminate length: ayak-ayakan, srepegan, and sampak. A brief
discussion of the melodic aspect of these forms has been given in the
second chapter. The position of the kenong and kempul is idiosyncratic
(see figure 42). The terms "ayak-ayakan," "srepegan," and "sampak" refer
to the form of the gendhing. However, they also provide the name of the
gendhing. Each pathet has its own ayak-ayakan, srepegan, and sampak. I
noted above that Sampak, laras sléndro pathet manyura, is probably the

---

23. One "gongan" is the period of a gendhing between two gong ageng
or gong suwukan strokes. "Kenongan" refers to the period of a gendhing
between two kenong strokes. "Kenongan" and "gongan" are terms commonly
used to indicate phrases or periods of gendhing. However, the term
"kenongan" is not applied in the shorter forms ayak-ayakan, srepegan, and
sampak. These forms will be discussed below.

24. Kerep 'frequent'; arang 'scarce' or 'far apart'. The number
after "kethuk" (for example, the "4" in "kethuk 4 kerep") indicates the
frequency of kethuk strokes within a kenongan. "Kerep" or "arang"
indicates the length of the interval between two kethuk strokes.

Figure 41. Gendhing Forms Consisting of Four Kenongan

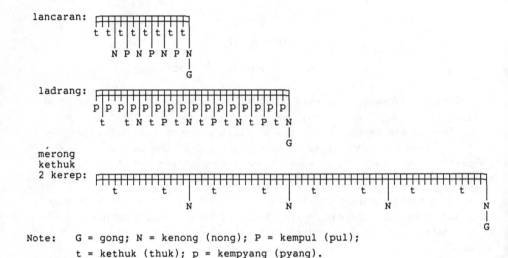

lancaran:

ladrang:

mérong
kethuk
2 kerep:

Note: G = gong; N = kenong (nong); P = kempul (pul);
        t = kethuk (thuk); p = kempyang (pyang).

Figure 42. Gendhing Forms Consisting of Two Kenongan

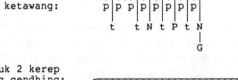

ketawang:

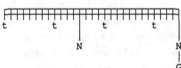

mérong kethuk 2 kerep
    ketawang gendhing:

oldest sampak.[25] *Sampak*, laras sléndro pathet sanga, is a new development;
Sampak, laras sléndro pathet nem, is even more recent (see figure 43).

---

        25. Jaap Kunst also mentions that "Sampak is heard only in pathet
manyura" (1973[1]:306). The scene *gara-gara* (a disturbance of the world)
in a wayang performance occurs in patḥet sanga. Because formerly pathet
sanga had no sampak, *Sampak*, laras slendro pathet manyura, was played to
accompany the tense or violent mood of the gara-gara scene. Ṭoday,
however, gara-gara is usually accompanied by *Sampak*, laras slendro pathet
sanga.

Figure 43.   Gendhing Forms of Indeterminate Length

ayak-ayakan:

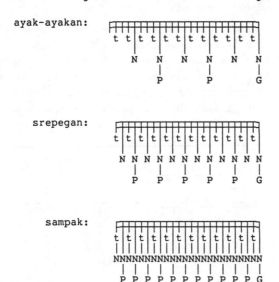

srepegan:

sampak:

Note: In these three gendhing forms, gong suwukan is usually played
         instead of gong ageng. For the *suwuk* (ending) of the piece, gong
         ageng is usually played. In *Ayak-ayakan*, laras sléndro pathet
         manyura, the gong suwukan takes the place of the kempul. Even so,
         the musicians can sense the finality of the gong played at the end
         of a gongan.

    "Gendhing," in the widest sense, means "a gamelan composition." In
the narrowest sense "gendhing" means "a gamelan composition that always
consists of two parts." The first part, mérong, has a solemn, peaceful, or
stately mood. The second part, inggah, has a lively mood. An inggah
section that is an abstraction of its mérong is termed *inggah kendhang*.
The kendhang plays a different pattern in this inggah section, but the
melody of the mérong is carried on to the inggah, though in an abstract
version. An inggah that does not have a melodic relation to the mérong is
termed *inggah gendhing*. Here both the drumming pattern and the melody of
the inggah differ from that of the mérong. Ladrang form can be included in
the inggah classification because some gendhing employ ladrang as their

inggah. Because inggah kendhang is an abstract version of the merong, its
melodic phrases are the same as in the merong. However, the kethuk is
played in a new position and the kempyang is added.

     In both inggah kendhang and inggah gendhing, the melodic phrases are
comparable, since the position of kethuk and kempyang is the same.
However, they are different in the length of kenongan or gongan, indicated
by the frequency of the kethuk in each kenongan. There are four kinds of
inggah: ladrang, or inggah kethuk 2 (each kenongan consists of two kethuk);
inggah kethuk 4 (each kenongan consists of four kethuk); inggah kethuk 8
(each kenongan consists of eight kethuk); and inggah kethuk 16 (each
kenongan consists of 16 kethuk).

Figure 44. Inggah Kethuk 4 of a Gongan Length

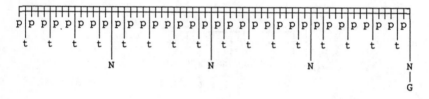

     It has been pointed out that gendhing are composed with equal metrical
units marked by the strokes of various gongs; the underlying feeling of a
gendhing is based on the smoothly flowing quality of the inner melody, as
discussed in chapter II. The marriage between the metrical units (with
their gong markers) and the inner melody typifies the musical style of
Javanese gamelan music.

     In this section, the relationship between inner melody and the various
gongs that mark gendhing forms will be discussed. The players of the
kenong and kempul usually play tones that coincide with the tones of the
inner melody of the gendhing. This kenong or kempul technique is called
kenong mbalung or *kempul mbalung*, since kenong or kempul strokes also
coincide with tones of the balungan. However, sometimes the kenong or
kempul tone anticipates the approaching tone of the inner melody. This
technique is called *kenong plèsèdan* or *kempul plèsèdan*. "Plèsèdan"
literally means 'slippery place'. Plèsèdan technique is an indication that
the kenong or kempul player feels the smooth pull of the inner melody
toward the tone that follows (see figures 45 and 46).

Figure 45. Example of Kenong Plèsèdan (Gendhing *Onang-onang*, laras pélog
            pathet nem, Excerpt)

```
          ‾‾ ‾ ‾‾ ‾‾ ‾‾   ‾ │G│ ‾ ‾ ‾‾ ‾‾   ‾‾ ‾ ‾‾
                            │—│        ·  ··  ·  ·    ··
rebab:    5 565 3 356 6 56 16565   3 2│56.│ . 6 1 126 1 2   126 5 3 565 5

balungan: 2   3   5  6  3  5   3  │2 │  6  6   .   .   6  5 3  5

kenong:   .   .   .  .  .  .    . │‾.6.‾│
```

Note: The circled part shows the place where the rebab flows smoothly
       toward the tone which follows and the kenong plèsèdan occurs.

Figure 46. Example of the Plèsèdan Technique for Kenong and Kempul (*Ayak-
            ayakan*, laras sléndro pathet sanga, Excerpt)

```
          ‾‾   ‾   ‾ ‾‾ ‾ ‾ ‾‾ ‾ ‾‾ ‾ ‾ ‾‾ ‾‾                               G
                        · ·   ·   · ·    ·   ·   ·  · ·
rebab:    65232  235 5  . 5 61.1. 1│1 .1│. 6 65. 616 6 1  16521 .62       1
                                   │    │                        ·
balungan: 3  2  3  5  3  2  3 │5 │1  6  5  6   5  3  2  1
                              │   │·
                                      ‾·
kenong:   .  5  .  5  .  5  . │.1.│. 6 . 6 . 1 . 1
                              │   │        ·     ·
                                      ‾·
kempul:   .  .  .  5  .  .  . │.1.│. . . 6   .   .   .   .
```

Note: The circled part indicates where kenong and kempul anticipate the
       motion of the inner melody.

A modern gamelan teacher using notation may explain kenong plèsèdan by
pointing out that it should be played whenever there is a repeated balungan
tone (*balungan nggantung*) immediately following the kenong stroke. But
this explanation can only hold for situations in which the musicians play
from notation. Traditionally, notation is not used in gamelan performance
or rehearsal. Thus, the kenong player must himself feel the flow of the
inner melody, since the kenong plèsèdan tone must be played just prior to
the sounding of the following balungan tone.

Another kenong and kempul technique is called *kenong kempyungan*, or
kempul kempyungan. When the balungan pitches 1 or 1 fall on the kenong or

kempul beat, the kenong/kempul played is an interval of a kempyung higher than the balungan tone, that is, pitch 5. This occurs usually in compositions in sléndro pathet sanga or pèlog pathet lima.

Some gamelan have an incomplete set of kenong consisting of only three tones (5, 6, and 1 in sléndro; 5, 6, and 7 in pélog). This set is believed to represent an older gamelan instrumentation.[26] With an incomplete kenong set the performance practice is as listed in figures 47 and 48.

Figure 47. Kenong Technique with Limited Number of Kenong Tones (Sléndro)

Tone of Inner Melody on Kenong Beat	Kenong Tone	Name of Technique
2	6	kempyungan
3	6	salah gumun
5	5	mbalung
6	6	mbalung
1	5	kempyungan
	or 1	mbalung

Figure 48. Kenong Technique with Limited Number of Kenong Tones (Pélog)

Tone of Inner Melody on Kenong Beat	Kenong Tone	Name of Technique
2	6	kempyungan
3	6	salah gumun
4	6	-------
5	5	mbalung
6	6	mbalung
7	7	mbalung
1	5	kempyungan

This method of playing an incomplete set of kenong, especially kenong kempyungan and salah gumun, gives a distinctive sound to the ensemble. However, a complete kenong set is preferred nowadays. With a complete

---

26. I have heard this from older musicians. According to Jaap Kunst, the older gamelan had only one kenong, tuned to lima (5). Then, kenong nem (6) and barang (1 or 7) were added. In a later development, a complete set with a kenong for every pitch of the laras was invented (1973[1]:161-62).

kenong set, the kenong player has more responsibility to make his part correspond to the inner melody.[27]

Other kenong techniques are known as *kenong monggangan* and *kenong goyang sungsun*. The only gendhing in which the monggangan technique is used is the first gongan of Ketawang *Suba Kastawa*, laras sléndro pathet sanga. In fact, this first gongan developed from an imitation of the Gendhing *Monggang* melody (from the archaic ensemble called *gamelan monggang*). Kenong is played in unison with the balungan melody in imitation of the Gendhing *Monggang* melody. Kempul is also played in *kempul monggangan* technique, in unison with the balungan and kenong, except that in the gong position kempul is omitted.

Figure 49. Kenong and Kempul Monggangan (Ketawang *Suba Kastawa*, laras sléndro pathet sanga, Excerpt)

```
balungan:  . 1 . 6 . 1 . 5 . 1 . 6 . 1 . 5
            N   N   N   N   N   N   N   N
            P   P   P   P   P   P   P   G
```

Kenong goyang sungsun is played in some kenongan of Ladrang *Sobrang*, laras pélog pathet barang, and Ladrang *Surung Dhayung*, laras pélog pathet nem. In this technique, the kenong is played three times. The first kenong stroke is on the normal kenong beat, and the second and third kenong strokes are played after the usual kenong beat.

Figure 50. Kenong Goyang Sungsun Technique (Ladrang *Sobrang*, laras pélog pathet barang, Excerpt)

```
balungan:  . . 5 6 7 2 3 2 . 2 7 6 5 6 7 2
                 N   .N  N P          N
```

The gong ageng or gong suwukan define the longest period in a gendhing. If there are enough musicians in a gamelan group, gong ageng is played by one player, and kempul and gong suwukan are played by another. Because the gong player must wait to play, especially in the larger

---

27. The addition of pitches and changes in the playing technique apply to the kempul as well.

gendhing forms, we might wonder how he keeps track of his part. In some
cases, a particular rhythmic cue is provided by the kendhang player as the
gendhing approaches the gong, signaling that the gong is about to be
played. For example, in drumming the mérong section, a drummer can retard
the tempo as he plays a particular pattern.

Figure 51. Kendhang Cue Leading to the Gong in the Mérong Section

```
                                                           G
        balungan:              .        1        6        5
                                                 .        .

        kendhang:   . - - 0 . - - 1 , , . , . , . ,
                                            slowing down
```

Note: The following symbols indicate drum strokes.
                – = ket
                0 = dhah
                1 = thung
                , = tong
                . = rest

In other kendhangan techniques, the kendhang player gives distinctive
rhythmic cues when approaching the gong, for example, in *kendhangan
kendhang kalih*[28] for ketawang and ladrang pieces.

    This practice of emphasizing the approach of the gong is limited. A
good gong player must be able to feel the flow of the inner melody
thoroughly. Though a gong is sounded relatively infrequently, playing a
gong ageng is a demanding task. The gong is the most important element in
gendhing, since it gives inner balance to the longest period of a gendhing.
However, a musician who is not skilled in playing gong ageng will often
miss his part. He may be restless, or even nervous, because he is not
accustomed to following the flow of the inner melody of the gendhing while
waiting to play.

---

    28. Kendhangan kendhang kalih are kendhang patterns played on
kendhang ageng and kendhang ketipung.

Melodic Phrasing[29]

Melodic phrases of gendhing are often symmetrically congruent with the periods marked by gong, kenong, kempul, and kethuk. For example, each kenongan of merong kethuk 2 kerep consists of two melodic phrases. The kethuk is played in the middle of each melodic phrase (see figure 52).

Figure 52. Melodic Phrasing in a Kenongan of Merong Kethuk 2 Kerep
           (Gendhing *Gendhiyeng*, laras pelog pathet nem, Excerpt)

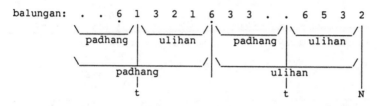

Note: padhang = 'question' (unresolved melodic phrase); ulihan = 'answer'
        (resolution of melodic phrase).

In general, this regular or symmetrical melodic phrasing applies to all gendhing. However, in some cases the flow of the inner melody runs against the usual melodic phrasing. This is a result of the marriage between the symmetrical unit implicit in gendhing form and an asymmetrical inner melody. Since the inner melody is the underlying feeling of a gendhing, it sometimes causes irregularity in the melodic phrasing of gendhing. For example, the middle of a kenongan of merong kethuk 2 kerep, which is supposedly the end of the first melodic phrase, cannot be felt as ulihan. Thus, the phrasing of this kenongan is as in figure 53.

It is apparent that the larger the gendhing form, the more varied the melodic phrasing. In the gendhing forms, merong kethuk 2 arang, merong kethuk 8 kerep, and merong kethuk 4 arang, melodies are phrased in several different ways, not necessarily following symmetrical melodic phrasing. An example of melodic phrasing in merong kethuk 2 arang gendhing is shown in figure 54.

---

29. Much of my material about melodic phrasing is derived from Martopangrawit's section on "padhang ulihan" (1972[1ᵇ]:26-40).

Figure 53.   Example of Irregular Melodic Phrasing in Mérong Kethuk 2 Kerep
             (Gendhing *Onang-onang*, laras pélog pathet nem)

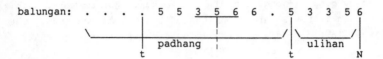

Note: The melodic movement in the underlined part cannot be felt as
        ulihan.

Figure 54.   Melodic Phrasing in Mérong Kethuk 2 Arang (Gendhing *Mega
             Mendhung*, laras pélog pathet nem, Excerpt)

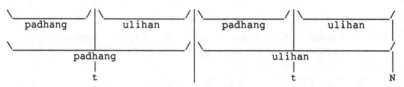

Figure 55.   Asymmetrical Phrasing in Mérong Kethuk 2 Arang (Gendhing
             Budheng-budheng, laras pélog pathet nem, Excerpt)

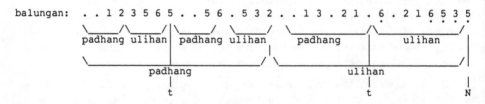

Note: The first half of the kenongan is mérong kethuk 4 kerep melodic
        phrasing. The second half is the "real" mérong kethuk 2 arang
        melodic phrasing.

However, gendhing mérong kethuk 2 arang do not always have such symmetrical
melodic phrases. In figure 55, the mérong kethuk 2 arang gendhing has
symmetrical melodic phrasing combined with the melodic phrasing of mérong
kethuk 4 kerep. Other possibilities of melodic phrasing of gendhing mérong
kethuk 2 arang are illustrated in figure 56.

Figure 56. Melodic Phrasing in Gendhing *Laranjala* (Mérong Kethuk 2 Arang),
laras pélog pathet lima

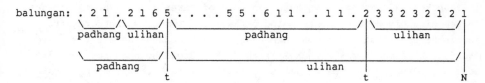

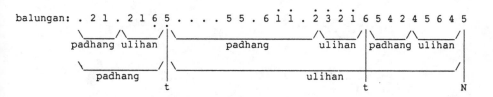

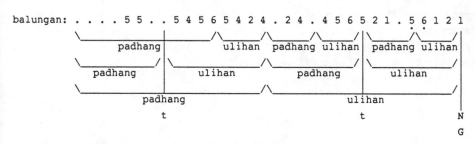

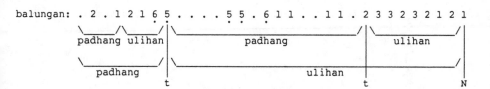

Some gendhing are known as *gendhing pamijèn* ('special', 'exceptional'). Depending on the positions of gong, kenong, kempul, and kethuk,
gendhing pamijèn can be included in either the first or second group of
gendhing forms (see p. 291). However, one gongan or one kenongan in these
gendhing will have an unusual length. For example, in the mérong and
inggah of Gendhing *Majemuk*, laras sléndro pathet nem (mérong kethuk 2

kerep, minggah kethuk 4), a gongan consists of five kenongan. In Ladrang
Srundèng Gosong, laras pèlog pathet nem, a gongan consists of four and one-
half kenongan. In Gendhing *Laler Mengeng*, laras slèndro pathet sanga
(mèrong kethuk 2 arang), a gongan consists of three and one-half kenongan.
In Gendhing *Miyanggong*, laras pèlog pathet nem, two gendhing forms are
combined: the first and second kenongan are kethuk 2 arang and the third
and fourth kenongan are kethuk 2 kerep. The second kenongan of Gendhing
bonang *Gondrong*, laras pèlog pathet barang (mèrong kethuk 4 arang), is only
seven-eighths of a kenongan. There are a few other gendhing pamijèn.

Figure 57. The Balungan of Gendhing *Laler Mengeng* (Mèrong Kethuk 2 Arang),
            laras slèndro pathet sanga

```
         t          .          t          N
     . 5565  .2.3  5616     . 6653  23.1  2353

         t                     t          N
     . 3323  55..  1121     . 1121  3212  .165
                                          ..

         t                     t          N
    .65.  5612  1312  .165   . 55..  5565  3561
    ..    ..          ..                   .

                          G
         t                N
    .3.2  .165  35.2  3565
    ..    .
```

A gendhing pamijèn results from the marriage of a smoothly flowing
inner melody and a symmetrically organized gendhing form. The flowing
inner melody, which carries the feeling of the gendhing, necessitates
irregularity in the melodic phrasing of the gendhing. This also results in
kenongan or gongan of unusual length.

CONCLUSION

It is apparent from the above discussion that the relationship between melodies played by instruments in the ensemble is an important aspect in the determination of Javanese gamelan melody. This relationship provides an understanding of how musicians intuitively conceive of the melody of gendhing as the result of their own inner creativity.

In a gamelan rehearsal or performance, each musician relates the part he plays to the melodies played on the other instruments. This practice is often employed during the learning period. At the same time, it also allows the musicians to gradually absorb the underlying feeling of gendhing as inspired by the melody of the whole ensemble. This underlying feeling of gendhing is the essence of Javanese gamelan melody--the inner melody as felt by the musicians.

Basically, inner melody is a continuous, smoothly flowing, melodic movement. The overall melodic motion of the inner melody of the gendhing exceeds the one-octave saron range[30] and can be as wide as two and one-half octaves.

Each musician must coordinate his conception of the inner melody with the range of his instrument and its performance technique when creating melodic patterns for a gendhing. In times past, this process allowed musicians to create a great variety of melodic interpretations in any given part. After years of evolution, standard melodic patterns and playing techniques have emerged, although different interpretations are still to be found in gamelan practice today. For this reason, Javanese musicians wisely use the term "garap" ('way of working', 'processing', or 'fashioning') when referring to the playing of an instrument. This means that the musician has to work, to fashion, or to model the melody of his part by coordinating his inner melody with the characteristics of his instrument.

---

30. Some theorists maintain that the framework of a gendhing is the saron melody, from which the other parts are derived.

In some cases, the rebab plays the part that is the closest
interpretation of the inner melody. This is due to the smoothly flowing
quality of its sound. However, the rebab frequently plays a more elaborate
interpretation. The inner melody is not played by any particular
instrument, but all instruments are inspired by it. The inner melody is
the spirit of the gendhing and the spirit of the Javanese gamelan.

WÉDHA PRADANGGA KAWEDHAR

[Knowledge of Gamelan Revealed]

by

Benedictus Yusuf Harjamulya Sastrapustaka

Translated from Javanese by

R. Anderson Sutton

(Unpublished manuscript, 1953-1978)

PREFACE[1]

My purpose in writing "Knowledge of Gamelan Revealed" is to carry on
the tradition of other scholars before me in an effort to broaden the scope
of our outlook on the art of *karawitan* and the science of this art.

The science of karawitan contained in this article has been in
existence for a long time. However, it has yet to gain the general
understanding of most students of the art of karawitan, because in former
times it was only transmitted orally in the form of moral lectures and
conversation.

I have gathered together, little by little, the opinions of elderly
experts in karawitan, from what I heard in the old days when they happened
to be talking to one another. (I have long since forgotten all their
names; two of these gentlemen said that these opinions should be kept
secret.) So, it is by the blessing of these experts that this article has
been made possible, even though I have been able to remember what they said
only with difficulty and after a long period of time.

It is still disappointing to me that no one can say who first held the
opinions contained in this article. Nevertheless, I hope it can shed some
light, without straying from reason, and that its basic content and message
can be understood.

Finally, because it is very unlikely that this article covers
everything sufficiently, I entrust all my shortcomings to the better
judgment of my readers.

Written [begun] on February 1, 1953 (the Javanese year 1885), with the
sangkala[2]

TRI   MARGA   AMBUKA   BUDI [Three Ways to Open the Mind]
[3]   [5]   [9]   [1]

or

PANCA   BRAHMANA   NGÈSTHI   SEMÈDI [Five Brahmans Contemplate Meditation]
[5]   [8]   [8]   [1]

Benedictus Yusuf Harjamulya Sastrapustaka

The Cryptic Literature (Sastra Sinandi)
Concealed in the Tones of the Gamelan

Before talking about the science of karawitan I would first like to explain about the wayang kulit [shadow puppet theatre] tradition, which goes hand in hand with karawitan and provides a point of reference for comparison in our investigation. The content and meaning of both karawitan and wayang are concerned with education.[3]

The feelings the Javanese have for wayang purwa (wayang kulit) are so deeply rooted that they cannot be changed. In fact, these feelings are not limited to the older generation; children who are still quite small already understand the wayang puppets and stories. For example, when they see the puppet Radèn Gathutkaca[4] appear, they jump for joy because they know he is an outstanding warrior. When they see Pétruk,[5] even before he has begun to talk they yell and laugh because they know that Pétruk is funny. When they see Patih Sangkuni,[6] they look away and grumble because Sangkuni has an evil heart. The same goes for the older generation; their opinions are the same.

Furthermore, for many people the wayang tradition provides images representing traits of the human character: goodness, patience, virtue, straightforwardness, and other desirable characteristics. The evil characteristics that are represented in the wayang are even more numerous.

If we now raise the discussion to the level of philosophical knowledge, it is said that wayang can symbolize the human being. A convenient example is the five Pandhawa brothers, often taken to represent the five senses. In describing someone's character one may refer to wayang. For example, one who is refined in temperament, resigned, straightforward, and detached is said to be like Darma Kusuma (a king in Ngamarta). One who is full of determination is said to be like Wrekudara.[7]

Because of the feelings people have for wayang, and for likening real people to wayang characters, accurate descriptions of this type make immediate sense to those who are listening. But, if we take a more rational stance, we see that the human body may be compared to a chest for

storing wayang puppets. Thus, we must understand that at times it is Durna
who comes out, at times ogres, at times the evil spirits in Krendha
Wahana.[8] We should not expect that just the good characters will appear.

This is the way everyone interprets the wayang tradition. It is no
different from the way we will interpret the science of karawitan, which I
have entitled "The Cryptic Literature Concealed in the Tones of the
Gamelan." People who enjoy matching up words will, of course, be able to
understand very well the words for the gamelan tones which are explained
below. But, if we really think about it for a moment, one who wishes to
trace the meaning of words is certainly not just matching words, but is
actually interpreting language. If this interpreting is not to lead to
misunderstanding, one must first have a feeling for what is to be
interpreted and an ability to think logically. In this way one can
evaluate the truth and error of the interpretation.

I would like you to know that when the elders in former times talked
about the wayang tradition, it was as if the wayang characters and stories
were real--it really was that way. Nowadays, more so than before, experts
in literature, mysticism, wayang, and education are taking an active
interest in wayang. Those involved in examining and interpreting wayang
would agree that the wayang tradition as it is--without changing the norms,
regulations, or principles--is a useful and important device for education
of the outer, public self (*lair*) and the inner, private self (*batin*).

In wayang it is easy to examine and analyze; we can see immediately
with our eyes. Because a form is visual, it is easily seen and straightaway enters our perception. Then we can easily interpret and experience
it. In the world of karawitan, it is by the sense of hearing (the ears)
that we perceive. Thus, the forms do not appear; one can perceive them
only by listening. If one is to interpret and experience by listening, the
setting must be calm, because one must pay close attention to sound. If
the setting is bustling with activity, one will hear and feel it (the sound
of gamelan) as nothing more than a sound.

We are now going to investigate and interpret the art of karawitan in
order to understand that the art of karawitan--which is thought to be only
for entertainment--is actually important for the physical (*lair*) and
spiritual (*batin*) education of all who study it in depth. Also, art is not
a tool for pleasure tainted with cynical allusions or coquettish flattery,
but a device for raising the grandeur of a people's spirit. Indeed, it is
very clear that this art can only give rise to a radiance or light which is

pure, if it resides within a person whose temperament is noble and refined. On the other hand, if it resides within a person whose temperament is crude and inferior, it can give rise to mischief and darkness instead.

Now, for our investigation into the science of karawitan we need to examine and interpret the meaning and sense of the names of the gamelan tones. There are five tones in the gamelan.[9]

a. tone *barang* ['thing']
b. tone *gulu* ['neck']
c. tone *dhadha* ['chest']
d. tone *lima* ['five']
e. tone *enem* ['six']

As we scrutinize the names of the gamelan tones, they seem very strange indeed. Let us proceed in our investigation and our search for knowledge. The first, (a), is the name of a tone as well as a word, 'thing' (*barang*). The second and third, (b) and (c), are the names of parts of the human body. The fourth and fifth, (d) and (e), take the names of numbers. The names of the gamelan tones raise various questions. Just what are their meanings and connotations? The names do not seem to go together. Of course there are meanings, but they will be explained later.

I would like you to know that the names of the five gamelan keys can have a broad scope of meaning if they are opened to thorough analysis and interpretation. The art of karawitan can teach us something about the individual human being. So, here we will talk about some of the broader scopes of meaning, with the hope that they will strike a responsive chord with my readers. I am not an expert in language, however. If I venture to discuss language, I will no doubt lose my way. So, what I am going to talk about are these ambiguous words which are rich in emotional content--albeit disguised. Indeed, these five words only serve as a foundation for the science of karawitan.

When people in former times gave a name to something, quite often the word they chose was difficult to understand. Especially when giving advice or explaining to their children or grandchildren, people did not speak frankly or openly, but rather by means of allusions, disguised and vague, which were not easy to interpret. Thus, those who were given an explanation had to know the intentions of the older generation and be quick to comprehend. Of course, once the meaning was made clear, one could see that their intentions were good, for they were concerned for the well being [of the children to whom they spoke].

Note. There is a simple matter which needs to be understood first of
all: the writing of the names of the gamelan keys.

I. Incorrect	II. Correct
a. tone barang	a. tone barang
b. tone gulu	b. tone gulu
c. tone dhadha	c. tone dhadha
d. tone 5	d. tone lima
e. tone 6	e. tone enem

Why is the writing of the names of the tones "5" and "6" with numerals
considered incorrect? Because the numerals 5 and 6 in this instance are
borrowed as labels, or names, for tones. The correct way to write them is
with letters ("lima" and "enem"), for they are nouns--names of the gamelan
tones--and not quantifying words.

Why borrow words from counting? This matter has been mentioned above.
The gentlemen of former times, when giving names, were secretive and
indirect. The words they used contained allusions and connotations whose
intent was educational. If, for example, one writes the names of the
gamelan tones with numerals 5 and 6, one would ask, "What is that tone?"[10]
Clearly, the writing with numerals is not correct. Also, the tones lima
and enem will inevitably be referred to in high Javanese as "*gangsal*" and
"enem," but that is another matter.

Let us proceed in our investigation and search for the meaning and
connotation of the names of the gamelan tones--names that are most unusual,
borrowed names of parts of the human body ("gulu" and "dhadha") and words
for counting ("lima" and "enem"). The route we shall travel in our search
is entitled "The Cryptic Literature Concealed in the Tones of the Gamelan."
This will consist of interpretation of the gamelan tones, based on their
names, meanings, and organization, which can assume orderly shape in the
form of a *gendhing*.

A. The tone *barang* ['thing'] suggests form (*wujud*). A thing cannot be
called a "thing" until it has form. In order to make clear the sort of
thing and form I mean, we can take this example. When two people meet in
the street, one does not at first focus on the other's arms, legs, and the
rest of the body, but instead on the face or head. The tone barang, then,
becomes the form of the head of a person. The tone barang suggests [the
following visual image].

Figure 1

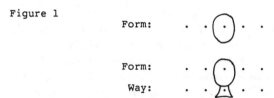

Form:

Form:
Way:

B. The tone *gulu* ['neck'] suggests 'way', 'passageway', or 'road' (*dalan*), for the neck is the passageway leading from the head.

C. The tone *dhadha* ['chest'] suggests 'life', or 'to live' (*urip*). The source of human life is, for the most part, in the chest.

Figure 2

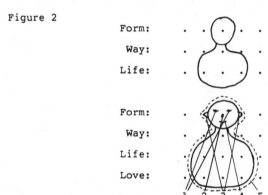

Form:
Way:
Life:

Form:
Way:
Life:
Love:

D. The tone *lima* ['five'] suggests 'love', 'passionate attraction' (*sengsem*). The attraction is not to sexual love, but to beauty of nature and art, springing from the five senses (*panca driya*):

1. *The eyes* are attracted (*sengsem*) to things or forms that are beautiful, lovely, nice, and so forth.
2. *The nose* is attracted to smells that are nice, pleasant, fragrant, and so forth.
3. *The ears* are attracted to sounds that are melodious, and so forth.
4. *The sensation of the tongue* is attracted to the taste of food that is delicious, and so forth.
5. *The sensation of the whole body* is attracted to feeling in a healthy condition.

E. The tone enem ['six'] suggests feeling (*rasa*). Why does enem
suggest feeling? Because feeling has six aspects. In the books, *Serat
Niti Śastra* and *Serat Dharma Śunya*,[11] and in Old Javanese (Kawi) and
Sanskrit, "*sadrasa*" means "six feelings" [*sad* = 'six'; *rasa* = 'feeling'].
Indeed, it is the "six feelings" which cause feeling to have six aspects.
Enem, then, suggests the aspects of feeling that come from the strength and
continual functioning of the five senses, which are necessary if one is to
feel and experience something.

Figure 3

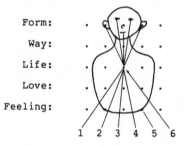

1. The feeling of sight: the eyes experience light, dark,
   brightness, and so forth.
2. The feeling of smell: the nose experiences smells that are
   fragrant, pleasant, rancid, acrid, musty, foul-smelling like
   urine, and so forth.
3. The feeling of hearing: the ears experience deafening noise,
   melodious sounds, and so forth.
4. The feeling of taste: the tongue experiences sweetness,
   deliciousness, bitterness, and so forth.
5. The feeling of touch: the body experiences roughness,
   smoothness, ticklishness, and so forth.
6. The inner feeling: moods, such as happiness, sadness,
   loneliness, grief, compassion, pain, and so forth.

This completes the exposition of connotations under the heading, "The
Cryptic Literature Concealed in the Tones of the Gamelan." Now I would
like to explain this "cryptic literature" so that it can be read and
experienced with short and complete sentences.

a. tone barang: form (*wujud*)
b. tone gulu: way (*dalan*)
c. tone dhadha: life (*urip*)
d. tone lima: love (*sengsem*)
e. tone enem: feeling (*rasa*)

We can read from

a b c d e: The form of the way gives life to [i.e., brings about] a love of feeling (*wujuding dalan nguripi sengseming rasa*).

e d c b a: The feeling of love gives life to the way of form *rasa sengsem nguripi dalaning wujud*).

b c d e a: The way of life loves the feeling of form (*dalaning urip nengsemi rasaning wujud*).

c d e a b: The life of love feels [experiences] the form of the way (*uriping sengsem ngrasakaké wujuding dalan*).

d e a b c: A love of feeling has the form of [i.e., is] the way of life (*sengseming rasa awujud dalaning urip*).

e a b c d: To feel [i.e., experience] the form of the way gives life to [i.e., gives rise to] love (*ngrasakaké wujuding dalan nguripi sengsem*).

Thus it becomes clear that in the art of karawitan, that which is dealt with and studied is nothing other than the expression of the connotations which are contained in the "cryptic literature" mentioned above.

Now, the tuning of the *rebab* is gulu--enem: the (passage)way to/of feeling (*dalaning rasa*). Therefore, the sound of the rebab, which is continuous, shows the passageway to/of feeling. The rebab can also determine the changes in register of the melodies of gendhing and can bring about feelings like happiness, sadness, and so forth.

If these five tones are mixed, arranged, and composed according to fixed principles, they then become the basis for various forms of gendhing. In fact, these very five tones--barang, gulu, dhadha, lima, and enem (form, way, life, love, and feeling)--when arranged into a gendhing, become images in sound with three qualities: pathet enem, pathet sanga, and pathet manyura. The reverberations of sounds with these qualities have a character which grows and a beauty that can be experienced with pleasure. Along with this grows the power of feelings such as joy, happiness,

pain, sadness, nobility, haunting fear, grandeur, contemplation,
compassion, love, displeasure, yearning, and excitement.

It has already been mentioned that three of the five tones (barang,
gulu, and dhadha) together comprise a symbolic image of the human body. The
tone lima suggests love--i.e., love for all sorts of beauty--springing from
the five senses, and the tone enem suggests feeling which penetrates into
the whole body and soul.

This completes our analysis and interpretation of the five tones,
barang, gulu, dhadha, lima, and enem, which together can represent the
human body and the passions and feelings that reside within it. It is now
clear that the meaning and aim of studying and devoting oneself to the art
of karawitan is, in fact, to train oneself (body and soul) to be sensitive
to beauty, with sharpness and quickness of cognition, refinement of
feeling, and determination of will.

Concerning Character

If we are sensitive in our examination of gendhing, whether in sléndro
or in pélog, we will see that each one has its own character.

Gendhing in pathet enem are plain, calm, or simple in character.

Gendhing in pathet sanga are noble, sad, joyful, painful, calm,
or peaceful in character.

Gendhing in pathet manyura are energetic, coquettish, or
arrogant in character.

All of this concerns gendhing in the sléndro tuning. As for the character
of gendhing in the pélog tuning:

Gendhing in pathet enem are noble, grand, or regal in character.

Gendhing in pathet lima are hauntingly frightening, contemplative,
or awesome in character.

Gendhing in pathet barang are compassionate, melancholy, crisp,
clear, or happy in character.

What has been stated above raises a question. How can one name the
character of gendhing in the first place? Before offering an answer, I
must explain that true study of and devotion to the art of karawitan/
gendhing can influence and refine one's sensitivity and sharpen one's

cognition. The feelings mentioned above lead to good conduct, charm, and
beauty, once one has experienced and understood them.

I would like to offer examples from the words of distinguished
philosophers from ancient times, before the Christian Era, quoted from
F. Atmodarsono's *Mardawa Swara* [1957:52].

Aristotle (384-322 B.C.): "Music for the soul of man is like a doctor
for a body that is suffering illness."

Plato (427-347 B.C.): "In the context of study, athletics should be
balanced by music."

Kong Fu Tse [Confucius] (551-479 B.C.): "If one wants to know the
quality of a certain country's government and customs, just listen to
its music."

Jaap Kunst writes in *Music in Java* [1973(1):131] about the Spanish
guitarist, Andrés Segovia, who toured Java in 1933:

When this musician was a little boy he used to hear the priest
depict the glories of Heaven, in which the chants of the blessed
souls were an important element, and the way he used to imagine
it was, that each of the souls would sing as his heart moved him,
and without giving heed to the song of the other souls. But,
since in Heaven everything is perfect, all these separate voices,
without wanting to, as it were, joined together into one
wonderful and glorious hymn. Now that was the very thing that
Segovia was reminded of on hearing for the first time the Paku
Alam[an][12] gamelan, with sindhèn and gérongan: to his hearing,
none of the parties seemed to trouble about the other voices, and
yet everything flowed together in the highest form of harmonic
unity, into one fascinating whole: truly "le ciel sur la terre."

The opinions of these distinguished people are sharp and profound. Why
are their opinions so profound? How can they distinguish between gendhing
that have various characters? Indeed, it is accomplished through the many
qualities that they possess, such as reverence of mind, sharp refinement of
sensitivity, quickness of cognition, patience and purity of heart, high
levels of thought, deep understanding, and inherent diligence and
intelligence. Even though the qualities listed above differ from one
another, when they are combined and work together, they can become a
powerful force which forms a container of wisdom. It is with this wisdom
that one can really experience [feel] the character of the gendhing that
one hears.

I would like you to know that the tones of the gamelan operate in the
same way. Although there are only five tones in the gamelan, when these
tones are laid out and arranged into a gendhing, bounded and governed by
the rules of pathet, and are played well according to principles--because
those who play their parts are all experts, knowledgeable in the art of
performing karawitan/gendhing--the result is a gendhing that possesses
great influential power. The influence of a gendhing, [once performed, is
like an arrow, no longer powered by the archer's bow, that][13] speeds toward
its target. ([In both the shooting of an arrow and the playing of a
gendhing,] there is the same give-and-take, action and reaction, and flow
of energy.)

Explanation. I am going to offer an example of how one art may send
its influence out beyond those who perform it. This means that one art can
influence, and be influenced by, other arts; there is give-and-take, flow
back and forth.

For example, in a certain place there is an informal gamelan
performance (*uyon-uyon*). All the people who are going to perform gather
together, making it more and more lively. Some of them are happy to meet
again, since they have not seen each other for a long time.

When all the gamelan players and male and female singers are there,
they begin to play a gendhing. The joyful sound of all those who are
performing and listening is really extraordinary. Then, right in the
middle of this enjoyment--with everyone listening to the melodious sound of
the gamelan, the soft and pleasant voice of the *pesindhèn* with her
appropriate *wangsalan* [short poetic form], and the strong sustained voices
of the *gérong*--as luck would have it, not far away from the place of the
uyon-uyon a funeral procession is passing by. (In former times, those who
accompanied the corpse sang *kidung* together in Arabic. Now these melodies,
when heard and felt, sound moving, melancholy, sad, painful, and troubled.)
The reverberation of the sounds of the kidung-singing seem as if they too
join in the mourning, as if they themselves could offer condolences.

When the people enjoying themselves at the uyon-uyon see and hear the
kidung-singing of the people in the funeral procession, they suddenly
become glum. Their enjoyment diminishes and a feeling of sorrow grows.
Conversely, the people who are singing kidung together hear the uyon-uyon--
the joyful sound of singing and gendhing--and all of a sudden they brighten
up. Their feeling of grief and sorrow diminishes and a joyful feeling
grows.

The strength of influence in the realm of art is this great. Likewise, in the realm of social interaction; if we are to become a strong and steadfast people, we must have the same give-and-take and flow back and forth in our lives together here on earth. The short moral lesson (*sari basa*)[14] below clearly states the means to bring about good, lasting, social interaction, free from harshness and hostility.

To Join in Happiness and to Join in Sadness

When one feels pity for someone who is miserable, there is still a glad feeling—albeit slight—which grows because one sees that person suffering. At least, one is happy that the person who is suffering such misery is someone other than oneself.

Be happy along with one who is happy; be sad along with one who is sad. There are many people who can feel someone else's sadness, but only a few who can feel happy that another person has been blessed with happiness. If one is able to understand someone else's sadness, then one is nearer to understanding one's own good fortune.

It is a virtue for one to fully understand someone else's good fortune. A pain in my little finger, even though it may only have been pricked by a needle, is sufficient to make me unhappy. Yet, the suffering or death of millions of people might not be able to affect me.

One who can understand the good deeds and kindness of others and can be happy when someone else is happy—she/he is the most fortunate of all.

Concerning Pathet

What is pathet? This is the familiar question so often heard in the realm of the art of karawitan. The explanation and answer are: . . . ? There should be an answer and an explanation that are easy to perceive so that this matter of pathet may be understood clearly. First of all, one must proceed slowly and carefully when investigating the word "pathet" along with its meaning. I would like you to know that there is, in fact, a usage of the word "pathet" that has absolutely no connection with gamelan (gendhing).

For example, when the elders gave advice or moral lessons to their children and grandchildren in former times, there was one who once said,

Listen all of my grandchildren and great-grandchildren, if you
wish to achieve your high aspirations, first all your desires
must be restrained (*dipathet*). You must keep your body strong;
otherwise its condition will weaken and deteriorate, and, along
with it, the condition of your soul. Every day people are certain to have various desires. I will give an example. Desire
flows continuously, like water in a river, and it must be dammed
up (be restrained, stopped; i.e., dipathet). When the water
(desire) has built up, concentrate your thoughts and look for
what you really desire. When you are sure you have found it,
open the dam and the water (desire) will rush out and carry you
quickly to the aspiration you wish to attain.

This was his moral lesson. It is very clear that this use of the word
"pathet" has no connection with gamelan (gendhing). For, if desire is
restrained (dipathet), the implication is that it is held back or checked.

Let us examine the usage of the word "pathet" that does have a
connection with the study of gamelan. When one learns to play gamelan (for
example, to play the *saron*), one learns that the striking of the keys must
be damped (dipathet). One damps only when one has already struck the next
key in the melody, so that the sounds of the keys do not overlap and blur
together, but yield a pleasing resonance or hum. If the striking of the
saron is damped right away, the sound is dull, with no resonance, and is
unpleasant to hear. The word "pathet," in both its nonmusical and its
musical usages, is used above as a verb. Verbs are words that express
action or doing. If, for example, the word "pathet" is made an active
verb, it becomes "mathet." Now, this verb may be conjugated by the rules
of the *tanggap tri purusa* [first-, second-, third-person passive]. The use
of these passive constructions means that the subject of the sentence is
not necessarily the one who carries out the action or the one who is
involved in the situation referred to by the verb. The object of a certain
action may also be the subject of a sentence. The prefixes for this
tanggap tri purusa, which express the subject of the predicate--i.e., the
one who performs the action--are of three kinds.

I.   ". . . is restrained/damped by me." First-person passive.
     dak (= tak) pathet   [low Javanese]
     kula pathet   [high Javanese]
     kawula pathet   [high Javanese: speaking to
                                a person of higher rank]

menira pathet   [court Javanese]
ingsun pathet   [high Javanese: king speaking
                            of himself]

II. ". . . is restrained/damped by you." Second-person passive.
kok pathet   [low Javanese]
dika pathet   [middle-level Javanese]
ijengandika pathet   [high Javanese: used in wayang]
sampéyan pathet   [high Javanese: only slightly
                            honorific]
panjenengan pathet   [high Javanese: speaking to a
                            person of higher rank]
pekenira pathet   [court Javanese: used in wayang]

III. ". . . is restrained/damped." Third-person passive.
di pathet   [low Javanese]
dipun pathet   [high Javanese]
dèn pathet   [Old Javanese: literary]
(It is not yet known who carries out the action.)

Before explaining about pathet in relation to gendhing, I would like
to offer the opinions of karawitan experts for the purposes of comparison.
Which of these various opinions can best serve in the science of karawitan
as a basis for understanding the principles and rules by which pathet may
be defined? I leave this up to the wisdom of my readers. The opinions are
given in the following quotation from R. M. [Radèn Mas] Wasisto
Surjodiningrat's *Gending Beksan Mataram* (1976:iii).

In the sléndro tuning there are three pathet, i.e., pathet
nem, sanga, and manyura; in pélog there are also three pathet,
which are, according to tradition, pathet lima, nem, and barang,
but in this book are reordered to become pathet nem, lima, and
barang. Experienced gamelan musicians can perhaps differentiate
one pathet from another but the understanding of pathet is a
difficult matter. There are several definitions of pathet that
do not offer much help; pathet has even become the subject of
a doctoral dissertation by the American gamelan scholar, Mantle
Hood, who received his degree from the University of Amsterdam.

According to Djojodipoera [1921], "Pathet is the couch or bed of
a melody." According to Djakoeb and Wignjaroemeksa [1913],
"Pathet serves to allow the gendhing to sit down." Dr. Mantle
Hood [1954:248] gives a definition of pathet which is longer than

half a page: "Pathet is a concept of tonality applied to two nonequidistant and distinct scale systems, the five-tone *sléndro* and the seven-tone *pélog*. . . . Each of the three pathet of both scale systems is associated with one of the three time-periods of *wayang* and with certain hours of the day or night in the following parallel pairs: sléndro pathet nem, pélog pathet lima-- sléndro pathet sanga, pélog pathet nem--sléndro pathet manyura, pélog pathet barang. . . ."

Ki Hadjar Déwantara, in his book, *Sari Swara* [1964], is able to give more practical guidance concerning pathet: "Pathet makes clear the register of the musical phrase or composition." The basic tone of sléndro pathet nem is gulu; of sléndro pathet sanga, lima; and of sléndro pathet manyura, nem; so that the stroke of the gong generally occurs with tones 2, 5, and 6, respectively. Change from pathet sanga to pathet manyura by going up one tone is possible; change from sléndro tuning to pélog is also frequent (although the reverse is not)--i.e., from sléndro pathet sanga to pélog pathet lima, from sléndro pathet manyura to pélog pathet barang, and occasionally from sléndro pathet nem to pélog pathet nem (*Raja Manggala* and *Merak Kasimpir* being two examples). For this reason the writer organizes the sequence of pathet in pélog as nem, lima, barang, and not the usual pélog pathet lima, nem, and barang.

I leave it up to the readers how they think and feel about the above quotation.

The idea of pathet that is discussed below may cause some confusion and be obscure to the reader, because the route to understanding this concept is quite roundabout. Nevertheless, our investigation had best continue, so that we may clearly feel the extent of people's understanding of pathet; we will use this understanding as a basis for the principles that follow.

Explanation. This concerns the writing of pathet enem (6), pathet sanga (9), and pathet manyura (?).

Incorrect	Correct
pathet 6	pathet enem
pathet 9	pathet sanga
(pathet manyura)	pathet manyura

Why is it wrong to write with numerals? It is wrong because numerals are

used to express a total or a sequence of something, such as "1 2 3 4 5 6 7
8 9 10," etc. Words, whether in root form or with inflections and affixes,
have literal meanings as well as figurative (borrowed) ones.[15] For
example, in the sentence, "That elephant is big," the word "big" is used
literally. In the expressions, "big-hearted" and "big man," it is used
figuratively. In the sentence, "There are 6 boys and 9 girls studying
gamelan," the "6" and "9" are use literally. "Enem" [lit. '6'] and "sanga"
[lit. '9'] are used figuratively in the following sentences: "Gendhing
Bondhèt is in laras sléndro pathet enem." "Gendhing *Gambir Sawit* is in
laras sléndro pathet sanga." "Gendhing *Kutut Manggung* is in laras sléndro
pathet manyura." This seems a sufficient explanation of the correct and
incorrect ways of writing, for the numbers "6" and "9" are borrowed here
and become nouns--the names of pathet. As mentioned above, they are
"borrowed" and used metaphorically. The spelling of the word must also be
complete: "pathet enem," not "pathet nem." What, then, is the difference
between the words "enem" and "nem"? It is not just in spelling, but also
in pronunciation.

"How many *saron* are there in all?"
"In all there are six (*enem*)."
"How many days has she/he studied gamelan?"
"She/he has studied gamelan for six (*nem*) days."[16]

Thus, it is advisable to write in full "pathet enem."

I would now like to reveal something about the word "pathet" in
connection with the words "enem," "sanga," and "manyura." "Pathet enem,"
"pathet sanga," and "pathet manyura" are compound words. Compound words
consist of two different words combined into one and are of two types:
(a) compounds made up of complete words, and (b) compounds made up of parts
of words (contractions). We may differentiate three kinds according to
their meanings.

    1. From nouns:

        nagasari [name of a flower and also of a popular snack; from *naga*
            'mythical serpent' and *sari* 'essence', 'nectar']

        gula batu ['crystallized sugar'; from *gula* 'sugar' and *batu*
            'rock']

        gandasuli [name of a batik pattern; from *ganda* 'smell' and *suli*,
            name of a tree]

        kwèlem [mixture of two kinds of manggo fruits; from *kwèni*, name of
            a type of long, stringy manggo, and *pelem* 'manggo']

2. From adjectives and adverbs:

silih-asih [name for the interplay of two contrasting metals on
a sheath cover for a Javanese dagger (the term connotes
sexual intercourse); from *silih* 'exchange', 'alternate',
'borrow', and *asih* 'love']

undha-usuk ['to have different levels'; from *undha* 'to let fly'
and *usuk* 'terrace', 'rib', 'beam']

lunglit ['emaciated', 'skin and bones'; from *balung* 'bone' and
kulit 'skin']

3. From verbs:

suduk-jiwa ['to stab oneself to death'; from *suduk* 'dagger',
'stab', and *jiwa* 'soul']

gotong-royong ['mutual cooperation'; from *gotong* 'to carry
together on the shoulders' and *royong* 'to lift noisily
together']

dhokkur ['to squat facing away from an exalted person'; from
dhodhok 'squat' and *mungkur* 'turn one's back to']

Once again, all these forms of compound words can be differentiated or
divided into two categories according to their meanings [i.e., the way
their meanings relate to the meanings of the constituent root words]:

I.   Those that drop the meaning of the constituent root words and
     unite those two words to produce a new meaning, such as *nagasari*
     (the name of a foodstuff and of a flower).

II. Those that retain the separate meanings of the constituent root
     words. In the expression *pager-bata* ['brick wall'], the meaning
     of *pager* is still "pager" ['fence', 'outside wall'], and the
     meaning of *bata* is still "bata" ['brick']. In the expression
     iwak-kebo ['water buffalo meat'], the meaning of *iwak* is still
     "iwak" ['meat'], and the meaning of *kebo* is still "kebo" ['water
     buffalo']. In the expression *pathet enem*, the meaning of *pathet*
     is still "pathet," and the meaning of *enem* is still "enem."

Explanation.

A. Compound words that drop the meaning of the constituent root words
to produce a new meaning may properly be called "joined compound words."
If they are given the [genitive or topic-marking] suffix -*é*, it is the
latter of the two words that receives the suffix: *nagasariné* ['the, his,
her, their, or its nagasari'], not *nagané sari*.

B. Compound words that retain the meanings of their constituent root
words may properly be called "unjoined compound words." If they are given
the suffix -é, it is the former of the two words that receives the suffix:
patheté enem ['the, its, or their pathet is enem'], and not *pathet enemé*.

There are several words that are nearly synonymous with the word
"pathet," all of which have the final syllable -*et*, such as *singget*
['separate', 'divide', 'partition'], *pepet* ['block off', 'bar'], *buntet*
['closed off at one end'], *sandhet* ['hold back', 'restrain'], and *gethet*
['mark off with a notch or a line', 'determine', 'fix']. For instance,
imagine a long house that is to be turned into a house with three rooms. It
is partitioned ("dipun singget") into three, and blocked off ("dipun
pepet"), or closed off ("dipun bunteti"), perhaps with Javanese bamboo wall
panels. Now there is a boundary between one room and another. Similarly,
when desires are held back ("dipun sandhet") they are given a boundary so
they will not become excessive, i.e., they are restrained. Wood that is
going to be sawed is notched off ("dipun gethet")--i.e., it is marked, or
bounded off--so that the lengths will be even. The meanings of the words
above are almost the same (synonymous). But, the particular situation
being described or explained of course determines how these words can be
used most appropriately.

Now, what is it really that is called "pathet"? For a question
phrased this way, there is already an explanation (given above). But, for
pathet in relation to enem, sanga, and manyura, the question must be
completed. One should ask, "What is it that is called 'pathet enem',
'pathet sanga', and 'pathet manyura'?" This question cannot be
satisfactorily answered in brief, but requires explanation and
clarification. Moreover, those who wish to understand this matter deeply
must be mature in their thinking and sharp in their sensitivities.

In the art of karawitan/gendhing we are dealing with *sound*, while the
gamelan serves as a tool. The art of karawitan is, in fact, the art of
sound, which one must practice with seriousness and in earnest. Beyond
this, one also needs the ability to use the five senses to perceive with
sensitivity, which may then stimulate the powers of memory and
intelligence. Of all that has its source in the five senses, it is the
power of hearing that is most important in this context. By using the
power of hearing, all sounds perceived from the gamelan, *lagu* ['melody'],
cèngkok ['formulaic melody'], gendhing, sindhèn, and gérong, can be
absorbed and can affect human thought, character, and feeling. Thus, when
one studies the art of karawitan with a basic understanding of its

principles, a harmonious feeling may arise between the power of the soul of man and the power of the soul of the gendhing.

On the other hand, the important power in a gendhing is its ability to make us aware of the specific feelings which characterize it, such as happiness, sadness, and so forth. The art of karawitan is always based on the power of hearing, so that such feelings can really be felt and absorbed. If one is going to make use of one's power of hearing in this context, one must be familiar with the sounds (*ngeng*) of the gamelan tones and be able to "read" them.[17] These are generally labelled with the notational signs 1, 2, 3, 5, 6, and ̇1. Furthermore, they should be changed around until one is really at home with the sounds of the gamelan tones.

Why must one be at home with "reading" the sounds of these tones? Because this is the way to seek out the characteristics of a certain gendhing and to feel that a gendhing is of a certain pathet.

Now, let us continue our investigation into the understanding of pathet with pure and clear thought. Even though the matter of pathet is very difficult to explain in brief, it is possible, nevertheless, to at least represent in abbreviated form the character and power of a gendhing that has influence on mankind, complete with the pure form of its pathet, as follows:

a. grambyangan for gendhing in pathet enem:
    enem – lima – dhadha – gulu (6 – 5 – 3 – 2)

b. grambyangan for gendhing in pathet sanga:
    gulu – barang – enem – lima (2 – 1 – 6 – 5)

c. grambyangan for gendhing in pathet manyura:
    dhadha – gulu – barang – enem (3 – 2 – 1 – 6)

This explanation is already sufficient for one to carefully analyze and seek out the distinguishing features of a gendhing whose *grambyangan* is like that given above. Yet, from this explanation a question is certain to arise. Why does the grambyangan in a certain pathet consist of only four tones, while the gamelan has five?

Explanation. The grambyangan for gendhing in pure pathet enem is simply 6 – 5 – 3 – 2. Although they may be rearranged, only these four tones are used. The excluded tone is barang (1). Why? If the tone barang (1) is used often in the realm of pathet enem, the feeling that it is a gendhing in pathet enem is lost. However, if the tone barang (1) is used only occasionally in pathet enem, but in the right places, this can feel pleasant and add to the beauty.

The grambyangan for gendhing in pure pathet sanga is simply 2 - 1 - 6 - 5. Although they may be rearranged, only these four tones are used. The excluded tone is dhadha (3). Why? If the tone dhadha (3) is used often in the realm of pathet sanga, the feeling that it is a gendhing pathet sanga is lost. However, if the tone dhadha (3) is used only occasionally in pathet sanga, but in the right places, this can feel pleasant and add to the beauty.

The grambyangan for gendhing in pure pathet manyura is simply 3 - 2 - 1 - 6. Although they may be rearranged, only these four tones are used. The excluded tone is lima (5). Why? If the tone lima (5) is used too often in the realm of pathet manyura, the feeling that it is a gendhing in pathet manyura is lost. However, if the tone lima (5) is used only occasionally in pathet manyura, but in the right places, this can feel pleasant and add to the beauty.

It has already been mentioned that the art of karawitan/gendhing is really the art of dealing with, and studying, sound. We perceive sound by means of hearing. Once we have heard sound (the sound of the gamelan), it is perceived by our feeling. Hearing and feeling together receive the sounds of the gamelan which have been made into a gendhing and then give rise to a sensation which may or may not be pleasant. The method presented above, derived from the grambyangan, is sufficient for seeking out all gendhing whose pathet is enem, sanga, or manyura.

Gamelan and Wayang Kulit

Concerning gendhing in pathet enem, pathet sanga, and pathet manyura that have a connection with the shadow play, there are two matters which are basic and central:

1. the matter of wayang kulit (purwa)

2. the matter of gamelan/gendhing

Gamelan/gendhing are needed to accompany the performance of wayang kulit. Of course, the gamelan/gendhing are controlled by the wayang play. Nevertheless, even though one rules and the other follows, they still join together--with give-and-take and a flow of energy back and forth--which is necessary in order to bring forth the clear form of truth that the wayang kulit has come to portray. Now, it is in the joining of the two that

pathet has grown and found its proper place, enabling it to become one with
the action of the wayang story (*lakon*), and to serve as a basic principle
down to the present time.

   In former times wayang kulit was usually performed at night, beginning
at 7:30, with a half hour for the *talu* ("talu" means 'begin'). Then, the
gendhing that introduced the beginning of the first scene was played. From
the beginning of the first scene (at eight o'clock) until midnight, the
gendhing were in pathet enem. From midnight to three o'clock the gendhing
were in pathet sanga, and from three to six o'clock they were in pathet
manyura.

   <u>Note</u>. I would like you to know that if we are going to investigate
the gendhing that accompany wayang kulit (in a wayang lakon), we must first
turn back and remember "The Cryptic Literature Concealed in the Tones of
the Gamelan," above. It will be used to investigate the sequence of
gendhing and their pathet. All of this will come from the tones barang,
gulu, dhadha, lima, and enem, which suggest form, way, life, love, and
feeling. Deriving, first, from the Cryptic Literature, then coming into
clearer focus in the imagination, the real truth that one finds in an all-
night wayang performance spreads forth.

   Why do gendhing and their pathet fit so nicely into place
sequentially? The reasons will be made completely clear in the explanation
below. The grambyangan for gendhing in pathet enem (which has been
explained above) is 6 - 5 - 3 - 2, enem, lima, dhadha, gulu (*rasa sengsem
nguripi dalan* ['the feeling of love gives life to the way']). If these
tones are juggled and rearranged they do not go beyond the bounds of that
sentence; for example, *dalaning urip nengsemi rasa* ['the way of life loves
feelings'], and so on, in other forms of rearrangement.

   Now, what is the excluded tone? The excluded tone is barang (1):
"form." How can there be flow back and forth between gendhing and wayang
lakon? The first act in a wayang performance begins at 8:00 P.M. and lasts
until midnight. The basic content of this section, and the issues it
raises, are mainly concerned with what will occur later. These issues are
also found within the gendhing in pathet enem. The grambyangan is
6 - 5 - 3 - 2 (*rasa sengsem nguripi dalan* ['the feeling of love gives life
to the way']; *dalaning urip nengsemi rasa* ['the way of life loves
feelings']; *sengsem nguripi dalaning rasa* ['love gives life to the way of
feeling']; *nguripi dalaning rasa sengsem* ['the feeling of love is given
life by the way']). At this point in the lakon there is no form, or, at
least, the form is not yet clear to the audience. (In other words, how is

the lakon going to proceed later on?) The tone barang (1), "form," is not present, because the form of the lakon is not yet clear. Suppose the grambyangan is shortened, by taking the first and last tones of 6 - 5 - 3 - 2, which gives us 6 - 2 (*rasa - dalan* ['feeling' - 'way']). At this point in the lakon we are just thinking about the direction the lakon will take later on, because it has not yet assumed definite shape (there is still no form).

The first section, lasting from 8:00 P.M. until midnight, has already ended. During the second section (midnight to 3:00 A.M.), we shift to gendhing in pathet sanga. The content and central issues of the lakon and the material that will be discussed are found in the grambyangan of pathet sanga: 2 - 1 - 6 - 5 (*dalane awujud rasa sengsem* ['the way has the form of (i.e., is) the feeling of love']; *sengseming rasa dadi wujuding dalan* ['the love of feeling becomes the form of way']; *wujuding rasa sengsem ambuka dalan* ['the form of feeling love opens the way']; *rasa sengsem dadi dalaning wujud* ['the feeling of love becomes the way of form']). If we describe the wayang period accompanied by gendhing in pathet sanga in summary form, we find we are discussing and depicting the ways of love, the forms of love, and the feelings of love. Suppose the grambyangan is shortened, by taking the first and last tones of 2 - 1 - 6 - 5, which gives us 2 - 5 (*dalaning - sengsem* ['the ways to/of love']). The way which leads to love and passion is clearly the subject matter of gendhing in pathet sanga. To reinforce this fact, the story is accompanied by turmoil in nature, which gives rise to fiery passions that first flicker and then flare up, out of control.

Therefore, the tone dhadha (3), "life," is absent. Here life is blocked out by love and passion, so that one is not conscious of his mortality. Such is the fiery power of passion in gendhing in pathet sanga.

After the section from midnight to 3:00 A.M. has ended, the section from 3:00 until 6:00 begins and we shift to gendhing in pathet manyura. The content and central issues of the performance, and the material to be discussed, are found in the grambyangan of pathet manyura: 3 - 2 - 1 - 6 (*uriping dalan awujud rasa*) ['the life of the way takes the form of feeling']; *rasa mujudake dalaning urip* ['feeling gives form to the way of/ to life']; *dalane awujud rasaning urip* ['the way takes form as the feelings of living']; *wujuding rasa nguripi dalan* ['the forms of feeling give life to the way']). If we describe the wayang period accompanied by gendhing in pathet manyura in summary form, we find the life of feeling, the ways of feeling, the forms of feeling. Suppose the grambyangan is shortened, by

taking the first and last tones of 3 - 2 - 1 - 6, which gives us 3 - 6
(*uriping rasa* ['the life of feeling']; *rasaning urip* ['the feeling of
life']); things become clearer and clearer. The basic issue in the section
of the play with gendhing in pathet manyura is the understanding of what
has come before in the gendhing in pathet enem and in pathet sanga. In
this case, the tone lima (5) is absent (love/passionate attraction). The
problem of love/passion has been left behind in the gendhing in pathet
sanga. So, the only thing left to do is experience life. What sort of
life? I will explain below.

Is the wayang performance over at this point? This question can be
answered very briefly: not yet. Gendhing in pathet manyura are not over
quite yet. There is an extension which is instrumental in doing away with
everything that hinders and disturbs the progress within the play. These
hindrances and disturbances are taken care of by what is called *Sampak
Galong* [the name of a gendhing]. In wayang it might be represented by a
warrior whose duty it is to eliminate trouble in a situation and get rid of
everything that blocks the road leading to his destination.

Now *Sampak Galong* can be abbreviated, through the "Cryptic Literature,"
as 2 - 3 (gulu - dhadha): *dalaning urip* ['the way to life'].

Note. *Sampak Galong* begins with tone 2 ("way") and ends with tone 3
("life"). In the portion of the wayang performance accompanied by *Sampak
Galong*, many characters fall in battle. They take their places [in the
afterlife] according to the degree of devotion they demonstrated while
still carrying out their duties on earth.

TRANSLATOR'S NOTES

1. The translator wishes to acknowledge the assistance of Drs. Mukidi Adisunarto in the early stages of this translation.

2. A "sangkala" is a cryptic way to represent a date in words or images. It has been used by Javanese poets since the fourteenth century as a means of dating poetry without including the actual numerals within the text. Each word used in a sangkala functions both as an ordinary word (with its lexical meaning) and as a sign for one of the digits from 0 to 9. When read from left to right, a sangkala presents a linguistic phrase or sentence; when read from right to left, it gives the date, digit by digit. Nowadays sangkala are found not only in newly composed poetry, but in introductions and prefaces to prose writings. They give the prose a poetic flavor that links it with the long tradition of Javanese literature.

3. This is education in a broader sense than formal schooling: enculturation, or learning manners and social values. Implied here, and stated explicitly below, is the notion of education of the outer, public self (*lair*) and the inner, private self (*batin*).

4. Raden Gathutkaca is one of the magically powerful sons of Bima, the second eldest of the five Pandhawa brothers in the *Mahābhārata* epic.

5. Petruk is one of the *panakawan* (clown servants) who aids the Pandhawa brothers, particularly the third eldest, Arjuna. In episodes based on the *Mahābhārata*, he invariably appears with all his brothers and his father, all of whom are panakawan and dearly loved by the Javanese audiences.

6. Patih Sangkuni is the conniving prime minister of the Korawa brothers, the rivals of the Pandhawas in the *Mahābhārata*.

7. Wrekudara is another name for Bima, the second eldest of the five Pandhawa brothers.

8. Durna is the teacher of the Korawas and Pandhawas in the *Mahābhārata* epic. In Javanese wayang, particularly in Yogyakarta (home of the

author), Durna is considered extremely evil. Krendha Wahana is the
kingdom ruled by Bathari Durga, the powerful ogre consort of the god
Shiva/Śiwa.

9. The pélog tuning system includes two additional tones (*bem* and
   pélog). The author lists the five names common to both the sléndro
   and pélog tuning systems. He has told me in conversation that this
   scheme works for the pélog tuning system as well as for the sléndro
   one, because the tone bem replaces barang, and the tone pélog
   replaces either dhadha or lima, depending on context.

10. This argument works better for Javanese than for English. Although
    we can ask, "How much is that pencil?" we can also correctly ask,
    "What is the price of that pencil?" In Javanese one cannot use the
    interrogative "*apa*" ('what', 'which') for questions dealing with
    quantities. Instead one must use "*pira*" ('how much', 'how many').

11. The *(Serat) Nīti Śāstra* is a "collection of Old Javanese moralistic
    maxims in Indian meters. . . . Several maxims are Old Javanese
    adaptations of Sanskrit ślokas" (Pigeaud 1967-1970[1]:104). The
    (Serat) Dharma Śunya is a didactic poem in Old Javanese said to date
    from the early fifteenth century (Poerbatjaraka 1952:55).

12. The Paku Alam is the prince of a small court (the Paku Alaman) in
    Yogyakarta.

13. This analogy with archery came up during a discussion with the
    author, and, in the opinion of the translator, helps to clarify a
    meaning that in the original text is only implied. The bow is no
    longer drawn; its power has been released and transferred to the
    arrow, which reaches far beyond the place where the archer stands.

14. "*Sari basa*" is the term for short moral lessons, which consist of
    straightforward advice together with the reasoning behind such
    advice. In contrast to parables, they are not narrative, but instead
    give only the essential message (*sari* 'essence') by means of language
    (*basa*).

15. The author uses the words "*barès*" ('straightforward', 'plain'), which
    I translate as "literal" (i.e., denotative); and "*éntar*," which I
    translate as "figurative" (i.e., connotative). The author explained
    in a personal interview that, by "borrowed," he means that a word
    used figuratively is separated ("borrowed") from the literal meaning
    of the word, and is used metaphorically, drawing only on the wider

connotations and inferences of the word and not on its literal
meaning.

16. In Javanese some of the number words assume different forms,
    depending on whether they are used as modifiers or not. According to
    Javanese grammar, the number words that end in vowels, such as "*lima*"
    (5), become nasalized ("*limang*") when used as modifiers preceding the
    words they modify. In this case, the author may seem to be splitting
    hairs, as "enem" and "nem" do not end in vowels; but the word "enem"
    is, he argues, the basic form of the word, and "nem" is derived from
    it, just as "lima" is the basic form of the word for "five" and
    "limang" derived from it. The author supports this opinion with
    reference to Dwijasewaya (1923[2]:110-11), where this difference
    between "enem" and "nem" is explained. Note also that, in Old
    Javanese, there existed a nasalized form of the word "nem"
    ("*nemang*").

17. I interpret this to mean 'to be able to know which tones one is
    hearing as one listens to a gendhing'; 'to have facility in aural
    perception and retention', but without necessarily writing down what
    is heard.

ICHTISAR TÉORI KARAWITAN
DAN TEKNIK MENABUH GAMELAN

[Summary of the Theory of Karawitan
and
Technique of Playing the Gamelan]

Compiled by Sulaiman Gitosaprodjo
Malang: Keluarga Karawitan RRI Malang (1970)

Translated from Indonesian by Judith Becker

TABLE OF CONTENTS

PREFACE[1]

Whenever we hear the sound of a gamelan, nearby or far away, we are influenced by its sound. Sometimes the sound gives us strength, sometimes the sound makes us sad. Sometimes the sound makes us tense, and then later we are happy to hear it. Gamelan influences our souls. This is the result of the efforts of our noble ancestors. Who does not feel transported to the realm of dreams when hearing Ladrang *Gonjang Ganjing* with pesindhèn and gérong? "It [listening to gamelan music] is like a dream of being carried to a heaven full of beautiful nymphs" (quoted from a Spanish guitarist who visited Indonesia in 1933). Who does not skip for joy when hearing *Pangkur*? Who does not feel sad when hearing Sendhon *Tlutur*? Who is not reminded of romance when hearing *Renyep*? In short, *karawitan* is the result of art which is noble, refined, beautiful, and can influence the soul of mankind.

Karawitan is a branch of Javanese art. The branches of art give input to one another. Gamelan music does not stand alone, but is closely connected with other Javanese arts.

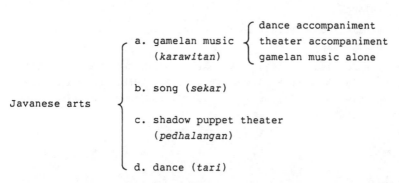

Javanese arts

a. gamelan music (*karawitan*)
- dance accompaniment
- theater accompaniment
- gamelan music alone

b. song (*sekar*)

c. shadow puppet theater (*pedhalangan*)

d. dance (*tari*)

Karawitan, then, does not stand alone, but rather is interconnected with the other branches of art. The art of gamelan playing is deep and broad. Rarely is any one musician skilled in playing all the instruments of the gamelan.

ACKNOWLEDGMENTS

Materials in this book were compiled from the following sources.

I. Lecture notes from the following:

R. L. [Radèn Lurah] Wignjosusastro, teacher at the Konservatori Karawitan Indonesia at Surakarta and lecturer at the Akademi Seni Karawitan Indonesia at Surakarta

R. M. P. [Radèn Mas Panji] Sutopinilih, teacher at the Konservatori Karawitan Indonesia at Surakarta

R. Ng. [Radèn Ngabèhi] Prajapangrawit, lecturer at the Akademi Seni Karawitan Indonesia at Surakarta

R. L. [Radèn Lurah] Martopangrawit, lecturer at the Akademi Seni Karawitan Indonesia at Surakarta

R. M. [Radèn Mas] Soekanto [Sastrodarsono], teacher at the Konservatori Karawitan Indonesia at Surakarta

II. Performance in several gamelan groups in Surakarta, Surabaya, and Malang

III. Bibliography [Full references are given in this volume's general bibliography.]

Atmodarsono (1956), Hadjar Dewantara (1935-1936), Kodiron (1964), Najawirangka (1936), Probohardjono (1961, 1963, 1966), Ranggawarsita (1957), Ronggosworo (1951), Soekanto (1954), Tedjosumarto (1958), and Tiknopranoto (1963).

CHAPTER I

GAMELAN

Instruments of the Gamelan

rebab: For a double set of gamelan instruments--two *prangkat* (sléndro and pélog)--it is best to have two rebab, one for sléndro, pélog bem and pélog barang, and one for pélog lima.

kendhang: There are five kinds of kendhang.
1. kendhang gedhé/kendhang gendhing (± 45 centimeters long)
2. kendhang wayangan (± 40 centimeters long)
3. kendhang batangan/kendhang ciblon (± 33 centimeters long)
4. ketipung (± 25 centimeters long)
5. penunthung (± 20 centimeters long)

gendèr barung: Every double set of gamelan instruments has three gendèr barung, one for sléndro, one for pélog bem, and one for pélog barang.

gendèr panerus: Same as gendèr barung.

bonang barung: Every double set of gamelan instruments has two bonang barung, one for sléndro and one for pélog.

bonang panerus: Same as bonang barung.

slenthem: Same as bonang barung.

saron demung: Same as bonang barung.

saron barung: Same as bonang barung.

saron panerus: Same as bonang barung.

kenong: Every complete double set of gamelan instruments contains ten kenong.

kempul: Every complete double set of gamelan instruments contains from six to ten kempul.

gong: Every complete double set of gamelan instruments contains three gong.

kethuk and kempyang:

    a. kethuk: Every complete double set of gamelan instruments contains
       two kethuk. For sléndro, pitch-level 2; for pélog,
       pitch-level 6.

    b. kempyang: Every complete double set of gamelan instruments contains
       two kempyang. For sléndro, pitch-level 1; for pélog, pitch-level 6.

celempung: Every complete double set of gamelan instruments contains two
    celempung, one for sléndro and one for pélog.

siter: The siter is the same as the celempung, only smaller and more
    portable.

siter panerus: The siter panerus is the same as the siter, except that it
    plays twice as fast as the siter and one octave higher.

gambang: Every complete double set of gamelan instruments contains two
    gambang, one for sléndro and one for pélog.

suling: Every complete double set of gamelan instruments contains two
    suling, one for sléndro and one for pélog.

Definitions

gamelan seprangkat: A complete set of gamelan instruments, sléndro or
    pélog. A double set, two prangkat, means a sléndro set plus a
    pélog set.

gangsa ['bronze']: Also called *prunggu*. Bronze is an alloy of copper and
    tin. Most sets of gamelan instruments are made of bronze. Sometimes,
    however, sets are made of iron or brass.

gamelan gedhé: A gamelan set containing many instruments of the knobbed
    type, made of bronze, such as those found at the studios of Radio
    Republik Indonesia [Indonesian National Radio].

gamelan sengganèn: A small set of gamelan instruments, not the knobbed
    type, but the slab type, made from bronze.

gamelan cilik: A small set of gamelan instruments of the slab type, made
    from iron.

wilahan: The slab parts of gamelan instruments, which are made from bronze,
    brass, or iron.

plangkan: The parts of the gamelan instruments that are made from wood
    [i.e., frames]. The different kinds of plangkan are:

a. rancakan: wooden frame of the bonang barung, bonang panerus, kempyang, kethuk, and kenong.

b. pangkon: wooden frame of the saron demung, saron barung, and saron panerus.

c. grobogan: wooden frame of the gendèr barung, gendèr panerus, and slenthem.

d. gayor: rack for hanging the kempul, gong suwukan, and gong gedhé.

pluntur: The cords that support the bronze keys or pots of the gendèr barung, gendèr panerus, bonang barung, and bonang panerus.

klanthé: The cords that support the pots or gongs of the kethuk, kempyang, kenong, kempul, gong suwukan, and gong gedhé.

Famous Gamelan

Surakarta:

a. At the Kraton:

   1. sekatèn gamelan: *Naga Jénggot*
                      Jimat

   2. sléndro gamelan: *Laras Ati*
                   Guntur Madu
                   Kaduk Manis

   3. pélog gamelan: *Pengasih*
                  Kancil Belik
                  Manis Rengga

b. At the Pura Mangku Negaran:

   1. sléndro and pélog gamelan: *Kanyut Mèsem*

   2. sléndro gamelan: *Udan Asih*
                   Udan Riris

   3. pélog gamelan: *Udan Arum*
                  Lipur Tamba Oneng

Yogyakarta:

    a. At the Kraton:

        1. sekatèn gamelan: *Naga Wilaga*
                                  Guntur Sari

        2. sléndro gamelan: *Harja Negara*
                                    Madu Kèntir
                                    Medharsih

        3. pélog gamelan: *Harja Mulya*
                                 Sirat Madu
                                 Megatsih

    b. At the Pura Paku Alaman:

        1. sléndro gamelan: *Pangawé Sari*

        2. pélog gamelan: *Telaga Muncar*

Instrumentation for Different Kinds of Gamelan*

Instrument	gamelan ageng	gamelan klenengan	gamelan gadhon	Notes
rebab	x	x	x	2 instruments
kendhang	x	x	x	5 instruments
gendèr barung	x	x	x	3 instruments
gendèr panerus	x	x	x	3 instruments
bonang barung	x			2 instruments
bonang panerus	x			2 instruments
slenthem	x	x	x	2 instruments
saron demung	x			2 instruments
saron barung	x	x		4 instruments
saron panerus	x			2 instruments
gambang	x	x	x	3 instruments
siter/celempung	x	x		2 instruments
siter panerus	x	x		2 instruments
kenong	x	x		minimum 6, maximum 10
kempul	x	x		minimum 6, maximum 10
gong kemodhong		x	x	pitch-levels 6, 5
gong suwukan	x			2 gongs (slèndro manyura: pitch-level 2; slèndro sanga: pitch-level 1)
gong ageng	x			2 gongs (slèndro manyura: pitch-level 6; slèndro sanga: pitch-level 5)
kethuk and kempyang (engkuk and kemong)	x	x	x	slèndro: pitch-levels 1 (kempyang), 2 (kethuk) pélog: pitch-levels 6 (kempyang), 6 (kethuk)
suling	x	x	x	2 instruments
keprak/kepyak	x			

*The instrumentation for *gamelan ageng* and *gamelan klenèngan* is fixed, while the instrumentation for *gamelan gadhon* is not.

CHAPTER II

LARAS

"*Laras*" is the arrangement of successive tones, from the lowest to the highest, and the harmonious intervals between the tones. The clear vibrations of the tones, and their relative positions, are known as "laras."

Western-style music uses a fixed standard of pitch. Thus, pianos all over the world are tuned in the same way. 'C' on a piano at the radio station in Malang is the same as 'C' on a piano at the radio station in Surabaya, or anywhere else.

Javanese gamelan does not have a fixed standard of pitch. For example, the pitch-level 6 sléndro on the gamelan at the radio station in Surakarta is not the same as pitch-level 6 sléndro at the radio station in Yogyakarta. If it were the same, it would be a coincidence.

There are two kinds of gamelan tunings: sléndro and pélog. According to the system of A. J. Ellis (1814-1890), one octave (6 - 6, [for example]) is equivalent to 1,200 cents. The five sléndro intervals are equal. The octave is divided into five equal parts (240 cents per interval). The seven pélog intervals are not equal.

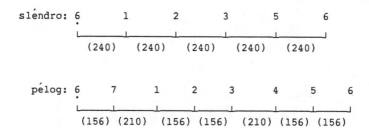

Intervals (Swarantara)

Gamelan intervals are as follows:

a. gembyang: In sléndro this interval has four intervening keys.

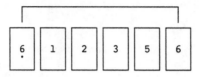

b. kempyung/adu manis: This interval has two intervening keys.

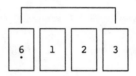

c. gembyung/salah gumun: This interval has one intervening key.

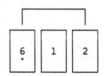

d. kempyang: This is the octave itself, conceived without intervening keys.

Tone Groupings (Nada-nada Kelompok)

Because the intervals between the sléndro tones are the same, sléndro does not have tone groupings. Because the pélog intervals are uneven, the pélog system has tone groupings.

group 1: 6 and 7
group 2: 1̣, 2, and 3̣
group 3: 5 and 6

Tone groupings are very important in the study of the rebab. In compositions in pélog pathet lima and pélog pathet nem, tone 7 is not played, so that the interval between 6 and 1 becomes the largest interval (156 + 210 cents = 366 cents). In compositions in pélog pathet barang, tone 1 is not played, so that the interval between 7 and 2̣ becomes the largest interval (210 cents + 156 cents = 366 cents).

Embat

"*Embat*" is the raising or lowering of the pitch of the gamelan keys when they are tuned.[2] *Embat laras ati* is coquettish. *Embat nyundari* is peaceful. *Embat lugu* is straightforward, frank, and open.

The equidistant tuning of the sléndro gamelan with 240 cents per interval, as well as the pélog intervals with 156 and 210 cents per interval, are only guides. In the end, it is the intuition of the gamelan-maker that determines the tuning of a gamelan.

Common Tones (Tumbuk)

"*Tumbuk* 6" means that pitch-level 6 is the same pitch on both a particular sléndro gamelan and a particular pélog gamelan.

Even though pitch-level 2 sléndro and pitch-level 2 pélog are usually not the same, sometimes they are made the same so that pitch-level 2 is also tumbuk. Also, pitch-level 5 sléndro is usually higher than pitch-level 4 pélog, but they are sometimes tuned the same, for example, in the gamelan [donated by] Paku Buwana X to the Paku Alaman in Yogyakarta.

A gamelan with both pitch-levels 6 and 2 as tumbuk:

sléndro	1	2.	3	5	6	1̇	
pélog		1	2	3	4	5	6	7	1̇

A gamelan with both pitch-levels 5 and 1 as tumbuk:

sléndro	1		2		3		5		6		i
pélog	1	2		3		4	5	6		7	i

The History of Sléndro and Péloq

It is not clear just when the sléndro gamelan had its origins. Some people think it started during the Śailéndra dynasty [Central Java, eighth and ninth centuries A.D.]. The remains of the Śailéndra palace are in the vicinity of Prambanan. It is clear, however, that the sléndro gamelan is older than the pélog. For this reason, the sléndro gamelan is used to accompany the performance of *wayang purwa*. The pélog gamelan, which originated in Kedhiri in the twelfth century, is used to accompany *wayang gedhog*. King Jaya Lengkara reigned in the kingdom of Purwa Carita in twelfth-century Kedhiri.

The pélog gamelan is derived from the sléndro gamelan by narrowing the intervals of the sléndro tuning system in the following manner. Pitch-level 5 is raised closer to pitch-level 6 and pitch-level 3 is lowered closer to pitch-level 2. Pitch-levels 5 and 3 are made to sound "awkward" (*dipélokan*),[3] thus producing the pélog tuning system. Pitch-level 4 is placed between pitch-levels 5 and 3, pitches 7 and 1 between 6 and 2.

Baranq Mirinq

"*Barang miring*" is the name of a tuning that is basically sléndro, but is mixed with pélog vocal pitches. For example, in Gendhing *Renyep*, sléndro [pathet] sanga, vocal tones are used which cannot be found on the keys of a sléndro gamelan. While singing in the sléndro tuning system, at certain fixed points some notes are borrowed from the pélog tuning system. The rebab, though an instrument and not a singer, can also play barang miring, because like a singer the rebab can produce all pitches. The notation of barang miring on a gamelan with tumbuk 6 is as follows:

sléndro	barang miring tone	notation
1	1 pélog	1̶
2	3 pélog	2̶
3	4 pélog	3̶
5	5 pélog	5̶
6	7 pélog	6̶

Barang miring evokes a mood of sadness and grief by reducing the size of the sléndro intervals.

Example: Gendhing *Renyep*, laras sléndro pathet sanga

balungan: .   6   5   .   5   6   1   2

voice and rebab: . 2 2 5 . 5 . 5 5 5 5 5̶ 5 2̶ 2 1 2

Definitions

suara pleng: two pitches, sounding together, perfectly in tune.

suara berombak: two pitches slightly out of tune.

suara nyliring: two pitches rather out of tune.

suara bléro: two pitches very much out of tune.

CHAPTER III

PATHET

"*Pathet*" indicates the register of a composition. For example, in
sléndro pathet sanga, the lowest pitch-level that sounds good is 5, and the
highest pitch-level that sounds good is 2. In sléndro pathet manyura, the
lowest pitch-level that sounds good is 3, while the highest pitch-level
that sounds good is 3.

The sléndro tuning system has three modes (pathet), with the following
registers.

sléndro pathet nem ['six'], low register:

```
     G             . . .
     2 3 5 6 1 2 3 5 6 1 2 3
     . . . .
```

sléndro pathet sanga ['nine'], middle register:

```
         G         . .
         5 6 1 2 3 5 6 1 2
         .
```

sléndro pathet manyura ['peacock'], high register:

```
           G         . . .
           3 5 6 1 2 3 5 6 1 2 3
```

The pélog tuning system has three modes (pathet), with the following
registers.

pélog pathet lima ['five'], low register:

```
               G
       1 2 3 4 5 6 1 2 3 4 5 6
       . . . . .
```

pélog pathet nem ['six'], middle register:

```
               G         . . .
         3 4 5 6 1 2 3 4 5 6 1 2 3
         . . . .
```

pélog pathet barang, high register:

$$
\begin{array}{c}
G \qquad \bullet\;\; \bullet \\
2\;\; 3\;\; 4\;\; 5\;\; 6\;\; 7\;\; 2\;\; 3\;\; 4\;\; 5\;\; 6\;\; 7\;\; 2\;\; 3 \\
\bullet\;\; \bullet\;\; \bullet\;\; \bullet\;\; \bullet
\end{array}
$$

In a sequence of compositions it is possible to go directly from a composition in sléndro pathet nem to a composition in sléndro pathet manyura because, in practice, the melodic patterns of sléndro pathet nem are a mixture of the melodic patterns of sléndro pathet sanga and sléndro pathet manyura, though mostly manyura.

In a sequence of compositions it is possible to go directly from a composition in sléndro pathet sanga to a composition in pélog pathet nem.

Pitch-level 7 rarely occurs in pélog pathet lima and pélog pathet nem. Pitch-level 1 rarely occurs in pélog pathet barang. If pitch-level 1 occurs in pélog pathet barang, it is a borrowed pitch and is used only to add to the beauty of the composition. (Pitch-level 7 occurs in Ladrang *Sembawa*, pélog pathet lima, and also in Ladrang *Gléyong*, pélog pathet nem.)

Pélog manyura, or pélog nyamat, is equivalent to pélog nem with a range from 3 - 3. For example, Ladrang *Pangkur Nyamat* means Ladrang *Pangkur*, pélog nem. The notation is the same as for Ladrang *Pangkur*, sléndro manyura.

Pélog sanga is equivalent to pélog nem, but with a range from 5 - 2. Gendhing *Bondhèt*, pélog pathet nem, and Gendhing *Onang-onang*, pélog pathet nem, were both originally played in sléndro sanga.

Pathetan sléndro manyura and pathetan sléndro sanga can be played in pélog pathet nem. Thus, the notation is in sléndro manyura or sléndro sanga, but the tuning is pélog and the mode is nem. For example, in *wayang kulit* the dhalang will sometimes sing *sulukan* in pélog, even though wayang kulit accompaniment is basically sléndro. In that case, the gamelan must follow the tuning system of the dhalang.

Examples of Compositions in the Different Pathet

sléndro pathet nem: Gendhing *Karawitan*
                       Gendhing *Kabor*
                       Gendhing *Kawit*

If a composition is in low register, it does not use a vocal introduction (*bawa*) or gérong. If, nowadays, there are pieces in sléndro pathet nem that use a vocal introduction or gérong, they have changed from their original form so that the vocal part lies far from the *balungan* [notated saron part]. Examples of such pieces are Gendhing *Titi Pati*, sléndro pathet nem, and Ladrang *Remeng*, sléndro pathet nem.

sléndro pathet sanga: Gendhing *Gambir Sawit*
        Gendhing *Bondhèt*
        Gendhing *Onang-onang*
        Gendhing *Renyep*

Since these compositions are in middle register, they may have a bawa and gérong. The compositions given above are very popular, and can be classified as cheerful compositions.

sléndro pathet manyura: Gendhing *Wida Sari*
         Gendhing *Montro*
         Gendhing *Perkutut Manggung*
         Gendhing *Lobong*

These compositions are in high register. Many compositions in pathet manyura can be classified as cheerful compositions.

pélog pathet lima: Gendhing *Candra Nata*
       Gendhing *Téja Sari*
       Gendhing *Logondhang*
       Gendhing *Kombang Mara*

As in the case of sléndro pathet nem, these compositions are in low register and, basically, do not use a bawa or gérong. Compositions in pélog pathet lima are characterized by refinement and serenity. Thus, it would be a mistake to play these compositions in a sprightly manner.

pélog pathet nem: Gendhing *Randhu Kéntir*
       Gendhing *Bondhèt*
       Gendhing *Onang-onang*
       Gendhing *Rujak Sentul*, etc.

As in the case of sléndro pathet sanga, these compositions are in middle register and, therefore, can have a bawa and/or gérong. The compositions above are popular pieces. They can be characterized as sweet (*manis*) and are easily understood by the public. Although not strictly conforming to tradition, compositions in pélog pathet nem can be played as popular songs (*langgam jawa*) with Western instruments.

pélog pathet barang : Gendhing *Bandhil Ori*
                      Gendhing *Wida Sari*
                      Gendhing *Montro*
                      Gendhing *Jangkung Kuning*

    As in the case of sléndro pathet manyura, these compositions are in
high register. Many compositions in pélog pathet barang are borrowed from
compositions in sléndro pathet manyura. "Borrowed" in this case means that
the compositions were originally in sléndro, then played in pélog with the
same notation, except that pélog pitch-level 7 is substituted for sléndro
pitch-level 1. "Borrowed" can also mean that the pathet is changed within
the same tuning system, for example, Ladrang *Pangkur*, sléndro sanga,
becoming sléndro manyura.

<u>Examples of "Borrowed" Compositions</u>

	Original	Borrowed
Ladrang *Pangkur*	sléndro pathet sanga (final gong 5)	pélog pathet barang (final gong 6, raised one pitch-level)
Gendhing *Bondhèt*	sléndro pathet sanga (final gong 5)	pélog pathet nem (final gong 5)
Gendhing *Onang-onang*	sléndro pathet sanga (final gong 5)	pélog pathet nem (final gong 5)
Gendhing *Perkutut Manggung*	sléndro pathet manyura (final gong 1)	pélog pathet barang (final gong 7)
Gendhing *Wida Sari*	sléndro pathet manyura (final gong 2)	pélog pathet barang (final gong 2)
Gendhing *Loro-loro*	sléndro pathet manyura (final gong 6)	pélog pathet barang (final gong 6)
Gendhing *Lobong*	sléndro pathet manyura (final gong 6)	pélog pathet barang (final gong 6)

Ladrang *Moncèr*	slendro pathet manyura (final gong 6)	pelog pathet barang (final gong 6)
Ladrang *Clunthang*	slendro pathet sanga (final gong 5)	pelog pathet nem (final gong 5)
		slendro pathet manyura (final gong 6)
		pelog pathet barang (final gong 5)
Ketawang *Suba Kastawa*	slendro pathet sanga (final gong 5)	pelog pathet nem (final gong 5)
Ketawang *Puspa Warna*	slendro pathet sanga (final gong 6)	pelog pathet barang (final gong 6)

The pathet must suit the time of day when the gamelan is played so that the mood or atmosphere (*suasana, rasa*) will be moving and beautiful (*nges*). Below is a guide to the hours of the day and the appropriate pathet.

slendro pathet nem: 8:00 P.M. - 12:00 midnight
and 8:00 A.M. - 12:00 noon

slendro pathet sanga: 12:00 midnight - 3:00 A.M.
and 12:00 noon - 3:00 P.M.

slendro pathet manyura: 3:00 A.M. - 8:00 A.M.
and 3:00 P.M. - 8:00 P.M.

pelog pathet lima: 8:00 A.M. - 12:00 noon
and 8:00 P.M. - 12:00 midnight

pelog pathet nem: 12:00 noon - 3:00 P.M.
and 12:00 midnight - 3:00 A.M.

pelog pathet barang: 3:00 P.M. - 8:00 P.M.
and 3:00 A.M. - 8:00 A.M.

CHAPTER IV

TITILARAS
[Notation]

sléndro:

old system	Kepatihan system
B = barang	1 = ji (siji)
G = gulu	2 = ro (loro)
D = dhadha (tengah)	3 = lu (telu)
L = lima	5 = ma (lima)
N = nem	6 = nem

pélog:

old system	Kepatihan system
P = panunggul (bem)	1 = ji (siji)
G = gulu	2 = ro (loro)
D = dhadha	3 = lu (telu)
Pl = pélog	4 = pat (papat)
L = lima	5 = ma (lima)
N = nem	6 = nem
Br = barang	7 = pi (pitu)

The old system of notation given above is no longer popular because it is felt to be old-fashioned and difficult compared with *Kepatihan* notation. Kepatihan notation, created by Patih Wreksadiningrat I of Surakarta in 1910, is the most commonly used system of notation in Java today. It is used for the notation of gendhing as well as sekar [instru-mental as well as vocal music].

sléndro registers:

$$2\ 3\ 5\ 6 \quad 1\ 2\ 3\ 5\ 6 \quad \dot{1}\ \dot{2}\ \dot{3}$$
low   middle   high

pélog registers:

$$1\ 2\ 3\ 4\ 5\ 6\ 7\ \underbrace{1\ 2\ 3\ 4\ 5\ 6\ 7}\ \underbrace{\overset{.}{1}\ \overset{.}{2}\ \overset{.}{3}}$$

low   middle   high

Pitch-level 1 is the lowest of sléndro or pélog, the lower limits of the register of the human voice. Pitch-level 3 is the highest in sléndro and pélog, the upper limits of the human voice. The range of notes given above can be played on the rebab as well as the gendèr. Thus, true notation is based upon the rebab and gendèr. Octave designations are very important and must be observed by the pesindhèn, gérong, rebab, gendèr, gambang, and siter.

Special notational symbols, according to the Chevé [Galin-Paris-Chevé 1884] (1804-1864) system of notation, are given below.

a. Octave dots: $\overset{.}{3}\ \overset{.}{2}\ \overset{.}{1}$ (high register)

   $\underset{.}{3}\ \underset{.}{5}\ \underset{.}{6}$ (low register)

b. Sustaining dots: 1 1 . .

c. Phrasing arcs: 6 $\underset{.}{1}\ 2$ 3

d. Vertical bar markers: 3 3 . . | 6 5 3 2

e. Small rhythmic lines indicate that the notes beneath the lines receive half the durational value of unmarked notes.

   6 $\overline{1\ 2}$ 3
   $\underset{.}{}$

   Rhythmic notation is needed for instrumental compositions and vocal parts accompanied by instruments. (For *sekar ageng*, *tengahan*, and *macapat*, however, which are not accompanied by instruments, rhythmic notation is not needed. On the contrary, they are more expressive since the singer is allowed freedom in matters of tempo and rhythm.)

Special notational symbols of the Konservatori Karawitan Indonesia at Surakarta are given below.

   gong   = ○
   kenong   = ∩
   kempul   = ∪
   kempyang = ' or ∨

        kethuk   = ∧

        enclosures for a repeatable unit = [ ]

Compositions are made up of *gatra*, which, in turn, are composed of
four saron strokes (*balungan*).

3   3   .   .   = 1 gatra (4 balungan)

$\overline{.\ 3}$ 5 $\overline{.\ 3}$ 6   = 1 gatra (4 balungan). The first and third
                              balungan are divided into two parts.

$\overline{\overset{..}{61}\ \overset{.}{2}}$ $\overline{.561}$ $\overset{..}{2\ 3}$ $\overset{.}{1}$ = 1 gatra (4 balungan). The first balungan
                              is divided into two quarters and one
                              half. The second balungan is divided
                              into four quarters. The third balungan
                              is divided into two halves.

Notational Examples

    Ladrang *Wilujeng*, sléndro pathet manyura

                buka: . 1 3 2   6̣ 1 2 3   1 1 3 2   . 1 2 6̣

                    umpak: [2 1 2 3   2 1 2 6̣

                             3 3 . .   6 5 3 2

                             5 6 5 3   2 1 2 6̣

                             2 1 2 3   2 1 2 6̣]

                ngelik: . . 6 .   i̇ 5 i̇ 6

                             3 5 6 i̇   6 5 3 2

                             6 6 . .   i̇ 5 i̇ 6

                             i̇ i̇ 3 2   . 1 2 6̣]

In practice, the bar-line symbol and the symbols for kethuk and
kempyang are often omitted because musicians can deduce them from the
notation.

Vocal Notation

    One phrase from sekar ageng *madayanti*, lampah 9, pedhotan 4-5, pélog
pathet manyura:

```
                     ....            ...   ...
  6     6     i     2123, i    i    i    123   1216
            Han - jrah  ing - kang, pus - pi - ta  a -  rum
```

```
                    ┌   4 wanda: Han - jrah   ing - kang
       9 wanda     ┤
                    └   5 wanda: pus - pi - ta   a - rum
```

    Gamelan notation is simple compared to Western notation, but it is
appropriate. The few symbols in gamelan notation provide enough
information for all gamelan musicians and singers to fill in their parts.
The quality of the realization of the notation depends upon the performers,
their ability, and their understanding of the rules of performance for each
instrument. The rules of performance, or the method of realizing the
notation on the various instruments, is embodied in gamelan theory. Most
of these rules are not written, but are common knowledge among musicians.
The quality of a gamelan performance will be high only if the musicians
understand theory and practice; notation is only a guide.

CHAPTER V

IRAMA

"*Irama*" has the following meanings:

a. tempo: the quickness or slowness of the composition or song

b. rhythm: the length or shortness of the notes

c. hiatus: the measurement of the time lapse between *dhing* and
    dhong

Dhing and Dhong

"*Dhing*" means 'weak sound' and is also called "*lagu*." "*Dhong*" means
'strong sound' (*antep*), and is also called "*guru*." "*Dhing-dhong*" or "*guru-lagu*" means the alternation between weak and strong notes. One gatra of a
composition is composed of four balungan consisting of two dhing and two
dhong. There are two kinds of dhing: small (*alit*) dhing and large (*ageng*)
dhing. Likewise, there are two kinds of dhong: small dhong and large
dhong. The arrangement of each gatra is as follows.

6	5	3	2
small	small	large	large
dhing	dhong	dhing	dhong

All melodic patterns of the gamelan instruments and the singers are
directed toward large dhong. Thus, if the person who notates the
composition makes a mistake in the placement of large dhong, it ruins the
melodic patterns of the pesindhèn and the gérong. For example, if pitch-level 6 is written as pitch-level 3, the pesindhèn and gérong will aim at
pitch-level 3; this would be a grave error.

The sound of dhong is stronger, and longer, than the sound of dhing.
The strokes of the kenong, kempul, gong, and kethuk always fall on dhong.
This is important so that the gamelan players can keep track of their place
within the formal structure.

Rhythmic levels (*tingkat irama*) are very important in gamelan music.
Actually, the length of any one note is only relative. The rhythmic levels
can be arranged as follows.

   a. Irama 1/2, or irama lancaran: Two strokes of the balungan occur
      every second. The saron panerus strikes at the same time as the
      balungan.

balungan:	3	1	3	2
saron panerus:	3	1	3	2

Irama lancaran is played in the buka of a fast piece and in the
playing of a fast piece.

   b. Irama tanggung, or irama I: One stroke of the balungan occurs
      every second. The saron panerus strikes twice for every balungan
      stroke.

balungan: 3   1   3   2
saron panerus: 3 3 1 1 3 3 2 2

Irama tanggung is played in all buka except the buka for fast pieces;
immediately after the buka of all pieces except fast pieces; and in all
pieces in the *sesegan* [literally, 'closely spaced'; figuratively, 'fast']
sections.

   c. Irama dados, or irama II: One stroke of the balungan occurs every
      two seconds. The saron panerus strikes four times for every
      balungan stroke.

balungan: 3   1   3   2
saron panerus: 3 3 1 1 3 3 1 1 3 3 2 2 3 3 2 2

Irama dados is played in all pieces when the tempo has become stable
enough so that the pesindhèn and gérong can sing.

   d. Irama wilet, or irama III: The example of the balungan/saron
      panerus is the same as for irama II. The difference is that the
      total number of balungan are doubled; the tempo is doubled while
      the number of kenong remains the same. The drummer plays the
      ciblon/kosèk alus style.

Irama wilet is played in (a) gendhing ladrangan, in which there are a
total of sixty-four balungan, four kenong, and three kempul per gong;
(b) gendhing kethuk 2 kerep, minggah 4; and (c) minggah sections of other
gendhing.

e. Irama rangkep, or irama IV: One stroke of the balungan occurs
every four seconds. The saron panerus strikes eight times for
each balungan.

balungan:	3	1	3	2
saron panerus:	22332233661166112233223311221122			

Irama rangkep is played in gendhing ketawang, ladrang, and in the
minggah section of other gendhing while the drummer plays the ciblon drum.

A change in irama in gamelan music is the change from one rhythmic
level to another. The limits of the rhythmic levels are not fixed, but
depend upon intuition. Understanding of the rhythmic levels is most
important for the drummer, who must control the rhythmic levels accurately.
Controlled irama is not erratic (*grag-greg*) like an automobile that is
almost out of gas. As soon as the tempo has leveled off, the drummer must
be able to feel the irama as regular and as steady as a metronome. Certain
other gamelan instruments must be particularly alert to the irama level
because they have the power to influence or spoil the irama. These
instruments are the siter, the saron panerus, the gambang, and the gendèr
panerus.

In gamelan music there can be various rhythmic levels within a single
composition--for example, from irama 1/2 to irama IV--as directed by the
drummer. When a drummer is skillful and careful, more than one rhythmic
level will often occur within a single kenong section. For example, in the
mérong section of *Gambir Sawit*, the first kenong section of the first
gongan consists of irama 1/2 and irama I. Unlike Western music, changes in
irama cannot happen suddenly.

CHAPTER VI

GENDHING

"*Gendhing*" has two meanings:

1. 'Any gamelan piece.' For example, "Gendhing *Pangkur*" means the piece *Pangkur*.

2. 'A particular formal structure.' The formal structure called "gendhing" consists of two parts.

    a. mérong: Sometimes has a ngelik and does not use kempyang.

    b. minggah: Sometimes contains an umpak and sometimes a ngelik, and uses kempyang.

Pieces that are not in gendhing form use kempul, while pieces in gendhing form do not use kempul.

The Formal Structures of Gendhing

1. Lancaran, irama lancaran (1/2), balungan nibani

        formula: 16 balungan per gong
                3 kempul per gong
                4 kenong per gong
                8 kethuk per gong
                16 kempyang per gong (irama II)

        schema: ⌃ . ⌃⌒ ⌃⌄ ⌃⌒ ⌃⌄ ⌃⌒ ⌃⌄ ⌃⌒ ⌃⌄ ⌃⊙

Example: Lancaran *Béndrong*, pélog pathet nem/sléndro pathet manyura [see appendix 1]

These pieces usually accompany dance (for example, *kiprah* dances). In practice, pieces in irama lancaran often become pieces in irama I or irama II. The drummer adjusts the irama to the dance movements.

2. Lancaran, irama tanggung (I), balungan mlaku

       formula: 16 balungan per gong
                 3 kempul per gong
                 4 kenong per gong
                 8 kethuk per gong
                16 kempyang per gong (irama II)

       schema: ⌢ . ⌢⌢ ⌢ᵛ⌢⌢ ⌢ᵛ⌢⌢ ⌢ᵛ⌢⊙

Example: Lancaran *Tropong Bang*, pélog pathet nem [see appendix 1]

    In addition to the accompaniment of wayang purwa, gendhing lancaran in irama tanggung may also be played for klenèngan.

3. Ketawang

       formula: 16 balungan per gong
                 1 kempul per gong
                 2 kenong per gong
                 4 kethuk per gong
                 8 kempyang per gong

       schema: ᵛ⌢ᵛ . ᵛ⌢ᵛ⌢ ᵛ⌢ᵛᵛ ᵛ⌢ᵛ⊙

Example: Ketawang *Suba Kastawa*, sléndro pathet sanga [see appendix 1]

    These pieces usually consist of the following sections: an umpak in which only the pesindhèn sings, and a ngelik in which both the pesindhèn and the gérong sing. The umpak and ngelik here can both serve as *inggah-inggahan*. Usually, ketawang are played in irama dados, with irama 1/2 and irama I heard as transitions. Also, gendhing for klenèngan are usually basically in irama dados with kendhangan kalih, or kendhangan satunggal. After the buka, the piece is in irama seseg [fast]. After one gongan, the piece goes into irama dados, kendhangan kalih. If the piece is to end (*suwuk*), the irama becomes seseg again in the penultimate gongan. In addition to irama II, ketawang may go to irama IV (rangkep), with kendhangan ciblon, according to need. This usually occurs in the accompaniment of the theater form, *kethoprak*.

4. Ladrangan

formula:

	irama II kendhang kalih	irama III kendhang ciblon
balungan	32 per gong	64 per gong
kempul	3 per gong	3 per gong
kenong	4 per gong	4 per gong
kethuk	8 per gong	8 per gong
kempyang	16 per gong	16 per gong

schema:

irama II

⌣ ∧ ⌣ . ⌣ ∧ ⌣ ⌢
⌣ ∧ ⌣ . ⌣ ∧ ⌣ ⌢
⌣ ∧ ⌣ . ⌣ ∧ ⌣ ⌢
⌣ ∧ ⌣ . ⌣ ∧ ⌣ ⊙

irama III

. ⌣ . ∧ . ⌣ . . . ⌣ . ∧ . ⌣ . ⌢
. ⌣ . ∧ . ⌣ . ⌵ . ⌣ . ∧ . ⌣ . ⌢
. ⌣ . ∧ . ⌣ . ⌵ . ⌣ . ∧ . ⌣ . ⌢
. ⌣ . ∧ . ⌣ . ⌵ . ⌣ . ∧ . ⌣ . ⊙

Example: Ladrang *Pangkur*, sléndro pathet sanga [see appendix 1]

Ladrangan may have the form of inggah-inggahan, which consists of an umpak, irama II and III, with pesindhèn and gérong and kendhangan ciblon; and a ngelik, irama III, with pesindhèn, gérong, and kendhangan ciblon. There are many ways to order a ladrang. The following is one example. After the buka, or bawa, the tempo is fast, irama seseg. Immediately thereafter, the tempo becomes irama dados, irama II. If the piece is going to irama III (*wilet*) kendhangan ciblon, the tempo quickens [as a signal, before slowing down], then proceeds through the transition (*angkatan ciblon*) to irama III. Irama III may go to irama IV, depending upon the skill of the drummer. If the piece is to end (*suwuk*), it must return to irama III beforehand.

5. Gendhing kethuk 2 kerep, minggah 4

formula:

	<u>merong</u> <u>irama II</u>	<u>minggah</u> <u>irama III</u>
balungan	64 per gong	128 per gong
kenong	4 per gong	4 per gong
kethuk	8 per gong	16 per gong
kempyang	– per gong	32 per gong

schema:

merong (irama II)

```
. . . ^ . . . . . . . . ^ . . . ⌒
. . . ^ . . . . . . . . ^ . . . ⌒
. . . ^ . . . . . . . . ^ . . . ⌒
. . . ^ . . . . . . . . ^ . . . ⊙
```

minggah (irama III)

```
.ᵛ.^ .ᵛ.. .ᵛ.^ .ᵛ.. .ᵛ.^ .ᵛ.. .ᵛ.^ .ᵛ.⌒
.ᵛ.^ .ᵛ.. .ᵛ.^ .ᵛ.. .ᵛ.^ .ᵛ.. .ᵛ.^ .ᵛ.⌒
.ᵛ.^ .ᵛ.. .ᵛ.^ .ᵛ.. .ᵛ.^ .ᵛ.. .ᵛ.^ .ᵛ.⌒
.ᵛ.^ .ᵛ.. .ᵛ.^ .ᵛ.. .ᵛ.^ .ᵛ.. .ᵛ.^ .ᵛ.⊙
```

Example: Gendhing *Gambir Sawit*, slendro pathet sanga [see appendix 1]

The formal structure of these pieces is complete, which means they consist of (a) a merong irama II with pesindhen, [sometimes] gerong and kendhangan satunggal; and (b) a minggah in irama III, with pesindhen, gerong, and kendhangan ciblon. Between the merong and the minggah [in irama III] there may be a minggah kendhang in irama II, pesindhen, gerong, and kendhangan satunggal. The transitional angkatan ciblon leads from the minggah kendhang [to the minggah in irama III]. (Not all gendhing use minggah kendhang; examples of some that do are *Gambir Sawit*, *Lobong*, *Cucur Bawuk*, etc.)

6. Gendhing kethuk 2 kerep (kenong 2), ketawang gendhing

      formula: 32 balungan per gong
              2 kenong per gong
              4 kethuk per gong

      schema: . . . $\overset{\wedge}{.}$ . . . . $\overset{\wedge}{.}$ . . . $\frown$

              . . . $\overset{\wedge}{.}$ . . . . $\overset{\wedge}{.}$ . . . $\odot$

Example: Gendhing *Kawit*, sléndro pathet nem[4] [see appendix 1]

    The formal structure of these pieces belongs to the category, gendhing kethuk 2 kerep, but each gongan contains only two kenongan. The minggah of these pieces takes the form of a ladrang. Thus, the merong is in gendhing form, while the minggah is not. As is usual, after the buka, or if the piece is to end, the tempo must quicken. The transition from merong to minggah must have the same gong tone as the minggah.

7. Gendhing kethuk 4 kerep, minggah 8

formula:

	mérong irama II	minggah irama III
balungan	128 per gong	256 per gong
kenong	4 per gong	4 per gong
kethuk	16 per gong	32 per gong
kempyang	– per gong	64 per gong

schema:

mérong (irama II)

```
...^ .... ...^ .... ...^ .... ...^ ...⌒
...^ .... ...^ .... ...^ .... ...^ ...⌒
...^ .... ...^ .... ...^ .... ...^ ...⌒
...^ .... ...^ .... ...^ .... ...^ ...⊙
```

minggah (irama III), kendhangan ciblon or kosèk alus

```
.ᵛ.^ .ᵛ.. .ᵛ.^ .ᵛ.. .ᵛ.^ .ᵛ.. .ᵛ.^ .ᵛ..
.ᵛ.^ .ᵛ.. .ᵛ.^ .ᵛ.. .ᵛ.^ .ᵛ.. .ᵛ.^ .ᵛ⌒
.ᵛ.^ .ᵛ.. .ᵛ.^ .ᵛ.. .ᵛ.^ .ᵛ., .ᵛ.^ .ᵛ..
.ᵛ.^ .ᵛ.. .ᵛ.^ .ᵛ.. .ᵛ.^ .ᵛ.. .ᵛ.^ .ᵛ⌒
.ᵛ.^ .ᵛ.. .ᵛ.^ .ᵛ.. .ᵛ.^ .ᵛ.. .ᵛ.^ .ᵛ..
.ᵛ.^ .ᵛ.. .ᵛ.^ .ᵛ.. .ᵛ.^ .ᵛ.. .ᵛ.^ .ᵛ⌒
.ᵛ.^ .ᵛ.. .ᵛ.^ .ᵛ.. .ᵛ.^ .ᵛ.. .ᵛ.^ .ᵛ..
.ᵛ.^ .ᵛ.. .ᵛ.^ .ᵛ.. .ᵛ.^ .ᵛ.. .ᵛ.^ .ᵛ⊙
```

Example: Gendhing *Bontit*, kethuk 4 kerep, minggah 8, pélog pathet nem
[see appendix 1]

The formal structure of these pieces is complete, which means they consist of: (a) mérong, irama II, kendhangan satunggal; and (b) minggah, irama III, kendhangan kosèk alus or kendhangan ciblon.

8. Gendhing kethuk 2 awis/arang, minggah 4

formula:

	mérong irama II	minggah irama III
balungan	128 per gong	128 per gong
kenong	4 per gong	4 per gong
kethuk	8 per gong	16 per gong
kempyang	- per gong	32 per gong

schema:

mérong

```
.... ...^ .... .... .... ...^ .... ...⌒
.... ...^ .... .... .... ...^ .... ...⌒
.... , ...^ .... .... .... ...^ .... ...⌒
.... ...^ .... .... .... ...^ .... ..⊙
```

minggah

```
.Y.^ .Y.. .Y.^ .Y.. .Y.^ .Y.. .Y.^ .Y.⌒
.Y.^ .Y.. .Y.^ .Y.. .Y.^ .Y.. .Y.^ .Y.⌒
.Y.^ .Y.. .Y.^ .Y.. .Y.^ .Y.. .Y.^ .Y.⌒
.Y.^ .Y.. .Y.^ .Y.. .Y.^ .Y.. .Y.^ .Y.⊙
```

Example: Gendhing *Laranjala*, pélog pathet lima [see appendix 1]

The formal structure of these pieces consists of a mérong and any minggah kethuk 4, as long as the gong tone is the same as the mérong (see *Gambir Sawit* [appendix 1]).

9. Gendhing kethuk 4 awis, minggah 8

formula:

	mérong	minggah
balungan	256 per gong	256 per gong
kenong	4 per gong	4 per gong
kethuk	16 per gong	32 per gong
kempyang	- per gong	64 per gong

schema:

mérong

```
....  ...:^ ....  ....  ....  ...:^ ....  ....
....  ...:^ ....  ....  ....  ...:^ ....  ...⌒
....  ...:^ ....  ....  ....  ...:^ ....  ....
....  ...:^ ....  ....  ....  ...:^ ....  ...⌒
....  ...:^ ....  ....  ....  ...:^ ....  ....
....  ...:^ ....  ....  ....  ...:^ ....  ...⌒
....  ...:^ ....  ....  ....  ...:^ ....  ....
....  ...:^ ....  ....  ....  ...:^ ....  ...⊙
```

minggah

same as (7) above

Example: Gendhing *Rondhon*, sléndro pathet sanga [see appendix 1]

The formal structure of these pieces is complete, which means they have both a mérong and a minggah. The inggah-inggahan kethuk 8 is the same as (7) above.

10. Gendhing *pamijèn*

The word "pamijèn" derives from the word for "one" (*siji*);[5] thus, every pamijèn is different, each pamijèn is singular. Furthermore, the formulas for gendhing pamijèn are inco..patible with the formulas of normal gendhing.

Example: Gendhing *Majemuk*, sléndro pathet nem, kethuk 2 kerep, kenong 5, minggah kethuk 4 [se° appendix 1]

11. Ayak-ayakan, Srepegan, and Sampak

These pieces do not have regular formal structures like the preceding.

Ayak-ayakan: The large gong is not played except at the very end. In
Ayak-ayakan, sléndro nem and sanga, the kempul is substituted for the gong except for the final gong. In
Ayak-ayakan, sléndro manyura, the gong suwukan is used
instead of kempul.

Before irama II, one kethuk per kenong; in irama II, two
kethuk per kenong.

Example: *Ayak-ayakan*, sléndro manyura [see appendix 1]

Srepegan: Only gong suwukan is played.

Example: *Srepegan*, sléndro manyura [see appendix 1]

Sampak (example): *Sampak*, sléndro manyura [see appendix 1]

12. Jineman/dolanan

Like ayak-ayakan, srepegan, and sampak, these pieces do not have fixed
formal structures. Jineman are often inserted into bawa. For example, the
jineman, *Jamuran*, may be inserted into the bawa, *dhandhang gula Padasih*,
sléndro sanga. Only gamelan gadhon instruments play for jineman. Rebab,
bonang, all saron, kethuk, and kempyang are omitted. For dolanan, all
instruments play except rebab. When dolanan are sung with gérong, the
instrumentation is the same as for jineman. However, the instrumentation
for these pieces is not fixed. It depends upon the composer or the
musicians.

General Guidelines about Gendhing

The term "minggah" means "from the mérong." "*Kalajengaken*" means
"from the inggah-inggahan."

Example: Gendhing *Randhu Kèntir*, pélog pathet nem, minggah Ladrang
Ayun-ayun, pélog pathet nem, kalajengaken Ketawang
Swala Gita, pélog pathet nem

A gendhing that follows (*gendhing lajengan*) must be of a lower level
than the preceding gendhing.

Example: 1. gendhing kethuk 2 kerep, minggah 4, kalâjengaken
         2. ladrangan
         3. ketawang
         (The order should not be reversed.)

The gendhing that follows must have the same gong tone as the
preceding gendhing.

Example: Gendhing *Randhu Kèntir*, Ladrang *Ayun-ayun*, and Ketawang
         Swala Gita all share gong tone 6.

The form of gendhing lajengan is not predetermined; the same is true
of inggah-inggahan. Gendhing kethuk 2 kerep can "rise" (minggah) to
ladrangan, for example, Gendhing *Randhu Kèntir*, minggah *Ayun-ayun*, pélog
pathet nem. *Randhu Kèntir* is a gendhing kethuk 2 kerep, while *Ayun-ayun* is
a ladrang (not an inggah-inggahan kethuk 4).

The ordering of a piece for *klenèngan* is usually as follows.

1. senggrèngan (After the playing of *senggrèngan* on the rebab,
   everyone should be quiet and composed.)

2. pathetan

3. bawa or buka

4. gendhing (and lajengan)

5. pathetan

The tempi of pieces played as klenèngan are generally slower than the
tempi of pieces used to accompany wayang purwa or dance.

Kinds of Gendhing in Which a Particular Instrument Plays a Leading Role

1. Gendhing Rebab

The rebab plays a leading role in the creation of melodic patterns.
The rebab must play the buka.

Examples: Gendhing *Karawitan*, sléndro pathet nem
          Gendhing *Gambir Sawit*, sléndro pathet sanga
          Gendhing *Titi Pati*, sléndro pathet nem
          Gendhing *Renyep*, sléndro pathet sanga
          Gendhing *Bondhèt*, sléndro pathet sanga
          Gendhing *Onang-onang*, sléndro pathet sanga

2. Gendhing Gendèr

The gendèr plays a leading role in the creation of melodic patterns. The gendèr must play the buka.

Examples: Gendhing *Kawit*, sléndro pathet nem
Gendhing *Kabor*, sléndro pathet nem
Ladrang *Dirata Meta*, sléndro pathet nem

3. Gendhing Bonang

The bonang plays a leading role in creating melodic patterns. The bonang must play the buka.

Examples: Gendhing *Babar Layar*, pélog pathet lima
Gendhing *Tukung*, pélog pathet barang
Gendhing *Singa-singa*, pélog pathet barang

The rebab, gendèr, gendèr panerus, gambang, suling, and siter do not play in gendhing bonang.

4. Gendhing Kendhang

The kendhang plays a leading role. The kendhang must play the buka.

Examples: *Gangsaran*
Pisan Bali
Kemuda [*Srepegan Kemuda*]
Ayakan-ayakan
Srepegan
Sampak

5. Gendhing Rebab, Buka Gambang

The gambang plays a leading role in the creation of melodic patterns. The gambang must play the buka.

Example: Ladrang *Sekar Gadhung*, sléndro pathet manyura

Definitions

ngelik: A section of a piece that is not basic or essential. Ngelik sections can occur in every kind of formal structure, but not all pieces have a ngelik section.

umpak minggah: A [transitional] section of a mérong that indicates the form of the following minggah. See *Gambir Sawit*, sléndro pathet sanga.

suwukan: A special closing section of a piece. See *Ayak-ayakan*, sléndro
pathet manyura.

kalajengaken: The word means to continue with another piece of a different
formal structure (*lajengan*). A lajengan can be attached to any form
except a mérong (which must be followed by a minggah)--for example,
Ladrang *Pangkur* kalajengaken Ketawang *Mijil Sulastri* [Ladrang *Pangkur*
followed by Ketawang *Mijil Sulastri*]. This is also true of minggah.
For example, from a gendhing kethuk 2 kerep it is possible to go to a
ladrang rather than a minggah kethuk 4 (Gendhing *Randhu Kèntir*,
minggah Ladrang *Ayun-ayun*, pélog pathet nem).

dados: The word means to continue with another piece of the same formal
structure--for example, Ladrang *Sembawa*, dados Ladrang *Playon*, pélog
pathet lima [Ladrang *Sembawa* followed by Ladrang *Playon*].

dhawah: The word means to continue from a buka bawa--for example, Bawa
sekar *retna asmara*, pélog pathet nem, dhawah Gendhing *Randhu Kèntir*
[bawa sekar *retna asmara*, pélog pathet nem, followed by Gendhing
Randhu Kèntir].

kaseling: An insertion into a piece of a given formal structure by a piece
of a different formal structure--for example, Ladrang *Ayun-ayun*,
kaseling Dolanan *Ilir-ilir* [Dolanan *Ilir-ilir* inserted into Ladrang
Ayun-ayun].

gendhing gérongan: Pieces based upon vocal forms with a gérong (of two or
more persons)--for example, Ladrang *Wilujeng*. (Ladrang *Pucung Rubuh*,
on the other hand, is not a gendhing gérongan.)

gendhing sindhèn: Pieces based upon vocal forms in which the buka is sung
by the pesindhèn--for example, Ketawang *Sinom Parijata* and Jineman
Uler Kambang.

Pieces with Special Functions

Many pieces have special functions. Those listed below are only a
sample.

To honor guests at a party or someone with a special cause:

Gendhing *Majemuk*, sléndro pathet nem

To change from sléndro pathet nem to sléndro pathet sanga:

Gendhing *Titi Pati*, sléndro pathet nem

For closing:

    Gendhing *Lobong*, sléndro pathet manyura

To prevent rain:

    Gendhing *Tunggul Kawung*, pélog pathet barang

For wedding ceremonies:

    Lancaran *Kebo Giro*, pélog pathet barang
    Ketawang *Monggang*, pélog pathet lima
    Ketawang *Kodhok Ngorèk*, pélog pathet barang
    Ketawang *Laras Maya*, pélog pathet barang
    Ketawang *Boyong Basuki*, pélog pathet barang
    Ketawang *Suba Kastawa*, sléndro pathet sanga
    Ladrang *Sri Wibawa*, sléndro pathet sanga

Pieces for Wayang Kulit

For opening court scenes (*jejer*):

1. For the opening court scenes in Kahyangan [the kingdom of the gods] and scenes in the kingdom of Ngamarta:

   Gendhing *Kawit* ['beginning'], minggah Ladrang *Kawit*, sléndro pathet nem

2. For the opening court scene at the kingdom of Ngastina:

   Gendhing *Kabor*, minggah Ladrang *Karawitan*, sléndro pathet nem

3. For the opening court scenes in all other kingdoms (for example, the kingdom of Dwarawati):

   Gendhing *Karawitan*, minggah Ladrang *Karawitan*, sléndro pathet nem

To create a peaceful atmosphere:

    Ayak-ayakan, sléndro pathet nem, sanga, or manyura

For a tense atmosphere:

    Srepegan, sléndro pathet nem, sanga, or manyura

For the most tense atmosphere:

    Sampak, sléndro pathet nem, sanga, or manyura

For a sad but calm atmosphere:

    Ayak-ayakan Tlutur, sléndro pathet sanga

For a sad but tense atmosphere:

    Srepegan Tlutur, sléndro pathet sanga

For the entrance of guests in the opening scene:

    Ladrang *Remeng*, sléndro pathet nem
    Ladrang *Dirata Meta*, sléndro pathet nem
    Ladrang *Léré-léré*, sléndro pathet manyura
    Ladrang *Kembang Pépé*, sléndro pathet manyura

For the accompaniment of cavalry (*kapalan*):

    Lancaran *Wrahat Bala*, sléndro pathet nem
    Lancaran *Manyar Séwu*, sléndro pathet nem
    Lancaran *Tropong Bang*, pélog pathet nem
    Lancaran *Kebo Giro Kedhu*, sléndro pathet sanga
    Lancaran *Kebo Giro Gambir Sawit*, sléndro pathet sanga
    Lancaran *Bubaran Nyutra*, sléndro pathet sanga
    Lancaran *Slébrak*, pélog pathet nem
    Lancaran *Singa Nebak*, sléndro pathet manyura

To accompany scenes in the chambers of the princesses:

    Gendhing *Titi Pati*, sléndro pathet nem
    Gendhing *Puspa Wedhar*, sléndro pathet nem
    Gendhing *Gantal Wedhar*, sléndro pathet nem
    Gendhing *Mas Kumambang*, sléndro pathet nem
    Gendhing *Lara Nangis*, sléndro pathet nem
    Gendhing *Lonthang*, sléndro pathet nem
    Gendhing *Kanyut*, sléndro pathet nem
    Ladrang *Gonjang Ganjing*, sléndro pathet sanga
    Gendhing *Renyep*, sléndro pathet sanga
    Gendhing *Gandrung Mangu*, sléndro pathet manyura
    Gendhing *Gandrung Manis*, sléndro pathet manyura
    Gendhing *Montro*, sléndro pathet manyura
    Gendhing *Damar Kèli*, sléndro pathet manyura
    Gendhing *Perkutut Manggung*, sléndro pathet manyura
    Ladrang *Pangkur*, sléndro pathet manyura
    Ladrang *Asmarandana*, sléndro pathet manyura
    Ketawang *Puspa Warna*, sléndro pathet manyura

To accompany scenes in the outer courtyard of the palace (*paséban njawi*):

    Gendhing *Kedhaton Bentar*, sléndro pathet nem
    Gendhing *Semu Kirang*, sléndro pathet nem

Gendhing *Kembang Tiba*, sléndro pathet nem
Gendhing *Prihatin*, sléndro pathet nem
Gendhing *Turi Rawa*, sléndro pathet nem
Gendhing *Capang*, sléndro pathet manyura
Gendhing *Tali Murda*, sléndro pathet manyura
Ladrang *Moncèr*, sléndro pathet manyura
Ladrang *Gègèr Sakuta*, sléndro pathet manyura

To accompany the scene when Wrekudara becomes king:

Ladrang *Liwung*, sléndro pathet manyura

To accompany scenes with Wrekudara and Gathutkaca:

Gendhing *Gendhu*, sléndro pathet nem
Gendhing *Dhandhun*, sléndro pathet nem
Gendhing *Kagok Madura*, sléndro pathet sanga

To accompany scenes with noble foreigners:

Gendhing *Udan Soré*, sléndro pathet nem
Gendhing *Sunggèng*, sléndro pathet sanga
Ladrang *Kandha Manyura*, sléndro pathet manyura

To accompany scenes in overseas kingdoms:

Gendhing *Lana*, sléndro pathet nem
Ladrang *Wani-wani*, sléndro pathet sanga
Ladrang *Babat Kenceng*, sléndro pathet sanga

For scenes in an ogre kingdom whose young king is in love:

Gendhing *Majemuk*, sléndro pathet nem

For scenes in an ogre kingdom whose king is not in love:

Gendhing *Guntur*, sléndro pathet nem

To accompany scenes of Bathari Durga:

Gendhing *Menyan Séta*, sléndro pathet nem
Gending *Lokananta*, sléndro pathet nem
Gendhing *Menyan Kobar*, sléndro pathet sanga

To accompany demonic characters:

Lancaran *Dolo-dolo*, sléndro pathet sanga
Ketawang *Dendha Gedhé*, sléndro pathet sanga

To accompany demons and giants in the forest:

    Ladrang *Jangkrik Génggong*, sléndro pathet sanga
    Lancaran *Bindri*, sléndro pathet sanga
    Ladrang *Embat-embat Penjalin*, sléndro pathet sanga

For the brief accompaniment of scenes with demons:

    Lancaran *Béndrong*, sléndro pathet manyura
    Lancaran *Ricik-ricik*, sléndro pathet manyura

For the accompaniment of scenes with a holy hermit and a young nobleman:

    Gendhing *Gambir Sawit*, sléndro pathet sanga
    Gendhing *Onang-onang*, sléndro pathet sanga
    Gendhing *Bondhèt*, sléndro pathet sanga
    Gendhing *Génjong*, sléndro pathet sanga
    Gendhing *Sumedhang*, sléndro pathet sanga
    Gendhing *Ganda Kusuma*, sléndro pathet sanga
    Gendhing *Lara-lara*, sléndro pathet sanga
    Ketawang *Langen Gita*, sléndro pathet sanga
    Ketawang *Raja Swala*, sléndro pathet sanga
    Ketawang *Puspa Warna*, sléndro pathet manyura
    Ketawang *Puspa Giwang*, sléndro pathet manyura

For the accompaniment of a young nobleman as he proceeds to the *prang sekar/kembang* ['flower battle']:

    Ketawang *Suba Kastawa*, sléndro pathet sanga
    Ketawang *Langen Gita*, sléndro pathet sanga
    Ladrang *Lompong Kéli*, sléndro pathet sanga
    Ladrang *Clunthang*, sléndro pathet sanga

To accompany scenes at Ngastina other than the opening scene:

    Ladrang *Uga-uga*, sléndro pathet sanga
    Ladrang *Kencèng Barong*, sléndro pathet sanga
    Gendhing *Gliyung*, sléndro pathet manyura

To accompany scenes at Ngamarta or Cempala [Radya] other than the opening scene:

    Gendhing *Candra*, sléndro pathet sanga
    Gendhing *Pujangga Anom*, sléndro pathet manyura

To accompany scenes in which Janaka becomes a priest:

    Gendhing *Jongkang*, sléndro pathet sanga

To accompany scenes concerning a sad king:

Gendhing *Tlutur*, sléndro pathet sanga
Gendhing *Laler Mengeng*, sléndro pathet sanga

To accompany scenes of Bathara Naradha or other gods:

Gendhing *Gègèr Soré*, sléndro pathet sanga

To accompany scenes at Madukara or scenes in which the king is of a serene character:

Gendhing *Bontit*, sléndro pathet sanga
Ladrang *Wilujeng*, sléndro pathet manyura

To accompany scenes, other than the opening scene, in the kingdom of Dwarawati:

Gendhing *Rondhon*, sléndro pathet sanga
Gendhing *Ramyang*, sléndro pathet manyura

To accompany scenes of miscellaneous kingdoms:

Gendhing *Bang-bang Wétan*, sléndro pathet manyura
Gendhing *Pucung*, sléndro pathet manyura
Ketawang *Pucung*, sléndro pathet manyura
Ladrang *Kandha Manyura*, sléndro pathet manyura

To accompany scenes of a young warrior who is lighthearted or romantic:

Ladrang *Sekar Gadhung*, sléndro pathet manyura
Ladrang *Jong Kèri*, sléndro pathet manyura
Ladrang *Sumirat*, sléndro pathet manyura

To accompany scenes of Gathutkaca in love:

Ketawang *Pawukir*, sléndro pathet manyura

Closing pieces played when the *kayon* is placed upright in the middle of the screen:

Gendhing *Lobong*, sléndro pathet manyura
Ladrang *Manis*, sléndro pathet manyura
Ladrang *Ginonjing*, sléndro pathet manyura
Ladrang *Mugi Rahayu*, sléndro pathet manyura

Introductory pieces played before the first scene of the play (*talu*):

Gendhing *Cucur Bawuk*, minggah Gendhing *Paré Anom*,
    sléndro pathet manyura
Ladrang *Sri Katon*, sléndro pathet manyura

Ketawang *Sukma Ilang*, sléndro pathet manyura
Ayak-ayakan, sléndro pathet manyura
Srepegan, sléndro pathet manyura
Sampak, sléndro pathet manyura

Gendhing *Lambang Sari*, kalajengaken Ladrang *Lipur Sari*, sléndro
     pathet manyura

Gendhing *Wida Sari*, kalajengaken Ladrang *Gonjang*, sléndro pathet
     manyura

CHAPTER VII

THE FOUR PRINCIPLES OF KARAWITAN
(*CATUR PRINSIP KARAWITAN*):
ETHICS, ESTHETICS, NORMS, AND IDEALS

The aim of the author in setting out a separate chapter with the above
heading, is that these matters are so important when viewed from the
perspective of ideal and pure striving [after knowledge]. It is hoped that
the reader will realize the importance of understanding the four principles
named above. Thus, after we understand, comprehend, and master karawitan
from the theoretical point of view, we must be able to apply it accurately.

Explanation of Terms. "Ethics" refers to proper behavior
(*kesusilaan*). "Esthetics" refers to beauty (*keindahan*). "Norms" refers to
all regulations that are not written, but are habitually followed.
"Ideals" refers to all positive aspirations aimed at physical and spiritual
improvement based on the philosophy of *Pancasila* [Five-point Indonesian
State Ideology].

The four principles of karawitan do not stand separately, but each
complements the others. If an artist (*seniman/seniwati*) should deviate
from any one of the above principles, he/she will become an artist who does
not truly know the meaning and aims of karawitan. Hence, the name of
karawitan, which should be held high, is debased.

Ethics

All the members of a gamelan group must keep the good name of the
group. For example, in all relations with other artists, or with people
outside the group, one must avoid undesirable consequences. One must avoid
giving support to the general opinion that to become involved in a gamelan
ensemble means to want to become a "*yaga*" [from *niyaga* 'gamelan player',
but with connotations of low status], or "*tlèdhèk*" ['dancing girl']. If
the rules of ethics are violated, the group will acquire a bad name and
will quickly be dispersed. The failure of a group of artists is usually

caused by the mistakes of the members of that group itself, whether the manager, instructor, or the members themselves have violated the above principle of ethics.

Esthetics

Karawitan, like all the arts, must be beautiful, both from the spiritual (*rochaniyah*) and the physical (*jasmaniah*) perspectives.

From the perspective of spiritual beauty the following elements are important:

1. The playing of a gamelan group must be smooth and harmonious (*harmonis, rempeg*). The situation must be avoided in which one person tries to show off his expertise to the disadvantage of others, for then the playing will not be harmonious. It must be remembered that gamelan playing is a collective activity.

2. In order to achieve the highest level of beauty, each player must control his/her ego. The theoretical and practical aspects of karawitan must be in balance.

From the perspective of physical beauty, the following elements are also important:

1. The place where the gamelan is kept must be clean, with mats, a platform for the gamelan, stands for notation, ashtrays, and a blackboard for purposes of study.

2. The gamelan players (*pradangga*) and vocalists, both male (*wiraswara*) and female (*swarawati*), should wear proper and clean clothing for rehearsals as well as for formal occasions (*pesta*).

3. The manner of sitting, standing, entering and exiting from the gamelan room, holding and setting down of the gamelan beaters (*tabuh*) must all be orderly. All bodily movements should appear beautiful.

Norms

Each gamelan player must know the norms or customs of gamelan playing in order to ensure the fluency and smoothness of the rehearsal or performance. Otherwise, confusion and disorder in playing will result. Among others, the following are various rules that should be understood:

1. The leader of the irama is the kendhang.

2. The leader of the gendhing (including vocal parts) is the rebab.

3. In the case of wayang kulit, the dhalang is in complete charge of everything. The players of kendhang, rebab, and gendèr must all follow the cues of the dhalang. To regulate irama, the dhalang may use a *cempala* and/or *keprak*. To direct the gendhing, the dhalang may sing a vocal introduction (*buka celuk*), provide vocal cues (*sasmita*), or request a particular piece through one of the wayang characters.

Ideals

The ideals [of karawitan] can be formulated in the following ways:

1. One should educate oneself to become an artist who is both skillful and wise (*berbudi luhur*).

2. One should teach students--from those in kindergarten to college students.

3. One should educate the society-at-large in karawitan--in government offices, villages, neighborhood compounds (*kampung*), and private groups.

4. The material to be taught can be taken from the inheritance of our revered ancestors, as long as it is not in conflict with the philosophy of *Pancasila*. To add freshness to the field of karawitan, new gamelan compositions (*kreasi baru*) may be added, as long as they too are based on the philosophy of Pancasila.

In conclusion, all gamelan musicians must cultivate these ideals for the glory and exaltation of the art of karawitan.

TRANSLATOR'S NOTES

1. The translator has compiled two versions of this manuscript, a handwritten copy (1969) and a stenciled version (1971). Sections have been reorganized with the approval of the author.

2. "Embat" is usually understood to mean the intervallic structure of a particular gamelan ensemble. See Martopangrawit, *Catatan Pengetahuan Karawitan*, in this volume. See also Hood 1966.

3. "*Pélo*" denotes a speech impediment. Deriving "pélog" from *di'pélo'kan* is a popular etymology in Java.

4. Ketawang Gendhing *Kawit* is usually designated as pathet manyura, although it is played in the pathet nem section of a wayang. See *Serat Sulukan Sléndro*, in this volume.

5. According to Gericke and Roorde (1901[1]:316-17), "*pamijèn*" is derived from the root "*piji*," whose verb form, "*miji*," means 'to select', 'to choose'. Thus, "*pamijèn*" would mean 'special', 'selected', 'chosen'; hence, 'exceptional', 'unusual'.

FAKTOR PENTING DALAM GAMELAN

[An Important Factor in Gamelan]

by

Ki Sindoesawarno

Translated from Indonesian by Stanley Hoffman

First published in *Sana-Budaja* I/3 (1956):136-48;
reprinted in *Udan Mas* I/2, 4 (1959):38-41, 85-88.

Introduction[1]

The word "gamelan" generally brings to mind images of large, round, bronze objects hung in a large wooden frame decorated with intertwined carvings of *naga*. Spread beneath them are a number of instruments of uncertain form, among which sit a number of men, some alert, others apparently drowsy. Two or three large and small drums attract the attention, not because of their appearance, but because of their sound. Also noticed are one or two rebab which look like mismade crosses. Thus we picture the gamelan. This description, however, includes only instruments, and instruments will not be discussed here. Rather, the sounds that come from these instruments will be the subject of this article--the art produced by the musicians, the art of playing, or *karawitan*. "Karawitan" is the art of music--vocal, instrumental, or the two together. In the art of karawitan, there is an important style, an essential factor which is called "*wilet*." This concept will be explained below.

If wilet is a factor of karawitan and therefore of art also, we may consider for a moment whether it is necessary to discuss art. Is it not enough that we merely enjoy art, that we just experience the beautiful feelings which it brings forth from the depths of the soul? Is this feeling not entirely subjective?

From psychology comes the concept that the experience of beauty is subjective. Similarly, the experiences of happiness, grief, anger, love, sorrow, remorse, fear, etc., are all subjective in nature. But, the feeling [perceiving] of beauty is a feeling separate and apart from the other emotions. Only, the emotion of [perceiving of] beauty may be accompanied by one or more other emotions. In any case, the emotion of [perceiving of] beauty is a subjective experience, and beauty is a subjective thing. This is clear and obvious. If there is an explanation that demonstrates the objectivity of beauty, then the truth of this explanation is certainly doubtful.

An art critic explains to us that a certain thing is beautiful, the reasons for its beauty, why it is beautiful, etc. We listen, discuss, and act as if we share this feeling of beauty as experienced by the critic.

Actually, we cannot entirely experience the beauty perceived by the critic
because to communicate such a feeling is not possible. What we call "the
experience of another's feeling" is in truth not experiencing at all, but,
rather, understanding--understanding that another has experienced beauty.
Psychologically, this understanding refers to apprehension by means of
analogy rather than through direct personal experience.

The above explanation may clarify the purpose of this article. It is
not my intent to give the reader the experience of beauty, but only to open
the way to understanding. The experience of beauty itself must lie within
the reader. Perhaps, with the aid of these explanations, the reader may
more easily achieve this experience and more easily understand why one can
enjoy listening to gamelan music for a whole evening, or listen without
boredom to familiar songs, or watch theatrical performances that we have
already heard or seen numerous times. These explanations will also
facilitate one's forming an opinion about new innovations in karawitan,
whether one is involved as a performer or as a member of the audience.

After a discussion of terms and facts about karawitan, we will turn to
recent innovations and conclusions.

<u>Lagu</u>

"Karawitan" is music--vocal, instrumental, or a combination of the
two. In karawitan, a series of notes (*nada*),[*] whether vocal or
instrumental, is called a "*lagu*" or "*lelagon*."

Vocal lagu are often called "*gendhèng*." The term "*tembang*" frequently
used now, is a common mistake. "Tembang" is a literary term which originally meant poetry or different forms of poetry. We all know how these
forms differ. Since tembang poetry (*macapat, kidung, kakawin,* etc.) is
always sung, the word "tembang" is now used imprecisely to refer to vocal
lagu in general. Tembang are usually sung without accompaniment. Types of
vocal lagu sung with gamelan include the following: *gérong, sindhèn,
sendhon, suluk, ada-ada, bawa, celuk,* etc. It is not necessary to explain
these terms here.

---

[*]"*Nada*" from the Sanskrit "*nada*," means 'sound' or 'tone'. "There are
two types of tones: *ahata* ['caused to vibrate'] and *anahata* ['not caused to
vibrate']. An ahata tone consists of a pitch and a quality. Anahata tones
are the words of God. Ahata tones give pleasure, anahata tones,
liberation" (*Naradha Purana*).[2]

In the context of gamelan, lagu are often called "*gendhing*," in its general meaning. Thus, "gendhing" and "gendhèng" refer to both vocal and instrumental pieces. In its more restricted meaning, "gendhing" refers to specific musical structures for gamelan pieces. Sometimes "gendhing" is applied loosely as an adjective modifying the name of a lagu where it indicates that the piece is a composition suitable for listening (*klenèngan* and *uyon-uyon*), rather than dancing (such as *bedhaya* or *srimpi*). Concerning the relationship of the vocal and instrumental parts, it should be understood that gendhèng and gendhing are on the same level, i.e., neither one is subordinate to the other.

In composing a lagu, the possibilities are unlimited; however, there are only three directions which can be taken. These are: from a low note to a higher note, from a high note to a lower note, and to sustain or repeat a note. A fourth possibility would be a mixture of the above three, and, in general, lagu are composed in this manner.

Like Indian, Arab, and Chinese melodies, lagu in karawitan always center on a single emotion or a certain idea that is manifested by the lagu. By his/her manner of filling in, adding to, altering, embellishing, or clarifying a lagu, a player or singer may influence and expand the lagu until its inherent atmosphere and emotion emerge. If the player or singer is a true and capable artist, he/she can elicit a trembling of the soul, transporting the listener into a world never dreamed of. Therefore, the musician must know the characteristics and nature of each lagu, and to which class of emotions it belongs. Misuse of a lagu of a given nature constitutes a great error in karawitan.

On the other hand, European melodies (*lagu*) constantly shift in mood; the use of contrasts is not rare. Changes of mood are used to strengthen the exposition of an idea. Players and singers follow these changes and endeavor to ascertain and accord with the emotions of the composer. To a certain extent, musicians must know the soul of the composer. Because of this, the name of the composer of a given piece (*lagu*) must be known. This is not necessary in karawitan.

Players and singers of karawitan fill, expand, embellish, and clarify a lagu. To give such treatment is to make use of *cèngkok*.

Cèngkok

The smallest meaningful unit of lagu is called "*gatra*." A gatra consists of four notes of the *balungan*, that is, four beats of the

slenthem, or four notes of the cantus firmus. Two gatra (eight notes of
the balungan) constitute one phrase of a lagu. Within such a phrase, the
first gatra is the antecedent (*padhang*), the second is the consequent
(*ulihan*). On another level, the first phrase of a piece is the antecedent
to the second phrase, or consequent. The third and fourth phrases are
similarly related. Furthermore, the first two phrases together form an
antecedent, followed by a consequent consisting of the second two phrases,
and so on.

As each phrase is played or sung, it is filled in, expanded, em-
bellished, etc. The series of notes and intervals (*sruti*)[*] used in this
manner are called "cèngkok." In principle, one phrase contains one
cèngkok. One antecedent-consequent also comprises one cèngkok. Thus, one
gongan may also be called a cèngkok. "Cèngkok" may then be defined as an
arrangement of phrases of a given lagu that are played or sung in the
process of filling in and embellishing a lagu.[**] The essential nature of
a cèngkok is neither its form nor its shape, but, rather, its course of
movement. The function of a cèngkok is to clarify and affirm the meaning
of the lagu, in order to give it movement and strength. Cèngkok is that
which gives soul and sense to a lagu.

In fact, the characteristics of cèngkok are individual and, hence,
local. Because of this, the number of cèngkok is theoretically unlimited.
But, it is easily seen that cèngkok are restricted by the technical
capabilities of instruments, by the rules of tuning, mode, and, of course,
by concerns of beauty. It is clear that cèngkok are bound by the course of
the balungan of the lagu. Thus, cèngkok always take into account the
fourth note of each gatra, or at least emphasize the eighth note of each
phrase.

The idea of recording all possible cèngkok is not strange. The number
of possible permutations of gatra, although quite large, is certainly
limited, and if only beautiful cèngkok are selected, a codification of
cèngkok for every practical use could be compiled. The method of studying
how to play the rebab and gendèr at the Konservatori Karawitan Indonesia is

---

[*] "*Sruti*," from the Sanskrit "śruti," means an audible distance: a
note-distance, space between tones, space between notes, or interval. In
Indian music, "sruti" is also used for the name of a unit of which there
are more than twenty per octave.

[**] This definition, as well as the definitions for other terms found
here, are peculiar to this article. In the case of varying terminology, it
is the definition assigned to a term, rather than the term itself, which
should be emphasized.

based on this speculation, as well as on the names for cengkok commonly
used by musicians. Taking into consideration that the function of cengkok
is to embellish and enhance the lagu, the danger of such a codification is
that it may destroy the creativity of musicians.

Finally, it may be noted that cengkok for gerong are metrical, while
those for sindhen, suluk, etc., are in a freer rhythm.

Luk and Gregel

In vocal music, there are instances in which a certain note must be
held for a long time. Such a note, provided it does not occur at the end
of a phrase, must also be filled in and expanded. The sequence of notes
and intervals used to expand a long note in vocal music is called a *"luk."*
A luk always moves to a note higher than the first, then returns, then
moves back and forth, leading to the following note. For example:

From a sustained i̇ to 3 in pélog:[*]

i̇ . . 2 .12 3 . . .23 2 . . . .3 i̇ . . 2 . i̇ .65 . . 5 .i̇ 6 . 5 . 65 3 . .

Like cengkok, luk give movement and style to the notes to which they
are applied. Luk in macapat, tembang gedhé, suluk, sendhon, etc., vary in
composition.

A note that moves to another note with a quick back-and-forth motion
may be called a *"gregel."* A gregel to a higher note has the shape fall-
rise-rise. For example:

A gregel from 2 to 3 is: 2 . i̇ 2 3

A gregel to a lower note has the shape fall-rise-fall. For example:

A gregel from 2 to i̇ is: 2 . i̇ 2 i̇

Gregel is a movement of notes that adds flavor to cengkok and luk; it
may both arouse and calm emotion. Luk and gregel are to cengkok as aroma
is to food or drink.

---

[*]Due to the practical considerations of using a typewriter, the
Kepatihan notation has been used. If there were enough equipment, it would
have been acceptable, and visually clearer, to use a staff or other
notation.

Wilet

Cèngkok may be written with the notational signs already agreed upon,
as with luk and gregel. Whereas metrical cèngkok are the simplest, cèngkok
in freer rhythm, such as in tembang (macapat and gedhé), sindhèn, suluk,
etc., may be written metrically only with a great deal of time and effort.
Even when notated in this way, the relative durations of the notes, as
indicated by the notation, will be altered by the musician according to his
own own feelings. He can (and may) stretch and compress the values of
notes until a variant, or *wilet*, results. The characteristics of such
variants are extremely individual and are characteristic of individual
players or singers. Thus, a wilet results from the subtraction from, and
addition to, the durations of notes in a cèngkok until living movement and
expressive style emerge.

The definition of "wilet" just given would seem to imply that wilet is
dependent upon cèngkok. This is most certainly not true, because wilet is
on a much higher level than cèngkok. This will perhaps be clearer when the
following comparison is made: cèngkok is like a sentence, while wilet is
the style and manner of uttering that sentence; or, cèngkok is like a
passport photograph whereas wilet is the actual person. Similar analogies
may be drawn.

But, because cèngkok and wilet are not on the same level, comparisons
of the type just made are not quite accurate. Wilet contains cèngkok
within it; wilet is a totality greater than the integration of its parts;
wilet is a movement which ceases the moment it is segmented, a living thing
that dies if analyzed part by part. To depict wilet in words is like
taking a fish out of water.

The life and movement of wilet is felt sincerely by musicians and
listeners alike. For this reason, wilet is always individual. The
essential characteristic of wilet is that it can cause the soul of the
listener to tremble and that it lends charm and grace to the lagu. Wilet
and cèngkok are very closely related; therefore, their meaning and
applications are often confused in everyday use.

Now that we determined the definitions of terms above, we shall
proceed with our observations of their application to the dynamics of
everyday musical practice.

Lagu, Player, and Listener

In karawitan, as explained above, a lagu centers on the single idea that it portrays. One performs the cèngkok in a lagu according to one's own feelings and skill, elaborating with one's own wilet.

Many lagu have been notated. Some have been published in books, others exist only in manuscripts, in museums, or in public or private libraries, and others have been written down by musicians and amateurs. All of these notations consist of the balungan alone, that is, only the slenthem part or cantus firmus. A few exist in full score as in European music, but these scores are used for ethnological or ethnomusicological purposes only. For the purposes of karawitan, such full scores are not necessary and are considered unsuitable for teaching.

We may understand the reasons for the practice of notating only the balungan if we realize that, in the opinion of musicians, it is neither necessary nor possible to notate cèngkok or wilet. This does not mean that cèngkok and wilet are unimportant; on the contrary, they are of great importance. But they must take on individual, personal characteristics. When notated, cèngkok and wilet resemble ready-made items and their individuality is lost. For this reason, musicians feel it is sufficient to notate only the balungan while they continue to create the cèngkok and wilet themselves.

Lagu are classified according to formal structure, tuning system, mode, final gong, and often by drumming style. Within this scheme, musicians further divide pieces according to mood and use. Musicians must understand the emotion or idea of a given piece and which piece is appropriate for a certain purpose. For example, in *wayang*, certain pieces are used for scenes taking place in Ngastina, and others for scenes in Ngamarta or Dwarawati, or for scenes featuring demons, holy men, etc. A similar division according to type is made for dance accompaniment.

The purpose of this system of classification can be understood if it is seen as a way of coordinating the manner of embellishing the lagu with meaning. Thus, cèngkok and wilet play an important role in the expression of a certain emotion. From this classificatory scheme we can also see that a given piece can express only one type of emotion. Gendhing *Méga Mendhung* ['dark rain clouds'] depicts a feeling of gloom, as if enveloped by fog, and this piece is usually followed by Ladrang *Remeng* ('hazy').
Pathet an sanga usually differs in mood from *pathet sendhon tlutur*, *ayak-ayakan* from *srepegan*, and *srepegan* from *sampak*.

A musician must know a lagu by heart, since knowing and memorizing pieces is an inherent obligation of one's position as an artist. Those who do not have a gift for memorization need to make notes to carry in their pockets wherever they go. Musicians who memorize easily are assigned to play the rebab or slenthem. A "musician of the front" means a musician who plays the gendèr, rebab, kendhang, slenthem, bonang, etc.; a "musician of the back" plays instruments that do not embellish the lagu, such as saron, kethuk, kempul, kenong, and gong. The terms "front" and "back" indicate a gradation, the front being higher than the back. The gendèr and rebab are the instruments that have the greatest freedom to make cèngkok and wilet, and these two instruments are played by musicians of the front.

It is evident from this that the rank of gamelan musicians is based, not only on the memorization of pieces, but also (and especially) on skill in creating cèngkok and wilet. Thus, cèngkok and wilet are greatly prized and valued by the musicians themselves.

Ordinarily, a singer of tembang macapat is on his way to becoming proficient after learning only eleven or thirteen macapat songs. In performing, he endeavors to perfect his skill in producing cèngkok and wilet with all their modifications. His success depends only on his own interest and talent. He rightly feels that his progress is measured by his use of cèngkok and wilet. The situation is the same with singers of tembang gedhé, bawa, suluk, etc. They establish themselves among their colleagues on the basis of their skill at executing cèngkok and wilet.

Instrumentalists and vocalists alike consider cèngkok and wilet essential factors in karawitan. With only slight exaggeration it may be said that lagu is an uncut stone, while wilet is a precious diamond.

In connection with lagu and performance, we may observe the relative vitality of tembang macapat and tembang gedhé. To the present day, tembang macapat remains a true people's art: not one melody has a known composer, all people sing them, embellish them, change them, create cèngkok and wilet for them. Furthermore, tembang macapat can be made into instrumental pieces while still maintaining their identity as tembang macapat. At present, the case of tembang gedhé is quite different. Very few people can sing them, and no one dares to alter their cèngkok. If their texts are changed, people find them difficult to learn and sing, and, once their wilet are altered, they are considered incorrect. This situation is very likely dependent on the development of language; that is, tembang macapat employ the language of today whereas tembang gedhé are composed in archaic style, which retards their development. But, musical-esthetic motivations

are not lacking: tembang macapat affords the singer much freedom to create
cèngkok and wilet, whereas tembang gedhé limits the singer to fixed cèngkok
only. The most that can be done with a tembang gedhé is to develop it into
a bawa (a vocal introduction [to a gamelan piece]), with cèngkok that are
largely influenced by instrumental idioms. But, transforming a tembang to
a bawa is not limited to tembang gedhé--tembang macapat may also be so
arranged. Thus, we are not far from the truth if we say that the
popularity of tembang macapat is due to the opportunity it provides the
singers to create wilet and cèngkok.

The vitality of lagu also depends on the freedom to create cèngkok and
wilet. Again we see that cèngkok and wilet are specific and essential
factors in karawitan. Listeners of karawitan also have standards. Even if
the makers of karawitan do have extensive material to start with, they
present their best to the audience, notwithstanding the freedom with which
cèngkok and wilet are created. Listeners calmly await surprises
(verrassingen), which may be presented at any time by the musicians and
singers. Certainly, many listeners have some technical knowledge or
theoretical understanding of the process involved. Intuitively or
consciously, they prefer singers skilled in cèngkok and wilet to those who
only render the basic melody faithfully; likewise, they prefer the humor
and intimacy of wilet to the discipline of established routine.

Clearly we may conclude that wilet is a specific and essential factor
in karawitan. Lagu, which provide opportunities for the creation of
cèngkok and wilet, evidently possess a strong vitality. Players themselves
feel they have progressed when they increase their ability with cèngkok and
wilet and listeners respond more to the life of wilet than to the dryness
of routine.

Has wilet always been an important factor? When did wilet become
specific and essential? These are questions that cannot be answered yet
because there are not enough aural remains and not enough sources in
libraries and archeological sites concerning music and esthetics. We can
only observe the karawitan of the present day, a system whose history and
development is clear only for the last fifty years. Perhaps our purview
can be extended back one or two more centuries, as the *Serat Centhini* and
the even older *Serat Panji Semirang* describe the performance of karawitan
in terms that seem to point to the existence of wilet. Possibly it can be
extended even ten centuries or more in light of the fact that the musics of
India, Arabia, China, and others also possess wilet as an essential factor.
This is a matter for further research.

Reason for Making Cèngkok and Wilet[3]

Something not yet mentioned, but very important to my position, is
irama. "Irama" originally meant 'to stop', i.e., 'duration of stopping'.
When used in the context of karawitan, "irama" refers to the length of the
stopping of the notes of the balungan, that is, the duration of time
between two notes of the balungan. The unit for measuring irama is the
time between two notes of the balungan.

Pieces that are played quickly, such that the time between two notes
of the balungan is the same as two time-units of the gambang [one note of
the balungan is played for every two notes of the gambang], are said to be
in a "very fast (*lancar*) irama" (*irama amat lancar*). Pieces in which the
time between two notes of the balungan is the same as four time-units [of
the gambang] are said to be in *irama tanggung*; if eight time-units, *irama
dados*; similarly, if sixteen units, *irama wilet*; if thirty-two units, *irama
rangkep*. So, in principle, irama may be doubled and its name changed. The
name of the irama is based on the number of gambang beats (time-units), not
on any absolute length of time. This means that a given irama may be
played fast or slow, depending on the "absolute value" of the gambang time-
units. This is usually referred to as "loose (*kendho*) irama" (i.e., slow)
or "tight (*kentjeng*) irama" (i.e., fast, tense). The word "*mlaya*" or
"*malaya*," meaning 'to walk', may have originally been related to this
understanding of loose and tight irama.[*]

With the above explanation we understand that the irama of every piece
in karawitan may be extended or stretched. This stretching of irama is
peculiar to karawitan. In other musics (*seni-swara*) there is certainly no
such phenomenon.

If the irama of a piece is doubled [literally, 'folded'], the name of
the piece remains the same, but the notes of the balungan sound (*mengumbang*
[literally, 'buzz']) longer, sometimes much longer. In this case, the
players and singers are forced to play ornaments (*fioritur*) and
improvisations in order to ensure that no long (or very long) note is
sustained meaninglessly. If there are four or eight long notes, the played
or sung ornaments constitute long improvisations called "cèngkok." As
explained above, cèngkok give individual character (*cachet*) to a piece.

---

[*]In present-day Indonesian, the term "*irama*" means rhythm (*rhythmus*),
which differs from [the concept of] irama in karawitan.

Suppose that the irama of a usually syllabic children's song were stretched so that the players and singers may (or rather, must) perform cèngkok. Indeed, this is what happens when a children's song is adapted to the klenèngan or uyon-uyon repertory. Because of the influence of individual and local styles on cèngkok, it is often difficult to recognize [an expanded and elaborated version of] a macapat song (especially, if the areas are distant, for example, Sunda and Madura, or Bali), even though the poetic rules (*pathokan*) remain the same.

What future is in store for wilet? Will wilet disappear? It is not possible to do more than grope for hints among the symptoms presently visible in modern innovations.

Innovations

Each of the components of lagu listed below is undergoing innovation:

1. tuning system (*laras*)
2. pathet
3. cèngkok
4. irama [meter]
5. instruments
6. playing style

We will examine such innovations in relation to the structure of karawitan, as presented above, and will also attempt to investigate the motives behind these innovations.

1. Tuning System

There are only five basic notes per octave in both sléndro and pélog. In the complete seven-tone pélog there are five basic notes and two auxiliary notes. However, since in seven-tone pélog there are two intervals that are nearly twice as large as the other intervals, there is room for the insertion of two new notes, bringing the total number of notes per octave to nine, and thus giving rise to nine-tone pélog.[*] This nine-tone pélog is by no means new to players of the rebab (much less Sundanese

---

[*]According to musicologists, these inserted notes may be obtained by the cycle of fifths (*deretan-kempyung*). Pelog is thus extended by one fifth in each direction. These two new notes are also a fifth apart in the circle of fifths (*lingkaran-kempyung*), the Pythagorean comma being easily eliminated.

rebab players!) who sometimes alter the notes dhadha [3] and barang [7] in
creating wilet. But in new compositions, especially those of
C. Hardjosubrata, nine notes are consciously used, with the result that
pélog is no longer a five-tone system with four auxiliary tones, but a
five-tone system with modulations to other varieties of pathet. In this
system, there are nine possible modulations and forty-five permutations or
arrangements of these modulations, although in fact only modulations within
the normal ambitus are practical. Such a nine-tone pélog was constructed
in 1934 by J. Kunst and R. [Radèn] Machjar Angga Kusumadinata,[*] and again
(independently of the influence of the the above) by R. [Radèn]
C. Hardjosubrata in 1952. Realization of pieces by Hardjosubrata followed
in 1954.

Such pieces have met with no response from the public as yet and
remain limited to the circle of theorists. The reason may lie in the
scarcity of nine-tone gamelan, or perhaps in the public feeling that beauty
lies in other areas (such as the freedom of wilet). Nevertheless, such
experiments clearly precede the development of public taste. Attempts to
unite sléndro, pélog, and the European diatonic scale in a *"gamelan gentha"*
by the late K. R. T. [Kangjeng Radèn Tumenggung] Wreksadiningrat in 1914
were repeated in 1948 at the cultural congress in Magelang and again in
1952 in Bandung. These attempts did not meet with lasting approval,
possibily because of shortcomings in the quality of the instruments.

2. Pathet

In fact, the new pieces by Hardjosubrata have added new pathet in a
tonal sense. Thus, five-tone pélog (with or without borrowed notes) can be
raised or lowered in frequency. Experiments that do not affect pathet
directly, but that change the positions of functional notes within a
pathet, have been made by Saudara Nartosabdo[4] in his humorous piece (*lagu
gecul*), *Gambang Suling*. In each pélog pathet, the distribution of
functional notes is as follows: *dhong, dhung, dhang, dhing, dhèng*. That
is, there are one tonic tone (*baku swara*); one dominant and one subdominant
tone (both called *daya swara*); two ordinary tones (called *warga swara*); a
borrowed tone; and, finally, an avoided tone (*nada sirikan*). In the above-
mentioned piece, Saudara Nartosabdo boldly uses an avoided tone as a
substitute tone (*lintasan*), resulting in a rather awkward-sounding piece.

---

[*]Saudara [Radèn] Machjar [Angga Kusumadinata] named the new notes
"pamiring" and *"panangis."*

But this awkwardness is intentional and is meant to add to the tension of the piece. Such pieces are apparently attractive by virtue of their awkwardness and may be included as adornments to klenèngan on listener's-request radio programs.

3. Cèngkok

It is the nature of cèngkok to be free and individual. When musicians are required to follow cèngkok that have been fixed by a composer, the result is what is called in European music "melody" (*mélodi*). Melody, too, manifests emotion, but it is the individual emotion of the composer. Through such melodies, a composer may freely express what is in his heart. This is the most common type of new composition and includes the following: children's songs sung in school (written by schoolteachers such as Hadisukatno, Hardjosubrata, Machjar A. Kusumadinata, and others); songs for every need--propaganda, satire, entertainment, comedy routines, etc. (in this regard, Mang Koko is proficient); serious songs for religious services (primarily by Atmodarsono and Hardjosubrata); and Western music, which uses pseudo-sléndro and pseudo-pélog (by Koesbini, Kamsidi, and others). In general, it is difficult to assess how much rationality and emotion each play a role. These pieces spread quickly among the people because of the beauty of their melodies or because of their frequent use in schools or on the radio. When played in gamelan, it is difficult to create cèngkok or wilet for them; rather, one is forced to play in a purely syllabic style, as in children's songs, which have already entered the gamelan repertory. Following the development of European music, the composers of these pieces wish to innovate and organize, to write canons and heterophony, to move in the direction of polyphony and harmony.

4. Irama, or Matra [Meter]

The basic meter (*matra*) of karawitan is quadruple. If triple meter is superimposed on quadruple meter, it is called "*salahan*," which refers to an intentional rhythmic deviation (*menyalahi irama*). The purpose of this deviation is to draw the attention of the other musicians; it is often used to signal the ending (*suwuk*) of a piece (as, for example, in signals given on the keprak or the drum). In fact, all pieces in quadruple meter can be executed in triple meter. This is demonstrated in compositions by Hardjosubrata (e.g., *Langen Sekar*, etc.) and in Sundanese children's songs (especially those by Machjar A. Kusumadinat-), all of which are in triple

meter. It may be noted here that if triple meter does indeed become more
common, it will give rise to new dance forms with new styles and
characters.

5. Instruments

Innovation with respect to instruments does not refer to construc-
tional changes resulting from "democraticization" in the gamelan--such as
new ways of carrying instruments, or new ways of caring for instruments.
Rather, it refers to the introduction of new timbres or tone colors.
Experiments with Western drums, brass, and string instruments have been
made in Central Java and in Sunda, but evidently they were no more
successful than attempts to introduce glass idiophones. Such experiments
have not been repeated. Yet, from time to time, the desire to use the
piano arises, perhaps because of its tone, perhaps for practical considerations. Such attempts are always frustrated by the problem of tuning.
Perhaps, if a piano were tuned to a generalized sléndro, or if a
generalized nine-tone pélog were developed and its tone were indeed found
desirable, these experiments could be pursued. In Sunda, *angklung* are
subject to exper-ments in the opposite direction, that is, not toward, but
away from, sléndro and pélog.

6. Playing Style

Innovations in style involve new ways of playing instruments so as to
incorporate stylistic features from the musics of other areas. Examples
are: (a) changes in instrumentation, such as the use of solo gendèr, solo
rebab, solo gambang, solo suling (!), or solo drum (!!) during the course
of a piece; (b) changes of arrangement, such as playing the *mérong* in
irama seseg (*lancaran*), use of *gérong milah* [syllabic *gérongan*] in
irama ciblon, stringing together "special" pieces as in listener's-request
radio broadcasts (*mana suka*), *lagu gecul* played in *irama rangkep*, etc.;
(c) dynamic changes, such as use of dynamics in sirepan; and (d)
instrumental techniques, such as playing the gendèr and bonang in the
Balinese manner, etc. These things have been done cleverly and boldly by
Saudara Cokrowasito [K. R. T. Wasitodipuro] and his associates. Such
experiments usually arise spontaneously during a piece, adding humour and
intimacy, but have not yet been used systematically. Apart from these new
creations, the creations of pieces in the traditional forms, with freedom
of cèngkok and wilet, still continues. Some results are good, others not

so good.   Some men associated with this are, for example, the late K. R. M.
H. [Kangjeng Radèn Mas Harya] Wiryadiningrat, the late R. Ng. [Radèn
Ngabèhi] Wirawiyaga, the late R. T. [Radèn Tumenggung] Wiraguna, the late
R. T. [Radèn Tumenggung] Danusuganda, the late Ki Demang Warsapradangga,
the late Ki Demang Gandasentika, and others; and presently, G. P. H. [Gusti
Pangéran Harya] Prabuwinoto, R. T. [Radèn Tumenggung] Warsodiningrat,
R. Ng. [Radèn Ngabèhi] Prawirapangrawit, R. Ng. [Radèn Ngabèhi]
Cokrowasito, R. T. A. [Radèn Tumenggung Arya] Sunarya, and various other
young, up-and-coming artists active in current music associations.

The innovations described above have been introduced only in the last
quarter century.   Actually, true innovation occurs only when new things
have become the property of a people or an extended society, either replacing old things or standing alongside them.   For these new things to become
the property of the people, the process of innovation requires more time.
In my opinion, the innovations described above are only experimental.   The
majority of the people are familiar with the musical structure described at
the beginning of this article, and they still sing, play, dance, and
perform shadow-puppet plays in the traditional manner, always speaking of,
thinking of, and making [music] based on the freedom of cèngkok and wilet,
whether consciously or not.   External influence from other musics, from new
new ways of thinking, from social, political, and economic structures are
certainly in evidence.   However, if we interpret the essence of karawitan
as the freedom of the individual as embodied by his freedom to choose and
create cèngkok and wilet (*bercèngkok dan berwilet*), then these external
influences can be considered as merely peripheral.   Karawitan itself,
issuing forth from the soul of a people witha long history, prevails
unsullied.

TRANSLATOR'S NOTES

1. This translation is a combination of the two published versions, incorporating material from the 1959 version that was not printed in the 1956 version. (See below, note 3.)

2. *Naradha Purana* is an unidentified manuscript.

3. The section entitled "Reason for Making Cèngkok and Wilet" appears only in the second edition of Sindoesawarno's article, reprinted in *Udan Mas* (1959), and not in the original edition published in *Sana-Budaja* (1956). Only the final paragraph of this section, beginning "What future is in store for wilet? . . ., etc." appears in the 1956 version.

4. The title, "Saudara," literally "brother," was used for a period immediately following the revolution in an effort to diminish status distinctions.

GENDHING JAWA

[Javanese Gamelan Music]

by

Radèn Mas Kodrat Poerbapangrawit
assisted by Mas Samoed Sastrowardojo

Translated from Javanese by
Judith Becker

(Jakarta: Harapan Masa, 1955)

AUTHOR'S NOTE

The source of much of the information presented in this book is R. T.
[Raden Tumenggung] Warsadiningrat, director of gamelan musicians in the
palace in Surakarta.   The compiler of this book wishes to humbly express
here his gratitude.

Kodrat Purbapangrawit

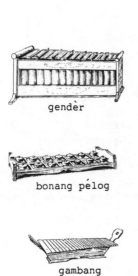

gendèr

gendèr penerus

saron penerus

bonang pélog

saron gedhé

slenthem

gambang

celempung

bonang sléndro

kendhang

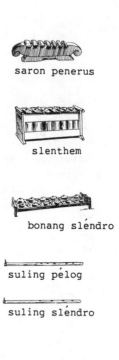

rebab

suling pélog

suling sléndro

kendhang

kepyak

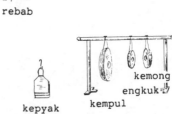

kemong

engkuk

kempul

gong

kethuk

kenong

INSTRUMENTS OF THE GAMELAN

Sléndro	Péloq
gendèr	gendèr (barang and nem)
gendèr penerus	gendèr penerus (barang and nem)
saron	saron
saron penerus	saron penerus
demung	demung
slenthem	slenthem
gambang	gambang (barang and nem)
bonang	bonang
bonang penerus	bonang penerus
celempung	celempung
suling	suling

rebab
kendhang gedhé
kendhang ciblonan
kendhang cilik
kendhang ketipung
teteg (small bedhug)
gong kemodhong
gong gedhé
gong suwukan

Sléndro	Péloq
kempul, lima	kempul, lima
kempul, nem	kempul, nem
kempul, tengah [dhadha]	kempul, barang
kempul, barang	
engkuk	-
kemong	-
kethuk	kethuk
kempyang	kempyang
kenong, lima	kenong, lima
kenong, nem	kenong, nem [equals slendro kenong nem, when tumbuk is nem]
kenong barang	kenong, barang
kenong, dhadha	kenong, panunggul
kenong, gulu	kenong, dhadha
kemanak	kenong, gulu
kecèr	

I. The Study of the Refinements of Gendhing
(Karawitaning Gendhing)

In a nutshell, the main body of knowledge of the refinements of
gendhing (*karawitaning/alusing gendhing*) comprises five areas:

1. the physical appearance and names of the instruments (*tetabuhan*),
   as illustrated in the drawings above;

2. *laras*, that is, the arrangement of tones from large to small, or
   small to large; or, in international terms, from low to high, or
   high to low;

3. *irama* (or *wirama*), that is, the pace of the pulse (*keteg*);

4. *pathet*, that is, the limits on the range--high or low--of a
   sequence of pitches; and

5. *gendhing*, that is, melody that has irama [i.e., is metrical].

II. Laras [Tuning]

There are two arrangements of tones, which are called "*laras*": *laras*
sléndro and *laras pélog*. Laras sléndro comprises five tones. From large
to small, the tones are arranged as follows.

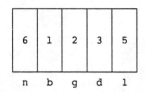

[Note: In this and the following diagrams, the following abbreviations are
        used: n = enem; b = barang; g = gulu; d = dhadha, or tengah;
        l = lima; pn = panunggul; pl = pélog.]

Laras pélog has seven tones. From large to small, the tones are arranged as
follows.

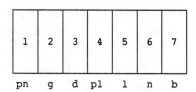

Of the seven pélog tones, only five are used in [pieces] in laras pélog. Thus, if the following tones are used [i.e., if the shaded keys are avoided],

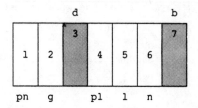

the [piece] is considered to be in laras pélog pathet lima. If the following tones are used,

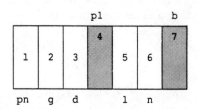

the [piece] is considered to be in laras pélog [pathet] nem (or bem). If the following tones are used,

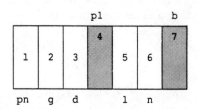

the [piece] is considered to be in pélog [pathet] barang.

The names of the tones in [laras] sléndro and [laras] pélog can refer
to the *wilahan* [keys (of an instrument)]; for example, "wilahan panunggul,"
"wilahan gulu," "wilahan dhadha," etc. Each of these keys can be
symbolized with a cipher; these ciphers are called "*titilaras*."

In [laras] sléndro, the wilahan are symbolized as follows.

barang	1
gulu	2
dhadha (tengah)	3
lima	5
nenem	6

In laras pélog, the symbols for the wilahan are as follows.

panunggul	1
gulu	2
dhadha (tengah)	4
pélog	4
lima	5
nenem	6
barang	7

Among the tones in sléndro and pélog there is a common tone, which is
called "*tumbuk*." Thus, "tumbuk 6" indicates that pitch 6 [nenem] in
sléndro and pélog is the same; and "tumbuk 5" indicates that pitch 5 [lima]
in sléndro and pélog is the same.

III. Irama

In the context of gendhing, "irama" refers to the even pace of the
pulse (*keteg*). If the pace is fast, it is called *seseg*; if the pace is
slow, it is called *tamban*.

The progression of irama from seseg to tamban or tamban to seseg must
be even and not jerky (*grag-greg*). An uneven irama is referred to as
"*irama rusak*" ['destroyed irama']. There are six varieties of irama:

1. irama lancar (a)

2. irama lancar (b)

3. irama siji ['one']

4. irama loro ['two']

5. irama telu ['three']

6. irama papat ['four'], or irama rangkep

If the pace of these irama is measured in seconds, the results are approximately as follows.

1. In irama (a) the pulse occurs every one-eighth second.

2. In irama lancar (b) the pulse occurs every one-fourth second.

3. In irama siji, the pulse occurs every one-half second.

4. In irama loro, the pulse occurs every second.

5. In irama telu, the pulse occurs every two seconds.

6. In irama papat, the pulse occurs every three seconds.

The above measurements of the pace of irama refer to the skeletal melody (*balunganing gendhing*, or *balungan*). The balungan is played by the slenthem, demung, and/or saron. The relative pace of this melody is determined by either the kendhang-player or the bonang-player.

IV. Pathet

Pathet is defined above as "the limits on the range of a sequence of pitches." The final tone of a sequence assumes the role of establishing the feeling (*rasa*).

In international music the sequence "do-re-mi-fa-sol-la-ti-do" can be raised or lowered to accommodate the range of the singer. It is the same for Javanese music; a sléndro piece can be raised or lowered according to the appropriateness of the feeling (*manut kepénaké rasa, manut patuté/ patheté*) produced by the change.

In sléndro there are three categories of pathet:

1. pathet enem

2. pathet sanga

3. pathet manyura

In pélog there are four categories of pathet:

1. pathet lima

2. pathet enem

3. pathet manyura

4. pathet barang

Let us return to the matter of establishing the feeling (*sèlèhing rasa*) of the piece. In laras sléndro, if the final tone falls on pitch (wilahan) 5, the piece is in pathet sanga. If the final tone falls on pitch/6, the piece is in pathet manyura. If the final tone falls on pitch 2 (*gulu*), the piece is in pathet enem.

If a [proper] feeling is to be established (*sumèlèh*), [the final tones] must be approached in a particular manner. Thus, the proper approach to pitch 5 from pitch 2 (*gulu*) is, moving from right to left,

> 5———6———1◂——2   (in pathet 9 [sanga]).

If the final tone is pitch 6, it must be approached, moving from right to left, from pitch 3 (*dhadha*),

> 6———1———2◂——3   (in pathet manyura).

If the final tone is pitch 2 (*gulu*), the approach will be from pitch 6, moving from right to left,

> 2———3———5◂——6   (in pathet enem).

In laras pélog, if the approach to a final tone on pitch 1 (*panunggul*) is from pitch 5, by way of pitch 4 (*pélog*) and 2 (*gulu*), then the pathet must be pathet lima.

> 1———2———4◂——5   (pélog pathet 5 [lima])

If the approach to a final tone on pitch 5 (*lima*) is from pitch 2 (*gulu*), by way of pitches 1 (*panunggul*) and 6 (*enem*), then the pathet will be pathet enem.

> 5———6———1◂——2   (pélog pathet 6 [enem])

If the approach to a final tone on pitch 6 (*enem*) is from pitch 3 (*dhadha*), by way of pitches 2 (*gulu*) and 1 (*panunggul*), then the pathet will be pélog pathet manyura.

> 6———1———2◂——3   (pélog pathet manyura)

If the approach to a final tone on pitch 6 (enem) is from pitch 3 (dhadha), by way of pitches 2 (gulu) and 7 (barang), then the pathet will be pelog pathet barang.

6———7———2◄——3   (pelog pathet barang)

Some examples of pieces in various pathet will be discussed below.

Gendhing [ladrang] Clunthang and [ladrang] Pangkur are usually played in slendro pathet 9 [sanga]. However, sometimes they are transposed to [slendro] manyura or pelog barang. When such a piece is transposed, the emotive quality changes, since the sequence of tones is higher/smaller (luwih dhuwur/luwih cilik).

Gendhing [ketawang] Puspa Warna is [an example of a piece] in pathet manyura. Gendhing Godheg and Krawitan are in pathet 6 [enem]. The counterpart of slendro pathet 9 [sanga] is pelog pathet 6 [enem]. The counterpart of slendro pathet manyura is pelog pathet barang, and that of slendro pathet 6 [enem] is pelog pathet 5 [lima].

Some pieces, such as [ladrang] Clunthang and [ladrang] Pangkur, can be played in slendro or pelog. However, other pieces are only played in pelog (e.g., Ganda Mastuti and Kombang Mara) or only in slendro (e.g., Gendhing Rondhon and Lagu Dhempel).

V. Gendhing

There are four categories of pieces in Javanese gamelan music: (1) vocal pieces (gendhing lesan); (2) instrumental pieces (gendhing thuthuk) [literally, 'struck pieces']; (3) instrumental pieces accompanied by voice; and (4) vocal pieces accompanied by instruments.

1. Vocal Pieces (Gendhing Lesan)

The category "vocal pieces" consists of three parts:

a. small pieces (gendhing cilik): children's pieces such as Lagu
    Ilir-ilir, Dhempo Talu Tameng, Cublak-cublak Suweng, Jamuran,
    Cempa Rowa. These are purely vocal pieces usually sung by small
    children.

b. medium pieces (gendhing sedhengan): slawatan, santi swara, and
    laras madya. These are usually sung by men, or sometimes women,
    to the accompaniment of terbang, kendhang, and sometimes also

kemanak. Terbang, kendhang, and kemanak are used to keep the
irama steady and to increase the beauty of the sound.

c. large pieces (*gendhing gedhé*): These are vocal pieces sung by both
male and female singers. A solo female singer begins the piece
with an introduction called "*celuk*" [literally, 'to call'], so
termed because the celuk often contains the name of the following
piece. The piece is accompanied by one *kendhang gedhé*, one
ketipung, one pair of kemanak, kethuk, kenong, and one gong gedhé.
The instruments serve to keep the irama steady, to mark off the
sections of the piece, and to increase the beauty of the sound.

2. Instrumental Pieces (Gendhing Thuthuk)

Instrumental pieces are called "gendhing thuthuk" ['struck pieces'],
because all the instruments used, except for the rebab and suling, produce
sounds by being struck. The melody (*lelagoné*) is produced on instruments,
which can be divided into the following categories:

(a) *balungan* ['skeleton', or 'framework']

(b) *rerenggan* ['ornamentation']

(c) *wiletan*[1] [(formulaic) melody]

(d) *singgetan* [sectional markers]

(e) *kembang* ['flowers', a kind of ornamentation]

(f) *jejeging wirama* [regulation of tempo]

The balungan of the gendhing is provided by the players of the slenthem,
demung, and saron. The rerenggan of the gendhing is provided by the
players of gendèr [barung], gambang, gendèr panerus, celempung, and bonang.
The bonang [barung] also serves to lead the balungan, and, if there is no
kendhang, to keep the tempo steady. The singgetan of the gendhing is
provided by the players of kempyang, kethuk, kempul, kenong, and gong. The
gong marks the longest phrase. The kembang of the gendhing is provided by
the player of the suling and the female solo vocalist [pesindhèn]. The
tempo of the irama is kept steady by the players of the kendhang and
ketipung.

The gendhing thuthuk can also be subdivided as (a) small, (b) medium,
and (c) large. The size of the piece is determined by the length of the
largest section in the piece (*singgetan kang dawa dhéwé*), that is, the
length of a single *gongan*.

3. Instrumental Pieces with a Vocal Part (Gendhing Gamelan lan Lésan)

Instrumental pieces with a vocal part are called *gendhing gérongan*, meaning "pieces that have a gérong part." The gérong, or vocal part, is performed by more than one male singer. The texts of the gérong part may be drawn from pre-existing texts in *kinanthi* or *salisir* meters, or may be created anew (i.e., not using a macapat meter), for example, the gérong of gendhing [ketawang] *Puspa Warna*, [ketawang] *Langen Gita*, [ketawang] *Tarupala*, etc. It is also the case with gérong of gendhing thuthuk used to accompany bedhaya and srimpi dances that the texts are not [necessarily] derived from macapat poetry.

4. Vocal Pieces with Instrumental Accompaniment

In this category of gendhing the vocal part is predominant, as, for example, in Gendhing *Mijil* or *Kinanthi*, which accompany the bedhaya and srimpi dances.

VI. More on Laras [Tuning]

Since Javanese gamelan do not yet use a standard system (*standaard*) of tuning, the tuning of any given gamelan merely reflects the preference of the gamelan maker. Thus, there are gamelan with so-called large [low-pitched] tunings (*laras gedhé*), medium tunings (*laras sedhengan*), and small [high-pitched] tunings (*laras cilik*). In Surakarta gamelan in the medium tuning, pitch lima (5) pélog corresponds to A [= 440 cycles per second] in the international system. A sléndro gamelan with tumbuk 6 in which pitch 5 of the parallel pélog gamelan corresponds to A [440 cps], would also be considered a medium tuning. Thus, both pélog and sléndro would be medium tunings, neither too high nor too low. However, when the tumbuk tone is pitch 5, then if the pélog is in a medium tuning, the corresponding sléndro will be rather high/small; and conversely, if the sléndro of a set with tumbuk on pitch 5 is in a medium tuning, then the corresponding pélog will be rather low/large.

In a double set with tumbuk on pitch 6, sléndro pitch 5 is equivalent to pélog pitch 4. In effect, therefore, there are two equivalent tones: sléndro pitch 5 is the same as pélog pitch 4, and sléndro pitch 6 is the same as pélog pitch 6.

In a double set with tumbuk on pitch 5, sléndro pitch 6 will be almost
equivalent to pélog pitch 7 (barang), and sléndro pitch 1 (barang) will be
almost equivalent to pélog pitch 1 (panunggul).

The sequence of seven tones in pélog approximates the sequence, do-re-
mi-fa-sol-la-ti [of Western solfège]. However, [the Western diatonic
scale] is not equivalent to the pélog tuning. The pélog tuning is
comprised of only five of the total seven tones. Even though laras pélog
and laras sléndro each consists of five tones, they can be distinguished
from one another by the size of the intervals (*godhagan/interval*) between
the tones. The intervals in laras sléndro are even (*ajeg*), whereas the
intervals in laras pélog are not. This may be roughly illustrated below.

sléndro:	6	1	2	3	5		
pélog lima:	1	2		4	5	6	
pélog enem:	1	2	3		5	6	
pélog barang:	2	3			5	6	7

The difference in intervals between pitches as shown in the diagram
above can also be demonstrated by the finger-holes of the suling. The
holes of a sléndro suling are evenly spaced, while those of a pélog suling
are uneven.

As far as I know, the intervals of sléndro and pélog have never been
measured exactly (in terms of vibration per second [*kedher/trilling*]),
since the tuning of sléndro and pélog gamelan is accomplished by ear
[literally, 'by mouth' (*swaraning lésan/cangkem*)]. Thus, there have arisen
low, medium, and high gamelan tunings.

Since the pitches of [laras] sléndro and pélog are used to realize the
melodies of gendhing (*lelagoning gendhing*), and since the melodies of
gendhing encompass low, medium, and high ranges, the use of merely five
tones is inadequate. To be complete, the five tones must be supplemented
by both a higher and a lower register.

Low register tones are found on the slenthem. Middle register tones
are found on the demung. High register tones are found on the saron
[barung]. Very high register tones are found on the saron panerus, or
saron peking. The number of tones found on each of the above-named
instruments is the same. The only difference lies in the registral range
of the pitches. The pitches found on the slenthem are referred to as one
gembyangan or *octaaf* in the low register; the pitches found on the demung

are referred to as one gembyangan in the middle register, etc. Therefore, the total range of a gamelan covers four gembyangan.

Even though laras sléndro and pélog derive from vocal tones (*swaraning lésan*), their realization in [particular] gamelan may diverge from those vocal tones. These divergences may or may not be intentional. If they are unintentional, they are referred to as "out of tune" (*bléru/ palsu*). If they are intentional, they are called *embat*.

There are three kinds of embat.

1. *embat nyendari*. Pitch dhadha (3) in the middle register is moved slightly to the left [i.e., it is lowered in pitch]. Therefore, the sound [interval] is increasingly closed up (*mingkup*). If pitch dhadha (3) is moved to the right [i.e., raised in pitch], the sound [or interval] will also be closed up (that is, moved closer to the neighboring tone).

2. *embat laras ati*. The interval from pitch dhadha (3) to the left [i.e., lower in pitch] is opened up (*megar*). So, too, the interval from pitch dhadha to the right [i.e., higher in pitch] is also opened up (making the distance to the neighboring interval greater). However, the opening up or narrowing of intervals is very slight, and can only be sensed by experts in gamelan tuning.

3. *embat colongan*. One of the tones is either moved closer to or farther away from its neighboring tone, according to the wishes of the gamelan tuner.

Thus, these differences of embat apply only to the tuning (*laras*) of a gamelan. There may also be gamelan without embat, that is, in which the tuning follows exactly vocal pitches that are not [themselves] out of tune. (For, vocal pitches that are not out of tune are without embat.)

On the other hand, when the pitches of a singer or a rebab player are realized as the melody of a gendhing (*lelagoning gendhing*), some of them will approximate the pitches of laras pélog, even though the gamelan played is laras sléndro. These tones are called *sléndro miring* or *barang miring*. This latter name refers to the similarity of the pitches of barang miring to the pitches of laras pélog pathet barang. In fact, the deviations in tuning (*miringing swara*) of the vocal pitches sometimes approximate laras pélog entirely, even though the instruments of the gamelan are tuned to sléndro. For example, the *tembang macapat* melodies called *mas kumambang* and *sinom logondhang* are purely pélog, but are frequently accompanied by a sléndro gamelan. This accompaniment is often *sampak* or *srepegan*.

However, the pélog gamelan is never used to accompany vocal melodies
in laras sléndro. Nevertheless, there is a kind of piece called *Kodhok
Ngorèk* which is played on a pélog gamelan, but accompanied by a gendèr and
gambang gangsa tuned to laras sléndro.

VII. More on Irama

It was explained above [see section III, "Irama"] that the kendhang
player determines the relative pace of the [balungan] melody. Sometimes it
is necessary for the kendhang player to effect a change in irama that is
called *mlumpat* ['leaping'] or *ditugel* ['cut off']. The explanation is as
follows.

As explained previously, the normal progress of irama that is not "cut
off" (*ditugel*) would require, for example, that from irama lancar (a) to
irama papat ['four'], the intermediate levels of irama--irama lancar (b),
irama siji ['one'], irama loro ['two'], and irama telu ['three']--would
have to be passed through. Whereas irama that is cut off may, for
instance, leap from irama lancar (a) to irama siji; or from irama siji it
may leap to irama telu. Or, from irama telu it may leap back to irama
lancar (b). Nevertheless, even if the irama is to leap, or is to be cut
off, the process must not be jerky (*grag-greg*). The emotional quality
(*lakuning rasa*) must still be even.

Leaps of irama are under the control of the kendhang player. This is
not, however, a matter of the kendhang player's personal taste, but follows
from the appropriate style of the piece being played. Many pieces cannot
be played with skips in the level of irama. On the other hand, there are
many pieces that may be played that way, or indeed, must be played that
way.

VIII. More on Pathet

Each of the sléndro pathet (nem, sanga, and manyura) and the pélog
pathet (lima, nem, barang) has its own melodies (*lelagon*). These melodies
fall under one of three categories: *pathet*, *sendhon*, and *ada-ada* (or
greget saut).

[Figure 1. Lelagon in the Six Sléndro and Pélog Pathet]

a. Sléndro Pathet 6 [Enem]

Pathet	Sendhon	Ada-ada
6 [Enem] Gedhé	Pananggalan	Gurisa
6 [Enem] Wantah	Tloloran	Hasta Kuswala Cilik
6 [Enem] Jugag	Tlutur	Hasta Kuswala Gedhe
Lasem		Mataraman
Kedhu		Budhalan
Lindur		

b. Sléndro Pathet 9 [Sanga]

Pathet	Sendhon	Ada-ada
9 [Sanga] Wantah	Rencasih	Sanga Wantah
9 [Sanga] Jugag	Tlutur	Manggalan
9 [Sanga] Ngelik		[Sanga] Jugag
Jengking		Palaran
Bimanyu		Bima

c. Sléndro Pathet Manyura

Pathet	Sendhon	Ada-ada
Manyura Wantah	Sastra Datan	Manyura Wantah
Manyura Jugag	Tlutur	Jugag
Manyura Ngelik		Bima
Manyura Gedhe		

d. Pélog Pathet Lima

Pathet	Sendhon	Ada-ada9
5 [Lima] Jugag	Tlutur	Pangkur
5 [Lima] Wantah		Durma
5 [Lima] Entek		Garjita Tawang

e. Pélog Pathet 6 [Enem]

Pathet	Sendhon	Ada-ada
6 [Enem] Gedhé 6 [Enem] Wantah 6 [Enem] Kemuda 6 [Enem] Manyura		Enem Wantah [Enem] Jugag

f. Pélog Pathet Barang

Pathet	Sendhon	Ada-ada
Barang Entek (Gedhé) Barang Wantah Barang Jugag Barang Onengan		Barang Wantah [Barang] Jugag

The rebab, gendèr, gambang, and suling play in the lelagon called pathet; the gendèr, gambang, and suling play in sendhon; and only the gendèr plays in ada-ada. Although pathet, sendhon, and ada-ada are referred to as melodies (*lelagon*), they do not have irama, in the sense of meter. Sometimes a melody that has irama is added at the end of a pathet; this is called *sarayuda*. For the playing of the metrical sarayuda, the kendhang and gong or kempul are required. And, in the accompaniment to wayang, even though no sarayuda is required at the end of a pathet, sendhon, or ada-ada, the kendhang and gong or kempul are used nevertheless.

The lelagon pathet, sendhon, and ada-ada listed above are used in the accompaniment to wayang kulit, or to increase the beauty (*tambah rerengganing jogèd*) of the dancing of *wireng*, *pethilan*, *bedhaya*, and *srimpi*. The lelagon pathet, sendhon, and ada-ada are sung with recited texts called *suluk* or *sulukan*.

IX. More on Gendhing

Above, in the section entitled "Gendhing" [V:4], we referred to the category of vocal pieces which have instrumental accompaniment; these pieces are used to accompany the badhaya and srimpi dances. The number of these gendhing is limited; I only know of eight.

1. [Bedhaya] *Ketawang Gedhé*
2. [Bedhaya] *Andhuk*
3. [Bedhaya] *Sumreg*
4. [Srimpi] *Suka Pratama*
5. [Bedhaya] *Dara Dasih*
6. [Srimpi] *Anglir Mendhung*
7. [Srimpi] *Mijil Yogan* [i.e., *Ganda Kusuma*]
8. [Bedhaya] *Pangkur* (not ordinary [ladrang] *Pangkur!*)

These vocal gendhing are referred to by gamelan experts as *gendhing kemanak*, or *gendhing kethuk kenong*. The experts consider gendhing kemanak to be exalted in their beauty. Vocal pieces of the small or medium categories cannot compare with the beauty of the highly esteemed gendhing kemanak.

Let us refer again to the second category of pieces listed under "Gendhing" above [V:2]--instrumental pieces (*gendhing thuthuk*). These gendhing can be divided into three categories--small, medium, and large-- according to the length of the gongan. The categories are characterized as follows.

(a)   small pieces: gendhing such as *sampak* and *srepegan*, in which there are two balungan strokes to each gongan; gendhing *ayak-ayakan*, with four balungan strokes per gongan; gendhing *Monggang*, *Kodhok Ngorèk*, [lancaran] *Kebo Giro*, [lancaran] *Béndrong*, etc., with eight balungan strokes per gongan; gendhing [ketawang] *Puspa Warna*, [ketawang] *Wala Gita*, etc., with sixteen balungan strokes per gongan; gendhing [ladrang] *Sri Katon*, [ladrang] *Clunthang*, [ladrang] *Manis*, etc., with thirty-two balungan strokes per gongan.

(b)   medium pieces: gendhing such as *Gambir Sawit*, *Bondhèt*, etc., [i.e., kethuk loro (2) kerep], in which there are sixty-four balungan strokes per gongan.

(c)   large pieces: gendhing such as *Damar Kèli*, *Lambang Sari*, etc., [i.e., kethuk papat (4) kerep], in which each gongan consists of 128 balungan strokes.

(d)   larger pieces: gendhing such as *Rondhon*, *Mawur*, *Semang*, *Agul-agul*, etc., [i.e., kethuk papat (4) arang, or kethuk wolu (8) kerep], with 256 balungan strokes per gongan.

A single gongan of a gendhing is referred to as "one cèngkok." Even though this gongan may be repeated numerous times, the gendhing is said to

have but one cèngkok. If there are two separate melodies, then the
gendhing is said to have two cèngkok, etc.

Gendhing with one or more cèngkok frequently have other melodies added
to them or substituted for one of their parts. One gongan or more can in
this way be substituted or added. There are two kinds of additions to a
piece: (a) *ngelik*, and (b) *umpak*. Ngelik usually involve the higher
registers. Some umpak are very short, others very long.

The umpak may be placed at the beginning, in the middle, or at the end
of a piece. If it is at the beginning, it begins immediately following the
gong of the introduction (*buka*). If it is in the middle of the piece, it
will be found preceding the gong, or immediately following a kenong. If it
is at the end of the piece, it will immediately precede the final gong of
the piece (*suwuking gendhing*). Umpak at the beginning and middle of
pieces, in addition to substituting for other parts of the main melody of
the piece, can never be repeated. However, if the umpak is at the end
together with a ngelik, it may be repeated numerous times.

Almost all gendhing of the medium and large category can be divided
into two parts: (a) *mérong*, and (b) *munggah* (or *unggah*). Gendhing with
mérong and munggah sections can comprise one cèngkok each, or more. Also,
the melody (*lelagon*) of the mérong may or may not be different from that of
the munggah. Gendhing in which the mérong and munggah have identical
melodies are referred to as *munggah gendhing*, while those with differing
melodies are referred to as *munggah unggahé dhéwé* ['with its own unggah'],
or "munggah gendhing (such and such)." Thus, gendhing with their own
unggah will have the same title to refer to the mérong and munggah
sections, even though the melodies may be different. However, if the
munggah is taken from another gendhing, it will carry the title of that
gendhing. For example, in Gendhing *Muntap*, after the umpak is played, the
piece proceeds to the munggah (*mangkat munggah*); in Gendhing *Gambir Sawit*,
after the ngelik is played, the piece proceeds to the munggah; Gendhing
Damar Kèli has its own unggah [the melody of which, however, is different
from the mérong]; and Gendhing *Ludira Madu* uses the munggah called Gendhing
Kinanthi.

Most pieces of the medium and large categories that have an umpak in
the middle of the piece, or a ngelik within the mérong, proceed directly to
the munggah after the umpak or ngelik.

[We shall now make reference again] to the third category of gendhing
mentioned above in the section "Gendhing" [V:3]--instrumental pieces with a

vocal part. The gérong part for gendhing that accompany the badhaya and srimpi dances is referred to as "*sindhènan badhaya*," and not as "gérongan." Thus, the vocal melodies used in the accompaniment of badhaya and srimpi dances are called "sindhènan badhaya."

Gamelan pieces that include a gérongan vocal part can also be divided into three subcategories: small, medium, and large. The small category includes pieces such as gendhing [ketawang] *Puspa Warna*, [ketawang] *Suba Kastawa*, [ladrang] *Clunthang*, [ladrang] *Sri Katon*, [ladrang] *Pangkur Paripurna* (which nowadays uses lyrics in *kinanthi* meter), [ladrang] *Sri Widada*, [ladrang] *Ayun-ayun*, [ladrang] *Loro-loro*, etc. The medium category includes pieces such as gendhing [kethuk loro kerep] *Gambir Sawit*, *Bondhèt*, *Montro*, *Wida Sari*, *Onang-onang*, etc. The large category includes pieces that are used in the accompaniment of the badhaya and srimpi dances, such as gendhing *Sinom*, *Kabor*, *Miyang Gong*, *Téja Nata*, etc.

All of the instrumental gendhing (*gendhing thuthuk*) mentioned above can be further differentiated according to the [most important] instrument. Thus, there are "gendhing rebab," "gendhing bonang," "gendhing gendèr," "gendhing gambang," and "gendhing kendhang." These categories may include pieces classified as small, medium, or large. The category takes its name from the instrument that the plays the introduction (*buka*)--if gendhing rebab, the rebab; if gendhing bonang, the bonang [barung], etc. In some categories all the instruments play; in others only some of them play. For example, for gendhing rebab, gendhing gendèr, or gendhing gambang, all of the instruments play. For gendhing bonang, the rebab, gendèr, gendèr panerus, gambang, and suling do not play, and there is no vocal part. Some gendhing kendhang are played with the instrumentation for gendhing rebab, some with the instrumentation for gendhing bonang. All instrumental pieces in which the bonang is used are played without celempung and engkuk kemong. For sléndro gendhing, if the bonang is not played, the engkuk kemong replaces the kempyang [which is used in pélog].

A. Balungan [Skeleton, or Framework]

The main part of a gendhing (*bakuning gendhing*) is carried by the slenthem, demung, and saron; this part is not subdivided (*ora nacah*) [literally, 'to chop, slice']). It is referred to as the *balunganing gendhing* ['framework of the gendhing']. The melody of a gendhing consists of gong periods of from 16 to 256 balungan strokes; these are divided into sections, like the verse lines (*pada lingsa*) of [certain] macapat poetic

meters (e.g., *kinanthi*, *salisir*, *juru demung*, *gurisa*, etc.). Just as each
line of verse contains eight syllables (*aksara/wanda*), so each section of a
gendhing consists of eight strokes, unless a dot (*cecek/titik* [indicating a
rest]) is substituted. The sum total of rests and strokes can only equal
eight.

The various divisions of a gendhing [melody]--depending on the
interspersal of rests--are referred to as *mlaku* [literally, 'to walk';
thus, 'with no interpolated rests'], *gantungan* [literally, 'hanging'; thus,
'to hang or sustain a single note'], or *nibani* [literally, 'to fall upon';
thus, 'to fall only on stressed beats', hence with interpolated rests].
Examples of these three varieties of melody [balungan] are provided below.

mlaku:	2	3	2	1	3	2	1	6
gantungan [for] one [beat]:	.	1	1	1	2	3	2	1
gantungan [for] two [beats]:	.	.	2	3	2	1	2	1
or	3	3	.	.	6	5	3	2
or	2	2	.	.	2	2	.	.
gantungan [for] three [beats]:	.	.	.	1	3	2	1	6
gantungan [for] four [beats]:	.	.	.	.	1	1	2	1
nibani:	.	3	.	2	.	1	.	6

The divisions of a gendhing [melody] given above are equivalent to one
eluk. There are also cases, however, where one eluk may consist of sixteen
balungan beats; this is referred to as *ngrancag* ['to hurry to the finish'].
In fact, there may be eluk that consist of thirty-two balungan strokes,
which are then referred to as "ngrancag banget" [*banget* 'very'; hence,
'extremely hurried']. An eluk of sixteen beats will usually be played by
two [saron] demung simultaneously. They will produce a [composite] melody
as follows:

```
2   3   2   3    2   1   2   1    6   5   6   5    3   5   3   5
```

The demung stroke that falls on the odd-numbered beats is referred to as
nglanangi ['to act the male part']; the demung stroke that falls on the
even-numbered beats is referred to as *medoki* ['to act the female part'].
This style of playing is called *imbal*--here executed on the demung. Demung
imbal technique may also be imitated on the slenthem, in which case the
slenthem part "falls behind" (*ngrèrèni*), as if inserting its part into the
composite demung imbal melody. This technique of slenthem playing is
referred to as *minjal* or *pinjalan* ['to act like a flea'; i.e., 'to leap'].

B. Kenongan [Kenong Playing]

There are five kinds of kenong playing.

1. *kenongan jumbuh* ['to be in accord'], in which the kenong tone is
    the same as the balungan tone with which it coincides (e.g.,
    kenong on pitch 6 when the balungan falls on 6, etc.).

2. *kenongan nunggal rasa (rasa kumpul)* ['to match the feeling'; 'to
    associate feelings'], in which, when the balungan falls on pitch 2
    (gulu), the kenong plays pitch 6, and when the balungan falls on
    pitch 1, the kenong plays pitch 5.

3. *kenongan salah gumun* ['settled, yet surprising'], in which, when
    the balungan falls on pitch 3, the kenong plays pitch 6.

4. *kenongan plèsèdan* ['as if sliding'], in which, when the balungan
    falls on pitch 6, [for example,] but the course of the melody
    suddenly shifts to another pitch--for example, pitch 3 (tengah)--
    then the kenong will play pitch 3. If the melody were to shift
    from pitch 6 to pitch 1, then the kenong would play pitch 1 [on
    the balungan tone 6], etc.

5. *kenongan sungsun* ['one after another'], *kenongan nitir*
    ['constant'], and *kenongan nibani* ['to fall upon'], in all three
    of which the kenong either divides the gongan in half or into
    quarters. Kenongan nitir refers to the technique used in gendhing
    sampak. Kenongan nibani refers to the technique used in gendhing
    ayak-ayakan, *srepegan*, and pieces like [lancaran] *Kebo Giro*. For
    gendhing such as [ketawang] *Puspa Warna*, [ladrang] *Sri Katon*,
    etc., on up to large-scale *gendhing gedhé* [i.e., kethuk loro (2)
    kerep and longer], the kenong also divides the gongan into
    quarters or halves, but this is not referred to as nitir or
    nibani. Kenongan sungsun refers to the technique used in the
    following gendhing: [ladrang] *Surung Dhayung*, [ladrang] *Sobrang*,
    [pélog pathet] barang, [ladrang] *Lèngkèr*, etc. The use of the
    technique is limited to appropriate parts of the melody; thus, not
    every kenong stroke will require the *sungsun* [reiterating]
    technique. The *sungsun* technique involves adding two additional
    kenong strokes to the basic stroke. That is, [where "tho" stands
    for a kenong stroke, and "gung" a gong stroke,]

tho . . tho . . tho . gung[2]

All gendhing with two kenong strokes per gongan are referred to as
ketawang. Gendhing in which each kenongan consists of eight balungan
strokes, and each gongan of four kenongan, are referred to as *ladrangan*.

C. Kethukan [Kethuk Playing]

There are six ways of playing the kethuk.

1. *kethuk ngganter* ['to beat steadily'], in which the kethuk is
    struck on every odd-numbered beat of the balungan (1, 3, 5, 7, 9,
    etc.), or between every beat of the balungan.

2. *kethuk kerepan* ['densely spaced'], in which for every eluk [i.e.,
    eight balungan beats] there are two kethuk strokes, falling on the
    second and twelfth beats.

3. *kethuk kerep*, in which for every two eluk [i.e., sixteen balungan
    beats] there are two kethuk strokes, falling on the fourth and
    twelfth beats.

4. *kethuk arang* ['sparsely spaced'], in which for every four *eluk*
    [i.e., thirty-two balungan beats] there are two kethuk strokes,
    falling on the eighth and twenty-fourth beats.

5. *kethuk banggèn* ['resisting'] occurs in the *unggah* [*munggah/
    minggah*] of a gendhing, two eluk [i.e., sixteen balungan beats]
    from the gong stroke. That is, [if we take "pyang" to stand for
    the sound of the kempyang, "thuk" for the sound of the kethuk, and
    "eng" for those balungan beats on which the kethuk or kempyang
    does not sound,] as follows:[3]

    thuk   eng   pyang   thuk   pyang   eng   thuk   eng
    pyang thuk pyang   eng   pyang   thuk pyang gong

6. *kethuk salahan*, which is a technique used exclusively in gendhing
    like [ketawang] *Puspa Warna*, [ladrang] *Sri Katon*, [ladrang]
    Gonjang Ganjing, etc. The kethuk strokes come between the
    balungan strokes, flanking the final kempul beat.[4]

The placement of kethuk strokes in a gendhing can be used as a means
of classifying different types of gendhing. For example,

1. *gendhing kethuk ngganter*: *sampak, srepegan, ayak-ayakan,*
   [lancaran] *Kebo Giro*, [lancaran] *Bendrong.*

2. *gendhing kethuk loro* ['*two*'] *kerepan*: [ketawang] *Puspa Warna,*
   [ladrang] *Clunthang*, [ladrang] *Gonjong Ganjing*, [ladrang]
   Sri Katon, [ladrang] *Pangkur*, [ladrang] *Asmarandana*, etc.

3. *gendhing kethuk papat* ['*four*'] *kerepan*: the unggah section of
   gendhing *Gambir Sawit*, [gendhing] *Onang-onang*, [gendhing]
   Titi Pati, [gendhing] *Bondhet*, etc.

4. *gendhing kethuk wolu* ['*eight*'] *kerepan*: the unggah section of
   gendhing *Lambang Sari*, [gendhing] *Damar Keli*, [gendhing] *Rondhon*,
   [gendhing] *Mawur*, [gendhing] *Jenthar*, etc.

5. *gendhing kethuk nemwelas* ['*sixteen*'] *kerepan*: the unggah section
   of gendhing *Agul-agul*, [gendhing] *Semang*, [gendhing] *Jalaga*,
   [gendhing] *Paseban* etc.

6. *gendhing kethuk loro* ['*two*'] *kerep*: the merong section of gendhing
   Gambir Sawit, etc.

7. *gendhing kethuk papat* ['*four*'] *kerep*: the merong section of
   gendhing *Lambang Sari*, etc.

8. *gendhing kethuk wolu* ['*eight*'] *kerep*: the merong section of
   gendhing *Agul-agul*, [gendhing] *Semang*, etc.

9. *gendhing kethuk loro* ['*two*'] *arang*: the merong section of gendhing
   Kaduk Manis,[5] [laras] slendro, [gendhing] *Laler Mengeng*,
   [gendhing] *Laranjala*, etc.

10. *gendhing kethuk papat* ['*four*'] *arang*: the merong section of
    gendhing *Rondhon*, [gendhing] *Sangu Pati*,[6] [gendhing] *Mawur*,
    [gendhing] *Jenthar*, etc.

D. Kempulan ['Kempul Playing']

The playing of kempul fulfills two functions: (1) substituting for the
gong; and (2) dividing the kenongan [i.e., period ending with a kenong
stroke] in half.

The kempul substitutes for the gong in gendhing such as *sampak*,
srepegan, and *ayak-ayakan*. The kempul divides the kenongan in half in such
gendhing as: (a) [lancaran] *Kebo Giro*, [lancaran] *Bendrong*, etc.; and
(b) [ketawang] *Puspa Warna*, [ladrang] *Gonjang Ganjing*, and other
[ladrangan] such as *Pangkur Paripurna*, *Asmarandana*, *Ayun-ayun*, *Jong Keri*,
Sri Widada, *Sri Karongron*, *Ginonjing*, etc. In all these pieces the
kenongan is divided in half by a kempul stroke, with the exception of the
first kenongan (i.e., immediately following the gong stroke) where the
kempul must not be played (i.e., there must be a rest on that beat). For,
to play the kempul in the first kenongan is characteristic of village
style. However, in pieces like [ladrang] *Ginonjing*, or [ladrang] *Éling-
éling*, which are played in fast tempo (*iramane lancar/sesegan*), the kempul
should be struck in the first kenongan. In fact, the stroke is reiterated
(*disungsun* ['played one after another']) so that for every kempul stroke,
two strokes are sounded.[7]

E. [The Playing of the] Kempyang

The kempyang is played in all gendhing that have kethuk kerepan; it is
not used in any other kind of gendhing. The kempyang is struck on the odd-
numbered balungan beats. In the case of balungan nibani [see section IX.A,
above, "Balungan"], the kempyang is struck on every rest, i.e., on the odd-
numbered beats of the balungan.

The engkuk, as a substitute for the kempyang, is played in the same
way. The kemong substitutes for the kethuk. Both engkuk and kemong are
only used in sléndro gamelan without bonang and demung, that is, in
gamelan klenèngan. In a pélog gamelan klenèngan, however, the kethuk and
kempyang would still be played.

F. The Playing of the Gongs (Gong-gongan)

Some gendhing require the playing of the *gong suwukan*, others require
the playing of the *gong gedhé*. In the former category are gendhing such as
sampak, *srepegan*, *ayak-ayakan*, [lancaran] *Kebo Giro*, [lancaran] *Bendrong*,

etc. The final gong in these pieces must, however, be the gong gedhé.
Gendhing that require the gong gedhé throughout are such pieces as
[ketawang] *Puspa Warna*, [ladrang] *Sri Katon*, etc., and all of the
gendhing gedhé [i.e., gendhing of kethuk loro (2) kerep and longer].
Nevertheless, sometimes at places in the melodies of such gendhing where a
gong stroke is not strictly called for a gong suwukan is played. This
technique is called *gong salahan* ['seemingly mistaken gong stroke';
'cadencelike gong stroke'], and is used only to decorate and enhance the
beauty of the sound. The "flesh and blood" of the piece is provided by the
rebab, gendèr, bonang, and other instruments.

X. Notation for Some Gendhing

Balungan (on slenthem, demung, saron):

sléndro:

| 6 | 1 | 2 | 3 | 5 | 6 |

pathet 9 [sanga]: (5) - 6 - 1 2

pathet manyura: (6) - 1 - 2 3

pathet 6 [nem]: (2) - 3 - 5 6

pélog:
laras 5
[lima]

| 1 | 2 | 3 | 4 | 5 | 6 | 7 |

pathet 5 [lima]: (1) - 2 - 4 5

laras 6
[nem]

| 1 | 2 | 3 | 4 | 5 | 6 | 7 |

pathet 6 [nem]: (5) - 6 - 1 2

laras barang

| 1 | 2 | 3 | 4 | 5 | 6 | 7 |

pathet barang: (6) - 7 - 2 3

Pélog pathet lima is the counterpart of sléndro pathet 6 [nem]. Pélog pathet nem is the counterpart of sléndro pathet 9 [sanga]. Pélog pathet barang is the counterpart of sléndro pathet manyura. Numbers in parentheses are final tones, comparable to <u>do</u> in international music.

Small Gendhing [Gendhing Cilik]

[Included here is the notation for Ladrang *Éling-éling*, kethuk 2 kerepan, pélog pathet nem, balungan mlaku and Ladrang *Sri Katon*, sléndro pathet manyura, kethuk 2 kerepan, balungan nibani. See appendix 1, volume 3. In appendix 1, Ladrang *Éling-éling* is designated as pélog pathet lima although the notation is the same.]

Small Gendhing, Lancaran Kethuk Ngganter

[Included here is the notation for Lancaran *Kebo Giro*, pélog pathet barang and Lancaran *Singa Nebah*, pélog pathet barang/sléndro manyura. See appendix 1, volume 3.]

Medium-sized Gendhing (Gendhing Sedheng)

[Included here is the notation for Gendhing *Montro*, kethuk 2 kerep, minggah kethuk 4 kerepan, sléndro pathet manyura and Gendhing *Gandrung*, kethuk 2 kerep, minggah kethuk 4 kerepan, pélog pathet nem/sléndro pathet sanga. See appendix 1, volume 3.]

Large Gendhing (Gendhing Gedhé)

[Included here is the notation for Gendhing *Godheg*, sléndro pathet nem, kethuk 4 arang, minggah kethuk 8 kerepan, and Gendhing *Gobet*, pélog pathet nem, kethuk 4 kerep, minggah 8 kerepan. See appendix 1, volume 3.]

NOTES

1. In the succeeding paragraph, explanations are provided for each of the
   listed terms except "*wiletan*." Perhaps the author intended to include
   the melodies of the rebab or male chorus (*gérong*) in this category,
   since they are not included in any of the other categories.

2. In the kenong sungsun ('one after another') technique the kenong stroke
   is repeated between the first and second beats and on the third beat of
   the gatra following the regular kenong stroke. This is illustrated in
   the notation for Ladrang *Surung Dhayung*, laras pélog pathet nem, below.
   (Note also the use of kethuk salahan technique in the final line
   leading up to the gong.)

```
         p   t   p           p   t   p   N
         .   .   5   6       1   2   3   2

             ___ N
         p N t   p   P       p   t   p   N
         .   1   6   5       .   6   1   2

             ___ N
         p N t   p   P       p   t   p   N
         .   1   6   5       .   6   1   2

         p   t   p t P t     p   t   p   G
         1   6   2   1       3   2   6   5
```

   (Key: p = kempyang, t = kethuk, N = kenong, P = kempul, G = gong.)

3. Kethuk banggèn can be indicated graphically as follows:

<u>t   .   p   t</u>   <u>p   .   t   .</u>   <u>p   t   p   .</u>   <u>p   t   p   G</u>

   Each underlined segment represents one gatra; two gatra represent one
   eluk in the author's terminology. Note that the normal sequence for
   the kethuk and kempyang in the unggah section would be:

<u>p t p .</u>   <u>p t p .</u>   <u>p t p .</u>   <u>p t p</u> G

4. See the last kenongan of the example provided in note 2 above.

5. According to Probohardjono (1964, 5th printing:25-26) and Djakoeb and
    Wignjaroemeksa (1919:29-31), the mérong section of Gendhing *Kaduk Manis*
    in laras sléndro is kethuk papat (4) kerep. Sumonagara (1936:15-16)
    classifies it as kethuk loro (2) kerep.

6. According to Mlojowidodo (1976[2]:116-17; 145-47), there are two
    versions of Gendhing *Sanga Pati* (also spelled "*Sangu Pati*"): one,
    kethuk papat (4) arang minggah kethuk wolu (8), and the other, kethuk
    loro (2) kerep minggah kethuk papat (4). The shorter version would
    appear to be a condensation of the longer. See also, Martopangrawit
    1975:107 for Gendhing *Sangu Pati* kethuk loro (2) kerep minggah papat
    (4) as used to accompany the srimpi dance.

7. The following example, from Ladrang *Éling-éling*, pélog pathet lima,
    illustrates the kempul sungsun technique.

```
            P   P           N
    6  5  3  2   1   2   3   5

            P   P           N
    6  5  3  2   1   2   3   5

            P   P           N
    1  1  .  .   1   2   3   5

            P   P           G
    3  2  3  1   3   2   3   5
```

In the first two kenongan, the kempul may play either pitch 6 or pitch
2; in the last two kenongan, the kempul may play either pitch 1 or
pitch 5.

SERAT SULUKAN SLÉNDRO

INGKANG JANGKEP LAN BAKU KANGGÉ NYULUKI TITINGALAN
WAYANG PURWA KATAMBAHAN KAWRUH-KAWRUH PADHALANGAN
INGKANG SANGET WIGATOS

[Songs of the Dhalang, in Sléndro]

[A Complete Manual of the Sulukan Used in a Wayang Kulit
Performance with Other Important Information about the
Art of the Dhalang]

by

Radèn Ngabèhi Samsudjin Probohardjono

Translated from Javanese

by

Susan Pratt Walton

[From 7th edition, Solo: Ratna, 1966]

PREFACE

Nuwun.[1] This publication of the seventh edition of *Sulukan Slèndro* includes some changes. The changes will help both scholars of *pedhalangan* ['the art of the dhalang'] and the student dhalang.

I have tried to make the poetic language used in the *sulukan* texts correct, following the language of the original texts, which are excerpts from *sekar ageng* and other poetry from Old Javanese books and from other similar books. However, because the spelling is so problematic in these old texts [due to different methods of transliteration from Javanese script], the spelling used here is free [i.e., not bound by any one spelling convention].

Sulukan consist not only of texts but also of long-held notes which occasionally are interspersed in the text. These long-held notes help evoke a pleasant feeling in the listener. They also make it easier for the dhalang to accommodate his melody to the melody of the instruments. The *o* and *e* sounds are called "*kombangan*" and the *a* and *ya* sounds are called "*ombak.*"

In addition, the dhalang often sings a vocal melody as the gendhing is played. His *wiletan* are free, although he must anticipate the *dhong-dhing* of the instrumental melody and he often intersperses the text with kombangan.

In the pathet nem and pathet sanga sections of the *wayang* play, when action on the screen [rather than narration or dialogue] is the focus, gendhing and sulukan in pathet manyura are often played. One example, among others, is the first major audience scene in the kingdom of Ngamarta or in the kingdom of the gods, which is accompanied by Gendhing *Kawit*, laras slèndro pathet manyura. Another example is the scene at the palace of Ngastina with Dèwi Banowati, which is accompanied by Gendhing *Damar Kèli*, laras slèndro pathet manyura, followed by the sulukan, *Pathet Manyura Ageng*. A third example is in the *gara-gara* scene when the panakawan Semar and his children cavort. The gara-gara occurs after the *prang gagal* [inconclusive battle at the end of the pathet nem section of the drama].

The panakawan episode should [theoretically] be in pathet sanga, but pathet manyura is traditionally used.

The method of learning sulukan used in this book involves correlating the cipher notation with the keys of a sléndro *gendèr*. A dot placed below a cipher indicates the low register; a dot placed above indicates the high register. Dots between ciphers indicate rests [or sustained tones].

In conclusion, herewith I present to you the seventh edition of *Sulukan Sléndro*. Nuwun.

Surakarta, November 20, 1966

S. Probohardjono

INTRODUCTION

Selections from Oral and Written Tests
for the Student Dhalang

Questions:

1. What does "sulukan" mean?

2. What is (a) *pathet*, (b) *sendhon*, and (c) *ada-ada*? Try to explain the distinction, role in the wayang, and the instrumental accompaniment associated with each one.

3. How many divisions based on a change of pathet are there in a full-night or a full-day wayang performance? Where, and around what time of day or night, does the pathet change?

4. In the first scene, which gendhing are usually heard? For each gendhing in the first scene, specify the laras, the kingdom with which the gendhing is associated, and the reason for which the gendhing is used.

5. What are (a) *janturan*, (b) *carita*, (c) *pocapan*, and (d) *antawacana*?

6. By what means are the dhalang's cues to the musicians in the gamelan communicated? How many types of cues are there, and how are they executed?

7. Distinguish the following types of stories: (a) *pakem*, (b) *carangan*, and (c) *carangan dhinapur*.

8. According to standard practice, how should the *gunungan* or *kayon* [mountain-/tree-shaped puppet] be placed in the banana trunk (a) before the wayang performance has begun, (b) in pathet nem, pathet sanga, and pathet manyura, and (c) after the performance has ended? Try to describe the position and stance of the gunungan as it is placed in the trunk. According to the rules of

puppet technique and philosophy, for what purpose is the gunungan placed in the trunk in these specific ways?

9. During the time of the Pandhawa, what are the names of the following people: (a) the kings, (b) their wives, (c) their children, (d) prime ministers in the kingdoms of (i) Ngastina, (ii) Ngamarta, (iii) Mandura, (iv) Dwarawati, (v) Pancalaréja, (vi) Mandraka, (vii) Wiratha, and (viii) Ngawangga?

10. How many levels and classes of dhalang are there, and what are the differences among those classes?

11. What personal characteristics and skills must a dhalang possess to perform a wayang? Try to differentiate and define them clearly.

12. According to ancient belief, a dhalang must also be rich in the knowledge of prayers and mantras. Try to list the mantras that a dhalang uses when performing a wayang, according to your understanding.

The answers to these questions begin on page 489.

Example of dhodhogan and kombangan of dhalang in Gendhing *Krawitan*, laras sléndro pathet nem, kethuk 4 kerep, minggah ladrangan[2]

buka:

Leng-leng ra-mya ni-kang / kang

R E P A N

S I R E P A N

Rows: A, B, C, D, E, F

Column end markers: G^3 6., N^6 6., G^6 6., N^6 6., G^5 5., G^5 5., G^2 2., N^1 6., G^3 6., N^6 6., $G^{3/6}$ 6., N^6 6., G^6 6.

Transition to minggah – – – –

Minggah Ladrang *Krawitan*

```
A  py  t     py    3     py  t     py  N6  py  t     py    P3    py  t     py  N6
   .   5     .     3     .   5     .   6   .   5     .     3     .   5     .   6
                                                                 6   6   6   6   6  56
                                                                 leng-leng ra-mya ni kang

   py  t     py    P     py  t     py  N6  py  t     py    P     py  t     py  G6
   .   1     .     6     .   1     .   6   .   2     .     1     .   2     .   6
         1 . 2 . 1 . 6       1 1 1 1 1 6 1     2 . . . . . . . 1            2 . 1 . 21. 6
         O                sa-sang-ka ku-me-nyar O                           O

B [ py  t    py          py  t     py  N5  py  t     py    P     py  t     py  N3
   .   3     .     5     .   6     .   5   .   3     .     6     .   5     .   3
                         6  6  6   6  6  616 5       1 . 2 . 1 . 6     5  6   6  6  65  3
                         mang-reng-ga rum-ning pu-ri O                 ma- kin tan-pa si-ring

   py  t     py    P     py  t     py  N2  py  t     py    P     py  t     py  G5
   .   5     .     2     .   3     .   2   .   3     .     5     .   3     .   2
         5 . 3 . 2          2  2  2  2  12           6 . 1 . 6 . 5     3  5  5  5  5  32  235
         O                  ha -lep i - kang u- mah  O                 mas lir mu - rub-ing la-ngit

C  py  t     py          py  t     py  N1  py  t     py    P     py  t     py  N1
   .   3     .     5     .   6     .   3   .   1     .     6     .   5     .   3
                         5  6  6  6  653 31          1 . 2 . 1 . 6     5  6   6  6  653  3.1
                         te-kwan sar - wa ma -nik    O                 ta-wing- nya si-na- wung

   py  t     py    P     py  t     py  N2  py  t     py    P     py  t     py  G3
   .   1     .     6     .   5     .   3   .   2     .     3     .   6     .   5
         1 . 2 . 1 . 6   5  6  6  6  6  653 32       2 . 3 . 5 . 6     2 . 6 . . 1 . 6 . 5
         O               sak-sat se- kar -ning su- ji O                O

D  py  t     py          py  t     py  N5  py  t     py    P     py  t     py  N2
   .   3     .     2     .   6     .   5   .   3     .     2     .   3     .   2
                                                     3 . 5 . 3 . 2     3  3   3  3  353  2
                                                     O                 ung-gwan Ba- nu- wa- ti

   py  t     py    P     py  t     py  N5  py  t     py    P     py  t     py  G5
   .   3     .     2     .   3     .   2   .   5     .     3     .   6     .   5
         3 . 5 . 3 . 2    5  6  6  6  653 235        6 . 5 . 3 . 5     3  6  6   6  6  616 5
         O                ywan a - mrem a - la- ngen O                 lan Na- ta Dur- yu- da- na

E  py  t     py          py  t     py  N5  py  t     py    P     py  t     py  N6
   .   3     .     2     .   3     .   5   .   2     .     1     .   2     .   6
                                                                            2 . 1 .. 21 6
                                                                            O

   py  t     py    P     py  t     py  N6  py  t     py    P     py  t     py  G6 ]
   .   1     .     6     .   1     .   6   .   2     .     1     .   2     .   6
                              1 . 2 . 1 . 6                                 1 . 1 . 2 .16
                              O                                             O
```

[The notation of *Ladrang Krawitan* above implies a repetition of the gongan marked "B" through "E." This repetition is optional. When there is no repetition of this section, and upon the final playing of the gongan leading to the suwuk (in gongan [D]), the dhodhogan is as follows.]

Key

d = rhythmic tapping on puppet box kethuk (*dhodhogan*)

P = kempul

py = kempyang

t = kethuk

N = kenong

G = kenong and gong together

[ ] = return to the sign [ ] and repeat section

[Note: The superscript ciphers above "N" and "G" indicate the kenong pitches.]

Explanation of Gendhing Krawitan

Gendhing *Krawitan* is a gendhing rebab, in the form of four kethuk kerep per kenong. On the second kenong, the gong sounds. This is followed by minggah ladrangan, in the form of two kethuk kerep per kenong. On the fourth kenong, the gong sounds. The piece is in laras sléndro pathet nem. Gendhing *Krawitan* is used for the first scene [in a wayang lakon], but not for a scene in the kingdom of the gods (Kahyangan), Ngamarta or Ngastina. Usually the gendhing is introduced by *Ayak-ayakan*, [sléndro pathet] manyura, without the ngelik section.

Formerly, in the palace at Surakarta, the gendhing used in the first scene was not preceded by *Ayak-ayakan*; rather, it began with the buka of the gendhing.

Following present-day performance practice, the mérong of Gendhing *Krawitan* is shortened. Thus, after the gong of cèngkok E, the kenong plays pitch 3 in plèsèd fashion. This section is repeated again and again until the *panjanturan* [major scene narration] is finished. It is then followed by cèngkok F, which is the transition to the minggah ladrang.

In the minggah Ladrang *Krawitan*, kosèkan drumming-style is used, along with the kombangan of the dhalang. The kombangan of the dhalang must anticipate the dhong dhing of the instrumental melody. When the dhalang reaches the words "saksat sekarning suji," then along with the kombangan there is a continuous knocking on the puppet box [in triplets; *dhodhogan ngganter*] until the second kenong of cèngkok D. After the *dherudhug* [triple rap on the puppet box, ♫. ♩], there is a *sirepan* and the tempo slows until the gong at the end of cèngkok D. The final gong is followed by the singing of the suluk, *Pathet Nem Ageng*.

[The endings of the phrases sung by the dhalang coincide with strokes on the kenong and gong. The beginnings of phrases are more flexible. Also, they are to be interpreted in free rhythm, which is not indicated in the notation.]

A. Sulukan in Laras Sléndro Pathet Nem

1. Pathet Nem Wantah

This sulukan is used after any gendhing in the pathet nem period, except for gendhing that have their own pathetan associated with them. Also, it is often used to indicate a transition [to a different mood or topic]. It begins with pitch tengah [3]. The text is taken from the *Bhārata Yuddha*, *kakawin*,[4] by Mpu Sedhah [and Mpu Panuluh; composed 1157 A.D.], canto V, [verse 1,] lagu *sardula wikridhita*.

```
3     3     3 3   3 2.3.   2.35   5    5 5 5  3.5.
Leng leng ra-mya-ni-kang,  sa  - sang-ka ku-me-nyar,

6.53.5.32.  6    6    6 6   6    616  5.   2.1.216.  3532
O            ma-ngreng-ga rum-ning pu - ri,  O         mang -

2   2   2  2  1.2.  3  5.6  3 5    532  2.  2.35. 2.35.  2
kin tan-pa si-ring, ha-lep i-kang u - .mah, mas   lwir   mu-

2   2   2.1  6165.  6....  12  2    2   2  2 1.2.
rub ring la - ngit,  O      te - kwan sar-wa ma-nik,

1.216.53. ( ompak 235.  356.  5356  .532 )
O
```

2. Pathet Nem Ageng

Pathet Nem Ageng is used after the suwuk of the gendhing that
accompanies the first major audience scene.   It begins on pitch tengah [3].
The text is taken from the *Bhārata Yuddha*, *kakawin*, by Mpu Sedhah [and Mpu
Panuluh], canto V, [verse 1,] lagu *sardula wikridhita*.

```
3    3    3  3   3  2.3.   2.35  5    5  5  5  3.5.
Leng leng ra-mya-ni-kang,  sa-   sang-ka ku-me-nyar.

6.53.5.32. 6  6     6  6  6    616.  5.   2.1.216.  3532
O              ma-ngreng-ga rum-ning  pu - ri,  O        mang -

2    2    2  2  1.2.  3  5.6  3  5    532 2.   2.35.   2.35.
kin tan-pa si-ring ha-lep i-kang u - mah, mas    lwir

2    2    2    2.1  6165.  6......  12  2    2    2  2  1.2.
mu-rub ring la - ngit,  O          te - kwan sar-wa ma-nik,

1.216.53. ( ompak  235.  356.  5356  .532 )  2  2    2    2  2
O                                              ta-wing nya si-na-

1.2.  6.165.  2..1.216.   3532 2    2  2  2    2  12.
wung, O       O           sak - sat  se-kar-ning su-ji,

3   56.   2  2  2  1216.  1.2.  3    5.6.  3    5   53
ung-gwan Bha-nu-wa-ti,  O      ywan a  - mrem  a - la-

2    2.35. 2.35. 2    2    2    21  6165.  6..... 1  2    2  2
ngen, mwang Na - ta  Dur-yud-da- na,   O        ma-wang Na-ta

2    2    2  1.2.  1.216.53.  ( ompak  235.  356.  5356  .532 )
Dur-yud-da-na,  O
```

3. Ada-ada Girisa Wantah

This ada-ada is used after Pathet Nem Ageng, and also to underscore intense emotion in any situation in pathet nem. It begins with pitch gulu [2]. The text is taken from the *Bhārata Yuddha*, *kakawin*, by Mpu Sedhah [and Mpu Panuluh], canto II, [verse 1,] lagu *prethitala*.

```
2.35 5    5  5  5  3.56.  3532 2   2  2   2 12.  2.35
Leng ngeng ga-ti-ni-kang,  a  - wan sa-bha sa-bha, ni  -

5    5  5  3.56.  3532 2   2  2  2 12.  6  6   6  6  6
king Has-ti-na,   sa - man-ta-ra tè-keng, te-gal Ku-ru Na-

6  56.  1   1  1  1  1  1   1  1  1  1 61.  2   2  2  21
rar-ya,  Kres-na la-ku si-rèng Pa-ra-su Ra-ma,  Kan-wa Ja-na-

6.  3 56.  3  5.3  2.  2  2   2  2   2.1  6.    3532 2
ka,  du-lur Na-rad - da, ka-pang-gih i -  ri   kang, te - gal

2  2  2  2    12.  235.  2   21 6.  3.....
mi-lu ri kar - ya,  sang  Bhu-pa- ti, ya
```

4. Ada-ada Girisa Jugag

This ada-ada is used to underscore intense emotion in any situation in the pathet nem period. It begins with pitch gulu [2]. The text is taken from [Serat] Brata Yuda, [macapat, canto VIII, verse 4,] by [R. Ng.] Yasadipura [I], [see Cohen Stuart 1860:15], sekar macapat *pangkur*.

```
2.35 5    5  5   5   5  5   3.56. 3532 2   2  2   2  2
Ju - mang-kah ang-gro su-sum-bar,  lin - dhu ge-ter pa-ter

2   2  2  2   12.  2.35 5  5  5   5  5  5 3.56.  3532
kang bu-mi gon-jing,  gu  - ma-lu-dhug gun-tur ke-tug,  go  -

2  2   2  2  2 12.  6  6   6  6   6  6  6 56.  1    1
ra rèh ga-ra ga-ra,  ka-dya be-lah bu-mi wu-kir, mang-gut-

1   1   1  1  1  1  1   1  1 61.  2   2  2   2  2
mang-gut, u- mob ja-la-dri pra-kem-pa,  pe-nyu-né ku-mam-

2    2.16 6.    3.....
bang wing-wring, ya
```

5. Pathet Nem Jugag

Pathet Nem Jugag is used to indicate a transition to any situation that has a calm mood during the pathet nem period. It begins with low pitch nem [6]. The text is in the sekar ageng *tebu kasol* meter.

```
6   6    6   6    6   6  6   6  56.  12   2  2   2    2
•   •    •   •    •   •  •   •  ••   ──
Han-jrah ing-kang pus-pi-ta a -rum,  ka - si-lir-ing sa-

2   2   2  1.2.  6.165.  3  5356  3532  2.    2.35.  2.35. 2
                 •
mi-ra-na mrik,  O        se-kar  ga - dhung, ko  - ngas  gan-

21 6.5.  6.....  12   2   2  2   2  2  2    2   1.2.
         •
da-nya   O       ma - weh ra-ras re-na-ning dri-ya,
             •                                    ̀

1.216.53.  ( ompak  235.  356.  5356 .532 )
    • ••             •••   •••   ••••  •••
O
```

6. Sendhon Pananggalan

This sulukan is used for *babak unjal* (the arrival of guests) in the first scene. It can also be used to indicate a feeling of anxiety (*èmeng*). It begins with pitch nem [6]. The text is from the [*Serat*] *Rama*, [*kawi miring*, by R. Ng. Yasadipura I, canto LIX, verse 3,] sekar ageng *swandana*.

```
6  6    6   6  6  6165   5.    3  2    2   2  2  2  1.216.
                   ̄ ̄ ̄               •
Si-yang pan-ta-ra ra  - tri, ha-mung cip-ta pu-ku-lun,

5 ..  2   2  2    2  2  12.  3  5356  3532  2.    2.35.  2.35.
O     tan na lyan ka-èk-si,  mi-la  ka  - tur, kang   cun-

2   21 6165.  3   3  3    3532  2.    3  5356  3   5   532
       • ••
dha-ma-nik,  pra-sa-sat ra  - geng, u -lun  kang su-mem-

2.    2.35.  2.35.  2  2   2  21  6165.  6     6  6    6  6
bah,  mung - gwing pa-dan-ta pra-bu,  myang ka-gung-an-ta
                                • ••

6   5.6.  3532 2   2   2  2    12.  3  5    5356 3  5
sing-sim,  sak  -sat sam-pun prap-ti,  ka-ton as - ta  pu-

532 2.    2.35.  2.35.  2   2   2  21   6165.  3.....
ku- lun  wu  - lat - en Na-ra-pa - ti,   A
                                   • ••
( ompak  .333  5235  6653  6532 )   2   2   2  2  21   1.216.  2.1.
                                    Ra-ma dé-wa-ning- sun,    O
                                                      •
( ompak  .111  2612  3123  1216  3565  2356 )
                •                  •    ••••  ••••
```

7. Sendhon Kloloran

Sendhon Kloloran is sung during the removal of puppets at the end of the *kedhatonan* [scene in the inner quarters of the palace]. It begins with pitch dhadha [3]. The text is taken from [*Serat*] *Brata Yuda*, *kawi miring*,[5] by [R. Ng.] Yasadipura [I], canto VII, [verse 3,] sekar ageng *bremara wilasita*.

```
3  3    356  6.53.  1 1 1  1    1  12  1.6.  2    2 2
Ga-lak  u - lat,   ka-di tha-thit a - ba -rung, kang pa-mu-

12.  3 3   3  6  5  353  21.   2.16.12.  3   3  6532  1.
lu,  a -lus ma-nis ma-weh kung, O        sem-ba-da    kang

6  5  3.  1    23  12  1216  ( ompak  ..36  .36.  3212 )  2  2
a- de-deg man- da  rang-kung,                             a -go-

2  12.  3 3   3  6  5  353  2.1.  2.1653
rèh pan, da-dya pan-tes ma-lar kung,  O

( ompak   555.  5365  5352  5356 )
```

8. Ada-ada Hasta Kuswala [Alit]

This ada-ada is sung when a prime minister or other official issues orders to the army troops. It begins with pitch nem [6]. [It is in the sekar ageng *hasta kuswala* meter.]

```
6  6   6  6   6  6  6   6  612.   2    2  2 2  2
Mun-dur ra-kya-na Pa-tih, un-dhang  mring pra wa-dya sa-

2.  2  2.35  2.  6  6    6  6  6  6  6   6  6  6  56.
mya sa-we - ga, u -myung ra-mya swa-ra-ning ben-dhé bè-ri,

5  5  5  5   5  5  356.532.  6  12  2  2  2 2   2
gu-bar gur-nang ka-la- wan,    pok-sur tam-bur su-ling pa-

2  2  2  235  2.  6  6  6  6  6  6  6  6  6  6
pan-dèn da-lu - dag, ban-dé-ra mi-wah ka-kon-dho war-na war-

56.  5  5  5   5  5  356.532.  5.32.16.  5  5   5  53  56.532.
na,  pin-dha ja-lad-dhi- yan,   O        a -sri ka-wur- yan
```

9. Ada-ada Hasta Kuswala Ageng

This ada-ada is played when a prime minister or other official returns
from issuing orders to the army troops. It begins with pitch dhadha [3].
[It is in the sekar ageng *naga bandha* meter.]

```
3.   6.    2 2    2 21  23.   3  5.6.  6   6 6.12
Grag grag, an-dhem-an-ing-kang, ja-ran  ngrik ma-ga -

6.   5    3 3 3  23.  2 2 2   2 2    21  23.21216.
lak, gen- ti ma-ni-tih, pa-me-kak-ni-ra  ri -sang,

12.1653.  2 2    2 2 21  23.21216.  i   i   i i i    i
O         su-dar-sa-na da- hat,        ken-dha-li ra-ngah man-

61.   2.16.53.  3.56  6   6  6.12  6. 3    3 3   2.3
jing, O          lak - lak-an ku  - da ngrik mi-jil rah,

2 2   2   2 2 21  23.2.16.  1.....   ( ompak  .111  2612
ka-dya tuk su-ma-ram- bah,         O

6163 5616 )  6.  2.   6.  2.   1.....  i   i  i   16 5.
             mung jir, mung jir, a      yak-sa te- mah-an,

2......  i   i  i  i 16 5.   1..... 2   2 2   2  2
O        kru-ra sru ma-na -ut,   a     yit-na sang Nar-pat-

21  6.   3.2165.
ma - ja,  O
```

10. Ada-ada Budhalan Mataraman

Ada-ada Budhalan Mataraman is sung when a prime minister or other official is about to order the troops to depart after all preparations have been made. It begins with pitch nem [6]. The text is taken from [*Serat*] *Brata Yuda*, [*kawi miring*,] by [R. Ng.] Yasadipura [I], [canto XIV, verse 2,] sekar ageng *wisalya harini*.

```
6  6   6  6   6  6  6.  6  6   6  6   6  65 5.   2.3 1
Én-jing bu-dhal gu-mu-ruh, sa-king na-gri Wi-ra-tha, gung-ing

1   1  1  16  5.  1  1   1  1  1  1  61.  2   2   2   2
kang ba-la kus-wa, a -bra bu-sa-na-ni-ra, lir sur-ya we-

2  2  2   2  2   2  2  235  6.  6   6  6  6    6 65 5.
dal-i -ra, sa-king ja-la-nid -di, har-sa ma-dhang-i ja-gad,

1  1  1   1  1   1 61.  2  2  2   2   2   2.1  6.
duk mu-ngup-mu-ngup a-neng, sa-pu-cak-ing-kang wu - kir,

3.2165.
O
```

11. Ada-ada [Greget Saut] Mataraman [Wantah]

This sulukan is used to underscore intense emotion in any situation during the pathet nem period. It begins with pitch nem [6]. The text is taken from [*Serat*] *Arjuna Sasra Bahu*, by [R. Ng.] Sindusastra, [canto II, verse 3,][6] sekar macapat *durma*.

```
6  6   6  6   6  6  6   6  6   6  6   56.  2.1 1  1  1
Ri-dhu ma-wor ma-nga-wur-a -wur wu-rah-an, te - nga-ra-ning

1  1  61.  1   1  1  1  1.6  5.  2.....  1  1  1  1  1
a -ju-rit, gong ma-gu-ru gang-sa, e      te-teg ka-dya bu-

1.6  5. 1  1  1   1  1 1   1  61.  2  2  2   2   2
tul- a, wor pan-jrit-ing tu-rong-ges-thi, re-ka-tak ing-kang,

2  2  2  2  2  2.1  6.  3.2165.
dwa-ja la-la-yu se - bit, O
```

11a. Ada-ada [Greget Saut] Mataraman

This version of Ada-ada Mataraman is used as an alternative to the
above, for intensifying the emotion in the *prang ampyak* [war of the
marching army], or to underscore intense emotion in any situation. It
begins with pitch nem [6]. The text is taken from [*Serat*] *Brata Yuda*, *kawi
miring*, by [R. Ng.] Yasadipura [I], sekar ageng *prit anjala*.[7]

```
6  6   6   6   6   6   6  6  6   6  6  56.  2.1   1   1
Ri-kat lam-pah-i -rèng ra-ta tan an-ta-ra, prap-tèng su-


1  1    1   61.  i   i   i   i  i.6  5.   2.... i   i   i   i
ku-ning har-ga, é-ram tu-mi-ngal ing,  E        pa-ku-won a-


i.6  5.  1    1    1 1   1   1  61.  2  2    2    2
sri- ne, ndhen-dheng sa-èng-ga pra-ja,  u-myung kang pra-


2   2 2 2   2   2  2.1   6.    3.2165.
dang-ga bu-sek-an kang jan - ma,  O
```

12. Ada-ada [Greget Saut] Mataraman Jugag

This is an abbreviated form [of Ada-ada Greget Saut Mataraman] and is
used to underscore intense emotion in any situation. It begins with pitch
nem [6]. The text is taken from [*Serat*] *Brata Yuda*, *kawi miring*, by
[R. Ng.] Yasadipura [I], canto XVIII, sekar ageng *sikarini*.

```
6  6   6  6   6    6   6   6   6   6   6  56.   2.1  1
Si-gra pa-reng mang-sah mung-suh la-wan  ro-wang, rok  a-


1   1   1  1 1 1   1   1 1   1  61.   2  2   2  2
ngem-bul-i  gu-mu-ruh kang su-rak u -myung, gu-bar bè-ri


2   2  2  2.1   6.   3.2165.
swa-ra wu-rah - an,  O
```

13. Pathet Kedhu

Pathet Kedhu is used after the prang ampyak. It begins with pitch nem
[6]. The text is in the sekar ageng *sulanjari* meter.

```
6   6  6   6   6  6  5.6.   2  2    2  2  2   1.216.
Myat la-ngen-ing ka-la-ngyan, a -glar pan-dam mun-car,

5.....   2  2  2   2  2  1.2.   3  5356  3  5   5   5   5.32
0            ti-non lir ko-ko-nang, su-rem  so-rot-e  tan pa-

2.      2.35.  2.35.  2   2  21  6.165.   i ....   2..i6.5.653.
dhang,  ka  -  sor   lan pa-jar-ing,    0        0

i  i  i   i  i  6i.  2..i6.53.2.356.  2   2   2  2    2  2
pur-na-meng ga-ga-na,  0              dha-sar-e  mang-sa ka-

2  1..216.  5.....  2  2  2  2  12.   3  5356  3   5   532
ti-ga,   0       hi-ma a -na-weng, ing u  - jung han- ca-

21  2.35.  2.35.  2   2   2  2   21  6.165.  6.....   12  2
la,  a  - se  - nen kar-ya wi -ge- na,    0        mi- wah

2  2   2  1.2.   1.216.53.   ( ompak  235.  356.  5356  .532 )
si-ning wa-na,   0

2   2  2   2  21  1.216  2.1.   ( ompak  .111  2612  3123
wrek-sa gung ti-nu- nu,   0

1216  3565  2356 )
```

14. Pathet Lasem

This sulukan is used after the suwuk of gendhing in laras sléndro pathet nem during scenes with a refined-looking foreign king, or other foreigners. It begins with pitch nem [6]. The text is taken from [*Serat*] *Aji Pamasa*, [canto V, verse 23,] by [R. Ng.] Ranggawarsita 1896(2):36, in the sekar tengahan *girisa* meter.

```
   . . ..
6...... 2..1.612.  6.5 5  5  5  5  5    5.6 5653.  3
───────  ────────  ──
 O        O        De- né u -ta-ma-ning Na - ta,   bèr

                          . .
3 3 3 3 3  356 6.  2..16.5.356.  2  2  2  2 2 2
bu-di ba-wa lak-sa - na,  O          lir-é bèr bu-di mang-

2 1.216.  5.....  3 3  3  3  3  3   3.56 6.  2..16.5.356.
  ────                           ──
ka-na,     O      li-la le-ga-wa ing dri - ya, O

                                                . .
2 2  2  2  2 2   2 1.2.  3   5356. 3  5   5 5
a-gung dè -nya pa-ring da-na,  ang-ge - gan-jar sa-ben
                        ──         ──

5.32 2.  2.35.  2.35.  2   2  2  2  2.1 6.165.  6.....
──       ────   ────               ──
di - na, lir - e     kang ba-wa lak-sa - na,    O

1.2 2 2  2 2  2   2 1.2.  1.216.53.  ( ompak  235.  356.
──             ──                               ...   ...
a - ne-tep-i pa-ngan-ki-ka,  O

5356  .532 )
....  ...
```

15. Pathet Lindur

Pathet Lindur is sung after the *prang gagal* [inconclusive battle]. It is also used as a signal of the upcoming change from pathet nem to pathet sanga. It begins with pitch gulu [2]. The text is in the sekar ageng *kilayu nedheng* meter.

```
2  2   2 2  1..216.  2.1.2165.  5..... 2  2  2 2
              ──                .. 
Nem-bang te-nga-ra,    O        O     mun-dur sa-wa-

2 1.2.  3 5356 3  5  5.32 2.    2.35. 2.35.  2 21
  ──            ──             ──
dya-ne,  ne-dya kon-dur ma- rang,  jro - ning pu-ra-

               .                              . .
6.165. 1..... 2..16.5653  i i   i i  61.  2..16.53.2.356.
.. ..                                 ──
ya,     O      O          cè-lèng ku-thi-la, O
```

2 2   2 2 2 1.216. 5..... 2   2 2 2   2 1.2.
sa-mya a- ma-ri-g̅i̅,   O̅   kang ka-tra-jang gi-g̅i̅r,

2.356   3   5   5.32   2.   2.35.   2.35.   2   21   6.165.   6.....
r̅i̅   - ra ka-r̅o̅   - w̅a̅k, s̅a̅ng - s̅a̅   - ya s̅a̅ -nget,   O̅

12 2   2 2   2   1.2.   1.216.53.   (ompak 235. 356. 5356 .532)
k̅a̅-dya re-but dhu-c̅u̅ng,   O̅

16. Sendhon Tlutur Wetah

This sendhon is used for scenes of lamentation, grief, and pity during
the pathet nem period. It begins with high-pitch gulu [2]. The text is
taken from [*Serat*] *Brata Yuda*, [*macapat*,] by Yasadipura [I], sekar macapat
dhandhang gula.

2..352.1656. 2 2   2 2 2   2 2   2 232   1.   1 1
O̅   Wu-kir sa-mo-dra ka-dya na-n̅g̅i̅s- i,   mé-ga

1 1 1 1 1   1 1.65 5.   2..1656.   2 2 2   2 2 2
mé-ga ru-ma-hap ma-n̅g̅an- d̅h̅ap, O̅   su-me-bar me-tu ri-

2 1..2.   3.56 6 6   6 6 612 6.   3   3 3   3 3
ris-e̅,   t̅e̅   -ja wang-ka-wa n̅a̅ - w̅u̅ng, lir mè-nget-i kang

3 3   2   3.5.   2   2 2 2   2 2.1 6.   1.6165.   2.32.1656.
ki-lat tha-t̅h̅i̅t, bre-ma-ra a- li-w̅e̅r-a̅n,   O̅   O̅

2   2 2   2 2   1..2. 3.56 6   6   6   6   6 612 6.
nèng ta-wang su-mung-s̅u̅ng, d̅h̅a - wuh ing-kang pus-pa w̅a̅r-s̅a̅,

3 3 3 3 3 3 3   3 3 3 32 3.5.   2   2   2 2   2
a-rum a-rum su-ma-wur a- ma-ra-t̅a̅- n̅i̅,   me - nuh-i ing pa-

2.1   6.   5.....   (ompak 555. 5352 2523 5616)
p̅r̅a̅ng -a̅n, A

17. Ada-ada Girisa Yaksa

This is the same melody as that of Ada-ada Girisa Wantah [no. 3,
above]. It is used after the suwuk of a gendhing for the scene of an ogre
king during the pathet nem period. It begins with pitch gulu [2]. The
text is from [Serat] Rama, [kawi miring, by R. Ng. Yasadipura I,] sekar
ageng sikarini.[8]

```
2.35  5  5  5  53   5.6.  3532  2  2    2    2  12.
Yak - sa go-ra ru - pa,  ri-  se-dheng sang Kum-ba,

2.35  5  5  53 5.6.   3532  2  2  2    2  12.  6   6  6
kar - na lu-ma-ku,    kan  mi-lu ling ing-kang, gam-bi-ra

6  6   56.  1   1   1   1 1    1  1 1 1   1 1.   2  2
ma-nga-rah, a - ngi-sis si-yung a- me-tu pra-ba-wa,   go-ra

2  2  216 6.   3  5356  3  5  53  2.   2  2   2  2  21  6.
ma-wa-lik-an,  lé-sus   a-pra-kem-pa, di-tya Dur-ba-lar-sa,

3532 2   2  2    2  12.  35.  2  2   21  6.   3.....
mrih cur-na-ning la-wan, wi - ra tri ro- dra,  ya
```

B. Sulukan in Laras Sléndro Pathet Sanga

1. Pathet Sanga Wantah

Pathet Sanga Wantah is sung to initiate the change from pathet nem to pathet sanga and is also used after gendhing in pathet sanga that are calm in mood. It begins with pitch gulu [2]. The text is taken from [*Serat*] *Rama, kawi miring*, by [R. Ng.] Yasadipura [I], canto IX, sekar ageng *prawira lalita*.[9]

```
2    2  2  2  2  2  2  2     2  2   2    2  2    2  2
Sang-sa-ya da-lu a- ra-ras,  a-byor kang lin-tang ku-me-

2.   21  1  1  1   1  1    1  1   1  1   1  1  1  1
dhap, tis tis su-nya te-ngah we-ngi, lu-mrang gan-da-ning pus-

1 61. 2..... 2  2  2   2  2  2   23.5  5.  1..... 2
pi-ta,  O     ka -re-ngwan ing pu-dya-ni-  ra, O     sang

2  2  2  2  2   2.16  6.   2.321 1  1  1   1  1
Dwi-ja-wa-ra mbre-nge- ngeng, lir  swa-ra-ning ma-du-

1    1.  1  1   1   1  1  1   1    6.1.   2.16.165.
brang-ta, ma-nung-sung sa-ri-ning kem - bang.  O
```

2. Pathet Sanga Jugag

This sulukan is used for indicating a transition to any situation that has a calm mood in the pathet sanga period. It begins with low-pitch nem [6]. The text is taken from *Bhārata Yuddha, kakawin*, by Mpu Sedhah and Mpu Panuluh, canto XXXI, [verse 7,] lagu *basonta tilaka*.

```
6  6   6  6   6  6  6   6  6  6   6  6  6  6.  2.321 1
As-car-ya Par-ta we-kas-an mu-wah e -ka-ta-na, ye-    ka

1  1   1  1  1   1    1  1  1  1   6.1.   2.16.165.
Wi-sang-ge-ni sang Hyang I -su-pra-dip-ta,  O
```

3. Pathet Sanga Ngelik

Pathet Sanga Ngelik is used after the suwuk of a piece for a scene in which a hermit gives audience to a *satriya* during the pathet sanga period. It begins with high-pitch panunggul [i̇]. The text is in the sekar ageng *pamular sih* meter.

```
i̇......    2.1̇6.1̇65.    2̇ 2̇    2̇  2̇  2̇   2̇.i̇.6  6.
─────      ─────                                ──
O          O         Ni-han  sis-wa u  -ma -  tur,


i̇.65.3532.    6  6    6  6    6  6  6  5..6.   i̇.65.3532.   2.3̇5
─────         ma-rang ri-sang ma-ha Yo-g̅i̅,     ─────        ───
O                                             O              sang


5  5   5  5   5  3.5.  1   1  1    1    1  1  1  1.   1  1  1
Wi-pra ka-di pa-r̅a̅n̅,  kar-sa-né Hyang Hu-ti-pa-t̅i̅, yo-ga sa-


1    1   1   6̇.1.   2̇.....   2   2  2  2   2 2    2.3.5   5.
lwir-ing war-n̅a̅,    O        kang gu-me-lar a-nèng b̅u̅ -   m̅i̅,


i̇.....   2  2  2 2   2  2.32  1.6.  2.321  1   1    1  1  1
─────    mu-gi u-lun te-d̅a̅h̅ - na,  tan -  dya sang Wi-ku an-
O


1   6̇.1.    2̇..1̇6.1̇65.
jar-w̅i̅,    O
```

4. Sendhon Rencasih

This sulukan has the same melody as that of Sendhon Pananggalan, laras sléndro pathet nem [but transposed up two pitch degrees]. It is used after the suwuk of a piece accompanying a scene with Prabu Yudhistira and other kings during the pathet sanga period. It begins with high-pitch gulu [2̇]. The text is from [*Serat*] *Brata Yuda*, *kawi miring*, [by R. Ng. Yasadipura I,] canto IV, [verse 1,] sekar ageng *sikarini*.[10]

```
2̇  2̇  2̇  2̇  2̇.1̇  1̇.   6   5    5  5   5  3.532.   i̇.....
Le-la-wa gu-m̅a̅n̅ -d̅h̅u̅l, nèng pang ke-bet ke-b̅e̅t,     O


5  5  5  5  3.5.  6  1̇.6i̇2  6  i̇  1̇.65  5.   5.6̇1.  5.6̇1.
lir mi-lu su-s̅a̅h̅, yèn t̅a̅    bi-sa m̅u̅ - wus, pa -   ge -


5  5   5.3   2.321.  6  6  6  6.165  5.   6   i̇.2.  6  i̇
né Pan-d̅h̅a̅ - wa,    tan a -na t̅u̅ - m̅u̅t, pri - b̅a̅ - di a -
```

```
i.65  5.  5.6i.  5.6i.  5  5  5.32  2.321.  2    2  2   2.321
─────     ────   ────           ────  ─────              ─────
min - ta, pra - jan - ta sa-pa  - lih,   kang se-kar tan -
```

```
i.    6 5 5  5 5 3.5.  6  i.6i2.  6  i  1.65 5.   5.6i.
─────                     ─────              ─────
jung, ru-ru am-be-la-sah, le-sah   ka-di su -sah, nge -
```

```
5.6i.  5  5.3  2.321.  6.....   ( ompak  .666  1561  2216  2165 )
─────          ─────    ─                 ···   ··    ·     ··
sah   ka -pi - sah,    A
```

```
5  5  5  5.3  3.532.  5..3.   ( ompak  .333  5235  2356  3532
         ───          ────
nge-sah ka-pi - sah,  O
```

```
6121  5612 )
·     ··
```

5. Sendhon Tlutur Wetah

Sendhon Tlutur is sung to express feelings of mourning, pity, sorrow,
deep emotion and so forth. It begins with high-pitch panunggul [1]. The
melody is the same as Sendhon Tlutur Wetah, pathet nem and pathet manyura
[but transposed down one pitch degree]. The text is taken from the [*Serat*]
Brata Yuda, [*kawi miring*, canto XLV, verse 1,] sekar ageng *patra suratma*
[*bangsa patra*].[11]

```
i..23i.6536.  i i  i i  i i   i i  i..6  6.   6
────────────
O             Su-rem su-rem di-wang-ka-ra king - kin, lir
```

```
6 6   6 6   6.53  3.  i..23i.6535.  1  1  1   1   1
                ──                             ·
ma-ngus-wa kang la - yon, O           de-nya i -lang ing-
```

```
1   1 1 1  6.1.  1.235  5  5  5  5  5.6i  5.   3  2   1
                 ───                ────
kang ma-ma-nis-e,   wa  - da-na-ni-ra lan - dhu, ku-mel ku-
```

```
2.3.  1   1 1 1 1  1.216  6.5.   6.5653.  3.56i.23i.6535.  1
────                      ───             ──────────────
cem  rah-nya ma-ra-ta - ni,   O          O                 ma-
```

```
1   1 1 1 1  6.1.  1.23 5   5.6i  5.   3  2  2  2  2
                                  ────
rang sa-ri-ra-ni-pun, me - les de  - ning lu-di-ra ka-wang-
```

```
12.3.  1  1 1 1   1  1.21  6.5.  3.....   ( ompak  333.  3253
─────                           ────
wang, ga-ga-na bang su-mi - rat, A
```

```
2312  3235 )
```

6. Sendhon Tlutur Wantah

Sendhon Tlutur Wantah is used to express feelings of mourning, sorrow, pity, and so forth. It begins with high-pitch panunggul [i]. [The text is a shortened version of Sendhon Tlutur Wetah, above.]

```
i..231.6535. i  i    i i    i i      i i  i..6 6.   6   6
O            Su-rem su-rem di-wang-ka-ra king-kin, lir ma-

6   6  6    6.53  3.   i..231.6535. 1  1   1 1   1    1
ngus-wa kang la  - yon, O            den-nya i-lang ing-kang

1  1  1   6.1.   1.235  5  5  5  5  5.61  5.  3  2   1  2.3.
ma-ma-nis-e,   wa   - da-na-ni-ra lan - dhu, ku-mel ku-cem

1   1   1  1  1.216 6.5.  3..... ( ompak  333.  3253  2312  3235 )
rah-nya ma-ra-ta-  ni,  A
```

7. Ada-ada Greget Saut Sanga Jugag

This ada-ada is used to underscore intense emotion in the pathet sanga period. It begins with pitch panunggul [1]. The text is taken from [Serat] Rama, kawi miring, canto XXIV, [verse 1,] sekar ageng basonta or sekar ageng ganda kusuma.[12]

```
1 1 1  1    1 1    1 1 1 1  1 1.   2  2
Bu-mi gon-jang gan-jing la-ngit ke-lab ke-lab, ka-ton

2  2  2   2  2 2  2   2  2.1  6.     1......
lir kin-cang-ing a- lis sang weh gan - drung, O
```

8. Ada-ada Greget Saut Wanawasa

This sulukan is also called Ada-ada Greget Saut Sanga Wetah, Sanga Jangkep, or Sanga Ageng. It is used for scenes of a satriya entering a forest or other such scenes. It begins with high-pitch gulu [2̇]. The text is taken from [*Serat*] *Rama*, *kawi miring*, canto XXIV, [verses 1 and 2,] sekar ageng *basonta* or sekar ageng *ganda kusuma*.

```
2̇ 2̇ 2̇   2̇   2̇ 2̇   2̇ 2̇   2̇ 2̇   2̇ 2̇   2̇.3 1̇
Bu-mi gon-jang gan-jing la-ngit ke-lab ke-lab, k̄a - ton
```

```
1̇ 1̇  1̇.65 5.  6 1̇61̇2 6 1̇  1̇.65 5.   5.3 2.1  1
lir kin-j̄ang-īng, ri-s̄ang  ma-wèh ḡan -drūng, s̄a - b̄a - rang
```

```
1 1 61.  6 1̇  1̇ 1̇   16 1̇2̇.  5.3 2   2   2 2 2.   6.
ka-du-l̄u,  wu-kir mo-yag m̄a-yīg, s̄a - king tyas ba-li-w̄ur, l̄u-
```

```
5 3  2  235 5.   2̇.3 1̇ 1̇ 1̇  165 5.   5.3 2.1 1 1
ma-ris a - ḡan-drūng, d̄uh a- ri Su-m̄i -tr̄a, t̄a - n̄a - ya pa-
```

```
1 61.  2 2   2  2   2 12.  1   6   6   6   6  6.
ran r̄eh, ka-bèh si-ning wa-n̄a,  nang-sa-yeng ma-ring-s̄un,
```

```
1.........
○
```

9. Ada-ada Greget Saut Sanga Wantah

This ada-ada is sung to underscore intense emotion in any situation [in pathet sanga]. It begins with high-pitch gulu [2̇]. The text is taken from [*Serat*] *Brata Yuda*, *kawi miring*, canto VI, [verse 9,] sekar ageng *kilayu nedheng*.

```
2̇ 2̇   2̇ 2̇ 2̇   2̇ 2̇   2̇ 2̇   2̇ 1̇2̇.  1̇ 1̇ 1̇ 1̇  1̇6
Ka-dang-mu pa-dha wa-rah-en dèn be-c̄ik, é-suk a-men-dh̄em-
```

```
5. 2̇.....  1̇ 1̇  1̇  165 5.  1 1  1 1  1  1  1  1
ā, e      ba-ris pra-yīt- n̄a, ha-ywa sa-ran-ta wong ing Dwa-
```

```
1 1 61. 2 2   2   2   2 2 2 2 2   21  6.  1......
ra-wa-t̄i, ti-num-pes pan i- ku a-wak Pan-dh̄a-wa, ○
```

10. Ada-ada Greget Saut Palaran

Ada-ada Greget Saut Palaran is used when the ogre chiefs and soldiers
are defeated during the *prang sekar* [battle between the hero and forest
demons]. It begins with high-pitch panunggul [i].

```
i   i i i   i i i i i  6i.   6   6   6   6   6.53
Rak-sa-sa kru-ra ka-gi-ri-gi-ri, geng-nya  lir pra-ba -

3.  5.6i i   i i i6 6.i. 6   6   6   6   6.53  3.   5 5
ta, a  - bang ka-we-la- gar, ma-ngu-wuh ing mung- suh, a-min-

5  53   3.5. 3.21  1   1   1 1   1   1 1   61.  2  2  2
ta la - wan, hang- gro kru-ra sru si-nga nab-da,  ka-di gé

2   2  2  2.16 6.  1.....
yun ma-nu-bruk -a,  o
```

11. Ada-ada Hasta Kuswala Sanga

This ada-ada is used for scenes in which a satriya is about to release
an arrow during the prang sekar. It is followed by [*Srepegan*] *Sri Martana*
in a fast tempo. It begins with pitch lima [5].

```
5   5   5   5 5 5  5.   5   6.i i   i i   i  1.23  i.
Men-thang gan-dhé-wa di-bya, bun-tar-an ri-nuk-mi ga - dhing,

6 5 5 5 5 5  35.   3  3   3   3   3  3    3  3
ka-ya ka-yu ku-mu-ning, a-nrus ing ja- ja  prap-tèng gi-gir

3  3  32  35.3.21. 5   6.i  i i i   i  1.23  i.      6 5
su-ra ra- ra,       man-jing pa-ke-kes-an-ing - kang, dha-rat

5   5   5  5   35.  3  3   3   32 35.3.21.  2.....
prap-tèng lan-car- an,  pa-nah tan ka-ton,      o
```

(ompak .222 3123 2532 1321)

This is followed by [*Srepegan*] *Sri Martana*, in a fast tempo, leading
into *Srepegan*, pathet sanga.

12. Pathet Sendhon Abimanyu[13]

This sulukan is sung during the removal of the satriya puppet after the prang sekar. It begins with pitch panunggul [1]. The text is taken from *Arjuna Wiwāha, kakawin,* by Mpu Kanwa, canto IV, [verse 4,] sekar ageng [lagu] *basonta tilaka.*

```
1  1  1  1  1  1   1  1   1    1  1   2.  3  5.  6.....
Li-la-ha-na ma-thi-ma-thi wruh-a   mèt w̄i- la-s̄a,  O
```

```
.
1..65.32.321.  1   1   1  1  1  2.  3   5.  6.....
————————————   ma-ngla-la-na ma-n̄ga-pit-ī,  O
O
```

```
.
1..65.32.321.  2   2   2  2    2    2  2.  2  2  2  2   2  2
————————————   ra-kwa ta-ngan sang Ar-ȳa, a-dan ma-han tu-kup-
O
```

```
                                .
2  2  2  2  2  2.35  5.  1.....  2   2    2  2   2.32  1.6.
                                                          .
a-ken ri-ka su-s̄u - nȳa,  O     ka-dyang re-ngen w̄u - l̄uh,
```

```
                                               .
2.1 1  1   1  1   1   1   6.1.  2.16.165.      1.....
—                                .   ..
a - ga-sah a- ti-nya mur - c̄a,  O            O
```

At the end of this sulukan, the dhalang raps the puppet box slowly five times, signalling *Ayak-ayakan,* pathet sanga.

13. Pathet Jingking[14]

Pathet Jingking is sung during the removal of the satriya puppets
after the prang sekar. It begins with pitch lima [5].

5   5   5   5 561 1. 2.16.165.3532. 2.35 6   61 6.5.
Tun-jung bang te-ra - te, e   i - rim i- rim

5.61 1.6.5. 2   2. 5 3 232 1.6. 3 3   35 3.2. 235
a - tap,   tap-ing ka-yu a - pu, a-gring-ing lu - lu -

5.   1..... 2   2   2 2 2.32 1.6. 5.61 1 1   1 1
mut, O   kang-kung-i- ra i - jo, sri - ga-dhing di-wa-

6.1. 2.16.165. 2   2. 5 3 232 1.6. 3 3   35 3.2.
sa,   O   ret-na-ning re-ja- sa, kem-bang ka- rang

235 5.   1..... 2 2   2 2 2.32 1.6. 5.61 1.   2.16.165.
sung-sang, O   bo-gem-é a- ra- ras, Ra - den, O

(in metered rhythm:)

         . . . .   5 6 1 6   2 1 6 .
                    kem-bang   i-   ra

         . . . .   5 6 1 6   2 1 6 .
                    ka- rang   sang   sang

                              N   P   G
([ompak]   2 3 5 6   5 3 1 2   3 2 1 6   2 1 6 5)

5   5   5 3.532.56. 1 1 6.1. 2.16.165. 5   5   5   5 5.61 1.
bo- gem-i- ra,   a- ra-ras, O   tun-jung bang te- ra - te

Dhodhogan follows, leading into *Ayak-ayakan* [pathet sanga].

14. Ada-ada Greget Saut Gathutkaca

This ada-ada is used in the exciting scene when Gathutkaca is about
to fly. It begins with high-pitch gulu [2]. The text is taken from the
Bharata Yuddha, *kakawin*, by Mpu Sedhah and Mpu Panuluh, canto XVIII,
[verse 1,] lagu *rajani*, or sekar ageng [lagu] *kawitana*.

```
. . .    . .    . .    . .   .                .   .    .   .
2 2 2    2 2    2 2    2 2  2.1  1.2.  1  1    1   1
I-ri-ka  ta sang Ga-thut-ka-ca  ki - non,  ma-pag Har-ka-
```

```
         .              .              .
1.65  5.  6  1.612 6  1  1.65  5   5.3  2.1  1  1  1   1  1
su - ta, te-kap - i -ra Kres -na,  Par -ta   ma-ne-her mu-ji
```

```
1   1  1  61. 2   2 2 2   2 2 2   2 2 2 2   2.16 6.
sak-ti ni-ra, sang i-nu-jar-an wa-wang ma-se-mu gar-ji- ta,
```

```
1.......
O
```

15. Ada-ada Greget Saut Wrekudara Mlumpat

This ada-ada is used when Wrekudara [Bima] is about to jump. It
begins with pitch gulu [2]. The text is taken from the *Dewa Ruci* story
[*Serat Bima Suci*, *kawi miring*, canto IX, verses 1 and 2; Prijohoetomo
1934:164. The meter is sekar ageng *wisalya harini*].

```
                        .
2.35  5   5 5   5    561  5    5.3  2.1  1   1  1
Can - cut gu-mre-gut man-jing,. sa - mo - dra tu-lya
```

```
6.1.   2  2 2 2   2 2 2 2 2   2 2 2   2..16 6.
dreng, wi-ra-ga-nya le-ga-wa ba-nyu su-ma-put wen - tis,
```

```
.         .  .    .  .   .                       .
2......   1  1    1  1   1 1..6  5   6  1.612  6   1  1.65
O         me-leg ing ang-ga-ni - ra, su-mi - ngep nam-peg -
```

```
5.  5..3  2..1  1   1  1   1 61.  2  2   2 2 2  21  12.
i,  mi - geg  jang-ga kang wa-rih, ka-ton na-ga ku-mam-bang,
```

```
1   6   6 6 6   6 6.  .1  1..  .1 1..  2  3  5    5.....
geng-nya sa-wu-kir a-nak, nga-kak ga-lak ku-me-lap, O
```

```
1.....
O
```

Dhodhogan follows, leading immediately into *Sampak Tanggung*.

16. Ada-ada Greget Saut Manggalan

This sulukan is sung after the suwuk of a gendhing accompanying an ogre king scene such as *Kresna Triwikrama* [Kresna in the form of an ogre] or other similar scenes. It begins with pitch panunggul [1]. [It is a transposition down one pitch degree of Ada-ada Girisa, laras sléndro pathet nem.] The text is taken from [*Serat*] *Rama*, [*kawi miring*,] sekar ageng *sikarini*.[15]

```
1..23   3   3   3   3.2  2.35.  2.321  1   1   1   1   61.
Yak  - sa go-ra  ru - pa,   ri -  se-dheng sang Kum-ba-

1..23 3   3   3.2  2.35.  2.321 1   1   1   1   61.   5   5   5
kar - na la-la - ku,   kan   mal-wa ling ing-kang, gam-bi-ra

5   5   3.5.  6   6   6    6  6.   6  6  6   6   6  56. 1   1   1
ma-nga-rah, a-ngi-sis si-yung a-me-tu pra-ba-wa,  lé-sus a-

1   1.65  5.   2   3..5   2   3.21 1.  i  i   i   i  1.65  5.
pra-kem - pa, go-ra     wa-lik- an, di-tya Dur-ba-lar - sa,

2.321  1  1   1    1  6.1. 2.3. 1   1   1.65  5.   2.....
mrih   cur-na-ning la-wan, wi - ra tri lo  - dra, ya
```

17. Ada-ada Greget Saut Tlutur

This sulukan is used for violent situations that are also mournful, moving, sad, or pitiful. It begins with high-pitch panunggul [1]. The text is taken from [*Serat*] *Brata Yuda*, [*macapat*,] by [R. Ng.] Yasadipura I, [canto XLV, verse 7,] sekar macapat *dhandhang gula*.

```
i   i   i   i   i  i   i   i   1.23  i.   6  5   5   5   5
Mi-wah pu-tra-né sam-pun nge-mas - i,  Ra-dèn Lak-sma-na-

5   5   5  5  35.  i.....  6  5   5  5  5  5  5   35.  3.21
man-dra-ku-ma-ra,  O     mi-wah pa-ra ri an-del- e,   Du -

1  1  1  1   1  6.1.  1.235  5   5  5  5   5  5  5.61  5.
sa-sa-na wus lam-pus,  la  - wan ré-ka Dur-ja-ya ma  - ti,

3  2   2   2   2 2  12.3. 1  1    1  1  1.21  6.5.   1.....
tu-win Ja-ya-susé-na,  ka-dang an-del-i  - pun,  O
```

Additions: Songs Sung by the
Panakawan in Pathet Sanga

1. Dhandhang Gula, Cèngkok Macapat

A song sung in a crude fashion by Pétruk when he departs to accompany
his master to the kingdom of the gods in heaven.

```
2   53 5  6.   6  i  2   2   16 i.2.   2  2   26 2.i.6.   6  6
Cip-ta è-meng é-mut ma-rang ngèlmi, nga-lam do-nya      dè-nya

6   6  65 5.6.   2  2   2   2  i.65  5.6i.2  65  i.6.5.   6  i
tan a- sa- ma,  se-mang se-mang pa - ngang - gep- e,     nga-ndhap

2  i  6   i.65  5.6i.  5  5   2  2.  2  3  5   2.32 1.6.   2  2
i-nga-ran lu -  hur,  ing-kang a-na  i-nga-ran se - pi,  se-pi

2  2  2   2 2.   1  1  6  2.   651  6.5.  5  6  1  2  2   2  2
i-nga-ran a-na,  a-na-nè tan  tam- tu,  tu-man ka-ta-man wa-ra-

2.  2  2   232 16.  6  6  6   6  6   16  6.12  2.  5  6  1
na kang nga-wer- i  tan we-ruh ma-rang kang we - rit, wa-ra-ta

6   2.  1.65  6.1.
tan was-pa -  da.
```

2. Gérong Kinanthi, Ketawang *Suba Kastawa*

This is a *buka celuk*, or vocal buka, that Pétruk sings when he departs to accompany his masters to heaven. Pétruk only introduces the piece; [after the buka celuk] the pesindhèn and penggérong take over.

```
                                                              N
    .    .2   2.23  1.    .23  2.1  616  5
         Mi-der-ing rat    a - nga- la- ngut,

                                                              G
    .16  1.65  2.32  1.    .23  2.1  616  5
    la - la -  na   nja -  jah  na - ga - ri,

                                                              N
    .    .2   2.23  1.    .23  2.1  616  5
         mu- beng te-pi   ning sa - mo - dra,

                                                              G
    .16  1.65  2.32  1.    .23  2.1  616  5
    su - meng - ka  a -   gra- ning wu - kir

                                                              N
    1.   .1   1.12  1     .23  2.   2321  6
         a - na-la- sak   wa - na - wa - sa

                                                              G
    .    .2   2.23  1.    .61  2.1  616  5
         tu- mu-run mring ju-  rang tre- bis
```

3. Gambuh, Cèngkok Palaran

This song consists of Togog's questions addressed to a satriya in the prang sekar.

```
i  i  i.  6  6i.  5  1.65.  2  2    23  2.1.  i  i  6   6i.  5
Si-ra sa- pa a - ran- mu, menyang ngen-di  pa-ra-ning se- dya -

1.65  1  6  1  2.321.  3  3  3  3    32  35.  1561  653.  2  2
mu,   dé-né wa- ni    na-sak te-ngah-ing wa - na - dri,  be-cik

2  2  2  3  23  2.1.  3  3  3  3    32  35.  213  2.1.
ba-li-a dèn gu- puh,  é-man la-mun prap-teng la - yon.
```

4. Cèngkok [Ketawang] *Langen Gita*

Semar sings this song in a free rhythm when his master is about to meet the ogre Cakil during the prang sekar.

```
                                            N
    .    .    .    .           .    .   6.5  5
                                        An- dhong,

                                            G
  .2   2   21   6.1         .5   65   326  6
   ti - nan-dur  te -        pi- ning  ge- dhong,

                                            N
    .    .   61    1         6   12.   616  5
              ar - gu                  lo - bang,

                                            G
  .2   2   21   6.1         .5   65   353  2
  lu- mem- bang pa -         ger  ba - lum- bang,

                                            N
  1.    .   .3   5.                2   53   2
             kem-bang             ang  -   grèk,

                                            G
  .2   6   23   1.          23   2.   616  5
  ru-mam - bat  a -         ngem-pèk  em- pèk.
```

5. Ketawang *Puspa Giwang*

Gareng sings this song in a free rhythm when he is about to meet the ogre Cakil during the prang sekar.

```
                                            N
  .2   2   2   2            2   23   35   5
  Pa- rab - e   sang        Ma - ra  ba- ngun,

                                            G
  .6   1   6   5            3   2   32   1
  se- pat dom - ba          ka - li  O -  ya,

                                            N
  .5   6   2   1            .5   6   2   1
   a - ja  do - lan         lan wong pri- ya,

                                            G
  .5   5   2   35           .13  2.1  616  5
  ge - ra - mèh  no-        ra  pra- sa - ja.
```

6. Lagu *Canthing Gléyong*

Pétruk sings this bawa when he is about to face the ogre Cakil during the prang sekar. This bawa is followed by Lancaran *Surabayan.*

```
i  2.   565 32.  6  1  2.  6  1  2.   2   3   5
Canthing gle-yong, man pa-man, man pa-man, wong bedhang

5   5   5    5   5    5   6   i  6.i.  5   6   i  6.i.
ke- pa-lang gedhong, mandheg ma-  yong, mandheg ma-yong,

5   2.   2.3  2.1.  1   6  1  2.3.  1   1  1.21  6.5.
mandheg ma - yong, ngen-te-ni se -  pi-ning u -  wong.
```

Same melody, but different text:

Canthing jali, man paman, man paman, wong bedhang kepalang kali, putung woté, putung woté, putung woté, dak sengguh putung atiné.

```
2   i   2.  6   i   6   6   2   2   2   i.
Yu mbak-yu, a - yo  mu-lih nyang o- mah-ku.
```

7. Cengkok *Hasta Kuswala Sanga*

Semar sings this song when he gives his master arrows during the prang sekar.

```
5   5   5   5  5  5   5   5   5   5   5.  5  6  i  i
A-yo  a-yo nju-puk pa-nah-é  nda-ra, a-yo nju-puk

i   i   i   1.23  i.  6  5  5  5   5   5   5   5  35.
pa-nah-é nda - ra, a-na ngi-sor wit ken-dha-yak-an,

3   3   3   3  3   3  3  3  3  32  35.3.21.  5  6i
a- yo a- yo nju-puk pa-nah-é nda - ra,      a- yo

i   i   i   i   i  1.23  i.  6  5  5  5   5   5  5
nju-puk pa-nah-é nda - ra, na-pa ni-ki na-pa ni-

35.  3  3  3  3   3  3  3  32  35.3.21.  2  2  2
ki, pa-nah-é nda-ra na-pa ni - ki,        na-pa ni-

2.   3  1  2  3   2  2  5  3  2  1  3  2  1.
ki na-pa ni-ki pa-nah-é nda-ra na-pa ni-ki.
```

C. Sulukan in Laras Sléndro Pathet Manyura

1. Pathet Manyura Wantah

This sulukan is used for the transition from pathet sanga to pathet manyura and after any gendhing in pathet manyura lacking its own pathetan. It begins with pitch dhadha [3]. The text is taken from the *Bhārata Yuddha, kakawin*, by Mpu Sedhah and Mpu Panuluh, canto VI, [verse 1,] lagu or sekar ageng *sasadara kawekas*, also known as lagu *wisarjita* or *widara gumulung*.

```
3   3   3   3 3   3   3.      3    3 3   3    3   3   3   3.
Mèh ra-hi-na se-mu bang, Hyang A-ru-na  ka-di né-tra-ning,

3.2  2   2   2    2   2   2    2   21   1.2.  3.....   3     3  3
O - ga ra-puh sab-da-ning ku-ki - la,   O         ring ka-ni-

3   3   3   3.5.6  6.  2.....  3   3   3    3    3..21 1.
ga-ra sa-ke  -  ter, O      ni ki-dung ning- a  -  kung,

3.532 2   2    2    2   2   2   1.2.  3.21.2.16.  1   1   1    1
lwir  wu-wus-ing wi-ni pan-ca,   O            pa-pe-tog-ing

1 1   1   61.   2.16.5.3.
a-yam wa-na,  O
```

2. Pathet Manyura Jugag

Pathet Manyura Jugag is sung to indicate a transition to any situation during the pathet manyura period that is calm in mood. It begins with pitch panunggul [1]. The text is taken from *Ramāyana, kakawin*, [canto XVI,] verse 31, sekar ageng [lagu] *bremara wilasita*.

```
1   1   1    1    1   1   1   1   1   1   61.   3.532 2     2
Jah-ni yah-ning ta-la-ga ka-di la-ngit, mam - bang tang

2   2   2    2 2  2   2   1.2.   3.21.216.  1   1    1   1   1 1
pas wu-lan u-pa-ma-ni-ka,     O          win-tang tu-lya ku-su-

1   1   1    1   6.1.   2.16.5.3.
ma ya su-ma-wur,  O
```

3. Pathet Manyura Ageng

This sulukan is used after the suwuk of Gendhing *Damar Kèli*, during
the scenes in the quarters of the queen, Dèwi Banowati, in the palace of
Ngastina. It begins with pitch panunggul [1]. The text is taken from the
Bharata Yuddha, *kakawin*, by Mpu Sedhah and Mpu Panuluh, canto V, [verse 2,]
lagu *sardula wikridhita*.

```
1   1   1    1  1  1  1  1  1   1  1  61.   2.1216.5653.
Ki-lyan sang-ka ri-ka ta ta-man a -re-pat, O
```

```
1   1   1   1  1   1  61.   2.1216.5653.  5......  6  6  6   6
rèh-nya-ba-lé kan-ca-na,  O                O         so-ba-bra ma-
```

```
6   6   6  6   6  6   6  5.6.  1.65.653.  3.5.6 6  6   6  6
he-ning pa-wal na-tar i -ka,  O           rok   mu-tya-ha-ra
```

```
6   5.6.  1.65.653.  3.5.6.  3.5.6.  3  3  3  32 1.216.  2  2
ra-ras, O            we    - dur   - ya ma-ra-ni-la,    ba-pra
```

```
2   2  2   2   2   1.2.  3   3  3.21  1.   2.16.5653.  3.56
ni pa-ger tun-jung-nya,  man-ten lu - meng, O          mun -
```

```
6   6  6   6   6  6  6  6   6   6  6   6.   1  1  1   1
tap in-ten-i ga-pu-ra-nya ma-ca-win-ten, sur-ya-kan-ta
```

```
1   6.1.   2.16.5.3.
jwa-la,  O
```

4. Pathet Manyura Ngelik

This pathetan is used after the suwuk of gendhing that accompany
scenes of holy seers (*pandhita*), princesses, and so forth, during the
pathet manyura period. It begins with high-pitch gulu [2]. The text is
derived from the *Arjuna Wiwaha*, *kakawin*, [canto XXVIII, verse 2,] sekar
ageng [lagu] *sudira draka* [or *rucira* (see Poerbatjaraka 1926:232)].

```
2......  123.21.216.  1.23   i   i   i   i   i   i  i  1.23
O        O            Re  -  rep ku-wung ku-wung ma-wi-let -
```

```
2.321.  2.16.5653.  6   6  6   6  6  6  6  5.6.  2.16.5653.
ing,  O             ngam-ba-ra, a- ni-la-ni-la,  O
```

3.56 6 6 6 6   6 6 56. 2 2 2   2 12. 3 3 3 3
$\overline{ja}$ -la-da-ra nge-mu u-$\overline{dan}$, ra-wi pra-ba-$\overline{nya}$, ka-lang-an-nya

3.56 6. 2̇...... 3 3   3 3 3 3.53 2.1. 3.532 2 2 2
$\overline{mak}$- $\overline{sih}$, O   ka-ton, wi-sé-sa $\overline{cih}$- na, $\overline{ha}$ - na-ni-ra

2   2 2 1.2. 3.21.216. 1 1 1 1 1   1 1 61.
sang hu-jwa-$\overline{la}$, O   ha-na-ni-ra sang hu-ja-$\overline{la}$,

2.16.5.3.
O

5. Sendhon Sastradatan

Sendhon Sastradatan is sung after the suwuk of a gendhing accompanying
scenes at Ngamarta and similar places, during the manyura period.   It
begins with high-pitch panunggul [1].   The text is taken from the *Bhārata
Yuddha, kakawin,* by Mpu Sedhah and Mpu Panuluh, canto XIII, [verse 1,]
sekar ageng [lagu] *wohing rat,* also known as *wawirat,* or *raga kusuma.*

1̇ 1̇ 1̇ 1̇   1̇ <u>1.6</u> <u>6.</u> 5   3 3   3 3 <u>3.2</u> <u>2.321</u>
Tat-ka-la Nar-pa Kres-na, tan tu-lus a-nya-kra ring,

<u>6.</u>...... 3 3 3 3 3   3 3 3 <u>2.3.</u> 5 <u>6561</u> 5 6 6
O   Re-si wa-ra Jah-na-wi-su-ta, ngka mung- gah si-ra

6 6 6   6.53 3. 3.56. 3.56. 3 3 3   3.2 1.216. 5
ka-lih ing $\overline{ra - ta}$, $\overline{te}$ - $\overline{her}$ tu-mi-yang-a - ken, i-

5   5 5 <u>5.65</u> <u>3.</u> 5 <u>6561</u> 5   6 <u>6.53</u> <u>3.</u> <u>3.56.</u> <u>3.56.</u>
kang sa-ro-ta - ma, tan wyar- than ma-ga - we, pu - pug

3 3 3   3 3.2 1.216. 1̇ 1̇ 1̇ 1̇ 1̇ 6.1. 5653 3
ni gu-na sang $\overline{Re}$ - si,   le-su ma-ri ka-$\overline{tar}$- u - jwa-

3 3 3 <u>23.</u> 5 6 1̇ 5 6 <u>6.53</u> <u>3.</u> <u>3.56.</u> <u>3.56.</u> 3
la te-kwan $\overline{suh}$, lu-mi-hat ri-sang $\overline{Wa}$ - ra, $\overline{Si}$ - kan - dhi

3 3 3.2 1.216. 5...... (ompak .555 6356 1165 1653)
ka-ra-$\overline{na}$ ni, A

3 3, 3 3 <u>3.2</u> <u>2.321.</u> <u>3.2.</u> (ompak .222 3123 5235 2321
gu-pe si-ra la - ga,   O

5616 3561)

6. Sendhon Tlutur Wetah

This sendhon is sung to convey feelings of intense emotion, sorrow, pity, mourning, and so forth. The text is taken from [Serat] Manuhara, by Kangjeng Gusti Pangeran [Adipati] Arya Mangku Negara IV [canto I, verse 1; see Mangku Negara IV 1953:29-42]. The meter is sekar macapat dhandhang gula.

```
2..352.1656.  2  2   2   2   2  2  2  2   2.1  1.   1
O                    Pu-teg-ing tyas da-ru-na geng king-kin, ka-

1  1  1  1   1   1  1   1.6  5.  2..352.1656.  2  2   2
gun-tur-an ing kra-ma sar-ka - ra,  E              ke-lud ka-

2   2   2  2   1.2.  2.356  6  6  6  6   6.12  6.   5   3  3
lim-put a-ngen-e,    nir    ka-bu-da-yan-i - pun, lir ka-ta-

3  3  3   3   3.2  2.3.5.  2   2   2   2  2  2.32  1.6.
man ing ngas-tra ban - ni,     bras-tha tan-pa u -pa-   ya,

1..6.5.  6.12...352.1656.  2  2  2   2   2 1.2.  2.356 6  6
O        E                 pu-wa-ra gung wu-yung wah - ya wi-

6  6  6.12  6.   5   3   3  3  3  3  3   3  3   3  32 23.5.
ya-di dri - ya,  dri-yas-ma-ra ma-ri-pih ma-rek nge-ne-ni,

2   2  2  2  2   2.32  1.6. 5......  ( ompak   555.   5365
sang-sa-ya ma-weh brang- ta,  A

3523  5356 )
```

7. Sendhon Tlutur Wantah

[This sulukan is the same as *Sendhon Tlutur Wetah*, above, but in an abbreviated version.]

2..3̇5̇2.1̇656. 2̇ 2̇ 2̇ 2̇   2̇ 2̇ 2̇ 2̇   2.1̇ 1̇.   1̇
‾‾‾‾‾‾‾‾‾‾
O̲   Pu-teg-ing tyas da-ru-na geng k̅i̅n̅g̅-k̅i̅n̅, ka-

1̇ 1̇ 1̇ 1̇ 1̇ 1̇ 1̇ 1.6 5. 2̇..3̇5̇2.1̇656. 2̇ 2̇ 2̇ 2̇
gun-tur-an ing kra-ma sar-k̅a̅ - r̅a̅, E̲   ke-lud ka-lim

2̇ 2̇ 2̇ 1.2. 2.356 6 6 6 6   6.1̇2̇ 6. 5 3 3
-put a-ngen-e̅, n̅i̅r̅ ka-bu-da-yan- i̅ - p̅u̅n̅, lir ka-ta-

3 3 3 3 3.2 2.3.5 2 2 2 2 2 2.32 1.6.
man ing ngas-tra b̅a̅h̅- n̅i̅, bras-tha tan-pa u -p̅a̅ -y̅a̅,

5...... (ompak 555. 5365 3523 5356)
‾‾‾‾‾
A̲

8. Ada-ada Greget Saut Manyura Wantah

This ada-ada is used to underscore intense emotion in any situation [in pathet manyura]. It begins with high-pitch panunggul [1̇]. The text is taken from [*Serat*] *Brata Yuda*, *kawi miring*, canto XLIII, [verse 1,] sekar ageng *sulanjari*.

1̇ 1̇ 1̇ 1̇ 1̇ 1̇ 1̇ 1̇ 1̇ 1̇ 1̇ 1̇ 1̇ 6.1̇.
Tan-dya ba-la Pan-dha-wa mbyuk gu-mu-lung ma-ngung-s̅i̅r̅,

356 6 6 6 6 56. 3̇..... 2̇ 2̇ 2̇ 2̇ 2̇ 2̇ 2.1̇
r̅i̅n̅g sa-ta Ku-ra-w̅a̅, O̲   kam-bah kong-kih sru ka-t̅i̅-

6. 2 2 2 2 2 2 2 2 2 2 2 1.2. 3 3 3
t̅i̅h, mi-rut ke-rut la-rut ka-tut pa-ra ra-t̅u̅, tu-win sa-

3 3 3 3.21 1. 2.....
gung pra di-p̅a̅ - t̅i̅, O̲

9. Ada-ada Greget Saut Manyura Wantah

This version of Ada-ada Greget Saut Manyura Wantah uses different cèngkok [i.e., different from that in no. 8]. It is used to underscore intense emotion in any situation. It begins with high-pitch panunggul [i̇]. The text is taken from [*Serat*] *Brata Yuda*, *kawi miring*, canto XXXVI, and is in the sekar ageng *sikarini* meter.

```
i̇  i̇   i̇  i̇  i̇    i̇  i̇   i̇  i̇   i̇  i̇  6i̇.  356  6
Pa-reng u-mang-sah lir pa-gut-ing ja-la-dri, pa- reng

6  6   6   6  6   6  6   6   56.  2  2   2   2  2   2   2
ma-nem-puh wa-dya tan pé-tung-an,  u-mang-sah si-lih rok ca-

2   2   2  12.  3  3   3   3    3  3   3  3    3  3  3.21
ruk ma-ru-ket, u-leng-ing kang ba-la des-tun tan pa ru -

1.     2.....
ngyan,  O
```

10. Ada-ada Greget Saut Manyura Jugag

This ada-ada is used to underscore intense emotion in any situation [in pathet manyura]. It begins with pitch gulu [2]. The text is taken from *Bhārata Yuddha*, [*kakawin*,] by Mpu Sedhah and Mpu Panuluh, canto XII, [verse 12,] lagu *girisa*.

```
2  2  2  2  2   2  2  2   2    2  2   2  2  2  2  2.  3
Ni-ya-ta la-rut-a sa-kwèh ning yo-dha sa-Ku-ru-ku-la, ya

3   3  3  3   3  3   3   3.21 1.  2.....
tan-a-ngu-tus-a sang sri Bhis- ma.  O
```

11. Ada-ada Greget Saut Wrekudara Mlumpat

This ada-ada is sung when Wrekudara is about to leap.   It begins with
pitch dhadha [3].

```
                                       ..
3.56  6    6    6  6  6     6.12   6     6.5   32   2   2
‾‾‾                                ‾‾‾         ‾‾   ‾‾
Ma - ngan-jur la-ku-ning a  -   ngin, gun - tur a-gra-

2    2   12.   3  3  3   3  3  3  3  3  3  23.   1  1   1  1
         ‾‾                              ‾‾‾
ning har-ga,  go-ra gur-ni-ta ka-gi-ri-gi-ri,  ho-reg bu-mi

                   :.:  :  :            :           .:
1   1   1  1.   3.5  2   2  2  2     2   2.16  6    1  2.3  1
‾‾             ‾‾                     ‾‾‾          ‾‾‾
pra-kam-pi-ta, pa - dho-la ma-ngam-bak am  - bak, u -dan dres

:   :.:                                                        
2   2.1   6    6.5  3.2  2  2  2   2  2  2   2  2  2  2
    ‾‾         ‾‾‾
wor le - sus,  ka - dya  pi-nu-sus gu-mu-ruh go-ra ma-wa-lik-

12.  3    3    3  3   3  3   32  23  2  1   1  1  1  1  1  1
‾‾                         ‾‾‾
an,  sin-dhung ri-wut ma-gen-tur-an, ku-mo-pak ma-we-tu ge-lap,

                                              .
2   2.   2  2.   2   3   5   6     6.....    2.....
‾‾       ‾‾
sè-tu  sè-tu  ban-da-la-yu,  O‾‾‾‾       O‾‾‾‾
```

12. Ada-ada Greget Saut Tlutur

This sulukan is used in violent situations to express feelings of
pity, deep emotion, and mourning.   It begins with high-pitch gulu [2].   The
text is taken from [Serat)] *Brata Yuda*, [*macapat*,] by Kyai [R. Ng.]
Yasadipura I, [canto XXXV, verse 25; Cohen Stuart 1860:95,] sekar macapat
durma.

```
:   :   :   :   :  :  :    :  :   :    :        :       .
2   2   2   2   2  2  2    2  2   2   2.35   2   1   6   6   6
                                     ‾‾‾‾
Ka-dya wu-kir ka-so-rot-an di-wang-ka  - ra, na-li-ka mèh

                .           .
6   6   56.    2.....      1   6   6   6   6   56.    5.32   2   2
                                             ‾‾‾     ‾‾‾‾
u-man-jing, O‾‾‾    rep ing ja-lad-dhi-yan,  mbe-  ra-nang-

                                              ..
2    2   2  12.   2.35  6   6   6   6   6  6.12   6   5   3   3
‾‾               ‾‾‾‾                      ‾‾‾‾
ing bu-sa-na,  ge - lar-é mang-ka-ra da  - di, ti-ning-kah-

2    3.5  2   2   2   2   2   2321  1.6.   2.....
‾‾             ‾‾‾‾               .
ting-kah, kang mung-gèng ing su-su - pit,  O‾‾‾
```

13. Sendhon Kagok Ketanon

This is one of Semar's songs, sung during the gara-gara scene before
the prang sekar. It begins with pitch nem [6].

```
                ..    ... .
6    6     612..352.1656..56..56..5.3.2.   3.56  6  6  6   6
Dhuh dhuh dhuh,                             dhuh  ya-na sun a-

                     ..
6   6.   6  6  6.12  6    5  3   3    3  3  3  3  2.35.   2
nem-bang, i-lir bum - bung té-bok kang dèn a-nam a- rang,  ba-

2  232  1.6.  2    2  2  1   2  6  1   5  5  5  3   56     6
                                                  . .
bo ba - bo,  dhuh ja-na ki-rag-ki-rig ka-ya di sem-prong bo-

6    6.
.    +
kong-e
```

13a. Sendhon Kagok Ketanon

This version of Sendhon Kagok Ketanon uses a different text [different
from no. 13, above].

```
..    ... .
612..352.1656..56..56..5.3.2.    3.56  6  6  6   6.12
E                                dhuh  ya-na ti-kus la -

6.   5   3  3  3   3  3   3  2.35.   2  2   232  1.6.   2
ngu treng-ga-lo kang sa-bèng lo-ngan,  ba-bo  ba - bo,  dhuh

2  2  1  2  6   1  5  5   5  3   5  6   1   6.
         .  .     .  .       .       .       +
ya-na ca-lu-rut-an ka-ya nggo-lèk-i  bé-dhang-e.
```

ADDITIONAL TEXTS FOR THE SULUKAN

I. Laras Sléndro Pathet Nem

1. Pathet Nem Ageng

Dwan sembah-nirèng hulun, kapurba ring sang Murbèng rat, O . . . , ing
sahananingkang, O . . . , yéka kang asung mring wadu, mawèh boga
sawegung, masih ring delahan, O . . . , dwan kanang amujwènga,
O . . . , (ompak) . . . , ring jeng Nataningrat, O . . . , O . . . ,
dutèng rat kotama, manggiha nugraha, O . . . , tarlèn siswa sagotra,
kang huwus minulya, O . . . , kang huwus minulya, O . . . , (ompak) .

[The text is taken from Serat Paniti Sastra, kawi miring, canto I,
verse 1; the meter is sekar ageng swandana.]

2. Pathèt Nem Wantah

Kontap kotamaning katong, dènya kretartèng budaya, O . . . , tétéla
malebdèng kayun, O . . . , Narèndra mbeg martotama, bebisik Sri
Padmanaba, Dwarawati prajanira, O . . . , mangkana ta sira prabu,
O . . . , (ompak) .

3. Pathet Nem Jugag

   a. Ramya wwang padha tusta anggarjita, tekapira nir mala mangayun
      ring, O . . . , trus hunggyaning, sang Sri Supadniwara,
      O . . . , tarlèn dwi lembana samya mangagnya, O . . . ,
      (ompak) .

   [This text is in the sekar ageng bremara wilasita meter.]

   b. Mudra mwang kutha sametri wimala, nahan puspanjalinira,
      O . . . , sasampunyan, mangkana mastuti, O . . . , ta sira
      rengen ucaranira, O . . . , (ompak) .

4. Ada-ada Girisa Wantah

   a. Raras kang alenggah, nèng dhampar kancana, sumorot prabanya,
      lir Bathara Indra, gumelar angèbegi, kang samya sumèwa, tinon
      kadi samodra pasang, kang samya trapsila, nganti wijil ingkang,
      sabda pangandika, sang Natadèwa, ya . . . .

      ["According to the dhalang, R. Sutrisno, this text was written
      by Ki Susiloatmojo (died 1973), a famous student of the Mangku
      Negaran dhalang Mas Ngabèhi Wignyosutarno" (Schumacher
      1980:84n; translation supplied).]

   b. Ana yaksa juga kagiri-giri, gengnyarga magalak, ahangkara
      ambegnya, gora godha tandya, krura mamangsa, tinampèl muka
      kaparsat, buta kabarubuh, piyak kayu pokah, belah bantala
      sirna, pinggang anggaota, swuh kapupuh, ya . . . .

      [This text is roughly derived from *Ramāyana*, *kakawin*, canto XV,
      verse 64; see Uhlenbeck and Soegiarto 1960:54-55.]

5. Ada-ada Mataraman Wantah

   a. Tandya kang bala bareng ngebyuki, gumregut umangsah mungsuh,
      aliru papan, O . . . , mrih lènaning lawan, caruk ruket rok
      silih ungkih, wus samya wuru ludira, O . . . .

   b. Mundur nembah sang Nindyamantri, harsa ambidhalaken wadya,
      minggah mring panggungan, O . . . , nembang tengara, gumrudug
      kang wadya prapti, samapta siyaga ing karya, O . . . .

   c. Muntap dukanirèng panggalih, dhoso wedaling kang pangandika,
      nètrandik angatirah, O . . . , kumejot padoning lathi, kadi gè
      yun mangrangsanga, lir kruraning sardulu, O . . . .

6. Pathet Kedhu

   Kacaryan tumingal, putra myang santana, O . . . , wadya samoha,
   dèra sang siniwi, sihnya amenuhi, O . . . , O . . . , meleg
   lumintu, O . . . , wit gusti sang prabu, O . . . , suka sih
   marang, pra mitra lyan nagri, samya sru kayungyun, O . . . ,
   atur warni-warni, O . . . , (ompak) . . . , sang sri kawuryan,
   O . . . , (ompak) .

7. Sendhon Tlutur Wantah

O . . . , katatangi tangising awengis, angemasi, O . . . ,
kasoring naya, nihanta yantiku dumèh, kadurus tam-tam laku, yèn
pinulur malah kapulir, O . . . .

8. Pathet Lasem

O . . . , O . . . , Dhuh sang prabu ningrat Narapati, sumbaga
prawirèng prang, O . . . , dibya sekti myang pekik warnané,
O . . . , sor Bathara Asmara, O . . . , kagunan myang
kaluwihanira, déwadi tan ana kang tumimbanga, nora wenang
mulat, O . . . , ing saktinta prabu, O . . . , (ompak) .

9. Pathet Lindur

Riris harda palwa nut ing warih, O . . . , O . . . , dresing
karsaningsun déning kanyut, manising lingira gusti, wohing
kamal mirahingsun, O . . . , O . . . , ésemira duk ing nguni,
O . . . , paparikan bantal dawa [or, "sidhat agung ing
narmada"; see Schumacher 1980:54], sajroning aguling,
pangucaping janma néndra, teka tansah dadi, O . . . , linduran
kéwala, O . . . , (ompak) .

[This text is in the sekar tengahan *lindur* meter.]

II. Laras Sléndro Pathet Sanga

1. Pathet Sanga Wantah

   a. Kagagas ing tyas dahat kéwran ing karyanira, datanpa antuk
      samya, myat rengganing prabata, O . . . , roning kadhep
      kumedhap, O . . . , lwir pangawéning sang dwija, lunging
      gadhung malengkung, O . . . .

   b. Mangkana lampahé wus prapta, jawining kitha rikat pangiriding
      rata, O . . . , kang swandana apindha, O . . . , panglayanging
      kagaraja, nagri katingal saking mandrawa, O . . . .

   c. Tan samar pamoring suksma sinuksmaya, winahya ing asepi
      sinimpen telenging kalbu, O . . . , pambukaning warana tarlèn
      saking, O . . . , liyep layaping aluyup, pindha pesating
      supena, O . . . .

(If this text is used in pathet manyura, the following line is
added at the end: "sumusuping rasa jati, O . . . .")

2. Pathet Sanga Ngelik

    a. O . . . , O . . . , Maweh ascarya langen isining wanadri,
        O . . . , mulat salwiring tuwuh kang arebut mangsa, O . . . ,
        mawantu tumuruning riris, mekaring sarwa puspita, O . . . ,
        mamrihira sang bremara ring sari, O . . . , miwah swaraning
        kukila kang, munggwing mandera raras rinungu, O . . . .

    b. O . . . , O . . . , Bremara reh manguswa umung, O . . . ,
        ambrangengeng kadi karunaning kaswasih, O . . . , aneng marga
        malat kung, sang Gondowastratmaja, O . . . , lengleng lalu
        angulati, O . . . , surya mangrangsang wayah, umyus
        amarawayanta, O . . . .

        [This text is taken from the *Serat Bima Suci*, *kawi miring*,
        canto III, verse 5 (Prijohoetomo 1934:153). It is in the sekar
        ageng *wisalya harini* meter.]

    c. O . . . , O . . . , Yeka caritanira, O . . . , risang
        Pandhusiwi, O . . . , duk nalika mesu brata, neng Indrakilardi,
        O . . . , pra jawata ngayubagya, O . . . , marang sang Pamadi,
        dadya sru ngeningken cipta, kontap Suranadi, O . . . .

        [Schumacher (1980:59n) remarks that this text is possibly taken
        from the *Serat Arjuna Wiwāha*, *kawi miring*, attributed to Paku
        Buwana III.]

3. Pathet Sanga Jugag

    a. Mulat mara sang Arjuna semu kamanungsan, kasrepan ri tingkah
        ing mungsuhniran padha kadang taya, O . . . .

        [This text is taken from the *Bhārata Yuddha*, *kakawin*, canto X,
        verse 12, and is in the *prethitala* meter.]

    b. Lenglenging driya mangu-mangu mangunkung, kandhuhan rimang lir
        lena tanpa kanin, O . . . .

4. Pathet Sendhon Abimanyu

    a. Elayana mati-mati wruha met wilasa, O . . . , O . . . , manglana
        mangapitira, O . . . , O . . . , gendhing Marioneng tambane si

jaka lara, lir thathit ing mandrakini, O . . . , ya nontona jaka
layar, mbang sri gadhing melathi lan kemuning, O . . . ,
O . . . , (dhodhogan leading to *Ayak-ayakan*, pathet sanga.)

[The text is derived from *Arjuna Wiwāha*, *kakawin*, canto IV,
verse 4 (Poerbatjaraka 1926:19), and is in the *basonta tilaka*
meter.]

b. Sigra lajeng lampahira, O . . . , O . . . , Nata ririh ginem
samargi-margi, O . . . , O . . . , mamikiri alus ngayem-ayem
ing driya, anglalembut sabarang pratingkah kang wus, O . . . ,
sadaya mawarna marta, mangkana ingkang winarni, O . . . ,
O . . . , (dhodhogan leading to *Ayak-ayakan*, sléndro pathet
sanga).

5. Ada-ada Greget Saut Sanga

a. Buta Pandhawa tata gati wisaya, indri yaksa sara maruta,
O . . . , pawana bana margana, samirana warayang, panca bayu
wisikan gulingan lima, O . . . .

[This text is derived from *Serat Candra Sangkala*, *kawi miring*,
canto I, verse 5 (Bratakésawa 1928:69-72). The meter is sekar
ageng *kusuma wicitra*.]

b. Ya ta umangsah sagung pra raja, sawadya sareng tempuh prang,
O . . . , ditya bareng gumregut, campuh mungsuh lan rowang,
mangsah athadah lwir bumi tangkep, O . . . .

c. Yaksa mangsah anggro galak lwir sardula, mamangsa gumregut,
O . . . , mangsah amangungkih, gumuruh surak, umung kang gubar
béri, swara mawurahan kadya rug gumuntur, O . . . .

d. Kadya rug gunturing wukir, bumi prakempa gora réh manengkeri,
O . . . , pamuking kang bala, maselur liweran mawor mawuru
getih, wus kathah kang pejah prajurit lan pra dipatya,
O . . . .

III. Laras Sléndro Pathet Manyura

1. Pathet Manyura Wantah

Mawéh ascarya langen isining wanadri, mulat salwiring tuwuh
kang arebut mangsa, O . . . , mawantu tumuruning riris,
O . . . , mekaring sarwa puspita, mamrihira sang bremara ring

sari, O . . . , miwah swaraning kukila kang munggwing mandéra
raras rinungu, O . . . .

[See additional text for Pathet Sanga Ngelik, above.]

2. Pathet Manyura Jugag

   a. Mulat mara sang Arjuna semu kamanusan, kasrepan ri tingkah ing
      mungsuhniran, O . . . , padha kadang taya mwang wanèha,
      O . . . .

      [See additional text for Pathet Sanga Jugag, above.]

   b. Lengleng umyat para sura marang, para waranggana patrapnya kang
      busana, O . . . , mangu-mangu ing tyas tumonton srining
      kalangyan, O . . . .

3. Ada-ada Greget Saut Manyura

   a. Sangsaya sru agalak ngamuk mrawasa, muntap krodha ngajrihi,
      O . . . , lir handaka sasra, angun-angun kruraya, asrèng
      asirung nétyandik, O . . . .

   b. Pinarbutan sira Arya Kumbakarna, déning pra wanara, samya
      ngarutug watu wukir, myang palu tal andugang andhupak,
      O . . . .

4. Ada-ada Greget Saut Manyura Jugag

   a. Korawa suka myat samya mangsah ngebyuki, bala Pandhawa panggah
      nanging kèh mati, O . . . .

   b. Gègèr kang bala Korawa déning bala Wiratha pupulih, sakethi
      pareng ngamuk mangkap kosik kahambah, O . . . .

   c. Jumangkah anggro susumbar lindhu geter kang bumi gonjing,
      gumaludhug guntur ketug gora rèh gara-gara, O . . . .

      [This text is the same as that for Ada-ada Greget Saut Girisa
      Jugag, laras sléndro pathet nem, above, no. A.4.]

   d. Kang nétya ngatirah andik jaja bang mawinga-winga wengis, duka
      yayah sinipi kumedhut padoning lathi, O . . . .

5. Sendhon Kagok Katanon

   a. O . . . , Dhuh Yana, jambu wana, kekapa munggwing dirada, babo
      babo, dhuh Yana kapok mara amitra wong kang tan lana.

b. Dhuh, dhuh, dhuh, dhuh, Yana sun anembang, temanten anyar, sing
    lanang wis brahi, sing wadon durung brahi, dhuh Yana, lagi
    cedhak, maratuwa nyela-nyela.

In addition, there are other, similar texts taken from various
literary sources. One can also compose one's own texts, utilizing new
material, as long as they are appropriate to the situation.

Selections from Oral and Written Tests
for the Student Dhalang[16]

Answers:

1. "Suluk," or "sulukan," can be defined as the *tetembangan* [poetry] that
    the dhalang sings when performing a wayang.

    The sulukan of the dhalang create a unified decorative effect and
    evoke images and moods of the story.

    Inherent in the word "suluk" are concepts of education, guidance
    in the attainment of perfection and completeness, wisdom of the
    venerated elders, and mysticism. This is so because the texts used in
    the dhalang's songs often include many words referring to instruction
    in mysticism, wisdom of the venerated elders, and guidance for the
    attainment of perfection and completeness.

    There are also scholars who explain the word "suluk" by using
    jarwa dhosok [folk etymology]. They split the word into *su* and *luk*.
    Thus, "suluk" means the *lak-luk*, or wilet, of a melody whose beauty is
    striking [*su* 'good'].

2. There are three types of sulukan: (a) pathet, (b) sendhon, and
    (c) ada-ada.

    a. The word "pathet" means 'proper and fitting' (*patut*),
        literally, 'to be suited', 'to be shaped', 'to belong in one's
        own group'. The word "pathet" also means 'to be restrained',
        'to be controlled', 'to be stopped', 'to be prevented from
        progressing beyond a certain limit'. Pathet[an] indicates the
        limited range of pitches within a given laras of a gamelan.
        Pathet[an] provide a feeling of contentment, peacefulness, and
        calmness. Pathetan are accompanied by the following
        instruments: (1) rebab, (2) gender, (3) gambang, (4) suling,

in addition to kenong, kempul, gong, and kendhang, which are performed in suitable fashion.

b.   The word "sendhon" comes from the root *sendhu* which means 'to nudge', 'to interrupt', 'to break continuity'. Sendhon are used to convey feelings of bewilderment, doubt, hesitation, reluctance, and so forth. Sendhon are accompanied by the following instruments: (1) gendèr, (2) gambang, (3) suling, in addition to kenong, kempul, gong, and kendhang, which are performed in suitable fashion.

c.   The word "ada-ada" means *adeg-adeg* ['a type of punctuation' or 'a door frame'], 'a support', 'root or base', 'stiffness', 'tension', and so forth. As examples, "*idep mangada-ada,*" which means 'the eyelashes standing tense and stiff', or "*ada-ada nyambut damel,*" which means 'a plan for initiating a project'.

Ada-ada are used for situations that are tense, unbending, firm, angry, fast-moving, full of energy, and so forth. Thus, ada-ada must be accompanied by soft dhodhogan (*tetegan*), like water dripping rather quickly, so as to produce an atmosphere of excitement. Ada-ada are accompanied by the following instruments: gendèr, kenong, kempul, gong, and kendhang, which are performed in suitable fashion.

It should be noted here that the kenong, kempul, gong, and kendhang are additional instruments. Their use in ada-ada is not essential, but preferable, because when used properly they add delight, beauty, charm, harmony, and enjoyment for the listener.

3.   Pathetan in laras sléndro can be divided into three groups: (a) pathet nem, (b) pathet sanga, (c) pathet manyura.

   a. Pathet nem is located in the low register.

   b. Pathet sanga is located in the middle register.

   c. Pathet manyura is located in the high register.

An all-day or all-night performance of wayang kulit purwa lasts, at the longest, for nine hours (beginning around nine in the morning or evening and ending around six in the morning or evening). The following is a guide to the times [of the pathet in a wayang]:

a. Pathet nem occurs from around nine o'clock to around twelve o'clock.

b. Pathet sanga occurs from around twelve o'clock to around three o'clock.

c. Pathet manyura occurs from around three o'clock to six o'clock for both day and night performances.

4. According to ancient rules, the gendhing heard during the *jejer* [first audience scene] or other scenes [*adegan*] of a wayang kulit are fixed and suited to the personalities of the puppets and to the situations shown on the screen.

a. The jejer in the kingdom of the gods (*Kahyangan*), or in the kingdom of Ngamarta, must be accompanied by Gendhing *Kawit*, minggah Ladrang *Kawit*, laras sléndro pathet manyura.

Gendhing *Kawit* not only complements the mood of the scene, but also indicates the idea of beginning or origin (*kawitan/wiwitan*). Thus, the origin of all creatures can ultimately be traced to the gods in Kahyangan, and the first kingdom of the kings of Pandhawa blood is Ngamarta.

b. Gendhing *Kabor*, minggah Ladrang *Krawitan*, laras sléndro pathet nem, is used only in the first jejer for King Suyudana of Ngastina.

In addition to complementing the mood of the scene, Gendhing *Kabor* conveys the meaning of invalidity or failure (*bobor*), haziness or vagueness (*kabur*), and failure to solidify [of a liquid] (*kabor*). Thus, Gendhing *Kabor* reflects the personalities of King Suyudana and the Korawas as indecisive, insipid, and ineffectual.

c. Gendhing *Krawitan*, minggah Ladrang *Krawitan*, laras sléndro pathet nem, is heard during the first jejer in any place except the kingdom of the gods, the kingdom of Ngamarta, or the kingdom of Ngastina when King Suyudana is ruling.

Gendhing *Krawitan* conveys a mood of refinement, melancholy, beauty, and tranquility. Thus, when played in the first scene, it is suitable for such countries as Dwarawati, Mandura, Mandraka, Ngastina (when not ruled by King Suyudana), Kumbina, Pancalaradya, and so forth.

In wayang kulit purwa, ogre kings or kingdoms that are considered foreign cannot be shown in the first jejer, because these kings and kingdoms are not regarded as models of good behavior or as religious leaders.

5. The dhalang's speaking techniques can be divided into three types: (a) *janturan*, (b) *carita* or *pocapan*, and (c) *antawacana*.

   a. "*Janturan*" is narration of action accompanied by *sirepan* [soft playing] of the gamelan. Therefore, the sound of the janturan must be in accord with the laras, lagu, and wilet of the gamelan. Every time the topic of narration changes, the lagu of the speech should also change, to conform with that topic of narration.

   b. "*Carita*" refers to the dhalang's narration spoken without gamelan accompaniment. If, however, the narration describes a very emotional scene, it can be accompanied by strong and clear dhodhogan on the puppet box, and by a gendèr playing *grimingan* in the ada-ada style. Pocapan, or *kocapan*, is the same as carita.

   c. "*Antawacana*" refers to the specific speaking style associated with each puppet. In addition to fitting each character with a properly high or low, heavy or light voice, the dhalang must attune his voice to the gendèr. Then, when he wants to sing suluk, his singing will not be out of tune or tonally incongruous.

   According to established practice, antawacana must be in accord with the different emotions, moods, and facial features of the characters.

   For example:

   When King Kresna appears in the first jejer, his voice is low, frequently sounding pitch 6. But, when King Kresna appears in pathet sanga and pathet manyura, his voice is high-pitched like the voice of Samba.

   The voices of Arjuna, Kamajaya, and others like them are like King Kresna's voic in the first jejer, but lighter, slower, smoother, and calmer.

The voices of Abimanyu and other *bambangan* [satriya who are born in the mountains] whose faces are black, are similar to Arjuna's voice, but lighter and higher.

The voices of Irawan and other bambangan whose faces are white, are like Abimanyu's voice, but have a more floating quality.

King Yudhistira's voice is like Arjuna's voice, but also has a floating quality.

King Salya, King Abiyasa, Drupada, Matswapati, Bismaka, Basudéwa, Dasarata, Bathara Indra, and others like them have voices in the middle range intoned to pitch 2 of the gendèr. Their speech is deliberate and clearly enunciated, the words sounding slow and heavy with frequent pauses. In a happy, startled, or angry mood, however, these characters speak faster and in a higher pitch.

Wrekudara's speech is low, steady, straightforward, and stiff, without any upward intonation. His voice is intoned to pitch 5 of the gendèr.

The voices of Gathutkaca, Antaréja, Antaséna, and others like them are like Wrekudara's voice, but not as stiff and steady.

Satyaki's speech is like Gathutkaca's, but smoother and somewhat long-winded.

Patih [chief minister] Udawa, Prabowo, Tuhayata, Jayatilaras, Kartamarma, Jayadrata, Séta, Utara, Wirasangka [Wratsangka], Ugraséna, Sangasanga, Wisatha, Jaladara, Durgandana, and others of their type have voices like Satyaki's voice, but not as heavy. All of these voices are intoned to pitch 6 of the gendèr.

King Duryudana's voice is like Gathutkaca's, but it is characterized by long, tense shrieks. If King Duryudana is startled, excited, or angry, his voice is higher-pitched.

King Baladéwa's voice is intoned to pitch 6 of the gendèr. His speech can become stern and staccato, but it also has a tender and relaxed quality. If King Baladéwa is startled, excited, or angry, he talks nonstop, stuttering frequently.

King Boma, Kangsa, Kéncakarupa, Rupakénca, Supala, and others of their kind have voices like Baladéwa. But their voices are more severe, loud, harsh, stern, and snarling. If startled or angry, these characters speak louder than does Baladéwa, but they do not stutter.

King Dasamuka's voice is like Boma's voice, but harsher, with louder and longer outbursts.

Samba, Satyaka, Drestadyemna, Rukmara, Rukmarata, refined-looking foreign kings, and other satriya of the proud type have high, arrogant voices intoned to pitch 6 of the gendèr.

Ogre kings and large ogres have low and nasal voices which come from the diaphragm. They speak rather tiresomely, at great length. Their voices are intoned to pitch 5 of the gendèr.

The ogre Pragalba and others of that type have voices like ogre kings' voices, but higher-pitched. Their voices seem to seep out of them [like escaping air]. They do not speak at such great length as the ogre kings.

The ogre Cakil has high-pitched, very rapid speech, which pours out as long, continuous, loud sounds punctuated by jerking movements. His speech is intoned to laras barang miring.

The voices of the ogre Kobis and the ogre Galiyuk are odd, out of tune, and nasal, like a person with a cold. Their shrieking is intoned to pitch 6 of the gendèr.

The ogre Térong, with his huge nose, has an exceedingly nasal voice.

Togog's voice is deep, loud, and rather nasal. He hums and mumbles as he talks.

Sarahita's high-pitched voice is marred by speech defects, odd deviations from the norm, and a rapid stammer. He often speaks in languages other than Javanese.

Semar speaks with his head raised and his speech is light but clear. It is characterized by rising shouts and noisy snickering. His speech is intoned to pitch 5 of the gendèr.

ted.   Due to
turned and
                              ce seems to come from the lower part of his
                              always roll his r's properly. He
                              nd grumbles.

puffy
ch is
nd demanding.
                              ech is moderate and easy-going and he laughs
                              he feels like it. His upper lip overhangs
                              ng in blowing sounds in his speech.
the ogre
dd.
                              the Gembor wanda,[17] seems to spout in a deep
                              from the back of his throat. He cannot roll
e most
classified
l and vocal
                              ech is awkward, ingenuous, and humorous. In
                              Bagong has a higher-pitched voice. He is
                              rd, simple-minded, and funny.

r almost the
uppet is
et is
than
is lower
speaks in
rth.
                              urna also has a high-pitched voice that is
                              sudden, bizarre shrieking. His speech is
                              ear and he is full of devious schemes.

                              aradha's voice is like Durna's, but his speech
                              He talks as if he has a cold.

pes:
                              ngkuni has a medium-pitched voice that is slow,
                              irited. He sounds as if he is constantly trying
                              reath--like a starving man.

amba
umètès
                              padi, Sumbadra, Kunthi Talibranta, and all the
                              characters whose faces are black-colored and
                              ther high voices that are intoned to pitch 2 of
                              Their speech is slow, patient, refined, and

unds'], or
boo as a
and (vi)
                              tisundari, Leksmanawati, and all other females
                              are calm and white-colored, have higher voices
                              ces of Dèwi Drupadi and the others like her.

at is
                              rikandhi, Banowati, Mustakawèni, Bathari Ratih,
                              f the same type have high voices like Drupadi's,
                              eak more quickly, sweetly, and coquettishly.

                              Rarasati, Nyai Sagopi, and other females whose
                              ither white or black, and with an aggressive
n in a   ize, have voices like that of Dèwi Srikandhi, but
eling   more humble.

Cangik's speech is high-pitched and protra
old age, she has a speech defect. Her head is u
she is still sexually energetic.

Limbuk has a low voice, which emanates fror
cheeks, and a distorted, pointed mouth. Her spee
tiresomely prolonged, and she is hard to please a

Bathara Yamadipati's speech is like that of
Pragalba, but slower, clearer, rather nasal, and

In sum, this describes the antawacana of the
important puppets. The rest of the puppets can be
with the above-mentioned types in terms of physica
characteristics.

When puppets whose antawacana are the same o
same are conversing, the elder or higher-ranking p
given a lower voice in order to clarify which pupp
speaking. For example, Wrekudara's voice is lower
Gathutkaca's or Antaréja's voices. Arjuna's voice
than Abimanyu's or others like him. Dèwi Srikandhi
a lower voice than does Dèwi Mustakawèni, and so fo

6. The dhalang's cues to the gamelan musicians are of three ty
    (a) *dhodhogan* or *kepyakan*, (b) movements of the puppets, an
    (c) verbal cues.

    a. There are six types of dhodhogan or kepyakan: (i)
        ['single']; (ii) *rangkep* ['double']; (iii) *ambanyu*
        ['like the sound of water dripping']; (iv) *geter*
        ['quivering'], *angganter* ['making loud and steady so
        nitir ['constantly beating a hollowed-out log or ban
        signal']; (v) *singgetan* ['boundary' or 'division'];
        tungkakan ['kicking with the heel'].

        i.   *Dhodhogan lamba* creates an atmosphere or wirama t
             peaceful, slow, and soothing.

        ii. *Dhodhogan rangkep* creates an atmosphere of energy,
             excitement, haste, and hurriedness.

        iii. *Dhodhogan ambanyu tùmètès* is like the sound of rai
             light sprinkle, slow but constant, and creates a f
             that a change of mood [is about to occur].

iv. *Dhodhogan geter* creates an atmosphere of energy, noise,
     passion, anger, and haste.

v.   *Dhodhogan singgetan* is the name of both the dhodhogan
     "dherudhug" sound [produced by a triple rap on the puppet
     box], and the kepyakan "cereceg" sound [produced by a
     triple rap on the kepyak]. It is used to separate one mood
     from another.

vi. *Dhodhogan tungkakan* refers to dhodhogan or kepyakan that
     interrupts or pushes the wirama and is used to speed up or
     slow down the wirama of the gamelan, and to signal the
     suwuk [conclusion] of a piece.

Dhodhogan can be executed by the hand or foot of the dhalang.
The cempala is grasped by the foot [or held in the hand].
Soft dhodhogan that does not drown out the dhalang's narration
is called "tetegan."

Kepyakan is usually used in the same way as dhodhogan, but
dhodhogan is more appropriate as a signal to the gamelan
musicians, since kepyakan produces a louder and more crashing
sound.

b.   The dhalang cues the musicians by moving the puppets in
     various ways. For example:

i.   In the scene after the *kapalan* scene, when the satriya
     mount their horses to go to another land, the satriya are
     followed by the *prampogan* [puppet depicting a marching
     army], which is moved from right to left several times.
     The placement of the gunungan in the higher banana log on
     the left side is a cue to the musicians to increase their
     tempo suddenly when playing srepegan. Then, the prampogan
     is placed in the upper banana log on the right side.
     Dhodhogan and kepyakan bring the srepegan to an end with a
     suwuk gropak [accelerated ending] or *sesegan*.

         The signal indicates that the progress of the army,
     represented by the prampogan puppet, is halted, hindered
     from going further, and forced to stop suddenly. Thus, the
     srepegan is to end in a suwuk gropak.

ii. During the scene of the prang ampyak, the soldiers of the
     army, represented by the prampogan puppet, work together to

clear a path through the forest. The penetration of the
prampogan into the gunungan [symbolizing the forest] is one
of the signs to the musicians to suddenly increase the
tempo of srepegan. This signal also indicates that the job
of the prampogan is finished--the forest barricade is
penetrated.

iii. After the prang ampyak, the gunungan flutters across the
screen, moving in a broad sweep from right to left a few
times. When the gunungan is raised up high and is placed
in the middle of the screen, leaning to the right a little,
this is the cue for the suwuk of srepegan. This cue, in
which the gunungan is raised and inclined to the dhalang's
right (as it would be when placed in the log), indicates
that the prang ampyak is over and that srepegan should be
concluded.

Indeed, srepegan must end in that way, because
presently the gunungan will be used again. As a suluk is
sung, the gunungan flutters in a broad, slow sweep across
the screen moving from right to left a few times. The
movements of the gunungan represent dust blowing, branches
of trees hanging by threads, and earth and rocks that have
fallen or been chipped away--all of this being cleaned up
by the soldiers.

iv. During the *prang gagal* or *prang simpangan*, after Kala
Pragalba is defeated by Patih Udawa, Kala Pragalba escapes
by taking a fork in the road. Then the tempo of srepegan
is increasingly accelerated. Patih Udawa chases Kala
Pragalba across the screen from right to left a few times.
Patih Udawa then stops in the middle of the screen, his
front arm hanging loose. This is the cue for srepegan to
change to a slow tempo, hence ayak-ayakan. When Patih
Udawa slows down and ceases his pursuit of Kala Pragalba,
this is the cue that the music must no longer be tense, but
slow and soft. Thus, srepegan changes to ayak-ayakan.

v. In the scenes of Wrekudara's leaping, he leaps as if he is
flying. This is accompanied by sampak. After Wrekudara
has leapt repeatedly, his front arm is placed in a loose
hanging position, then rotated and raised high and stiff.

Then he starts walking rapidly. This is the cue that the tempo of sampak must accelerate. The action indicates that he has, or has almost, arrived at his destination; his trip is almost completed. Therefore, the tempo of srepegan should accelerate and the piece end quickly.

In order to save time after ending a piece, the dhalang can immediately request another piece with a different melody and wirama by cueing the musicians. For example, after the suwuk of srepegan or sampak, a dhodhogan of five slow raps can be played, resulting in a direct transition from srepegan or sampak to ayak-ayakan.

c. The dhalang's utterances that are verbal cues to the musicians are of several types:

i. Kombangan, long-held tones, sung to "o" or "e," which follow the melody and wirama played by the gamelan. After a dhalang has finished the janturan [narration of an important scene, intoned to background music played softly], kombangan is heard. This is a sign to the musicians that the janturan is finished, and, therefore, they should no longer play softly (*sirep*).

ii. If, in the middle of a gendhing, ayak-ayakan, srepegan, or sampak, the dhalang's hands are both at work and he is unable to give a clear signal, or the signal is not heard by the musicians, then the dhalang often will utter the words, "wau ta," as a request to the musicians to play softly (sirep), stop, and so forth.

iii. In order to request a gendhing, a dhalang can sing a *buka celuk*, or vocal buka.

As examples:

```
                                    G
6   1   2   3   2 · 2   1   6   1   3   1   2
·               ·
Sam-pun mi-yos wa-hu-ta Sri Na-ra  Na-ta
['A noble king goes forth']
```

which is followed by a gendhing in laras sléndro pathet manyura. Or,

$$\overset{\text{G}}{3 \quad 1 \quad 3 \quad 2 \quad \underset{\cdot}{5} \quad \underset{\cdot}{6} \quad 1 \quad 2 \quad 1 \quad \underset{\cdot}{6} \quad \underset{\cdot}{4} \quad \acute{5}}$$

Tan-dya bi-dhal gu-mu-ruh sa-king na-ga-ra
['Like thunder (they) quickly depart the country']

followed by Lancaran *Tropong Bang*, laras pélog pathet nem.

iv.   In addition to buka celuk, *wangsalan* [riddles] are
      frequently used to request certain gendhing.

For example:

"*Wus nitèni konduring Nata*" ['the King's return has been
noted'] refers to Gendhing *Titi Pati* [*nitèni* 'observed'
from the root *titi*; also, *titi* 'time'; *pati* 'death' or
'king'], laras sléndro pathet nem.

"*Lir surya kalingan méga*" ['like the sun obscured by
clouds'] refers to Ladrang *Remeng* ['cloudy'], laras sléndro
pathet nem.

"*Kawentar yèn mengku karya*" ['it is known that they are
engaged in an important task'] refers to Gendhing *Kedhaton
Bentar* [*kedhaton* 'palace'; *bentar* 'split in two' (rhymes
with kawentar)], laras sléndro pathet nem.

"*Pindha riris wanci sonten*" ['like a misty rain in the late
afternoon'] refers to Gendhing *Udan Soré* [*udan* 'rain'; *soré*
'late afternoon'], laras sléndro pathet nem.

"*Pindha peksi kineplokan*" ['like a bird scared away by
clapping'] refers to Ladrang *Peksi Kuwung* ['peacock'],
laras sléndro pathet nem.

"*Pindha liman nèng madyaning paprangan*" ['like an elephant
in the middle of a battlefield'] refers to Ladrang *Dirata
Met* [*dirata/dirada* 'elephant'; *meta* 'angry'], laras sléndro
pathet nem.

"*Pindha kinembong bojaning temantèn*" ['like an invitation
to partake of a wedding feast'] refers to Gendhing *Majemuk*
['many people eating a ritual meal together'], laras
sléndro pathet nem.

"*Gora swaraning akasa*" ['a loud sound from the skies']
refers to Gendhing *Guntur* ['thunder'], laras sléndro pathet
nem.

"*Netepaké jamangé kaya jebol-jebola*" ['he adjusts his headband so vigorously, the ties are about to snap'] refers to Ladrang *Bedhat* ['the breaking of ties, strings'], laras sléndro pathet nem.

"*Pindha manyar sasra bareng aneba*" ['like a thousand *manyar* birds flocking together'] refers to Lancaran *Manyar Sèwu* [*manyar* 'a kind of bird'; *sèwu* 'one thousand'], laras sléndro pathet nem.

"*Pindha maésa binereg*" ['like herded water buffaloes'] refers to Lancaran *Kebo Giro* [*kebo* 'water buffalo'; *giro* 'angry'], laras sléndro pathet sanga.

"*Pindha sekar menur dadu*" / "*Pindha sekar gambir mangambar*" ['like a pink jasmine flower' / 'like a fragrant *gambir* flower'] refers to Gendhing *Gambir Sawit* [*gambir* 'flowers used for weddings'; *sawit* 'a kind of batik pattern worn by both bride and groom'], laras sléndro pathet sanga.

"*Ngambar gandaning kusuma*" ['the fragrance of flowers spreading everywhere'] refers to Gendhing *Ganda Kusuma* [*ganda* 'fragrant'; *kusuma* 'flower'], laras sléndro pathet sanga.

"*Ngencengi busanané*" ['straightening or tightening one's clothing'] refers to Ladrang *Babat Kenceng* [*babat* 'membrane'; *kenceng* 'tight'], laras sléndro pathet sanga.

"*Kadya pandam kéntir ing warih*" ['like a light drifting over water'] refers to Gendhing *Damar Kèli* [*damar* 'light'; *kèli* 'drifting'], laras sléndro pathet manyura.

"*Lir sabdaning kukila*" ['like the voice of a bird'] refers to Ladrang *Kandha Manyura* [*kandha* 'voice', 'speech'; *manyura* 'peacock'], laras sléndro pathet manyura.

"*Pindha peksi munggwing gantangan*" ['like a bird hanging in a high cage'] refers to Gendhing *Perkutut Manggung* [*perkutut* 'peacock'; *manggung* 'cooing constantly'], laras sléndro pathet manyura.

"*Pindha kenya tinari krama*" ['like a young girl who has been proposed to'] refers to Gendhing *Montro* ['flower of the cucumber'; or *montro-montro*, 'a frown'], laras sléndro pathet manyura.[18]

"*Ing tyas kadya ginonjing*" ['trembling in his heart']
refers to Ladrang *Ginonjing* ['shaken'], laras slendro
pathet manyura.

"*Katon mamanising praja/wadana*" ['the beauty of her face is
evident'] refers to Ladrang *Manis* ['sweet' or 'beautiful'],
laras slendro pathet manyura.

"*Pating kendharah kuncane*" / "*Pating kadhedher kuncane*"
['with one's clothing dragging on the ground' / 'the folds
of his ceremonial sarong were open and disheveled'] refers
to Ladrang *Moncer* ['a hanging ornament'], laras slendro
pathet manyura.

"*Kadya mliwis lumakweng toya*" / "*Kadya kumricik swabawane*"
['like wild ducks waddling in water' / 'like the sound of
falling water'] refers to Ladrang *Ricik-ricik* ['constantly
raining'; also known as Ladrang *Mliwis* ('wild duck')],
laras slendro pathet manyura.

"*Waktune mangsa kasanga*" / "*Samya reren sangandhaping
randhu wana jajar sanga*" ['during the ninth month' /
'together they rest under nine rows of forest kapok trees']
indicates the transition from the pathet nem period to the
pathet sanga period of the wayang.

"*Lamat-lamat swaraning kukila manyura*" ['the sounds of the
peacock are faintly heard'] indicates the transition from
the pathet sanga period to the pathet manyura period of the
wayang.[19]

7. In former times, only a few stories were used for wayang kulit purwa,
    and, since there were also only a few dhalang, it was easy to
    differentiate the *pakem* stories from the *carangan* stories.

    a. The pakem stories, forming the basic repertoire, consist of
        selections from the *Mahābhārata*, *Pustaka Raja* [by R. Ng.
        Ranggawarsita, composed late nineteenth century], *Ramāyana*,
        Arjuna Sasra [*Bau*], and so forth. The stories include, among
        others, "Rabinipun Parasara" ['The marriage of Parasara'],
        "Pandhawa Dhadhu" ['The Pandhawa play at dice'], "Bale Sigala-
        gala" ['The house of resin'], "Jagal Bilawa" ['The butcher
        Bilawa'], "Brata Yuda" ['The great war'], "Pejahipun Sumantri"
        ['The death of Sumantri'], "Anoman Duta" ['Anoman as envoy'],
        and so forth.

b. The carangan stories are branch or subsidiary stories stemming
    from the basic repertoire, including, among others, such
    stories as "Partadéwa," "Makutha Rama" ['The crown of Rama'],
    "Tuhu Wasésa," "Rama Nitis" ['The reincarnation of Rama'], and
    so forth.

c. The carangan dhinapur stories are selections taken from other
    repertoires that have been adapted to wayang kulit purwa.
    They include such stories as "Kunjarakarna" [the name of a
    demon] from the *Budha Carita*[20] cycle; "Semar Ambarang Jantur"
    [Semar as itinerant storyteller], also known as "Karta Wiyoga
    Maling" [Karta Wiyoga as thief] from the wayang gedhog cycle;
    "Bancak Dhoyok Ambarang Jantur" [Bancak and Dhoyok as
    itinerant storytellers], "Sekar Sumarsana Wilis" [Green
    sumarsana flower], from the wayang gedhog cycle of *Panji
    Angreni*, and so forth.

The three types of stories are now very difficult to differentiate
because there are so many newly created stories and many basic stories
that have been altered. In the words of the old saying, "a dhalang is
never short of stories." Nevertheless, faint traces [of either a
pakem or a carangan story] are discernible if one looks carefully.

8. In a wayang performance, the gunungan puppet is used to represent a
mountain, a log, a large tree, a gate, a house, the earth, water,
wind, fire, clouds, and so forth.

   In addition, the gunungan is also used to separate one scene from
another. For example, after the scene in the kingdom of Ngastina, the
Korawa depart for another place. The placement of the gunungan in the
middle of the screen separates that scene from the next.

   According to standard practice, the conventions for placing the
gunungan in the banana log, from the time before the wayang kulit
begins to the time after the wayang ends, are as follows:

a. Before the wayang begins, the gunungan is placed straight up
    in the higher log, in the middle of the screen.

b. (1) During the pathet nem section, the gunungan is placed in
        the middle of the screen in the lower log, inclining to
        the dhalang's right at an angle of about 110 degrees.

   (2) During the pathet sanga section, the gunungan is placed
        straight up in the lower log, in the middle of the screen.

(3) During the pathet manyura section, the gunungan is placed in the middle of the screen in the lower log, inclining to the dhalang's left at an angle of about 110 degrees.

c. When the wayang is finished, the gunungan is placed straight up in the higher log again, in the middle of the screen, covering the puppets of the last scene.

Conventions governing the various positions of the gunungan, as described above, have the following aims: (1) to make the technique of puppetry easy to execute, beautiful, and practical; (2) to make the positions of the gunungan representative of universal events; and (3) to illustrate symbolically a profound philosophy. This is explained below.

d. Before the wayang kulit has begun, the gunungan is placed straight up in the higher log, in the middle of the screen. Aside from making the "stage" more beautiful and more pleasing, the gunungun makes it seem not so bare, but decorated. The position of the gunungan also symbolizes the fact that, before the creatures of the world were created and before the existence of the sphere of desire, the universe was empty, like the skies. But, in spite of that emptiness, in the innermost depths of the empty world and skies there was actually a center of activity. This center, upright and just, located above everything else, eternally operates in accordance with the laws of destiny. This is the significance of the positioning of the gunungan before the wayang performance has begun, upright in the higher log, in the middle of the screen, which is otherwise still, empty, and void.

e. After the wayang kulit has started--that is, when there is activity and movement--the gunungan is placed in the lower log, in the middle of the screen, leaning to the right in pathet nem, standing upright in pathet sanga, and leaning to the left in pathet manyura. These positions of the gunungan symbolize the progression of the sun--rising in the east, moving to the west, and setting in the western horizon--and the everlasting and uninterrupted occurrence of days and nights. Thus is time created and all the movement and activity that are ruled by time.

A map illustrates the movement of the sun from right to
left. For example, on a map of Java, Surabaya is placed on
the right side representing the east and Jakarta is placed on
the left side representing the west. The sun originates from
the direction of Surabaya and progresses westward toward
Jakarta, that is, from east to west, or from the right side to
the left. Analogously, during a performance of wayang kulit,
the gunungan first inclines to the right; then, as time
progresses, it inclines to the left. In the middle time-
period, the gunungan is upright, like the sun directly
overhead in the middle of the sky. Then it moves to the left,
setting on the left side--that is, on the western horizon.

Also, the positions of the gunungan during a wayang kulit
symbolize a philosophy of being. There are three realms
called "Triloka" or "Tribuwana": (1) the realm that predates
creation and all creatures is called "Guruloka" [place of
Guru, or Śiwa]; (2) the realm of creation, of creatures and
sounds, the sphere of desires, that is, the earth (*arcapada*),
is called "Janaloka" [place of men]; (3) the realm that
follows all creation, when all creatures are dead and have
vanished from the earthly world--that is, the realm of spirits
or of gods--is called "Indraloka" [place of Indra].

Moreover, [the three placements of the gunungan] also
remind us that there are three great powers, or forces, that
intertwine to become one, called "Trimurti": (1) Sang Hyang
Brahma, whose power it is to bring life to all creatures and
things; (2) Sang Hyang Wisnu, who is empowered to protect,
care for, and maintain all things; and (3) Sang Hyang Śiwa,
whose power it is to destroy all creation. Gradually, this
belief changed in the minds of some, so that Śiwa became the
Creator, Wisnu the Protector, and Brahma the Destroyer.

Therefore, to symbolize [this trinity of deities], stages
or divisions are grouped in units of three in a wayang
performance. For example, (1) the initial placement of the
gunungan in the higher log, then in the lower log, and finally
in the higher log again, covering the puppets of the last
scene; (2) [the division of the wayang play into three
sections:] pathet nem, pathet sanga, and pathet manyura; and
(3) the practice of removing the gunungan from the higher log

in the beginning of the first scene, then shaking and stopping
it three times.

f.   During pathet nem, the gunungan is placed in the lower log in
the middle of the screen, inclining to the dhalang's
right. When not in use, the gunungan is always stuck on the
right side of the dhalang, not only because this position is
the most practical, but also because the gunungan then covers
the extra puppets on that side. When the gunungan is used to
to indicate a change of scene in the middle of pathet nem, it
is easy for the dhalang to replace it in a position inclining
to his right. Furthermore, the position of the gunungan,
inclining to the dhalang's right, is suitable for pathet nem
in which everything must be clearly enunciated, slow, orderly,
and beautiful.[21]

In addition, this placement of the gunungan symbolizes
and represents the notion that during the period from birth to
adulthood, or from childhood to approximately twenty-five
years in an individual's life, there arises a personal concern
with worldly matters. Everything that [the young person] sees
he covets, desires, and considers important (*nengenaken*)--
hence, the symbolism of the gunungan at the beginning of the
play (i.e., in pathet nem) being placed to the right (*tengen*)
of the dhalang.

When one has reached adulthood--the period from about age
twenty-five to fifty years--one begins to form
interpretations, ideals, and opinions that are upright
(*jejeg*), just, and constant. Although still recognizing the
importance of worldly matters, one now exercises adult
judgments, based on experience and study. As a symbol of that
idea, the gunungan is placed straight up (*jejeg*) in the log
during the middle of the play--that is, representing the
middle period of one's life--during pathet sanga.

When one has become old--that is, the period from around
age fifty until one's death--one begins to set aside
(*ngiwakaken*, [literally 'to set on the left side']) worldly
matters. Due to the effects of old age, such as ever
decreasing strength, shortness of breath, loss of teeth,
failing eyesight, wrinkled skin, and so forth, one no longer
enjoys things. One no longer places an important value on

things. In fact, it is said that when one becomes very old, one yearns for death. Not only is one not concerned with this world, one actually wants to leave it behind. This is symbolized by the gunungan at the end of the play, during pathet manyura, when it is inclining to the dhalang's left.

g. When a person dies, only his corporeal body remains, because the refined and pure part, called the "spirit" (*nyawa*) or "soul" (*sukma*), has already returned to nothingness. That is, one can no longer be seen, or sensed, by mortals. The spirit originates from nothingness and returns to nothingness. That is, the spirit originates in that which (*Ingkang*) creates life and returns to it. Thus, only the corporeal body remains to be destroyed by burial, cremation, abandonment to the elements, or other means of disposal. At the end of a wayang performance, the return of the gunungan to its original position, standing straight up in the higher log in the middle of the screen, is symbolic of this idea. The gunungan covers the bodies of the puppets of the last scene, whose story is now finished, leaving behind only traces of the good and evil doers, the contemptible, the ordinary, and the prominent people of this world. The gunungan is initially placed in the higher log, and later returned to the higher log, just as it comes from nothingness and returns to nothingness.

9. The dhalang must be thoroughly versed in the names of the kings, their wives, noble families, prime ministers, officials, and their subordinates from every kingdom. He must also be familiar with rules [concerning wayang] found in old writings and established pakem. This matter should not be treated carelessly, lest the good name of all dhalangs and the art of wayang kulit itself be damaged.

Some of the names of the kings, their wives, relatives, prime ministers, officials, and so forth, from the time of the Pandhawa and Korawa, are listed below.

a. In the kingdom of Ngastina (Hastina/Gajah Oya), the king is called Prabu Suyudana (Duryudana/Jayapitana/Anggendarisuta/ Kurupati). His beloved queen is Dèwi Banowati whose garden in the palace is called Kadi Lengeng.

They have two children: (1) Raden Laksmana Mandrakumara, crown prince of Ngastina, who lives in the *kasatriyan*

[nobleman's residence] of Saroja Binangun; and (2) the
princess, Dèwi Laksmanawati.

Suyudana's *patih* [prime minister] is his uncle, Patih
Harya Suman (Patih Sangkuni/Sakuni/Sangka-uni), a younger
brother of Dèwi Anggendari of Gandhara. He is the Adipati of
Gandhara and lives in the *kepatihan* [residence of the patih]
of Plasa Jenar.

Prabu Suyudana is the first-born of one hundred children
in the Korawa family. The last-born is a daughter, Dèwi
Drusilawati (Dèwi Drusilah/Dusalah). She marries the king of
Sindura (Sindu/Sindu Kalangan/Bana Keling). The king of Bana
Keling is Prabu Jayadrata (Prabu Sindupati/Sinduraja/
Sindukalangan/Semaniputra/Sapwaniatmaja). In the kingdom of
Ngastina, Prabu Jayadrata uses only the titles "Radèn" or
"Harya."

Those Korawa brothers who are often mentioned or shown on
the screen are, among others: (i) Radèn Dursasana, from the
kasatriyan of Banjar Jungut, who is the king's first younger
brother; (ii) Radèn Durmuka, from the kasatriyan of Sekar
Cindhé; (iii) Radèn Durmagati, from the kasatriyan of Sobrah
Lambangan; (iv) Radèn Kartamarma, from the kasatriyan at Tirta
Tinalang; (v) Radèn Citraksa, from the kasatriyan of Cindhé
Dadu; and (vi) Radèn Citraksi, from the kasatriyan of Cindhé
Biru.

The commanding general of Ngastina, related by marriage
(*paripéan*),[22] is Prabu Karna (Suryaputra/Suryatmaja/Basusèna),
king of Angga (Ngawangga). However, in the kingdom of
Ngastina, he only uses the title "Adipati."

The king's spiritual advisor is Pandhita Durna (Dhang
Hyang Kumbayana), from the shrine or hermitage of Soka Lima.
Pandhita Durna has one child, a son, named Bambang Haswatama,
a nobleman from Padhanyangan. He also serves in the kingdom
of Ngastina as one of the leaders of the army.

b. In the kingdom of Ngamarta (Cintaka Pura/Indra Prastha/Batana
    Kawarsa), the king is Prabu Puntadéwa (Yudhistira/Dwijakangka/
    Darmaraja/Darmakusuma/Darmatanaya/Darmawangsa/Darmaputra/
    Gunatalikrama/Sang Ajatasatru). His queen is Dèwi Kresna

(Dèwi Drupadi). They have one child, a son, named Radèn
Pancawala. In the *Mahābhārata*, Prabu Yudhisthira is said to
have been married also to Retna Dèwika, from the kingdom of
Sibi, who bears him one child, a son, Radèn Yodèya. The
king's patih is Patih Handakasumilir (Patih Tambakganggeng).

Prabu Puntadèwa is the first of the five Pandhawa
brothers: (1) Prabu Puntadèwa; (2) Radèn Wrekudara (Sèna/
Bimasèna/Bratasèna/Kusumayuda/Kusumadilaga/Wayuninda/
Bayutanaya/Judhipati/Gandawastratmaja), of the kasatriyan of
Munggul Pawenang; (3) Radèn Arjuna (Janaka/Pamadi/Margana/
Parta/Palguna/Dananjaya/Indratanaya/Kandhi Wrehatnala/Kirithi/
Kuntadi/Kumbalyali/Kunthiyatmaja/Pandhuputra), of the
kasatriyan of Madukara and the garden retreat called
Madèganda; (4) Radèn Pinten (Radèn Nakula) from the kasatriyan
of Bumi Retawu; and (5) Radèn Tangsen (Radèn Sadèwa) from the
kasatriyan of Sawo Jajar.

c. In the kingdom of Madura, the king is Prabu Baladèwa
(Balarama/Kakrasana/Sangkarsana/Jaladara/Halayuda/Basukiyana/
Kusumawalikita). His queen is Dèwi Irawati. They have one
child, a son, named Radèn Wisatha. Prabu Baladèwa has two
prime ministers, one for court affairs named Patih Prabawa,
and one for affairs outside the court named Patih Pragota.
The king's mount is a white elephant called Kyai Puspa Denta.

d. In the kingdom of Dwarawati (Dwaraka/Narmakodaka), the king is
Prabu Kresna, who may also rightfully be called Bathara
[mythological deity] Kresna (Prabu Arimurti/Wisnumurti/
Danardana/Janardana/Madusudana/Wasudèwaputra/Narayana/
Narasinga/Kèsawa/Padmanaba). He has three queens: (1) Dèwi
Jembawati, daughter of Bagawan [hermit] Kapi Jembawan and Dèwi
Trijatha of the hermitage of Ganda Madana; (2) Dèwi Rukmini,
daughter of Prabu Rukma (Prabu Bismaka) of the kingdom of
Kumbina; (3) Dèwi Satyaboma, daughter of Prabu Satyajit of the
kingdom of Lèsan Pura. Prabu Kresna has three children by
Dèwi Jembawati: (1) Radèn Gunadèwa, whose body is covered with
hair, which explains why [out of shame] he spends his whole
life at the hermitage of Ganda Madana; (2) Radèn Samba (Radèn
Kilatmaka), crown prince of Dwarawati, who lives in the
nobleman's residence of Parang Garudha; (3) Dèwi Titisari, who

eventually marries Bambang Irawan, a son of Radèn Arjuna.
Dèwi Rukmini bears Prabu Kresna one child, Radèn Partajumena,
who lives at the nobleman's residence of Dhadha Paksi. Dèwi
Satyaboma bears Prabu Kresna one child, Radèn Satyaka, who
lives in the nobleman's residence of Tambak Mas. In addition,
as a god, Prabu Kresna receives in marriage Dèwi Pratiwi of
the heavenly kingdom of Éka Pratala, who bears him a son and a
daughter: (1) Harya Sitija (Bambang Sutija), who eventually
becomes king of Traju Trisna (Pratisya/Prasti Tistha), and who
is called Prabu Boma Narakasura; (2) Dèwi Sitisundari, who
eventually marries Radèn Abimanyu. In the carangan story
called "Sukma Ngumbara" ['The Wandering Soul'], Prabu Kresna,
as a result of prayer, receives a child named Dèwi
Kuntharawati, who is married later to Pétruk. Prabu Kresna's
prime minister is Patih Udawa, the son of Demang Sagopa of
Widara Kandhang.

Harya Satyaki, who is the younger brother of Dèwi
Satyaboma, serves in the kingdom of Dwarawati and becomes a
commanding general there. He is also crown prince of Lésan
Pura, and a nobleman from Swala Bumi.

e. The kingdom of Pancala Radya, or Cempala Radya, is ruled by
    Prabu Drupada (Sucitra/Prabu Pancalaraja). His queen is Dèwi
    Gondowati. They have three children: (1) Dèwi Drupadi (Dèwi
    Kresna), who eventually marries Prabu Puntadéwa; (2) Dèwi
    Srikandhi, who eventually marries Radèn Arjuna; and (3) Radèn
    Drestajumna (Trusthajumna), crown prince of the kingdom of
    Pancala. Prabu Drupada's prime minister is Patih Drestakètu
    (Trusthakètu).

f. The kingdom of Mandraka (Madra/Madraka), is ruled by Prabu
    Salya (Salyapati/Narasoma/Somadenta/Mandradipa/Mandrakéswara).
    His queen is Dèwi Satyawati (formerly Éndhang Pujawati), the
    beloved daughter of Bagawan Bagaspati of the hermitage of
    Harga Belah. They have five children: (1) Dèwi Irawati, who
    eventually marries Prabu Baladéwa; (2) Dèwi Surtikanthi, who
    eventually marries Prabu Karna; (3) Dèwi Banowati, who
    eventually marries Prabu Suyudana; (4) Radèn Burisrawa, crown
    prince of Madraka and a nobleman from Cindhé Kembang; and (5)
    Radèn Rukmarata, who lives in the nobleman's residence of
    Tanjung Anom. Prabu Salya's prime minister is Patih Tuhayata.

g. The kingdom of Wiratha (Matswasabha/Matswaloka) is ruled by
Prabu Durgandana (Matswapati/Basuwendra/Wirateswara/
Matswanata). His queen is Dewi Rekathawati (Dewi
Sutiksnawati). They have four children: (1) Raden Seta,
(2) Raden Utara, (3) Raden Wratsangka (Wiratsangka), and
(4) Dewi Utari, who eventually marries Raden Abimanyu and who
bears him a son, Prabu Parikesit of Ngastina. Prabu
Matswasabha's prime minister is Patih Nirbita, son of Raden
Setama and Dewi Kandhini. Raden Setama is the elder brother
of Resi Abiyasa.

h. In the Kadipaten of Ngawangga (i.e., the kingdom of Angga),
Prabu Karna (Suryaputra/Suryatmaja/Jaka Radeya/Basusena)
rules. He serves in the kingdom of Ngastina as commanding
general, with the title Adipati. His queen is Dewi
Surtikanthi. They have two children, a son and a daughter:
(1) Raden Warsakusuma (Warsasena/Karnasuta/Karnatmaja); and
(2) Dewi Karnawati. In the carangan story called "Dewa
Kusuma," Dewi Karnawati is married to Bambang Dewa Kusuma, son
of Raden Arjuna. Prabu Karna's prime minister is Patih
Hadimanggala, son of Demang Pralebda, younger brother of
Demang Antagopa of Widara Kandhang.

10. The word "dhalang" is derived from the syllables *dhang* and *lang*. It
may be explained as follows. "Dhang," or "dhah" [as in *dhang hyang*
or *dhahyang*, titles for priests], is similar to "sang," an honorific
title, as in "sang raja" ['the honored king'], "sang pandhita" ['the
honored priest'], "Dhang Hyang Durna" ['the honored Durna'], and so
on. "Lang" means 'to go away', or 'to leave', as in "ilang," which
indicates wandering about without a clear sense of direction or goal;
"balang," which means 'to be flung away quickly and forcibly, like a
stone that is thrown'; or "kalangan," which means 'to move in
circles'. Thus, the word "dhalang" means an honored person who is
constantly moving [from one place to another] in order to help
whomever may be in need. It also means a savior, a person who can
heal sickness, sadness, or other disturbances by means of exorcism.
He is also one who can summon the images, or *ayang-ayang* ['shadows']
of the spirits, gods, and other noble beings who no longer live on
earth. Indeed, it is in these activities that the wayang performance
has its origins.

Others derive the word "dhalang" by folk etymology (*jarwa dhosok*) from "ngu*dhal*-udhal piwu*lang*" ['to disseminate knowledge'], or from "ngu*dhal*-udhal wayang lu*lang*" ['to spread the art of wayang kulit'].

As the art of the dhalang developed, five types of dhalang came to be distinguished:

a.   The *dhalang sejati* ['pure dhalang'] serves to guard the peace, performs ceremonies that exorcise disturbances, hardship, and suffering, and teaches the art of mysticism, achievement of well-being, and tranquility of heart. He does not covet material payment for his services, but in former times was paid through offerings and the like.

b.   The *dhalang guna* ['powerful dhalang'] serves to disseminate knowledge, teachings, mystical gnosis, and cultural knowledge, aimed at establishing the peace, well-being, nobility, and glory of the community.

c.   The *dhalang wasésa* ['authoritative dhalang'] serves to disseminate information, teachings, and the laws of proper living, aimed at securing tranquility, nobility, and glory based on the authority of society or government.

d.   The *dhalang purba* ['dhalang of antiquity'] serves to provide examples [of good behavior] through his art. By performing he can arouse feelings of harmony in people so that their actions are virtuous and lead to peace, tranquility, and honor.

e.   The *dhalang wikalpa* ['dhalang of doubt/hesitation/confusion'] performs his art solely with a view to personal material gain.

11.   When performing a wayang, a dhalang must exhibit certain personal characteristics, traits, and skills, namely the following five: (a) *gendhung*, (b) *gendheng*, (c) *gendhing*, (d) *gandhang*, (e) *gendhèng*. They are differentiated below.

a.   "*Gendhung*" means 'daring' or 'bold'. When performing a wayang, a dhalang must be bold and confident no matter who is present. He cannot be afraid or timid in front of his audience. For this reason, he must be rich in his understanding of material and spiritual matters, in his skills as a dhalang, and in his knowledge of mysticism, ethics, the laws of the land, spiritual power, and so forth. If the dhalang does not have experience and thorough understanding in these matters, he will feel afraid, awkward, and confused. As a consequence, his performance will clash with the rules of puppetry, resulting in a poor performance drained of vitality. With poor luck, he may even be the victim of a lawsuit or have other major difficulties.

b. *"Gendheng"* means to consider one's own needs, ignoring the needs of others. A person who is gendheng is not deranged, but reflects on his own feelings a good deal. If, in the middle of a performance, the dhalang suddenly starts to think of something else--something other than the wayang performance at hand--he is sure to be careless and become distracted from the wayang.

c. *"Gendhing"* refers to the lagu, irama, and wilet of gamelan music. The dhalang must be highly trained in gamelan music. He must control and guide the musicians and he must accommodate the music to the elements of the wayang: sulukan, kepyakan, dhodhogan, puppet movements, and staging. These elements give the wayang its dignity, harmony, beauty, and inner meaning.

d. *"Gandhang"* means 'a clear and resonant voice', but not an excessively loud one. The speech of a dhalang must be clear, distinct, intelligible, and capable of touching the feelings and emotions of those who are watching and listening.

e. *"Gendhèng"* means 'a protective roof'. The dhalang must be able to shelter and protect the well-being and tranquility of his audience and everyone else, making them feel refreshed, secure, healthy, and whole. It is hoped that the dhalang will contribute to the development of honor, nobility of character, and tranquility in all aspects of life.

12. In former times, the dhalang said prayers while performing a wayang. Thus, he had to memorize prayers of supplication, prayers of worship, and *mantra* [sacred formulas][23] begging for peace and good luck for himself, for those in need, for the entire family who sponsored the wayang performance, and for the audience. He prayed for universal concord, well-being, and tranquility for everyone in the world.

In addition, the dhalang had to be diligent in his practice of asceticism and meditation, because the efficacy and strength of the mantra depend on the depth (or shallowness) of his asceticism and meditation.

In former times, the prayers of supplication, prayers of worship, and mantras of the dhalang were recited in Sanskrit or Old Javanese. Gradually they were changed to modern Javanese or Javanese with Islamic influences. Examples of prayers and mantra, taken from dhalang *primbon* [manuals] that have been preserved, are mentioned below.

   a. For every wayang performance, from the time the dhalang leaves his house to the time the performance begins, between different subjects in the course of the wayang, and until the end of the wayang, the dhalang repeatedly recites the mantra: "Aum awignam astu nama Siddem." "*Aum*" is a reverential name for the Highest Spirit/God. "*A*" means 'no' or 'not'. "*Wigna*" means 'hindrance', 'obstacle', 'trouble', 'disturbance', 'grief'. "*Astu*" is 'to worship' and 'to respect'. "*Nama Siddem*" means 'to the most perfect God'. Thus, the phrase means "Oh, honored and greatest God, may my humble offering of devotion to you meet no hindrance, trouble, or other obstacle. May you provide an easy road for me. May this wish be fulfilled. Amen."

   The Sanskrit language of the above phrase has been gradually changed to "Hong wilahéng mangastawa Siddhem," or "Hong wilahéng sekaring bawana langgeng."

   b. The *Serat Kramaléya*[24] mentions various mantra recited by the dhalang from the time he sits down under the oil lamp until the first scene. Pressing his navel, he recites from memory a Javanese Buddhist mantra requesting power and compassion: "Hong awigenam pranawa, saméh mamohya mandel sri, syuh syuh ruwat kala suha ripwa hyong pasung pangasih." The intention of this mantra is to beseech both the compassion of the Ruler of All Creatures and the benevolence of the audience.

   After that mantra, the dhalang grasps the wick of the oil lantern with tongs, and, making the flame burn brighter, he recites the following mantra: "Hong Nurrada, Hyong ri Hyang Nurrada hagni," which means 'May Hyang in his aspect as Light illuminate the world and illuminate my heart'.

After that mantra, the dhalang strikes the puppet box to
cue the gamelan to play. The dhalang removes the kayon, or
gunungan, from the log, lowers it, and makes it vibrate slowly
and gracefully, stopping three times, until the gunungan
reaches the level of the lower log. He blows on the tip of
the gunungan three times, presses the tip with the fingers of
his left hand, and rests the gunungan on the top edge of the
puppet box while reciting the auspicious mantra: "Rep sidhem
pramanem padha, korup racut racut dadi, nèng aku tunggal
kahanan, tunggal sir rasa sejati, tetep madhep mring mami. La
lla ha llallohu Allohu, muga-muga paringa idi sejati,
niyatingsun ambuka gancaring carita." ['May all be totally
silent. May separate things come together and become one, one
with my intention of pure *rasa*; may (my intention) ever be
steadfast. There is one God and Allah is his name. May I be
given leave to open up the path of this story.']

c. In a number of *primbon* handed down by various dhalang of
    former times, the mantra for wayang performance are mentioned
    as follows:

    1. When preparing to leave his house, the dhalang recites
        the mantra: "Hong lelembut padhanyangan sira sing
        ana . . . (referring to the dhalang's house, yard,
        village, or district), kang asmara désa, kang asmara
        bumi, bapa biyang babo kabuyutan, réwang-réwangana aku,
        katekana sasedyaku, katurutana sakarepku, titah lanang,
        titah wadon kang andudulu marang aku, teka dhemen teka
        welas, teka asih, awit saka idining Hyang, Hyang kang
        Murbèng Dumadi." ['Hong, guardian spirits, you who
        reside at . . . , protector of the village, protector of
        the earth, father and mother and ancestors, come to my
        aid, strengthen my resolve, grant my wishes. May all the
        men and women who are watching me be pleased,
        compassionate, and loving, by the will of Hyang, who
        rules all creation.']

        Holding his breath, the dhalang then stamps upon the
        ground three times. The mantra quoted above can also be
        used by someone who is about to depart for work, such as
        a trader about to go to sea. When the dhalang reaches

his destination, he recites the mantra again, but the
name of the dhalang's house is replaced with the name of
his new location.

2. When the gamelan has begun to play the *talu*, the dhalang
    recites the following mantra: "Sang Basuki Naga Bumi,
    Dhanyang perayangan ing omah kéné, désa kéné, réwang-
    réwangana aku, katona becik banget anggonku andhalang,
    aja pati-pati bubar kang padha nonton, yèn durung rampung
    anggonku andhalang." ['Sang Basuki,[25] Serpent of the
    Earth, protective spirits who are residing in this house
    and in this village, may you come to my aid, and may my
    performance be seen to be excellent. May the spectators
    who come stay until the performance ends.']

        Sitting while reciting this mantra, the dhalang
    holds his breath and stamps three times on ground that
    has been covered with a straw mat.

3. The first time the dhalang adjusts the flame of the oil
    lamp to make it burn brighter, he recites the following
    mantra: "Hong sang Hyang Purba Sukma jatining Tunggal,
    sang Hyang Nurcahya urubé mrabani sabawana, kang padha
    andulu marang saliraku, teka kédhep, teka lerep, teka
    welas, teka asih, atas saka karsané Hyang Purba Sejati."
    ['Hong, Holy Powerful Spirit, Essence of Unity, God of
    Radiance, may this flame illuminate the whole world. May
    people who come to see me be respectful, attentive,
    compassionate, and loving, by the will of the Powerful
    and True God.']

4. Before the first scene of the performance, the dhalang
    raps on the puppet box with a cempala to signal the
    gamelan to play as he recites the mantra: "Gunung agung
    palinggihanku, petak gelap lindhu prabawaku." ['A great
    mountain is my seat, and my power is the crash of thunder
    and violent shaking.'] While reciting this mantra, the
    dhalang raps three times, either with his foot or his
    right hand, on ground that has been covered with a straw
    mat.

5. Upon first removing the gunungan from the log, after
    taking hold of its tip, he recites the following mantra:

"Hu mangun kung awakku kaya gunung, kul kul dhingkul, rep rep sirep [teka]²⁶ kedhep, teka lerep, teka welas, teka asih, saha karsaning Allah." ['Give me the strength of a mountain, that the spectators may bow down to me, that they be silent, that they be respectful, attentive, compassionate, and loving, by the will of Allah.']

d.   The book, *Mantra Yoga*,²⁷ mentions various mantras recited by the dhalang, including the following:

1.   When the dhalang first sits under the oil lamp, pressing his navel he recites the mantra "Aji Semar Kuning" to beseech compassion:²⁸ "Matak ajiku Semar Kuning, alungguha angigela, dewa, dewa asih, manusa asih, wong sabawana asih marang badan sariraku, awit saka karsane Hyang Purba Jati." ['As I recite the incantation (*aji*) Semar Kuning, may (Semar) reside in me and dance, that all the gods and mortals in the whole world may love me, by the will of the Powerful and True God.']

2.   As the dhalang pulls the wick of the oil lantern for the first time, he recites the following mantra to beseech silence: "Sari Ruwi urubing cahya bening, cahyaning Hyang, rupa kula rupa teja, rupa amiyak sarining rasa, rep rep wong sabawana, kedhep tresna asih, alok arum arum kesdik jaya rupa." ['Essence of clear light, the divine light, may my actions be infused with this light, which can open up the essence of *rasa* (in the spectators). May all mortals in the world be calm, compassionate, and loving. May my performance cause cries of delight, may fragrance spread,²⁹ may I be clever and perfect in my actions.']

3.   As the dhalang removes the gunungan for the first time, he grasps its tip and recites the mantra: "Kap kap laka. Hyang Lata Walhujwa, nyuwun buka, sirep sirep asih asih wong sabawana, saking karsaning Hyang kang Maha Kawasa." ['Oh Red Climbing Plant, venerable Lata Walhujwa, I beg leave to begin. May all the people of the world be quiet and full of compassion, by the wish of God, Whose Power is greatest.']

NOTES

1. "Nuwun" or "kula nuwun" (literally, 'I beg your leave/permission') is a standard greeting and closing for formal letters, books, and conversations.

2. The notation presented here is a modification of the original, made in consultation with Sri Joko Raharjo, a former student of the author as well as a teacher of dhodhogan and sulukan at the Akademi Seni Karawitan Indonesia. We feel this modification better represents Probohardjono's intentions, which may have been misrepresented due to carelessness on the part of the typist or printer. The passage of the original that differs from the notation presented here is as follows:

Gendhing *Karawitan*, 1st gongan, 2d kenogan

	t		.t		t		t		G^6
....	66..	6616	5323	5653	2165	3561	3216
	d			dddd	dddd	dddd	dddd

2d gongan, 1st kenongan

	t		t		t		t		N^6
3565	2232	5653	2126	.666	3356	3532	.356
dddd	dddd	ddddherudhug	(instruments play sirepan)

Also, the dhodhogan for the suwuk section has been added to this notation.

3. By request of the author, explanations and notations for the sulukan have been taken from the sixth edition of *Sulukan Sléndro* (1962). The rest of the text, including the section "Songs Sung by the Panakawan in Pathet Sanga," follows the revised seventh edition (1966).

For translations (into Dutch, Indonesian, and German, respectively) of most of the sulukan texts, as well as attributions of provenance, the reader is referred to Uhlenbeck and Soegiarto 1960, Sutrisno 1977, and Schumacher 1980.

4. Following Pigeaud (1967[1]:179-81, 237-40), the versions of the story
   of the "Great War" between the Korawa and Pandhawa brothers--taken
   originally from the Indian *Mahābhārata*--will be distinguished as
   follows.

   a. *Bhārata Yuddha*, *kakawin*, refers to the twelfth-century Old
      Javanese version, written in Sanskrit-derived *kakawin* meters.
      This poem has been edited and translated by Poerbatjaraka and
      Hooykaas (1939), and by Sutjipto Wirjosuparto (1968).

   b. *Serat Brata Yuda*, *kawi miring*, refers to the eighteenth- and
      nineteenth-century versions, written in modern Javanese
      (though in an archaic style), in *sekar ageng* meters. These
      versions have never been published and can only be found in
      manuscript form (in libraries in Indonesia and The
      Netherlands).

   c. *Serat Brata Yuda*, *macapat*, refers to the modern Javanese
      version in sekar macapat meters written ". . . by
      Yasadipura I, still in the reign of Paku Buwana III [reigned
      1749-1789], and probably re-edited by his son [Yasadipura
      II]. . . . [This latter version] was published by A. B. Cohen
      Stuart in 1860, provided with collations with the Old Javanese
      text. Probably the kawi miring text [see note 5] is also the
      work of Yasadipura I" (Pigeaud 1967[1]:240).

   Analogously, the Javanese versions of the Indian *Ramāyana* epic are
   distinguished as *Ramāyana*, *kakawin* (edited and published by Kern
   1900); *Serat Rama*, *kawi miring* (unpublished); and *Serat Rama*, *macapat*,
   by Yasadipura I (edited by C. F. Winter 1846; see also Jasadipura
   1925).

5. The literary idiom known as "kawi miring" (literally 'sloping kawi')
   consists of modern Javanese paraphrases of the Old Javanese kakawin
   literature. "These paraphrases are simplified versions; ordinary,
   generally understood expressions are substituted for difficult Old
   Javanese and Sanskrit ones" (Pigeaud 1967[1]:237). The meters in
   which these paraphrases were written are the modern Javanese sekar
   ageng meters, which, like the Old Javanese kakawin meters, are
   characterized by two- or four-line stanzas and fixed numbers of
   syllables per line, but in which no distinction is made between long
   and short vowels. (Such a distinction is generally thought to be
   operative for kakawin meters.)

Probohardjono usually refers to kakawin meters as "lagu" and the kawi miring meters as "sekar ageng." Where he has written "sekar ageng," and where the kakawin version is clearly implied, the editor has added "lagu" in square brackets. See, for example, pages 469 and 475.

6. The provenance of the original version as "canto II, verse 3" is given in Sutrisno 1977:13. However, this verse does not correspond to canto II, verse 3, in the published version (Sindoesastra 1868:4). We have been unable to locate this text in the published edition.

7. Schumacher (1980:94), on the basis of verse boundaries and phrasing, identifies the meter of this text as *sardula wikridhita*.

8. Since Probohardjono says this text is from "*Rama* in sekar ageng meter," he is probably referring to the kawi miring version. According to Uhlenbeck and Soegiarto (1960:63), only the first line of this text can be traced to the first line of *Serat Rama Jarwa* [*kawi miring*], while the rest of the sulukan cannot.

9. According to Sutrisno (1977:16), this text is related to *Bhārata Yuddha*, *kakawin*, canto V, verse 8, which is in the *sardula wikridhita* meter. Probohardjono elsewhere repeats his contention that *prawira lalita* is correct (Probohardjono 1961:40; no. 83, app. 1, *Sekar* in vol. 2).

10. Uhlenbeck and Soegiarto (1960:61) cite the original verse as canto III, verse 1.

11. Since Probohardjono says that this text is from the "*Brata Yuda* story in a sekar ageng meter," it can be inferred that he is referring to the kawi miring version (of Yasadipura I). Tjan Tjoe Siem (1938:251) points out that the sulukan text is not identical with either the kawi miring or the macapat versions of *Brata Yuda*, but represents a "combination" of the two. The sources in the two versions are: kawi miring, canto LVIII, verse 1; macapat, canto XLV, verse 1 (see Cohen Stuart 1860:119 for the text of the macapat version). Soetrisno (1977:20) identifies the sekar ageng meter as *bangsa patra*. Tjan Tjoe Siem calls the meter *maésa bayangan* (1938:168). The meter of the macapat verse is sekar macapat *dhandhang gula*.

12. Sutrisno identifies the meter as sekar ageng *basonta* (1977:21). See Schumacher 1980:100.

13. This sulukan is sometimes called "Sendhon Abimanyu" or "(Pathet)
    Sendhon Elayana."

14. This sulukan is also called "Pathet Jengking" with the folk etymology
    jengking, from *jeng* (*ngajeng* 'front'), and *king* (*wingking* 'back'),
    because the song begins and ends the same way. See Schumacher
    1980:62; also see Warsadiningrat 1979:42-43 (translation to appear in
    volume 2 of this work).

15. See note 8, above, in reference to the same text as that of Ada-ada
    Girisa Wantah, sléndro nem.

16. See questions on pages 443-44, above; these are the answers.

17. "Wanda" refers to differences in puppet iconography--e.g., inclination
    of head, slenderness of body, vertical attitude of body, costume,
    coloring--that distinguish a character in a particular mood, stage of
    life, or aspect. For instance, Sutrisno (1964:8) lists twelve
    separate wanda for the Wrekudara puppet, each with a different proper
    name and characteristics. See also the discussion in Brandon
    1970:50-51.

18. According to Soedarsono (private communication), Javanese custom
    forbids a young woman to smile when she has been proposed to, since
    such open expression of feelings is considered unrefined; her
    expression is referred to as "*montro-montro*," or "*lontro-lontro*."

19. For a more complete rendering of each wangsalan, see Heins
    1970:101-27.

20. The best known text by the name *Budha Carita*, or *Buddhacarita*, is by
    Aśvaghosa, who lived in India in the late first or second century A.D.
    The text relates the life stories of the historical Buddha (see Müller
    1969). The story of the demon Kuñjarakarna is not included in the
    published editions of the *Buddhacarita*. There is, however, a
    rendering of it in the fourteenth-century Old Javanese kakawin,
    Kuñjarakarna. See Zoetmoelder 1974:374-81 and Teeuw and Robson 1981.

21. In Javanese, "right" and "left" have somewhat different symbolic
    meanings than in English. "Nengenaken" (from *tengen* 'right') means
    literally 'to put in the right-side position', and, by extension, 'to
    give prominence to'. "Ngiwakaken" (from *kiwa* 'left') means 'to put in
    the left-side position', and, by extension, 'to set aside', 'to give
    no consideration to'. Though the polarity right/left, as analogous to

good/bad, is not as clear-cut as it is in English, more positive
values are associated with the right side in Javanese, as in English.

22. Suyudana's and Karna's wives are sisters. Hence, they are brothers-
    in-law (*sedulur ipé*).

23. For an explanation of the philosophy and practice of mantras, see
    Bharati 1970:101-63.

24. We have been unable to identify this text.

25. Basuki is the fourth son of Hyang Guru (Śiwa).

26. Two other printed versions of this mantra include the word "teka" at
    this point; see Sastroamidjojo 1964:182 and Hooykaas 1973:144.

27. We have been unable to identify this text.

28. Semar is the god of love or compassion. According to Sastroamidjojo
    1962:35, *kuning* 'yellow' is symbolic of desire and enjoyment.

29. According to A. L. Becker (private communication), the puppet's aroma
    is a sign that the puppet has become possessed by the spirit of the
    character. Also, in preparation for a wayang kulit, the puppets are
    passed through the smoke of burning incense.